Cambridge Studies in Social and Emotional Development

General Editor: Martin L. Hoffman

The transition to parenthood

The transition to parenthood

Current theory and research

Edited by

GERALD Y. MICHAELS
Northwestern University Medical School

WENDY A. GOLDBERG
University of California, Irvine

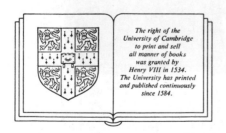

The right of the
University of Cambridge
to print and sell
all manner of books
was granted by
Henry VIII in 1534.
The University has printed
and published continuously
since 1584.

CAMBRIDGE UNIVERSITY PRESS

Cambridge

New York   New Rochelle   Melbourne   Sydney

Published by the Press Syndicate of the University of Cambridge
The Pitt Building, Trumpington Street, Cambridge CB2 1RP
32 East 57th Street, New York, NY 10022, USA
10 Stamford Road, Oakleigh, Melbourne 3166, Australia

First published 1988

Printed in the United States of America

Library of Congress Cataloging-in-Publication Data
The Transition to parenthood.
(Cambridge studies in social and emotional development)
Includes index.
1. Parenthood. 2. Pregnancy. I. Michaels, Gerald Y.
II. Goldberg, Wendy A. III. Series.
HQ755.8.T73 1988 306.8′74 87–32649

British Library Cataloguing in Publication Data
The Transition to parenthood: current theory
and research. – (Cambridge studies in social
and emotional development).
1. Parenthood – Psychological aspects
I. Michaels, Gerald Y. II. Goldberg,
Wendy A.
306.8′74 HQ755.83

ISBN 0 521 35418 8

To my mother, Ruth Michaels, with love
G.Y.M.

In loving memory of my father, Merrill Goldberg
W.A.G.

Contents

List of contributors *page* ix

Editorial preface xi

Introduction. Perspectives on the transition to
parenthood *Wendy A. Goldberg* 1

**Part I. The transition to parenthood as a challenge for
adaptation by individuals, couples, and families**

1 Motivational factors in the decision and timing of
pregnancy *Gerald Y. Michaels* 23

2 The power of parenthood: personality and attitudinal
changes during the transition to parenthood 62
Toni C. Antonucci and Karen Mikus

3 Psychological issues in adjustment to first
parenthood *Nicolina M. Fedele, Ellen R. Golding,* 85
Frances K. Grossman, and William S. Pollack

4 Changes in marriage during the transition to
parenthood: must we blame the baby? 114
Philip A. Cowan and Carolyn Pape Cowan

**Part II. The transition to parenthood under
conditions of risk**

5 Medical perspectives on pregnancy and birth:
biological risks and technological advances 157
Linda Hughey Holt

6 Effects of infant risk status on the transition to
parenthood *M. Ann Easterbrooks* 176

7 The transition to parenthood: special tasks and risk
factors for adolescent parents *Joy D. Osofsky,* 209
Howard J. Osofsky, and Martha Ourieff Diamond

**Part III.   Intervention strategies for individuals,
couples, and families**

8   Social networks and the transition to parenthood   235
    Benjamin H. Gottlieb and S. Mark Pancer

9   Intervention programs for the transition to parenthood:
    current status from a prevention perspective   270
    S. Wayne Duncan and Howard J. Markman

10 Family support programs for new parents   311
    Sharon L. Kagan and Victoria Seitz

    Conclusion. The transition to parenthood: synthesis
    and future directions   *Wendy A. Goldberg*   342
    and Gerald Y. Michaels

    Index of names   361
    Index of subjects   372

Contributors

Toni C. Antonucci
Institute for Social Research
University of Michigan

Carolyn Pape Cowan
Department of Psychology
University of California,
Berkeley

Philip A. Cowan
Department of Psychology
University of California,
Berkeley

Martha Ourieff Diamond
Child and Adolescent Psychiatric
Hospital
University of Michigan Medical
School

S. Wayne Duncan
Department of Psychology
University of Denver

M. Ann Easterbrooks
Department of Child Study
Tufts University

Nicolina M. Fedele
Department of Psychiatry
Boston University School of
Medicine

Wendy A. Goldberg
Program in Social Ecology
University of California, Irvine

Ellen R. Golding
Beth Israel Hospital
Harvard Medical School
and Charles River Hospital

Benjamin H. Gottlieb
Department of Psychology
University of Guelph

Frances K. Grossman
Department of Psychology
Boston University

Linda Hughey Holt
Northwestern University
Medical School and Evanston
Hospital

Sharon L. Kagan
Bush Center in Child
Development and
Social Policy
Yale University

Howard J. Markman
Department of Psychology
University of Denver

Gerald Y. Michaels
Department of Psychiatry and
Behavorial Sciences
Northwestern University
Medical School

Karen Mikus
Family Resource Program
Perry Child Development Center

Howard J. Osofsky
Department of Psychiatry
Louisiana State University
Medical Center

Joy D. Osofsky
Department of Pediatrics and
Psychiatry
Lousiana State University
Medical Center

S. Mark Pancer
Department of Psychology
Wilfrid Laurier University

William S. Pollack
Harvard Medical School and
McLean Hospital

Victoria Seitz
Yale University Child Study
Center and Department of
Psychology

Editorial preface

The purpose of this volume is to bring together the work of leading scholars in several disciplines and subdisciplines related to the study of the transition to parenthood. Each chapter is designed to add to our understanding of what makes the transition easy or difficult: to explain why some individuals and relationships experience mainly growth during the process whereas others undergo strain. Of special importance in this volume is the inclusion of the perspectives of men, women, couples, and familes under normative and risk conditions. Factors discussed that influence the transition to parenthood range from individual motivation and personality characteristics to formal and informal support systems. In addition to supplying integrative reviews, a number of the authors bring firsthand research findings and new theoretical models to their chapters. Each chapter concludes with methodological and/or conceptual suggestions to guide further research.

Following an introductory chapter that offers perspectives on the transition to parenthood, the chapters in Part I examine typical or normative development during pregnancy and the first year of new parenthood. Factors that promote dimensions of growth and change for individuals, couples, and families are discussed. The chapters in Part II consider biomedical and psychosocial risk factors that affect the parent and infant. Parent risks, such as maternal age, and infant risks, such as premature birth, are discussed in conjunction with adaptive and maladaptive modes of response to risk conditions. The chapters in Part III cover both informal and formal means of assisting prospective and new parents. Interventions suitable for the pre-conception, pregnancy, and postnatal periods are presented, and prescriptive recommendations are offered. A concluding chapter by the editors follows this section.

We are privileged to have such an outstanding group of contributors for this volume. We are grateful to them for their careful work and for their patience with the process of preparing an edited volume. At Cambridge University Press, we thank Susan Milmoe for her interest in our idea for this book, Helen Wheeler for her diligence and graciousness throughout all phases of production, Mary Nevader for her expert copy editing, and Martin Hoffman, the series editor, for his review. We are indebted to Jill Vidas at the University of California, Irvine, for preparing numerous drafts of several of the chapters, and we acknowledge Dale Arnesen, Fran Renner, and Carol Wyatt for helping us at many critical points. In a volume about families, we wish to thank our own for their support and encouragement, particularly our spouses, Carolyn Michaels and Samuel Gilmore. Finally, we have learned a great deal from one another through our collaboration. We note in closing that we shared equal responsibility for the planning and editing of this volume and in the writing of the final chapter.

Introduction
Perspectives on the transition to parenthood

Wendy A. Goldberg

The transition to parenthood has been an area of lively interest since the landmark study of LeMasters in 1957, which culminated in perceptions of the transition as a crisis experience for adults. Since then, numerous studies, including many dissertations, have been written on the topic. The transition-to-parenthood research has its roots in the discipline of sociology; nonetheless, today it represents an area of active inquiry in several disciplines, with sociology, psychology, and medicine being the most prominent. A volume published in the late 1970s, *The First Child and Family Formation* (Miller & Newman, 1978), counted psychologists, sociologists, physicians, and anthropologists among its contributors. More recently, a special issue of the *Journal of Family Issues* (Cox, 1985), a family sociology publication, contained empirical studies by sociologists, psychologists, and psychiatrists. The present volume takes its place in this interdisciplinary forum. The contributors represent many areas of psychology (developmental, clinical, community, social, personality), social policy, psychiatry, and obstetrics. More telling, perhaps, is the fact that many of the authors transcend traditional disciplinary boundaries in their academic affiliations, locating themselves in interdisciplinary programs and departments. This broadened perspective is reflected in the scope of their chapters.

The transition to parenthood, as the term typically is used, refers to the fairly brief period of time from the beginning of a pregnancy through the first months of having a child. From a biological perspective, the transition begins with the child's conception. From a psychological and sociocultural perspective, however, there is no requirement that the transition to parenthood be limited to the period after conception. The expectations and events that precede conception, especially as they concern decisions about whether and when to have a child, will affect the transition experience. In this book, the emphasis is on the pregnancy, birth, and months following birth; as well, attention is given to the preparatory period before conception.

The study of the transition to parenthood is important not only because it represents a milestone in the new parent's development, but because it marks the beginning of the new child's development. The new parent's capacity to make a successful adjustment at this time may set a future course of effective, competent parenting, whereas serious difficulties in adjustment may lead to, or exacerbate, marital discord and promote difficulty in providing for the child's needs. Preventive and therapeutic interventions may be required to alter an unfavorable trajectory and ensure the healthy psychological growth of the individual parent and child, the marital couple, and the family system.

The transition to parenthood in life-span perspective

The transition to parenthood may be the most universally occurring adult developmental transition, with psychological, sociocultural, and biological components, all of which interact and influence one another (Michaels, Hoffman, & Goldberg, 1982). From a theoretical standpoint, the study of the transition to parenthood is important because of the unique position it holds at the interface of individual models and systems models of behavior. Research on individual psychological development, studies on the development of the marital dyad, and work on family development are unanimous in viewing the transition to parenthood as a pivotal adult developmental event. Several issues come to the fore when the transition to parenthood is placed in a life-span framework. In this section we highlight a few of them.

The timing of parenthood

There is a tendency in developmental models of child development (e.g., Piagetian models, Freudian models) and adult development (e.g., Erikson, 1963, 1968; Levinson, 1986) to anchor change to age. The transition to parenthood, rather than occurring at a particular age, typically occurs within a particular age range, from the teenage years through the thirties.

Age can serve as a marker for the level of life experiences that one has accumulated and the influence of history or cohort effects on one's life (Rossi, 1980). Certainly, becoming a parent for the first time at age 20 is qualitatively different from becoming a parent for the first time at age 35. Mercer (1986) refers to issues surrounding the timing of parenthood as the energy of youth versus the perspective of maturity. Smoothing the transition for late childbearers might be the self-confidence, self-knowledge, contentment, and financial security that may accompany age and accomplishments, and the strong motivation to become a parent that may characterize those who postponed childbearing. Thus, deliberate late-timers seem to be creating a "readiness for parenthood in the spheres of self and life and work" (Daniels & Weingarten, 1982, p. 21). However, late childbearers also face challenges and potential problems regarding the coordination of children with heightened career demands and diminished levels of physical energy; as well, they confront age-related medical risks associated with late-age pregnancy and advanced age during the childrearing years (see Holt, Chapter 5, this volume). Those who delay childbearing may also have a sense that they are "off-time" in regard to societal expectations for the timing of first parenthood (Neugarten & Datan, 1973).

The new parent in his or her late teens and early twenties faces a different set of issues. This individual is attempting to coordinate parenthood with a fledgling career and marital relationship or the postponement of career and educational opportunities to accommodate the demands of childrearing. Advantages for younger parents include a high level of physical energy and a perspective that the demands of parenthood are not so disruptive because these young adults are not set in their ways. The younger teenage parent faces his or her own set of problems, including a lack of psychological readiness for parenthood and marriage, health risks, dependence on others for economic support, and interruption of basic educational paths (Jones, Green, & Krauss, 1980; Mercer, 1980; Wise & Grossman, 1980; see also Osofsky, Osofsky, & Diamond, Chapter 7, this volume).

From her study of women ranging in age from 19 to 40, Mercer (1986) concluded that, despite the perceived advantages and disadvantages of early and late timing, most of the new mothers were satisfied with their choice. Perhaps cognitive dissonance was operative, or perhaps other factors intervened to facilitate the transition. Across ages, the extent of support available from one's social network, therapeutic interventions, and social programs mediates the ease of the transition to parenthood (see Gottlieb and Pancer, Chapter 8; Duncan and Markman, Chapter 9; and Kagan and Seitz, Chapter 10, this volume).

Support from family, friends, and formal institutions should assist both women and men as they become parents. However, despite the attention given to new fathers in other areas of parenthood, most of the data on the timing of parenthood have been collected from women and concentrate on the consequences of variations in the timing of parenthood for adult women's lives; far less attention has been given to the impact of timing on men's lives. Particularly interesting is the phenomenon of being the biological parent of an infant when one is in "late middle" or "senior" age – a phenomenon that can be experienced only by men. These older fathers fall into one of two groups: those who become parents for the first time in later life and those who experience a hiatus of some years between childrearing (i.e., men who had children by a previous marriage a decade or two earlier). The latter group could be subdivided into men who had previously been stepparents and men who had been biological parents.

Psychologically, the motive to become a father later in life may reflect a different balance of factors than it does earlier. The desire to become a parent for the first time in older middle age may be intertwined with a sense of one's mortality and a desire to reproduce to ensure one's contribution to the future. (Erikson's [1963] notion of generativity is relevant here.) The prioritization of parenthood relative to other domains may also differ. A man who becomes a parent when he is in his fifties or sixties is likely to be at a very different point in his occupational life cycle than the modal new father in his twenties. In the context of a middle-class lifestyle, the older father probably has passed the intensive career-building years to find himself with an established, settled work life that allows him to devote considerable time to his new family. The motivation to be highly involved with his young child may also be indicative of a desire for compensatory family experiences. If an older father had children from an earlier marriage whose arrival coincided with the peak years of his career trajectory, he might feel that he had missed the best years of his children's lives because of his absorption in work. The birth of children later in life may be viewed as an opportunity to enjoy experiences that were missed before.

The transition to parenthood as a developmental challenge

Variations in the timing of parenthood are related to the types of developmental tasks faced by the individual.[1] The concept of developmental task has found some prominence among life-span researchers and can be integrated into the conceptualization of the transition to parenthood as a life-span event. Havighurst (1972), who first popularized the concept of developmental tasks, describes these as "tasks that arise at or near a certain time in the life of an individual, the successful achievement of which leads to his happiness and to success with later tasks – whereas failure leads to unhappiness in the individual, disapproval by society, and difficulty in later tasks" (p. 2). Duvall (1977) states that developmental

---

[1] Gerald Michaels's contribution to the material presented in this subsection and the one following is gratefully acknowledged.

tasks derive from two origins: physical maturation and cultural pressures and privileges. Different tasks become salient at different points in development and through interaction with the expectations of familial and extrafamilial agents.

The particular developmental tasks faced by the individual at the point in the life cycle when she or he becomes a parent bear on the quality of the experience (i.e., the ease of adjustment or extent of crisis). As indicated in the quotation above, the developmental task concept embodies the idea that a particular task must be accomplished at a particular point in development and that the achievement of the task at this point is necessary for success in achieving future developmental tasks. These points in time are often thought to be "developmental crises" that the individual must struggle with and resolve. Erikson's (1963) theory of development through the life span taking place through a series of eight psychosocial crises, each with a critical period for resolution, is one of the best-known personality theories utilizing this approach.

There have been a number of studies examining the question of whether parenthood represents a crisis in terms of psychological upheaval for the individual and for the family. The prevailing view is that for a minority of families, perhaps 20%, a true crisis occurs, whereas for the majority of families, parenthood would better be considered a transition period that does not provoke a major life crisis, though it may provoke a series of minicrises (see, e.g., chapters in Miller & Newman, 1978; see also Cowan & Cowan, Chapter 4, this volume). Duvall (1977) wrote that at the point of crisis there occurs "the teachable moment" when the body is prepared for, culture is pushing for, and the individual is reaching out for the achievement of some developmental change. Thus, the individual is highly motivated for developmental change at the point of crisis.

The concepts both of critical period and of life crisis imply that there is potential for sudden, long-lasting change that, if it does not occur at this time, will not occur afterward when the individual has readjusted and ended the crisis or when the critical period has ended. The concept of critical period, even more than the concept of crisis, suggests that there is a particular adaptive and nonadaptive outcome to the period in question.

The transition to parenthood as a stage of family development

Whereas in the concepts of life events, crisis, and developmental task described above parenthood is viewed from the perspective of individual development, first parenthood has also been studied in the context of stages of family development (Duvall, 1977; Hill & Hansen, 1960; Hill & Rodgers,

1964; Mattessich & Hill, 1987; Rodgers, 1973, 1977). The family development approach, which integrates many of these concepts, has a long theoretical and research tradition anchored by the work in the late 1940s by Elizabeth Duvall and Reuben Hill. These authors, drawing on the theoretical writings on individual development of such men as Lawrence Frank, Robert Havighurst, and Erik Erikson, took the changing age and sex composition of the family over time as the basis for identifying a series of changing developmental tasks that characterize families over the life span (Hill, 1978). Essentially, the family development approach is a marriage of interests in the life cycle of families and the life cycle of individuals (Mattessich & Hill, 1987).

In the family developmental approach, the total family system is considered the unit of analysis and the individual is treated as one point in the family structure. Individual change is viewed as part of the structural and role changes that are occurring in the family. The individual's unique experience usually is not a subject of focus in family developmentalists' analyses, which emphasize interpersonal behaviors and interdependent relationships. Also, the focus of family developmentalists' interests typically is on the family as a circumscribed entity, and thus the emphasis is on family interactions and changes within the composition and role structure of the family. How first parenthood affects the individual's interests and behaviors outside the family context has received less attention (Peterson, Hay, & Peterson, 1979; Rodgers, 1973).

The family developmental perspective makes several important theoretical contributions to the understanding of individual changes that take place during the transition to parenthood. First is the life-cycle focus itself. The transition to parenthood is not seen as an isolated developmental event, but is viewed within the context of the entire sequence of concrete developmental events that characterize family life. Although the number of family career stages varies in the literature, a seven-stage model is often used (Mattessich & Hill, 1987). The second stage in this typology occurs when the couple has their first child. Next, there is value in viewing individual development as, in part, being embedded in family development. Changes in the family system certainly influence the direction and character of changes in the individual and the individual's adaptation to change. In the context of the transition to parenthood, the nature of the individual parent's adaptation to parenthood will bear on the nascent parent–infant relationship and the infant's development. Thus, the individual development of the new parent and child may be influenced profoundly by "developmental changes" in the family system. Finally, the concept of developmental tasks particular to the transition to parenthood can apply both to the individual and to the family as a whole (Duvall, 1977). A sensitivity to the family context of individual and couple adjustment during the transition to parenthood can be found in the chapters in this volume.

Setting the stage: world fertility patterns

Before we embark on an overview of the contents of this volume, we wish to place the transition to parenthood in sociocultural perspective. Because the bulk of psychological and sociological research on the transition to parenthood is conducted with samples of white middle-class Americans, it is too easy to accept the idea that their behavior patterns are indicative of all parents in the United States and other nations. It is beyond the scope, or intent, of this volume to present the transition to parenthood in cross-cultural perspective. Yet we wish to provide a context for the discussions to follow, and choose to fulfill this goal by presenting, albeit briefly, data on the demographics of the transition to parenthood. First, we shall highlight world fertility patterns, giving emphasis to major factors that influence reproductive behavior worldwide. Then, to set the stage for the remainder of this volume, which focuses on U.S. samples, we shall discuss current U.S. trends.

The data presented in this section have been culled largely from two major sources: the World Development Reports of the International Bank for Reconstruction and Development and the Current Population Reports of the U.S. Bureau of the Census. These reports are compilations and integrations of large-scale survey data. Extant large data bases present an underutilized (except by demographers) resource for transition-to-parenthood researchers. Brief descriptions of four sources that seem particularly relevant to U.S. social scientists who study the transition to parenthood are provided in the Appendix at the end of this chapter.

Many of the demographic data are framed in terms of birthrates for various age ranges of women. The number of live births per 1,000 women (the raw birthrate) provides some insight into current population growth. More precise information about the trajectory for population growth is yielded by the total fertility rate, which is the sum of birthrates specific to each age group of women. Essentially, the total fertility rate indicates the number of children a woman would have in her lifetime if she experienced the current age-specific fertility rates of all women (i.e., a woman's lifetime level of childbearing) (Cherlin, 1981; International Bank for Reconstruction and Development, 1984). Thus, the total fertility rate measures changes in the volume of children born over time to women of a particular cohort (Cherlin, 1981).

In mid-1987, the world population reached 5 billion, with the population growing at a rate of about 150 babies per minute ("Zagreb baby," 1987).

From the perspective of the World Bank, the economic and political consequences of population growth are of paramount importance. High rates of fertility prevail in countries where citizens have little education, low and unsteady incomes, and poor health and family-planning services. In developing countries, especially in rural areas, the average family consists of four or more children (International Bank for Reconstruction and Development, 1984). Having many children is perceived to be an economic boost because of child labor contributions, the need to have children to take care of parents in later years, and high infant and child mortality. Unfortunately, to the extent that population growth limits development opportunities, the economy of many of these countries as a whole will suffer if fertility rates remain high (International Bank for Reconstruction and Development, 1984). By contrast, in developed countries, many children per family would pose economic constraints at the individual level because of mothers' time out of the labor force, the costs of alternative care, and the minimal contribution of children to household chores or income. The inverse association between fertility rates and income that is found both among and within countries is not without notable exceptions – for example, in China, where fertility is lower than the norm for income level, and in Algeria, where fertility is higher than the norm for income level (International Bank for Reconstruction and Development, 1984). However, in general, there is a linear, inverse relation between level of fertility and level of income.

The status of women in countries, particularly the educational opportunities for girls and employment opportunities for women, has a strong influence on fertility rates (International Bank for Reconstruction and Development, 1984; see also Hoffman, 1978). These trends are in the predictable direction: The more education a woman receives in her youth, the fewer children she will bear, in part because education implies the postponement of marriage, and therefore childbearing, and because more education is associated with being better informed about birth control methods. In the United States, the inverse association between level of education and fertility is evident: 1985 birthrates were highest among women without a high school degree (98.2 per 1,000), far lower for high school graduates (68.3 per 1,000), and lower still for women who had at least some college education (52.3–61.3 per 1,000) (U.S. Bureau of the Census, 1986; see also Rindfuss, Bumpass, & St. John, 1980). Critics of the thesis that education directly limits fertility argue that the viability of this link is contingent on another factor, namely, the opportunities for women to use that education in acquiring gainful employment (Graff, 1979; Handwerker, 1986).

Across countries, urban women who work full time in "modern occupations" (e.g., in industry) tend to have fewer children, although there are exceptions (International Bank for Reconstruction and Development, 1984). Changes in the patterns of labor force activity, such as the number of employed women, have been found to influence the overall fabric of family life (e.g., family income, marital relations) and fertility behavior (Cherlin, 1981; Davis, 1984; Hoffman, 1978; Oppenheimer, 1974; Waite, 1980). Hoffman (1978) observed that, to understand the relationship between the employment of women and fertility in the United States, we need to uncover the reasons that employed women have fewer children. Women who cycle their life roles such that there is a break between completing their education and getting married may bear fewer children. Researchers have found that employment during this hiatus after education and before marriage results in later age at marriage and, consequently, lower fertility (Cramer, 1980; Jones, 1981; Masnick & Bane, 1980).

It is important to distinguish between employed women who are career-absorbed and do not desire any or many children and employed women who have few children because of a lack of suitable, affordable, alternative care (Hoffman, 1978). Social change toward family supportive programs likely would have a major impact only on the fertility of the latter group. As social policies change to include parental leaves for care of newborns, public-supported childcare, and other family-related benefits, women who limited fertility for lack of alternative care arrangements might be motivated to bear and rear more children, whereas the high-work-committed group would still be expected to remain childless or bear few children.

Attitudes and beliefs can also influence employment and thereby fertility behavior. Women's beliefs about the rewards and costs of employment for their own and their children's well-being coincide with their actual employment behavior (Beckman & Houser, 1979; Greenberger, Goldberg, Crawford, & Granger, 1988) and intentions for future employment (Hock, Gnezda, & McBride, 1984). Women who perceive higher costs than benefits of paid work are less likely to be employed or to become employed while their children are young.

Even though personal beliefs and social changes may influence women's and men's decisions about whether and when to have children, there is some question as to whether reproductive behavior is a function of a deliberate, rational decision-making process. "Rationality models" may apply only to certain people under certain circumstances: Factors ranging from an internal locus of control to religious affiliation to congruency in husband–wife preferences may mediate the relationship between rational preference and actual fertility behavior (Crosbie, 1986; see also Crawford & Boyer, 1985, regarding the salience for women of their husbands' childbearing preferences).

Current U.S. fertility patterns

Amid reports of another baby boom, current U.S. trends represent at best an echo of the baby boom, a result of the original baby boom generation moving into their prime childbearing years. Actually, birthrates have not varied greatly since the mid-1970s; since then, the total number of births has ranged between 3.1 and 3.5 million babies born per year. Compared with the boom years that peaked in the late 1950s, American fertility rates since the mid-1970s have remained relatively low and stable. As well, women in the past decade have been consistent in the number of children (2.0–2.1) they expect to bear (U.S. Bureau of the Census, 1986). (The "replacement level" is considered to be 2.1, two to replace parents and one-tenth to cover infant mortality.) These low actual fertility rates are expected to continue through 1990 (U.S. Bureau of the Census, 1986; Masnick & Bane, 1980).

In the year ending June 1985, 3.5 million women in the United States gave birth (U.S. Bureau of the Census, 1986). About 40% of these women gave birth to their first child. The average rate of first births for adult women has remained steady since 1980. However, rates of first-time births vary by age. The average rate declines with age: Young women 18 to 24 had the highest rate of first-time births (53.5 births per 1,000 women), followed by women 25 to 29 (38.7 per 1,000) and women 30 to 44 (8.0 per 1,000). Despite popular notions that a great number of modern women postpone childbirth until their thirties, most women 30 to 44 years old already had given birth to their first child: First births were only 21% of all births for women over 30 years of age. Nonetheless, compared with their parents' generation, women today are older when they give birth to their first child (Wilkie, 1981).

The birthrates reported above apply to the population of adult women 18 to 44 years of age. These average statistics belie the variations based on such factors as race, marital status, and educational level. Based on 1985 data, birthrates were higher for Hispanic than non-Hispanic women, higher for black women than white women in the 18 to 24 age range, higher for white women than black women aged 25 to 29, and equal for black and white women over 30. As would be expected, women who bear children are usually married: Birthrates were roughly three times higher for married women than for divorced women, widowed women, or never married, single women (U.S. Bureau of the Census, 1986).

Is the pattern of low marriage, high divorce, and low fertility rates an anomaly of the current generation? Several researchers argue not: When rates are the unit of analysis, the patterns reflected in today's generation are consistent with the trends of this century but represent a departure from the patterns of the previous generation (i.e., the parents of today's parents; Cherlin, 1981; Masnick & Bane, 1980). The generation of individuals who came of age in the 1940s and 1950s appears to be the century's "deviant" generation because it departed from the trends toward leveling off of marital rates, declining fertility rates, and increasing rates of divorce that had prevailed since the turn of the century. Thus, taking marital patterns as an example, the postponement of first marriage practiced by the baby boom generation is a delay only if the parents' generation is the frame of reference (Cherlin, 1981). In 1984, the median age at first marriage was 25.4 years for men and 23.0 years for women (U.S. Bureau of the Census, 1986), which is similar to the ages found earlier in this century, but about 1½ years later than the ages for the generation of individuals who came of age in the 1940s and 1950s (Cherlin, 1981).

In this century, lifetime levels of childbearing have followed an inverted U shape, with its peak among the cohort of women who married and had children just after World War II. The period from 1946 to 1964, which delineates the baby boom, witnessed yearly birthrates of greater than 100 births per 1,000 women, with the peak of 123 per 1,000 in 1957 (U.S. Bureau of the Census, 1986). (The peak year using total fertility rates as the index was 1960, in which the total fertility rate was 3.8 children.) Put another way, more than twice as many babies were born during the postwar baby boom than were born during the 1930s (Masnick & Bane, 1980). This rise in fertility was discrepant with the overall decline in fertility rates in the United States since 1880 (Cherlin, 1981). Thus, if it had not been for the marriage and fertility patterns of the 1940s and 1950s, "today's young adults would appear to be behaving normally" (Masnick & Bane, 1980, p. 2). It is only when patterns set by the baby boom generation are compared with their parents' patterns that we see postponement in the median age at first marriage and first parenthood, fewer children born and spaced farther apart, and sharp increases in the divorce rate.

Fertility patterns are typically presented in terms of women's behavior. Obviously, the family life circumstances of men are also affected by social and economic factors. The active participation by men today in childrearing has been commented on by many in the popular press and has been studied extensively in the academic community (e.g., Lamb, 1977; Parke, 1979, 1981; Pleck, 1985). Yet when 1980 patterns are compared with 1960 patterns, it is apparent that 1980s men spend less of their lives in family environments with young children present (43% reduction since 1960; Eggebeen & Uhlenberg, 1985). Of course, as these researchers suggest, it may be that men today who choose to become fathers are more active in their parenting role than fathers were decades ago, leading to an increase in the quality, if not in the quantity, of parenting behavior. Perhaps men are achieving greater visibility in their role as fathers and are receiving more support than heretofore for prioritizing this role in their lives.

There is some indication that social policies are beginning to accommodate the needs of men and women as parents in the 1980s. More than 100 countries, and all industrial nations except the United States, have statutory laws that provide job-protected maternity leave, and many provide paternity leave as well (Kamerman, Kahn, & Kingston, 1983). In Europe, for example, the average paid maternity or paternity leave is 5 months; West Germany, Austria, and Finland provide 100% of pay for periods ranging from 14 to 35 weeks (*Congressional Quarterly Weekly Report*, 1986).

In comparison, progress on a parental leave policy in the United States has been modest. The 1978 Pregnancy Discrimination Act clarified that short-term disability policy must treat pregnancy and childbirth as it would any other disability. In January 1987, the U.S. Supreme Court upheld a California state law that grants pregnant employees the right to a 4-month leave to have a child and guarantees their job upon return. Several attempts have been made to introduce *federal* family and medical leave legislation to guarantee to both men and women the right to take several months of protected leave from their job to care for a newborn infant, a newly adopted infant, or a seriously ill child. The House Education and Labor Committee approved legislation in June 1986 to require medium-size and large companies to grant employees up to 18 weeks of unpaid family and disability leave; however, the 99th Congress closed session without taking action on this bill (*Congressional Quarterly Weekly Report*, 1987).

Thus, although it has one of the highest percentages of women with young children in the labor force, the United States falls well behind other advanced industrial nations in its policies to help parents care for newborns. The reasons for this country's lag are perplexing, but the advances in other nations likely reflect their small, homogeneous populations and pronatalist policies (Kamerman et al., 1983). If the demand for American women's labor is sustained amid a climate of low birthrates, profamily policies may become instituted in order to maintain women's employment rates and increase birthrates.

In summary, developing and developed countries have generally adopted different positions in regard to population growth, the former trying to limit fertility and the latter facing at- or below-replacement levels of population growth. National and individual levels of income and the status of women (their educational and occupational attainments) are primary correlates, if not determinants, of fertility behavior. In the United States, the birthrate has remained low and stable for a decade. The marriage and

family patterns enacted by contemporary U.S. adults during their reproductive years are at odds with the patterns set by the previous generation
but are reminiscent of trends that dominated the first half of this century.
The United States, which has lagged behind other advanced industrialized
nations in its parental leave policies, is starting to witness some momentum
in the move toward federal legislation to assist parents in the care of their
young. With these world and national trends on fertility as a backdrop,
we now turn to an overview of the chapters in this book.

Overview of this volume

The transition to parenthood as a challenge for adaptation by individuals, couples, and families

Since the late 1970s, social science researchers have embarked on intensive
study of psychological processes that underlie the decision to become a
parent. In Chapter 1, Michaels discusses the motivational basis for the
transition to parenthood. He first reviews a number of theoretical frameworks for the study of the motivations to become a parent, including psychoanalytic theoretical writings and the work of population researchers.
The discussion then turns to previous research in which motivations for
having children are cast within a values framework. Particular attention
is given to Hoffman and Hoffman's theoretical model describing the salient
values parents place on having children. Michaels also describes research
in which he and his colleagues are utilizing and expanding this model. He
concludes with a discussion of methodological issues related to assessing
the motivation to become a parent and offers suggestions for future research on the value of children to parents.

The transition to parenthood presents an opportunity for normal adult
personality growth and change. In Chapter 2, Antonucci and Mikus examine the effects of the transition to parenthood on men's and women's
personality and attitudes. The parental role in adult development is of
importance symbolically (e.g., proof of femininity or virility), practically
(e.g., the labor-intensive demands of childrearing), and emotionally (e.g.,
issues concerning dependence, autonomy, and intimacy). Antonucci and
Mikus examine the "power of parenthood" to promote change in adult
self-concept and personality, and discuss factors, such as prebirth personality characteristics, that may mediate the extent of influence of the
transition to parenthood on personality. The authors discuss two process
models that explain how personality is affected by parenthood: (1) the
concept of "possible selves" and (2) the "act-frequency" approach to

understanding personality dispositions. In the final section, the authors cover areas of adult personality that may be expected to change with the advent of parenthood, such as self-esteem, personal efficacy, and level of maturity.

The birth of a first child brings a potential for psychological complications and an opportunity for adaptive responses. Fedele, Golding, Grossman, and Pollack in Chapter 3 follow the historical roots of clinical interest in this area in their review of research on postpartum psychopathology. They expand their coverage of psychopathological responses to pregnancy and parenthood to include the unique array of responses experienced by men. Then, in a contemporary clinical approach that integrates object relations theory with family systems theory (a "relational systems" approach), the authors present a model to explain normal adaptation of mothers, fathers, and couples to the transition to parenthood. These contributors propose that affiliation and autonomy are two dimensions of psychological development that have particular salience for adjustment during periods of transition. Research evidence is supplied to support the significance of autonomy and affiliation for individual (both female and male) and family development and to underscore the critical role of flexibility in predicting the individual's and family's adaptation to first parenthood.

For decades, the birth of a first child has been viewed as an impetus for change in the marital relationship. The introduction of a third party, the infant, into a preexisting dyadic relationship, the marriage, has been considered by many to have a strong negative impact on the quality and functioning of the husband–wife relationship. Cowan and Cowan in Chapter 4 take issue with this position that blames the baby for causing distress in the marriage. The authors emphasize that the process of change must be examined in order to understand how some couples fare well whereas others have difficulty during the transition to parenthood. Following an integrative review of the sociological literature on the transition as crisis or not, Cowan and Cowan present a five-domain structural model of marital and family adaptation. The five elements of the model constitute an ecological perspective that covers the development of both problems and adaptations for men, women, and their families during the transition to parenthood. To illustrate how structural changes affect marital quality, a process model of marital change is presented and applied to the oft noted finding of decline in marital satisfaction following the birth of a child and to the question of whether the baby is really the cause of the decline.

The transition to parenthood under conditions of risk

In Chapters 1 through 4, the adjustment of individual adults, couples, and families is examined under normative circumstances: a low-risk pregnancy and the birth of a "normal" infant. In Chapters 5 through 7, the focus is on various conditions that place the adult and child at risk, both medically and psychosocially.

Pregnancy and birth entail a host of physiological changes and extensive contact with the medical system. In Chapter 5, Holt offers insights from the perspective of a medical professional. She discusses the physical changes that occur during each trimester of pregnancy and their impact on the expectant mother. Couples' wishes for a healthy baby, and sometimes for a "natural" birth, are presented alongside prevailing medical wisdom, demands on the doctor–patient relationship, and the advances and limitations of obstetrical technology. Holt covers a variety of risk conditions, including advanced maternal age and multiple births. The advent of new technologies for screening and monitoring risk is discussed, and issues raised by new technologies, such as the need to balance fetal risk and maternal risk (e.g., fetal monitors, cesarean birth), are given careful attention.

Parental adaptation under conditions of a high-risk pregnancy or the birth of an at-risk infant is the topic addressed by Easterbrooks in Chapter 6. Appearance, threshold for stimulation, soothability, and cuddliness are some of the dimensions on which premature and handicapped infants' needs seem to differ from their full-term, intact counterparts. Easterbrooks gives special attention to the impact on parents of a preterm birth, because prematurity is a major and fairly common infant risk factor that is considered to be the most pressing concern in perinatal medicine. The circumstances faced by parents of "premies," including separation from the infant and high financial costs, are discussed as they affect parental and couple adaptation. Easterbrooks also examines the implications of infant risk status for mother–infant and father–infant behavioral interactions, in terms of both the quantity of contact and the nature of the interaction. Easterbrooks concludes that favorable adaptation for parents and infants depends on both characteristics of the infant and the amount and quality of support in the caregiving environment.

The potential for individual change during the transition to parenthood may have a parallel in the physiological and emotional changes that occur in adolescence. What results when these two events co-occur, that is, when adolescents bear children, is the question addressed by Osofsky, Osofsky, and Diamond in Chapter 7. The authors place adolescent preg-

nancy and parenthood in the larger context of the transition to parenthood.
They elucidate the psychology of adolescence (i.e., psychodynamic tasks
faced by adolescent girls and boys) and discuss changes in cognitive development during adolescence in order to provide a basis for understanding
the impact of pregnancy and parenthood on adolescent development. The
authors evaluate the medical, social, educational, and relationship issues
(boy–girl, parent–infant) that typify the experience of adolescent pregnancy
and parenthood. Opportunities for growth are considered and factors that
mitigate risk are presented; however, the authors take the position that
the early timing of parenthood does threaten the fulfillment of developmental tasks of adolescence.

Intervention strategies for individuals, couples, and families

The unique needs of families during the transition to parenthood have
spurred a number of intervention strategies designed to prevent the occurrence of maladaptive interaction patterns and to promote the growth
and development possibilities of this major life transition. Preventive intervention strategies include the mobilizing of existing strengths and resources that the individual and the couple already possess. Obtaining
needed support from members of the expectant and new parents' informal
social network is one way to do this and is the topic addressed by Gottlieb
and Pancer in Chapter 8. The authors examine the interplay between the
couple's social network and its psychosocial needs during three stages of
the transition to parenthood: pre-conception, pregnancy, and the postnatal
period. Characteristics of the social network, such as its size, composition,
and density, are integrated with types of social support (e.g., emotional,
cognitive guidance, tangible aid), as they bear on the needs and demands
of the husband and wife during the three stages. Gottlieb and Pancer provide evidence for reciprocal influence between the couple and their social
support network. They discuss the impact of the transition to parenthood
on the structure of the network and elucidate the positive and negative,
direct and indirect influences of the social network on the couple.

In recent years, innovative therapeutic interventions have utilized a
prevention model of mental health rather than a medical or treatment model
to assist couples who are trying to decide whether and when to have children, how best to prepare for childbirth, and how to enhance their adaptation to the demands of parenting. These types of intervention programs
and approaches for couples during the transition to parenthood are reviewed by Duncan and Markman in Chapter 9. Programs that emanate
from a wide range of disciplines, including public health, psychology,

medicine, and nursing, are evaluated within a prevention framework. Also discussed are the effects of these programs on mothers and fathers as individuals as well as on their marital relationship. To guide future work in this area, Duncan and Markman offer recommendations regarding conceptual, design, measurement, and clinical issues pertinent to the development and evaluation of future programs.

The changing needs of families and fiscal constraints on federally funded social service agencies are responsible in part for the emergence of a new system of support programs that are defined outside traditional bureaucracies. In Chapter 10, Kagan and Seitz concentrate on these new family support programs. After reviewing the historical antecedents of the programs, Kagan and Seitz discuss contemporary family support programs within a framework that integrates the audience that is targeted (e.g., mainstream families, high-risk families) with the types of services provided (e.g., information and referral, parenting education, infant care). Despite the diversity of programmatic goals and orientations, some implementation and evaluation issues are common across programs for new parents. The authors discuss these issues, and then offer suggestions for these programs that bear on the role of government, networking among programs and the need for more research on the effects of these programs.

In the final chapter, Goldberg and Michaels provide a conceptual and methodological synthesis of the preceding chapters. The major points and findings of each chapter are highlighted in an integration of correlates and predictors of competency and risk across the transition to parenthood. Also presented are types and goals of intervention strategies for individuals and families at various phases of the transition. The chapter includes suggestions for future research, covering both conceptual and methodological issues.

Appendix

Information on the sources below was adapted from Watts and Hernandez's (1982) report for the Social Science Research Council. These sources may be helpful to social scientists who are conducting research on the transition to parenthood.

Census. Every 10 years, data are compiled at national and local levels on key indicators for the demography of children and families and the socioeconomic resources available to the child in the home. These indicators include age, race, sex, education, employment status, occupation,

18 W. A. GOLDBERG

income, household composition, family formation and dissolution, and housing quality.

Current Population Survey. Since 1947, the Current Population Survey has provided yearly information that is more detailed than the census data. It is the source of most labor force data and includes supplements on marriage and fertility, school enrollment, and income.

National Center for Health Statistics: vital records. The vital records contain basic birth and death information. In addition to information on the number of children added to the population each year, they include data on the demographic characteristics of the children's parents and the amount of prenatal care received.

National Survey of Family Growth. Predecessors of this survey are the Growth of American Families Studies first conducted in 1955 and the National Fertility Surveys. They are rich sources of data on social, economic, and demographic characteristics of women and their sexual activity, contraception usage, reproductive behavior and attitudes, and marriage patterns.

References

Beckman, L. J., & Houser, B. B. (1979). Perceived satisfactions and costs of motherhood and employment among married women. *Journal of Population, 2,* 306–27.
Cherlin, A. (1981). *Marriage, divorce, remarriage.* Cambridge, MA: Harvard University Press.
Congressional Quarterly Weekly Report. (1986). *44*(26), 1437–1520.
Congressional Quarterly Weekly Report. (1987). *45*(3), 101–36.
Cox, M. J. (Ed.). (1985). The transition to parenthood [special issue]. *Journal of Family Issues.* Beverly Hills, CA: Sage.
Cramer, J. C. (1980). Fertility and female employment: Problems of causal direction. *American Sociological Review, 45,* 167–90.
Crawford, T. J., & Boyer, R. (1985). Salient consequences, cultural values, and childbearing intentions. *Journal of Applied Social Psychology, 15,* 16–30.
Crosbie, P. (1986). Rationality and models of reproductive decision-making. In W. P. Handwerker (Ed.), *Culture and reproduction* (pp. 30–58). Boulder, CO: Westview Press.
Daniels, P., & Weingarten, K. (1982). *Sooner or later: The timing of parenthood in adult lives.* New York: Norton.
Davis, K. (1984). Wives and work: The sex role revolution and its consequences. *Population and Development Review, 10,* 397–417.
Duvall, E. C. (1977). *Marriage and family development,* 5th ed. Philadelphia: Lippincott.
Eggebeen, D., & Uhlenberg, P. (1985). Changes in the organization of men's lives: 1960–1980. *Family Relations, 34,* 251–7.
Erikson, E. (1963). *Childhood and society,* 2nd ed. New York: Norton.
Erikson, E. (1968). *Identity, youth, and crisis.* New York: Norton.

Graff, H. (1979). Literacy, education and fertility, past and present: A critical review. *Population and Development Review, 5,* 105–40.

Greenberger, E., Goldberg, W. A., Crawford, T. J., & Granger, J. (1988). Beliefs about the consequences of maternal employment for children. *Psychology of Women Quarterly, 12,* 35–59.

Handwerker, W. P. (1986). Culture and reproduction: Exploring micro/macro linkages. In W. P. Handwerker (Ed.), *Culture and reproduction* (pp. 1–29). Boulder, CO: Westview Press.

Havighurst, R. J. (1972). *Developmental tasks in education.* New York: McKay.

Hill, R. (1978). Psychosocial consequences of a first birth: A discussion. In W. B. Miller & L. F. Newman (Eds.), *The first child and family formations* (pp. 392–401). Chapel Hill: University of North Carolina, Carolina Population Center.

Hill, R., & Hansen, D. (1960). The identification of conceptual frameworks utilized in family study. *Marriage and Family Life, 22,* 299–311.

Hill, R., & Rodgers, R. (1964). The developmental approach. In H. T. Christensen (Ed.), *Handbook of marriage and the family* (pp. 171–211). Chicago: Rand McNally.

Hock, E., Gnezda, M. T., & McBride, S. L. (1984). Mothers of infants: Attitudes toward employment and motherhood following birth of the first child. *Journal of Marriage and the Family, 46,* 425–31.

Hoffman, L. W. (1978). Employment of women and fertility. In L. W. Hoffman & F. I. Nye (Eds.), *Working mothers* (pp. 81–100). San Francisco: Jossey-Bass.

International Bank for Reconstruction and Development. (1984). *World Development Report 1984.* New York: Oxford University Press.

Jones, E. (1981). The impact of women's employment on marital fertility in the U.S., 1970–1975. *Population Studies, 35,* 161–73.

Jones, F. A., Green, V., & Krauss, D. R. (1980). Maternal responsiveness of primiparous mothers during the postpartum period: Age differences. *Pediatrics, 65,* 629–35.

Kamerman, S., Kahn, A., & Kingston, P. (1983). *Maternity policies and working women.* New York: Columbia University Press.

Lamb, M. E. (Ed.). (1977). *The role of the father in child development.* New York: Wiley.

LeMasters, E. E. (1957). Parenthood as crisis. *Marriage and Family Living, 19,* 352–5.

Levinson, D. (1986). A conception of adult development. *American Psychologist, 41,* 3–13.

Masnick, G., & Bane, M. J. (1980). *The nation's families 1960–1990.* Boston: Auburn House.

Mattessich, P., & Hill, R. (1987). Life cycle and family development. In M. B. Sussman & S. K. Steinmetz (Eds.), *Handbook of marriage and the family.* (pp. 437–69). New York: Plenum.

Mercer, R. (1980). Teenage motherhood: The first year. *Journal of Obstetric, Gynecologic and Neonatal Nursing, 9,* 16–27.

Mercer, R. T. (1986). *First-time motherhood: Experiences from teens to forties.* New York: Springer-Verlag.

Michaels, G. Y., Hoffman, M., & Goldberg, W. A. (1982, August). *Longitudinal investigation of value systems changes at the transition to parenthood.* Paper presented at the meetings of the American Psychological Association, Washington, DC.

Miller, W. B., & Newman, L. F. (Eds.). (1978). *The first child and family formation.* Chapel Hill: University of North Carolina, Carolina Population Center.

Neugarten, B., & Datan, N. (1973). Sociological perspectives on the life cycle. In P. B. Baltes & K. W. Schaie (Eds.), *Life-span developmental psychology: Personality and socialization.* (pp. 53–69). New York: Academic Press.

Oppenheimer, V. K. (1974). Women's economic role in the family. *American Sociological Review, 42,* 387–406.

Parke, R. D. (1979). Perspectives on father–infant interaction. In J. D. Osofsky (Ed.), *Handbook of infant development* (pp. 549–90). New York: Wiley.

Parke, R. D. (1981). *Fathers*. Cambridge, MA: Harvard University Press.

Peterson, G., Hay, R., & Peterson, L. (1979). Intersection of family development and moral stage frameworks: Implications for theory and research. *Journal of Marriage and the Family, 79*, 229–35.

Pleck, J. (1985). *Working wives/working husbands*. Beverly Hills, CA: Sage.

Rindfuss, R., Bumpass, L., & St. John, C. (1980). Education and fertility: Implications for the roles women occupy. *American Sociological Review, 45*, 431–47.

Rodgers, R. H. (1973). *Family interaction and transaction: The developmental approach*. Englewood Cliffs, NJ: Prentice-Hall.

Rodgers, R. H. (1977). The family life cycle concept: Past, present and future. In J. Cuisenier (Ed.), *The family life cycle in European societies* (pp. 39–57). The Hague: Mouton.

Rossi, A. (1980). Aging and parenthood in the middle years. In P. B. Baltes & O. G. Brim, Jr. (Eds.), *Life-span development and behavior* (Vol. 3, pp. 137–205). New York: Academic Press.

U.S. Bureau of the Census. (1986). *Fertility of American women: June 1985* (Current Population Reports, Series P-20, No. 406). Washington, DC: U.S. Government Printing Office.

Waite, C. J. (1980). Working wives and the family life cycle. *American Journal of Sociology, 86*, 272–94.

Watts, H., & Hernandez, D. (1982). *Child and family indicators: A report with recommendations*. Washington, DC: Social Science Research Council.

Wilkie, J. R. (1981). The trend toward delayed parenthood. *Journal of Marriage and the Family, 43*, 583–92.

Wise, S., & Grossman, F. K. (1980). Adolescent mothers and their infants: Psychological factors in early attachment and interaction. *American Journal of Orthopsychiatry, 50*, 454–68.

Zagreb baby hailed as 5 billionth person. (1987, July). *New York Times*, p. 7.

Part I

The transition to parenthood as a challenge for adaptation by individuals, couples, and families

1 Motivational factors in the decision and timing of pregnancy

Gerald Y. Michaels

Social scientists studying reproductive behavior in the latter half of the twentieth century are witnessing a monumental change in the psychology of human fertility. The issue of whether and when to have children is no longer a biological given or an unavoidable cultural demand, but a matter of true individual choice. The widespread use of contraceptive technology has enabled couples who do not want to become parents to avoid doing so in most instances. At the same time, the decline in pronatalist values has led to a situation in which those who do not want to have children can make this choice without the fear of extreme social criticism or ostracism. Furthermore, new medical technologies are making childbearing possible for couples who want children but who previously would not have been able to conceive, and our society is at the brink of further developments that, though highly controversial, will allow couples to make decisions not only about whether to have a child, but about the characteristics of the desired child.

However, this increase in choices has had the effect of raising to the forefront the question of why an individual wants to have a child and become a parent. Previously, the question of what values and satisfactions children provide, and at what cost to other life goals and values, presented itself much less frequently. Now faced with a choice, prospective parents sometimes report that they do not know on what basis to make their decision. Miller (1983) writes, "Many cannot seem to find within themselves a real motivational basis for their decision, as though some important kernel of desire is missing; others feel extremely ambivalent, torn in a double-approach conflict (e.g., having children versus having a career) or a double avoidance conflict (e.g., not wanting to take care of children versus not wanting to be childless)" (p. 1203).

Furthermore, the existence of choice does not necessarily indicate that the prospective parent has made an informed choice, that is, has actually thought about his or her motivations for having a child or is aware of the

23

real motivations that underly this choice. In this case, the motivations still exist, but not in the individual's awareness. In addition to furthering our understanding of basic human motivations and values, one purpose of the psychological research on motivations for parenthood is the practical one of assisting couples in making informed and personally meaningful choices. Moreover, understanding the motivational patterns that underly fertility choices may help in the prediction of worldwide fertility patterns, which have a huge impact on social and economic conditions in the United States and throughout the world.

This chapter begins with a brief historically oriented overview of a number of approaches to the study of motivation for parenthood. It then turns to the model of motivation for parenthood that has produced the most empirical research, the values of having children approach developed by Hoffman and Hoffman (1973). Past research tying this model to fertility behavior is reviewed, and then two studies by this author and his colleagues that develop the ideas of the Hoffman and Hoffman theoretical model are discussed. The final sections of the chapter are devoted to a methodological and theoretical critique of this field of research and to suggestions for further study.

Historical overview

A historical overview of the literature on motivation for parenthood begins with the long-controversial area of whether there are innate (unlearned) factors that make having children rewarding. The earliest writers who held such a belief spoke of a "maternal instinct" (e.g., Deutsch, 1945; Soddy, 1964; Wengraf, 1953). Pohlman (1973) suggests avoiding the term "instinct" because it is too vague. He distinguishes six possible areas in which innate factors can logically play a role: (1) sex relations, (2) having a fetus in the uterus, (3) delivery and childbirth, (4) breastfeeding, (5) skin contact with and cuddling of the baby, and (6) caretaking of an infant or older child. The area of sexual relations, however, is usually not included in the concept of "maternal instinct," and Pohlman notes that all the other areas pertain primarily to mothers. However, Benedek (1959) speculated that there also might be a drive toward fathering.

More recently, theoretical writing in the area has postulated a more modern version of the parental instinct viewpoint in which motivation for parenthood is considered to have evolutionary survival value, ensuring the passing of one's own genes to future generations (e.g., Barash, 1977). At the same time, as a result of the feminist movement, there is increased sensitivity to the possible manifestations of a "pronatalist" bias in societal attitudes and even in scholarly arguments concerning an innate component of motivation for parenthood. Although most psychologists who have done research in the area favor an explanation based on learning, there is no conclusive evidence that can distinguish innate and learned factors and entirely rule out the innate component. Evidence of individual adults or even cultures in which women do not want children is not itself sufficient to rule out innate factors, since it is possible that socialization has suppressed the innate tendency (Pohlman, 1973).

In general, the proponents of an innate parenthood motivation have not attempted to identify the psychological manifestations of the hypothesized motive. This task has been left to the psychological theories of motivation for parenthood. The earliest attempts to understand the psychological experience of motivation for parenthood were made by psychoanalytic writers. Psychoanalytic theorists traced motivation for parenthood to the dynamics of childhood personality development, rather than seeking the roots of the desire to have children in conditions of adulthood. Furthermore, they focused on unconscious motives having to do with psychosexual dynamics, ego formation, and the internalization of parental representations. In keeping with the emphasis on distinctions in the development of males and females, different processes of development of motivation for parenthood were posited for mothers and fathers, though the primary emphasis was on mothers.

The girl's motivation to become a mother was attributed by some psychoanalytic writers to "penis envy"; having a baby, especially a boy, was thought to be a penis substitute (Deutsch, 1945). Other psychoanalytic writers postulated the girl's oedipal attachment to her father to be the origin of her wanting to have children; that is, she fantasizes having children by him. In keeping with the emphasis of psychoanalytic theory on defensive operations, it was also suggested that a woman might be attracted to having a larger family because she unconsciously feels that if her oedipal interests are divided among many children, the intensity of any one relationship will be reduced and she may feel less guilty over her forbidden impulses (Rainwater, 1965). Still other psychoanalytic writers focused on the other side of the oedipal struggle, the woman's intense competition with her mother, as the basis of her desire to have children. A woman may hold unconscious wishes to have a baby in order to replace her mother, and having a larger family may represent a wish to outdo the mother (Deutsch, 1945; Hoffman & Wyatt, 1960). Similarly, competition with siblings may be a motivation for some women.

A different etiology of men's development of motivation for parenthood was suggested by the psychoanalytic writers. Freud (1909/1955a, 1911/

1958, 1918/1955b, 1923/1961) believed that the boy's wish to have a child arose during the oedipal period from regression to an earlier identification with the mother. This was thought to serve two purposes. By wishing to be impregnated by the father and bear his child, the boy was said to both invite the father's love and to avoid fantasized castration for his competitive, aggressive, oedipal strivings. Freud called this wish the "negative oedipal complex" (1923/1961). Later, a number of psychoanalytic writers changed their focus from the negative oedipal complex to the boy's wish to be like the mother because of his envy of her creative power (Boehm, 1930; Jones, 1927/1961a, 1933/1961b).

With the advent of ego psychology, the psychoanalytic focus shifted from instinctual gratifications to processes of identification. The child's motivation to have a child was seen as part of his or her internalization of a crucially important aspect of the parent's behavior, the caretaking role. One aspect of the child's motivation was thought to emerge from the struggle to deal with the concept of separateness from the mother. The child attempts to internalize the mother's parenting role in order to recreate psychologically the lost infantile relationship he or she once had with the mother. Involved in this process of identification is the attempt to do for oneself what one's mother has previously done.

Other ego psychologists, still within the psychoanalytic tradition, suggested that an important motivation for having children comes from seeing the child as an extension of the ego or the self, with the love one has for oneself then invested in the child. This is essentially a narcissistic motivation (Fleugel, 1947a,b). An important part of the extension of the ego that parenthood provides is its extension into the future after one's own death (Fleugel, 1947b). However, not all ego psychologists consider the motivation for having children to be so narcissistically centered. Erikson (1950) viewed it as an important expression of a generativity motivation in which the psychological experience is one of wishing to give something altruistically to the next generation.

Motivation for parenthood in population research

Given the problem of world overpopulation and the impact of population size on social and economic trends in the United States, it is quite understandable that the early psychoanalytically based writings on motivation for parenthood were followed by attempts to define the values and costs of having children in order to predict various aspects of fertility behavior. From the perspective of the fertility researchers, the values of having children are considered one of a group of antecedent or independent variables that are thought to influence fertility decisions, behaviors, or out-comes. Other variables also considered to influence fertility by the pop-ulation researchers were outlined by Beckman (1982). The list includes demographic and background factors, such as age, age at marriage, eth-nicity, and socioeconomic status; psychological traits, such as locus of control, sex role traditionalism, and personal efficacy; attitudinal factors, such as knowledge and acceptability of birth planning, attitudes regarding contraception, sexuality, and abortion; biological factors, such as subfe-cundity and sterility; social-psychological factors, such as power in the family, openness of communication, and social support; and developmental factors, such as age of previous children, life-cycle stage, and one's own socialization experiences.

Including psychological variables such as the values of having children into an overall model of fertility behavior enabled population researchers to address the individual level of human fertility. Jaccard and Davidson (1976) wrote, "If we are to understand fertility-related behavior, it is clear that we must not only describe variation in fertility but also determine the process by which social and economic variables operate through psy-chological variables to influence desired family size" (p. 330).

Vinokur-Kaplan (1977) pointed out that the use of a values of having children model to predict fertility behavior bears a close resemblance to the behavioral decision-making framework used in mathematical and social psychology (e.g., Edwards, Lindmann, & Phillips, 1965). According to this approach, a decision about whether to take a particular course of action is determined by the expected value of the action, defined as the degree to which it is perceived to be the optimal way of obtaining desired goals and avoiding undesirable outcomes or both. Not only the decision to have a child, but other family-planning-related behaviors can be studied as outcome variables of such decision making. These include attitudes toward birth control (Blake, Insko, Cialdini, & Chaikin, 1969; Crawford, 1973; Kothandapani, 1971), contraceptive use (Davidson & Jaccard, 1976), abortion (Smetana & Adler, 1979), mother's employment (Beckman, 1978; Beckman & Houser, 1979), desired family size (Inazu, Langmeyer, & Lundgren, 1974; Kirchner & Seaver, 1977; Werner, Middlestadt-Carter, & Crawford, 1975), and the decision to have another child (Townes, Beach, Campbell, & Wood, 1980).

One group of studies attempting to relate the values of having children to fertility behavior using the behavioral decision-making approach was done by Lee Beach and his colleagues (Beach, Campbell, & Townes, 1979; Beach, Townes, Campbell, & Keating, 1976). Beach developed the Hi-erarchy of Birth Planning Values, a hierarchically organized set of 20 value categories related to having a child. The subject first assigns weights to each value to indicate perceived utility to him or her. The subject then assigns subjective probabilities to the categories to indicate how likely it will be that the values will be fulfilled if one is going to have a child in the next 2 years. Using this model, predictions were made about whether each subject was likely to have a (another) child within the next 2 years. The best predictions (73% correct) were made for those couples who had not yet reached their desired family size.

Campbell, Townes, & Beach (1982) administered the Hierarchy of Birth Planning Values to 199 middle-class married couples with zero to four children; all of the couples were currently using a contraceptive. They found that the values of husbands with no children differed from those of husbands with one or more children, but that there were no differences in the values of husbands with one to four children. Wives, however, showed a somewhat more articulated pattern in that there were value differences between women with zero, one, and two children. Husbands and wives within the same party were quite similar in the extent of their overall parenthood motivation. Couples with no children were ambivalent about having a child; couples with one child were quite positive about having another child; couples with two children were negative; couples with three or four children were again ambivalent.

Examining the specific values in the Hierarchy, the authors found that, for both husbands and wives, across the different parity levels the strongest values were "parent/child relationships – the opportunity to establish a close affiliative relationship with another human being" – and "child's education – the opportunity to participate in the education and training of the child." The major costs of having a (another) child were "educational/vocational – the negative impact of a child upon attainment of parents' educational and vocational goals" – and "material – the material well-being of the family." Each parity level also had some values and costs that were specifically salient to itself. For couples who had not yet had children, "parents age – the desire to have a first child while one is young" – was an important motivation. Another important value for nonparents was "relatives – producing a grandchild for one's parents and a niece or nephew for one's siblings in order to enhance affiliation with one's family of origin." Thus, both socialization to the role of parent and family expectations are very important motivations for having a first child.

Parents with one child already also had specific motivations not shared by parents at other parity levels. The most important value was "siblings – to provide a companion or playmate for the first child." The authors suggest that these parents have accepted the cultural bias against the one-child family. Furthermore, wives with one child viewed having another child as more important for "self-concept – enhancing their own maturity" – and for "the self–spouse relationship – enhancing closeness with their husbands" – than women of other parities. Husbands with one child attached significantly greater importance to "prospective child – the positive qualities of an additional child which are expected to have a positive impact on the family."

Hoffman and Hoffman's theoretical model

The values of having children theoretical model that has received the most attention and has been studied most extensively both in the United States and internationally was developed by Hoffman and Hoffman (1973). The Hoffman and Hoffman model identifies a set of nine basic values or satisfactions that children may provide.

The nine value categories refer to functions that children serve or needs they fulfill for the parent. Each value is based on an underlying psychological need, but at the same time, the values are influenced by cultural, social, and economic factors. Thus, the model may be seen as spanning or linking psychological and sociological approaches. The nine value categories are as follows:

1. *Adult status and social identity*. This value fulfulls the need to be accepted as a responsible and mature adult member of the community.
2. *Expansion of the self*. This value fulfills the need to have someone carry on for oneself after one's own death, as well as the need to have new growth and learning experiences and to add meaning to life.
3. *Moral values*. This value satisfies the need for moral improvement, including becoming less selfish and learning to sacrifice, making a contribution to society, or satisfying one's religious requirements.
4. *Primary group ties and affection*. This value satisfies the need to express affection and attain intimacy with another person, as well as to be the recipient of such feelings from someone else.
5. *Stimulation and fun*. This value fulfills the need to add the interest to life that children can provide.
6. *Achievement and creativity*. This value fulfills the need for accomplishment, achievement, and creativity that can come from having children and helping them grow.
7. *Power and influence*. This value satisfies the need to have influence over another person.
8. *Social comparison*. This value satisfies the need to have prestige or a competitive advantage over others through comparing the behavior, appearance, or accomplishments of one's children with those of other children.
9. *Economic utility*. This value satisfies needs related to economic usefulness and the fact that children can sometimes help with the parents' work or add their own income to the family's resources.

An important additional concept of the Hoffman and Hoffman model is the "alternatives hypothesis." This hypothesis predicts that individuals or groups who have less access than others to alternative means of satisfying a particular need will value children more highly for this quality. The extent to which one holds a particular value is dependent on (1) the intensity of the felt need underlying the value, (2) the extent to which children are seen as a potential source of satisfaction of the need, and (3) the availability of alternative sources of need satisfaction.

Aside from the nine "values of children" categories, a set of costs of having children (e.g., financial costs, interference with mother's working) were identified (Hoffman, 1975). However, the costs of having children figure much less prominently in the research that has utilized the Hoffman and Hoffman "values of children" model. Finally, two other concepts of the model that have received little direct research attention are "barriers," which are factors such as economic problems, poor housing, or maternal health problems that make it difficult to achieve a particular value, and "facilitators," which are factors such as prosperity or good housing that make it easier to achieve a particular value.

The "values of children" international study

Using the Hoffman and Hoffman theoretical model as the primary conceptual framework, a seven-nation research study of the values and costs of having children was conducted in 1975. The data were collected in Korea, Indonesia, the Philippines, Taiwan, Thailand, Turkey, and the United States. The U.S. sample consisted of 1,569 married women under age 40 and about one-fourth of their spouses. Identical interviews were conducted in each country, the topics covering values of having children, alternative sources of need satisfaction, costs of having children, and costs involved in the alternative sources of need satisfaction. The interview also covered desired family size, sex preference, family plans, contraceptive behavior, decision making, and sociodemographic factors.

Research reports focusing on values of having children in the U.S. sample have utilized two broad measures from the interview. One measure is an open-ended, structured interview item about the advantages of having children: "I want to ask you about the advantages and disadvantages of having children. First – what would you say are some of the advantages of having children compared with not having children at all?" The researchers developed a coding scheme for this item consisting of 65 types of responses and coded a maximum of four different responses per subject. They wrote that they were guided in their selection of categories by the

Hoffman and Hoffman (1973) nine-value schema, but the categories were also empirically based in that they were adopted from actual responses to the interview. Hoffman, Thornton, and Manis (1978) found that almost all the responses could be categorized into one of the nine dimensions, though two dimensions, "social comparison" and "power and influence," were infrequently coded in the U.S. sample. The "social comparison" category was combined with "achievement and creativity," whereas the "power and influence" category was retained.

The second "values of children" measure from the interview with the U.S. sample was a structured measure consisting of a 22-item list of reasons for having children. The subjects were asked to rate the importance of each reason on a 3-point scale: *very important, somewhat important,* or *not important.* The items that comprised the scale were derived in part from pretest responses to the open-ended question.

Hoffman et al. (1978) found general concordance between the responses from the open-ended and structured measures. For both measures, "primary group ties and affection" and "stimulation and fun" were the values most highly endorsed by the U.S. subjects. The values "expansion of the self," "adult status and social identity," and "achievement and creativity" fell in between. "Economic utility," "power and influence," and "morality" were rated least important. Minor variations for the two measures were found; for example, achievement and creativity were rated higher on the structured measure. Hoffman et al. suggest that this may have occurred because this value was acceptable to most people but not likely to be one of the four top values (the ones coded) for the nonstructured measure.

Differences on some of the values were also found between men and women. Women rated primary group ties and affection and stimulation and fun, as well as the aspect of expansion of the self that focuses on one's current life, as more important on the nonstructured measure. Men rated the aspect of expansion of the self that focuses on achieving immortality through children higher than did women. On the structured measure the largest difference between the sexes was for the value adult status and social identity, which women consistently rated higher. Of the items in this category, the item with the greatest differences was "because it is part of being a woman/man." The researchers suggest that men are apparently much less likely than women to view having children as an integral part of their sex role.

In general, on both measures parents rated the "values of children" categories more highly than did nonparents. Parents particularly rated children as being more important as a source of adult status and social identity. They also rated stimulation and fun higher, as they did that aspect of expansion of the self dealing with one's current life. The only categories rated higher by nonparents were achievement and creativity and that aspect of expansion of the self dealing with leaving something behind after one's death. To explain the higher valuing of achievement and creativity among nonparents, the authors suggest that this value may be more highly satisfied in anticipation than in the actual day-to-day life of being a parent.

Investigation of the "alternatives hypothesis"

Hoffman et al. (1978) then examined the relationship of various social, economic, and demographic variables to these values of having children, paying particular attention to variables thought to be relevant to the "alternatives hypothesis." The results were mixed. In support of the alternatives hypothesis was the finding that two groups of subjects who presumably have less access to economic resources – those with less education and subjects who were black – were more likely than other subjects to highly value economic utility considerations as an advantage of having children. Also, economic utility and security in old age was more often cited as an advantage of having children by respondents with a rural background, which is consistent with the view that in urban environments children lose the economic utility they once had as helpers on the farm. Furthermore, subjects living in an urban environment were found to value children more for meaning and purpose, which is consistent with the hypothesis that urbanization increases the perception that children are important sources of satisfying this value. Jews and those with no religion rated the value "immortality" higher. The authors speculated that since Christianity places more emphasis than Judaism on life after death, children are not as necessary for the expression of this value.

Nonsupportive of the alternatives hypothesis was the lack of findings for higher education, higher employment, and holding an egalitarian sex role definition, all of which were expected to provide women with alternative sources of satisfaction for values of having children associated with achievement, creativity, and competence. Also, in general the strength of the relationships between background and demographic variables and values of having children was small. Some possible reasons for this are discussed later in the chapter.

Values of having children and attitudes toward fertility

Hoffman and Manis (1979) used responses to the open-ended values question described earlier to examine the relationship between values and the number of children desired by women in the U.S. national sample. When they included appropriate controls, they found items from three values related to desired family size: "Children give you something useful to do," which is associated with the category adult status and social identity; "Children make you feel like a better person," which is associated with the morality category, and "Children have general economic utility," which is associated with the value economic utility and security in old age. Other relationships of values of having children to desired family size differed with parity. For example, valuing children for the enhancement of the marriage was a salient motivation for wanting a child or another child among women with no children or one child, but it was not a salient motivation for wanting to have additional children among subjects who already had two or more children. Valuing children for immortality, a value that includes "interest in passing on one's beliefs, family name or part of oneself," was frequently a motivation for having a first child or only one child and was also a motivation for wanting additional children among respondents who already had a large family (four or more children).

Hoffman and Manis noted that the values that were related to a larger desired number of children are infrequently cited in the United States compared with other countries, which fits with the low birthrate here. Still, these values may be important in understanding the desire for large families among particular individuals or subgroups of the population. For example, black respondents both experienced a desire for more children than did whites and more frequently cited economic utility as a value of having children. Similarly, larger family size was desired by women who valued having children because it gave them "something useful to do." Since nonemployed women also more often gave this response, the authors suggested that a woman who is not employed may believe she needs more than two children to keep herself involved in useful activity.

The focus on desired family size represents a very important and underinvestigated area for future research. Hoffman and Manis explain that one would not expect a linear relationship between values of having children and number of children desired, since some values may be satisfied by having one child, whereas other values may require or benefit from a large family. For example, achieving adult status could be largely established by having a first child, though additional children could help cement this status. Values like stimulation and fun and economic security in old age may be better satisfied by having more than one child. Hoffman and Manis also mention, but do not elaborate, the idea that some values may be related to a desire for another child at a particular stage of life rather than be related to the total number of desired children. This brings up the important question of how values of having children relate to the timing of childbearing and suggests that aspects of fertility attitudes other than total number of children desired should be investigated.

Hoffman and Manis also suggest that situational factors may influence the relationship of values of having children to fertility attitudes. This may occur in a number of ways:

1. Social conditions can define the circumstances in which value satisfaction is highest. For example, the authors point out that the way in which children are seen as promoting the marital relationship in the United States, where companionship marriages predominate, would be different from the way they are seen in a country where marriage is more often evaluated in terms of economics, extended kinship, or childbearing functions.
2. Social conditions can determine whether a small number of "quality" children can satisfy the parents' need for achievement satisfaction through their children. In other situations, achievement satisfaction may be more dependent on the number than on the quality of children.
3. Social conditions can determine the number of children necessary to satisfy the value. Thus, satisfaction of the value "completion of the family" may require a different number of children in one culture or subculture than another, since it is defined by the social milieu.
4. Social conditions can affect the shape of the relationship between values and fertility attitudes and behaviors. As an example, the authors state that, although there may be an association between number of children desired and valuing children for security in old age, social conditions will determine when there is a point of diminishing returns. The authors explain that in high-mortality countries, the value "security in old age" requires a parent to have a sufficient number of children to guarantee that one child will be living when the parent reaches old age. Also, in cultures where women have no independent economic resources, multiple children may be needed to achieve economic security in old age.

Hoffman and Manis did not directly investigate the relationship between fertility attitudes and costs of having children. They do suggest that economic considerations usually place an upper limit on the number of children desired. However, although costs may set the upper limit, the values that children satisfy will set the lower limits, and when values of having children are strong enough and no alternatives are available, individuals will go to considerable length to have children.

Costs of having children

Compared with the values of having children, the costs or negative values have been a less extensively investigated component of the theoretical model. In a 1975 article, however, Hoffman did report on the costs of having children in a subsample of the U.S. married couples of her larger study. The subsample was composed of parents who already had one or more children. Hoffman first categorized the types of responses given to the open-ended interview item "What are some of the disadvantages or bad things about having children, compared with not having children?" From her data she identified 10 cost categories. The cost most frequently given by both women and men was "loss of freedom," which included all responses that centered on the idea that children in some way tie the parent down or restrict his or her activities. The second most important category for both sexes was "financial costs." Though the rank orderings of these values for men and women were identical, men actually cited financial costs more frequently than did women, whereas women cited loss of freedom more frequently than did men. This finding probably reflects the pressures of the different traditional roles of breadwinner and housewife. The third most important negative value for both sexes was labeled "traditional worries." The responses that comprised this category included worries over the child's health, safety, and well-being. The fourth category contained specific aspects of the parenting role that the respondents found unpleasant. These included things like having to change diapers or discipline the child. The fifth most frequently cited negative value for women was interference of the child with the mother's working. This, however, was the ninth or lowest-ranking value cited by the men. The fifth negative value for the husbands and the sixth for the wives was "worry because of the troubled world," which included worry that children might turn out badly, not because of the parenting they received, but because the world is plagued by crime, war, and pollution. The seventh most important value for women and sixth most important value for men was interference of the child with the marital relationship. The eighth value for women and seventh for men was "worry over one's own ability to parent." The ninth value for women and eighth for men was "children are lazy" and the tenth most frequently cited value for both women and men was "concern about overpopulation." What seems most notable about the ordering of these negative values is the similarity between husbands and wives.

Hoffman also presented couples' reasons for not wanting to have more than a stated number of children. Financial matters were most frequently cited by both women and men of all current family sizes, including those with no children. Hoffman suggested that this finding may indicate that the current trend toward smaller family size could be reversed in the future if the economy were to become very prosperous.

Husband–Wife and level of parity differences in values

Vinokur-Kaplan (1977) studied 141 American couples, 71 with one child and 70 with two children. To assess values, husbands and wives were asked during separate interviews to sort 27 cards, each with a value of having children written on it, into a 5-point rating scale ranging from *very important* to *not at all important,* and then to rank-order the nine most important values. The 27 values were based mainly on the Hoffman and Hoffman 9-category scheme, but also included a tenth category, "health and well-being." However, the individual items were not identical to those used in the international values of children study, and the authors did not assume a priori that having another child would always work toward the satisfaction of the value.

The results showed substantial similarity between the values of couples at the two parity levels. There were only four highly rated values on which the two groups differed: The value "to give each of your children the companionship they need from brothers or sisters" was rated higher in the one-child families, whereas "to make sure that the workload of your husband or wife is not too difficult or demanding," "to make sure that your workload is not too demanding," and "to feel healthy and energetic" were all rated higher by the two-children parents. However, when the couples were asked whether these values would be enhanced or interfered with if they had another child, the two-children parents were always more likely than the one-child parents to state that the value made them not want to have another child. This was also true for values that had to do with the exclusive relationship with one's spouse and with one's own personal time, work, and interests. Thus, important life values tended to lead couples away from wanting more children as parity increased.

Correlations between husband's and wife's value system ratings revealed associations ranging from .39 to .45. Thus, there is considerable similarity in values of having children between spouses. However, these correlations were lower than those between spouses regarding their stated desires and intentions of having another child, which ranged between .60 and .80. This probably reflects the influence of additional intervening variables other than the values. Also, spouses may arrive at similar decisions based on different value considerations.

Vinokur-Kaplan was one of the few investigators to attempt an empirical analysis of the internal relationships among the values in order to identify salient values of having children dimensions. She subjected the importance ratings for the 27 value items to smallest space analysis (Bailey, 1974; Lingoes, 1973) and found that these values could be accounted for quite adequately by two dimensions that include five value clusters. The dimensions and clusters held for both the one-child and two-children parents. Cluster I reflected desires and norms regarding family size and composition, particularly having a balance of types of children in the family.

Cluster II consisted of values having mainly to do with personal achievement and fulfillment, including meeting needs for personal affection, stimulation, affiliation, and belonging. Cluster III focused on the need for achievement and fulfillment in the social area and included contributing to one's community and society. Cluster IV focused on the need to maintain physical resources such as time and energy, including the wish to have time alone with one's spouse and ensuring a manageable workload. Cluster V focused on economic maintenance and included maintaining an acceptable standard of living and being able to provide for one's children's education.

Vinokur-Kaplan then interpreted the two dimensions underlying these values. The first axis can be seen as a continuum with one pole representing "maintenance and fulfillment of personal existing role demands" and the other pole representing "enhancement and extension of oneself and one's roles through change." The second axis can be seen as a continuum with one pole representing "a concern for family group life and its demands" and the other pole representing "concern emanating from being part of, and participating in, the larger social system." Subjects who intended to have another child tended to have scores located at the poles of enhancement of the self and concern for the family unit. Subjects who were least likely to have another child had scores located at the poles reflecting concern for maintenance of current role demands and concern for being part of the larger social system. Vinokur-Kaplan's space diagram thus suggests a potentially useful theoretical organization of the motivational structures underlying fertility behavior.

Relationship of values to sex roles and parental identification

Working within the same general approach to values of having children, Gerson (1980) designed a measure of parenthood motivation that had six components: (1) a question concerning the respondent's eagerness to have children, (2) a ranking of the satisfaction of childrearing compared with nine other activities of adulthood, (3) a rating of the appeal of various stages of childrearing, (4) a rating of motivation to have a child relative to potentially serious difficulties of pregnancy and childbearing, (5) a rating of role conflicts particular to parenthood, and (6) a rating of the overall benefits and costs of children. The list of benefits was derived from Kirchner's (1973) factor analysis of college students' motivations for wanting children, whereas the list of costs of having children was based on Hoffman's (1972) exploratory study of parenthood motivation, also in a college sample. Each of these six scores was standardized and then the six component scores summed to obtain a global measure of motivation for parenthood.

Gerson (1980) then administered the questionnaire to a large group of unmarried, childless, female college students with a mean age of 18.7. She believed that this was a group for whom the choice of whether to have children was a relatively open one, since most of the students had broad exposure to feminist attitudes and broad career options. She then examined the relationship between the global parenthood motivation score and a number of demographic and psychological variables.

Three variables for which significant and unique variance components were found in a hierarchical multiple regression analysis merit special consideration. First, memories of one's mother being loving was related to parenthood motivation. Gerson (1980) notes that this finding supports Benedek's (1960) focus on early "positive-satisfying" experiences as a basis for wanting children, as well as Erikson's (1950) belief that nurturance in adulthood emerges out of the "basic trust" developed early in the mother–child dyad. Gerson (1980) suggests that what Wyatt (1967) described as the principle of inner duality, which is a wish to nurture and simultaneously identify with a child one is nurturing, may be a salient experience only for individuals who have enjoyed the early gratification that Benedek and Erikson discussed.

Second, sympathy for the women's liberation movement was strongly negatively associated with parenthood motivation. This finding supports other research (Bram, 1974; Lott, 1973) and suggests, according to Gerson, that motherhood may be associated with an inferior status or that women with high feminism scores are especially cognizant of the problems of balancing career and childcare responsibilities.

Third, femininity scores on the Bem Sex Role Inventory (Bem, 1974) were positively related to parenthood motivation. Since femininity scores were also related to perceptions on the Parenthood Relations Questionnaire (Siegelman, 1965) of mother care, father care, perceived maternal success in childrearing, and happiness of family life, Gerson (1980) suggests that women with high femininity scores on the Bem scale especially consider parenthood to be reciprocally gratifying to parent and child – hence, their increased parenthood motivation.

There was no confirmation, however, that "feminine" women on the Bem measure are more likely to consider childrearing as essential to their female identity, since a correlation between femininity scores and endorsing beliefs such as "If a woman fails to have a child she violates her true nature" was not significant.

A finding of a nonsignificant relationship between maternal identification and parenthood motivation was inconsistent with the prediction of both psychoanalytic theory and social roles theory. However, Gerson (1980) points out that studies of parental identification among college women have often produced unexpected and confusing findings and that the Semantic Differential measure (Osgood, Suci, & Tannenbaum, 1975) used to assess identification may have failed to capture important aspects of the identification process.

In evaluating Gerson's study one must keep in mind that the subjects were unmarried college students for whom long-range considerations of parenthood might influence future life-course directions but who were not, as a group, in a position to decide now to have children. It is possible that in the context of a dyadic or marital relationship both the salience of particular parenthood motivations and their interrelationships with other factors would differ. Furthermore, by combining the components of parenthood motivation into a single index, Gerson lost the opportunity to study how various components of motivation for having a child (or not having a child) interact with the sex role and parental identification measures that were studied.

Values of having children in adolescent parenthood

My own research with Raeford Brown (Michaels & Brown, 1987) has begun to examine the utility of Hoffman and Hoffman's theoretical model for understanding motivation for parenthood among adolescent parents. An important conceptual problem may have slowed this line of research. Since only approximately 9% of pregnant adolescents report having made a purposive decision to have a baby (Alan Guttmacher Institute, 1981), it might mistakenly be concluded that values of having children, which according to the Hoffman and Hoffman theoretical model are expected to exist within the awareness of the individual, could not possibly be involved for the majority of this group. However, there is no reason to suspect that strong motivation to have a child cannot exist in the subjective experience of an adolescent who nevertheless would still not make a purposive decision to have a child. Russell (1980) argued that the motivations for adolescent pregnancy and parenthood are essentially similar to the motivations of adults who are becoming parents, which she believes are ultimately tied to our culture's valuing of children, parenthood, and family building. Furthermore, even if motivational processes do not play a major role in the conception, as the pregnancy progresses, motivational processes are certainly involved in decisions about pregnancy outcome (i.e., whether to keep the baby, place the baby for adoption, or have an abortion), and among those adolescents who decide to keep their children, motivational processes are likely to play an important role in the type of caregiving arrangements that are made for the baby.

The Michaels and Brown study explored three questions: (1) What is the relationship between values of having children and number of adolescent pregnancies an individual has had? (2) Is there support for an expanded version of Hoffman and Hoffman's alternatives hypothesis that takes into account psychological as well as demographic barriers to seeking alternative need satisfaction outside of parenthood? (3) Are the values of having children categories related to the pregnant adolescent's expected involvement in childcare activities or to postpartum reports of involvement in childcare?

The second question requires some explanation. We expected that relationships similar to those found with the U.S. national sample of adults between demographic variables and values of having children would occur among adolescent parents. Specifically, we predicted that four demographic variables – having a low socioeconomic background, being black, living in a rural setting, and not being employed or being employed for few hours – would be associated with higher values of having children. However, we believed that, although demographic variables may determine the objective availability of alternative resources for satisfying needs, the objective availability of alternatives does not guarantee their psychological availability to the adolescent. Thus, if an adolescent has been socialized from an early age to consider motherhood to be the primary arena in which she can expect to satisfy basic needs, she will be unlikely to consider other opportunities, even if these are objectively available. This type of socialization may be especially strong in a family where the adolescent's own mother gave birth to a child at an early age, since in such families seeking gratification through teenage parenthood is modeled by the adolescent's primary identification figure. We therefore predicted that there would be a positive relationship between the strength of the adolescent's values of having children and the age at which her own mother gave birth to a first child.

Furthermore, even in situations in which the adolescent may be oriented toward the possibility of attaining alternative need satisfactions, she may lack the social skills necessary to utilize these alternatives. The kinds of alternative need gratifications available to the adolescent often require an ability to negotiate the intricacies of adultlike social relations. Such negotiation in turn would seem to require the development of a sufficient degree of what might be conceptualized as "social maturity" on the part of the adolescent. Thus, adolescents with greater social maturity might value having children to a lesser degree than other adolescents because they would have greater ability to make use of alternative sources of need gratification. To examine this hypothesis, we employed a measure of social maturity that was developed especially for an adolescent population. Domains assessed by this measure included the adolescent's social competence, self-knowledge, independence, and goal-directedness.

Question 3 focused on the possible relationship between values of having children and expectations, as well as postpartum reports, of involvement in child caregiving by the adolescent mother, the baby's father, and extended family members. First, since it has been speculated (Hoffman & Hoffman, 1973) that it is mainly through direct child caregiving that the psychological needs thought to underlie the values of having children categories can be satisfied, we hypothesized that the strength of an adolescent's values of having children would be associated with expectations during the pregnancy and reports after the baby was born of extensive personal involvement in infant care by the adolescent herself. Second, we hypothesized that strongly valuing having children would be associated with the adolescent expecting and reporting greater involvement in infant caregiving by the baby's father. An important part of the potential satisfactions of having a child comes from the possibility of sharing the parenting experience with the father, and in fact achievement of a number of the Hoffman and Hoffman values of having children categories, such as primary group ties and affection, may not be possible unless the adolescent maintains a close relationship with the baby's father and can involve him in caregiving. Third, although we expected that highly valuing having children would be related to the adolescent mother's expectations and reports of her own and the baby's father's involvement in infant caregiving, we predicted that the strength of her values of having children would be negatively related to the extent to which she expected or reported that her own mother and father would perform the infant caregiving tasks.

The subjects in our study were 95 adolescent mothers and expectant mothers enrolled in three school-age parent programs in a midwestern state, one located in a large metropolitan area, a second in a small metropolitan area, and the third in a small town in a rural setting. The average age of these adolescents was 17 years. Their backgrounds ranged from lower to middle socioeconomic status (SES). Sixty-one percent were white and 39% were black. All the subjects had chosen to give birth and keep their babies.

For the study we modified the Hoffman and Hoffman structured values measure slightly by adding several new value items specifically relevant to adolescents: "to create life," "to establish independence from your parents,'' and ''because it is part of being an adult.'' Also, the original item ''because children bring love'' was replaced by two items, ''because you can have someone to love'' and ''because you can have someone love you.''

The social maturity scale was constructed for the study with an eye toward assessing issues relevant to the social maturity of adolescent mothers. Titled the ''How Are You Feeling Questionnaire,'' it consists of a series of self-rated items developed in consultation with a group of adolescents and their school teachers. The items focus on the following areas: the degree to which the adolescent feels she is a responsible person; the degree to which she feels a sense of purpose in her life; the degree to which she believes she knows herself; the degree to which she considers herself an independent person; the degree to which she feels independent from her parents; the degree to which she feels comfortable handling financial matters; the degree to which she feels comfortable being considered an adult at this point; and the degree to which she feels comfortable living on her own. Test–retest reliability, established with another subject sample, was .91.

Finally, the adolescents were asked to complete the Activity with the Child Questionnaire, a modification of a scale used by Goldberg, Michaels, and Lamb (1985), in which they were required to indicate, for the time periods when they were not at school, what proportion of a list of common infant caregiving activities was presently being done (or was expected to be done once the baby was born) by the adolescent mother herself, by the baby's father, by the adolescent's own mother, by her own father, and by other people. The 15 items comprised three dimensions of infant caregiving: (1) physical maintenance activities (e.g., ''buys child's clothes''), (2) physical caregiving activities (e.g., ''bathes child''), and (3) attachment activities (e.g., ''hugs and kisses child''). Each potential caregiver received a score for each activity dimension.

A preliminary analysis of the data showed that the strongest value for having a child was stimulation and fun, followed by achievement and creativity, primary group ties and affection, power and influence, expansion of the self, adult status and social identity, morality, and economic utility and security in old age. The rank ordering of values for the adolescent mothers was very similar to that for the adult mothers studied in the U.S. national sample by Hoffman et al. (1978). In fact, the only difference was that, in the adolescent group, power and influence had the fourth highest average item score and adult status and social identity had the sixth highest, whereas in the U.S. national sample this pattern was reversed.

It was predicted that higher scores would be associated with a higher incidence of pregnancy in this adolescent parent population. For 88% of the adolescents, this was a first pregnancy, whereas 12% had experienced one or more previous pregnancies. Despite the relatively small variability in pregnancy rates, we did find a small but significant positive association between number of pregnancies and two value categories: valuing children as a means of expanding the self and valuing children for their ability to provide stimulation and fun.

We next examined the alternatives hypothesis in its expanded version, that is, our prediction that adolescents who had less access to alternative outlets for need gratification, due either to demographic barriers (race, SES, rural–urban environment, hours employed) or to psychological barriers (low social maturity, low age of the adolescent's own mother at first parenthood), would show higher value of having children scores. The greatest number of significant findings occurred for the psychological variable social maturity, which was negatively associated with six of the eight value of having children categories: economic utility and security in old age, strengthening primary group ties and affection, adult status and social identity, moral reasons, power and influence, and achievement and creativity. The second psychological factor, age at which the adolescent's own mother had her first child, was related to two value categories. The younger the adolescent's own mother's age, the more likely the daughter was to value children as a means of economic utility and security in old age and in order to achieve adult status and social identity.

Some support was also found for the expected relationships between the demographic variables that may regulate opportunities for need satisfaction outside of parenthood and values of having children scores. Being black was positively related to the values economic utility and security in old age, adult status and social identity, power and influence, and expansion of the self. The number of hours the adolescent was employed was negatively related to valuing children as a means of achievement and creativity. Low SES and living in a rural environment were positively associated with valuing children as a means of strengthening primary group ties and affection. Furthermore, within this group of adolescent mothers age was positively associated with three values of having children categories: expansion of the self, stimulation and fun, and morality.

A series of stepwise multiple regression analyses was performed with the psychological and demographic variables as the predictors. Six of the eight value categories were significantly predicted by the overall model derived in the stepwise multiple regressions. For five of the six values, social maturity was the strongest single predictor, with own mother's age

at first parenthood, race, and employment also contributing independently
to the variance in the stepwise regressions.

To examine the relationships between values of having children and
family members' current and expected participation in child caregiving,
separate analyses were conducted for the adolescents who were still pregnant and those who were already parents. The strongest findings were
those for the pregnant adolescents. The more the pregnant adolescents
expected to engage in the physical care of the child, the more they valued
children as a source of achievement and creativity. The more they expected
that the baby's father would provide for the child's physical maintenance,
the more they valued having children for primary group ties and affection
and for stimulation and fun.

The more the pregnant adolescents expected their own mothers to engage in attachment behaviors with the child, the less they tended to value
children in order to attain primary group ties and affection, stimulation
and fun, expansion of the self, adult status and social identity, achievement
and creativity, and power and influence. Also, the more the pregnant adolescents expected their mother to provide for the physical maintenance
of the child, the less they tended to value having children for primary
group ties and affection and for stimulation and fun. The more the pregnant
adolescents expected their own father to engage in attachment behavior
with the child, the less they tended to value having children in order to
achieve adult status and social identity and power and influence. Also,
the more they expected their father to engage in direct physical care of
the child, the less they tended to value children as a means of attaining
power and influence. All these findings were in the expected direction.

These results generally support the utility of the values of having children
model as a theoretical framework for adolescent pregnancy and parenthood. Particularly interesting was the study's support of the alternatives
hypothesis. The results for the demographic variables support Hoffman
et al.'s (1978) previous findings with adults and suggest that, when an
adolescent has fewer alternative sources for need satisfaction in her cultural milieu, she is likely to turn to children as a valued source of need
satisfaction. It should be pointed out, however, that although the assumption is made that these demographic factors result in there being
fewer alternative sources of need gratification, it is not yet known how
this process operates and so we cannot yet explain why a particular demographic variable is related in the predicted direction to some values of
having children but not to others.

The expanded version of the concept of "barriers" was also supported
by this study and suggests that a useful distinction can be made between

the psychological barriers to alternative sources of need satisfaction and the cultural or demographic barriers to these sources. Quite early in life, cultural and demographic factors may set lifelong limits on available sources of need gratification. Then, within this overall context, such socialization experiences as having an identification figure who became a parent at an early age herself may more directly influence the adolescent to look to having children for primary need gratification. Finally, the adolescent's individual level of social maturity may limit her ability to attain the alternative need satisfactions that her culture and socialization experiences have made available to her. During adolescence, gratification of psychological needs through having children may seem to be easier to attain than long-range sources of need gratification. In this light, the social maturity measure, which generated the strongest findings, may reflect both the adolescent's ability to formulate long-term future goals that require extended preparation and training and her ability to delay gratification now with the confidence that long-term gratification will follow later.

The findings that high scores on the values of having children categories were related to the pregnant adolescent's expectations that she and the baby's father would be more involved, and that her own mother and father would be less involved, in childcare activities show that there is a strong link between motivation for parenthood and expectations about the parental role. However, there were only weak findings between values of having children and reports of actual child caregiving among the adolescents who were already parents. Although many other factors may intervene between motivations, on the one hand, and actual parenting behavior, on the other, at this point we have not yet demonstrated that values of having children influence quality of parenting. However, the finding of a relationship between values of having children and number of pregnancies is important in confirming that values do play a role in adolescents' fertility behavior.

A longitudinal study of values of parenthood

Clearly lacking in the previous research on values of having children is a longitudinal study in which individuals' and couples' values are assessed early in their relationship and then followed across the period of early family formation and eventually across all the stages of family development. Such a study could focus both on preexisting values as predictors of later fertility behavior and on the impact of parenthood as well as other events of family life on values of having children. Furthermore, if such a study assessed husbands' and wives' values separately, the role of congruence or lack of congruence in the overall motivation to have children could be studied with regard to such outcome variables as marital adjustment, family stress, the child's psychological development, and ultimately the development of the child's own attitudes and values about childbearing.

In 1982 Rosenbaum and O'Leary undertook a longitudinal study of beginning marriages recognizing the importance of the transition to parenthood. This author was invited to include measures of parenthood values, affording a unique opportunity to study motivation for parenthood in a longitudinal fashion. The larger study has followed a group of approximately 400 couples from the period of their premarital engagement through the first 18 months of their marriage.[1] Data on premarital values of having children were collected from half the sample, whereas the entire sample completed the value measures at each of the follow-up points. The subjects in the study resided in two locations, a middle-sized metropolitan area of central New York State and a suburban area outside of New York City. The couples were recruited from a number of sources including community and church contacts, newspaper advertisements, and radio announcements on local stations.

The measure of values of having children was a compilation of items from the original structured interview item of the international study described earlier and items from Gerson's (1980) motivation for parenthood instrument. Included in the measure was a list of 31 values of having children and 32 costs of having children, which the respondent was requested to rate on a 4-point scale of relative importance as a reason for wanting (or not wanting) a child. After rating each value or cost individually, the respondent was asked to go back and rank-order the five most important reasons from each list. Also, in addition to the values of having children measure, couples in the study were asked a series of fertility planning questions and questions regarding their communication about having children.

Only the data from the premarital assessment of values of having children have been analyzed to date, but this analysis brings the search for meaningful dimensions of values of having children one step closer to fruition. At the time of these assessments, which occurred 6 weeks before their marriage, the average age of the prospective husbands was 25.3 years, whereas that of the prospective wives averaged 23.4 years. Both men and women had an average of two years of college education. They had been dating an average of 3⅓ years and had been engaged an average of 13

[1] This research was supported by NIMH Grant 1RO1MH35340-01A12K to Daniel O'Leary.

months. The average income of the men was $17,600, whereas that of the women was $12,600. The female respondents wanted 2.5 children and expected to have their first child in 3.3 years, whereas the male respondents wanted 2.4 children and expected their first child in 3.4 years. However, 5.4% of the men and 3.5% of the women reported that they did not want any children.

Separate principal components factor analyses were performed for the values and the costs. On the basis of these analyses, three positive motivational dimensions and three negative motivational dimensions were identified. The first positive factor was labeled "Competency and Fulfillment." Items that loaded highly on this factor focus on the interest and excitement that having children brings to life and include "to experience the honesty and freshness of children," "to watch them grow and develop," "because life is more interesting with children," and "children add interest and spice to family life." The second positive value was labeled "Mutual Dependency." Here, the items loading highly focus on the role that having children plays in promoting positive interdependency. Three items focus on the gratification that being needed and important brings to the parent: "to have someone who needs you," "because children will look up to you," and "to be remembered after you are gone." One item focuses on the security of being able to depend on one's children, "to have someone to depend on when you are old," and another item focuses on the child's role in promoting interdependency between the spouses, "to strengthen the bond between you and your husband/wife." The third positive value factor was labeled "Conventional Reasons." The items that loaded highly on this factor focus on the belief that having children is an integral part of one's self-definition and include "because it's part of being a man or woman" and "because it would seem odd not to." Other items loading highly on this factor focus on the wish to fit in and be accepted by important others who expect the couple to have children: "to be like other couples you will know" and "to please your parents or other relatives." Finally, an additional item focuses on having a child because it is expected by one's religion: "because of your religion."

Three factors also emerged from the principal components factor analysis of the costs or negative values of having children. The first factor was labeled "Restriction." The most highly loaded items focus on the variety of ways in which having a child ties the parent down and include "You are not as free to leave the house," "You are not as free to travel," "It leaves you too little time for yourself," and "the loss of privacy," as well as the more general item "because you would not be as free to do what you would want to do." Another highly loaded item focuses on the work of raising a child: "It is a lot of work"; another focuses on the loss of time available to spend with one's spouse: "because you couldn't spend as much time with your husband/wife."

The second negative value factor was labeled "Negative Feelings Evoked by Children." The items loading highly on this factor focus on the variety of negative feeling states that can be aroused by having children. The most highly loaded items focus on the disappointment that children can bring to the parents: "They might turn out badly through no fault of your own" and "because children may disappoint you when they grow up." Another item focuses on how having a child may reflect the parent's selfish motivations, which presumably are not consistent with a person's ideal self-image: "People have them for selfish reasons." Another item states simply, "Children are not particularly fun to be with," and another focuses on negative feelings evoked by problems with disciplining children: "because children are hard to discipline and control." Worries caused by children's health are another area tapped by this factor: "because of worries children cause when they are sick." Still another negative feeling has to do with the perception that children may make one feel old: "You no longer feel young." Finally, the item "You are not free to end a bad marriage" expresses the fear that children could be the cause of one's staying in an unhappy marital situation that one would otherwise leave.

The third negative value factor was labeled "Concerns about the Child Being Poorly Cared For." Items loading highly on this factor focus on the potential inability of both the parents and society as a whole to provide an environment in which healthy development of a child can take place. Some difficulties reflect the parent's fear of inadequacy: "because you would not be able to give enough care and attention to your child," "because your husband/wife and you are too young for a child," and "because having a child would be a financial burden to your family." Other items reflect a pessimistic view of the world's future capacity to care for its children: "because you are concerned about the problem of overpopulation" and "because the world is a mess, so why bring someone into it."

A comparison can be made between the values of having children dimensions obtained from the factor analysis and the nine dimensions of Hoffman and Hoffman's (1973) model. Each of the three positive value factors contains highly loading items from several of the Hoffman and Hoffman categories. Our Competency and Fulfillment factor includes items from three of Hoffman and Hoffman's original categories as well as seven items from the Gerson measure. Our Mutual Dependency factor includes items from five of the Hoffman and Hoffman categories, and our Conventional Reasons factor includes items from three Hoffman and Hoffman categories, as well as one item from the Gerson measure. It would seem, therefore, that the factor analysis delineates a simpler and substantially different conceptual schema of salient values of having children dimensions. The relative utility of this schema, as well as its stability across the period of family formation, will, of course, have to be further investigated.

The three costs of having children factors may provide a conceptual schema for examining why an increasing number of couples are choosing not to have children, as well as for understanding the ambivalent motivations behind decisions about having children. Of the three factors, the Restriction dimension is most often the topic of discussion in newspaper and magazine articles on the low birthrate in the United States (Three's a crowd, 1986). However, the second factor, Negative Feelings Evoked by Children, is less often discussed. It may be that the fears of emotional vulnerability brought on by parenthood may be just as salient an issue for modern couples, especially for dual-career couples who are directing considerable emotional energy and resources outside the family. When the wife has invested emotionally in a career, the additional positive feelings of the Competency and Fulfillment factor may be outweighed by the potential negative feelings, disappointments, and worries that children may cause, and there may be a fear that preoccupation with such feelings could diminish the individual's ability to function well in the career.

Some relationships were found between factor scores for these new values and costs of having children categories and the engaged couples' fertility attitudes and behavior. For both men and women, higher scores on the Competence and Fulfillment factor were significantly associated with wanting more children and wanting a first child in a fewer number of years. Similarly, the extent to which these men and women valued children for the second factor, Conventional Reasons, was associated with wanting a greater number of children. In contrast, the extent to which children were valued for Mutual Dependency was unrelated to these fertility attitudes, nor were any of the costs of children factors related to these fertility attitudes.

The relationship of the values of having children factors to the couples' reported use of contraceptives, as well as to their intention to prevent having a child immediately, was also examined. For women, Mutual Dependency was significantly positively associated with reports of "actively trying to have a child" and "just letting nature take its course." Competency and Fulfillment was also positively associated with "just letting nature take it course," whereas Conventional Reasons was associated with reports of not using contraceptives. Again, the costs of having children factors were not related to these contraceptive use attitudes and behaviors for women. For men, however, the only significant relationship for a positive or negative value factor and these variables was for the Concerns about the Child Being Poorly Cared For factor. The less importance given this value by the men, the more likely they were to report that they were actively trying to have a child.

A small number of women in our sample reported that they were already pregnant at the time of the premarital interview. We examined the relationship between the value factors and current pregnancy status and found that women who were pregnant were significantly more likely to rate highly the Mutual Dependency factor, whereas men whose fiancée was pregnant were significantly less likely to rate highly the Concerns about the Child Being Poorly Cared For factor.

We also examined the relationship between the value factors and history of abortions among the women in our sample. Women who rated highly the Competence and Fulfillment factor had had a greater number of previous abortions than other women, although high scores on the Restriction factor were also associated with a higher number of abortions. These seemingly contradictory findings may be explained by the fact that abortion may be resorted to either when a pregnancy is unwanted (e.g., due to a high rating of Restriction) or when the pregnancy might be wanted so much (e.g., Competence and Fulfillment) that the woman allows herself to get pregnant but then later decides that she cannot provide for the child sufficiently.

Age and sex differences were also examined with regard to the scores on the values and costs of having children factors. There were very few differences. Age was unrelated to any of the values or costs factors for the same sex. However, age of the woman was negatively related to the importance attached by men to Restriction as a reason not to have children. Thus, men with older fiancées were less likely to worry that their lifestyles would be overly constrained by having children. Sex differences were found for only one factor. Again, this was for Restriction, women rating this a more important reason for not having children than men.

Methodological issues

Although from the standpoint of population studies, the values of having children model reflects a growing sophistication about the need to address psychological variables in fertility, from the standpoint of a useful psychological model of motivation for parenthood, it needs further refinement:

1. A shortcoming of the alternatives hypothesis is that it has been con-

ceptualized and applied mainly at the group or population level. Though some groups may typically have less access than others to alternative sources of need satisfaction outside parenthood, there may be considerable overlap among the groups, and within each group (e.g., blacks, rural dwellers) there may be considerable variability in the existence of alternatives. It will be necessary to build into research on values of having children methods of assessing the subjects' unique set of alternatives, barriers, and facilitators.

2. More attention should be given to the concept of barriers and facilitators. It may sometimes be difficult to distinguish a situation in which there is an absence of alternative sources of need satisfaction from a situation in which such alternatives are seen to exist but barriers impede the individual's ability to attain them. With an expanded view of barriers to include psychological impediments, it becomes hard to say whether an alternative resource to which there is a psychological barrier exists as a resource at all. Yet the distinction is practically important because it suggests two different intervention approaches, one directed at changing external conditions and one directed at promoting psychological changes in the individual.

3. In its present form the values of having children model does not provide for measuring the intensity of the needs underlying the values of having children categories. There may be both innate and environmentally caused differences in need intensity. Need intensity may also differ developmentally, and in some cases the felt intensity of a need may depend on the gratification of more basic needs (Maslow, 1959, 1962). Furthermore, there is not always a direct relationship between the intensity of a need and the ease of its satisfaction, since some needs are recurrent and require continuous satisfaction. Differences in the ease with which particular needs are satisfied may influence such factors as motivation to have a second child. Hoffman and Manis (1978) make brief mention of these issues but do not suggest how to incorporate assessment of needs in a practical way into their model.

4. The values of having children model does not give consideration to the place of the values of having children within an individual's overall value system. Indeed, there are important needs that children cannot satisfy, and the decision about whether to have a child will be based on a cost–benefit analysis that includes the entire value system hierarchy, as well as alternative means of satisfying all one's primary life values.

5. Little attention has been given to the interaction between a husband's and wife's values of having children. It has yet to be determined whether values and costs tend to become more similar over the course of a mar-

riage, or whether initial differences or growing differences in values are a prognostic sign of poor marital adjustment or parenting distress. The issue of individual versus couple values may have implications for the prediction of fertility attitudes and behaviors. It may turn out that the best predictor of fertility behavior is some sort of "couple value of having children system" that is built from the husband's and wife's individual values but not reducible to the sum of each spouse's individual values. If this is the case, further attention will have to be given to the measurement issues involved in using a couple versus individual level of analysis.

6. There are probably individual differences in ability to conceptualize and explain motivations for having children based on education and intellectual ability. Hoffman, Thornton, & Manis (1978) found that respondents with 17 or more years of education gave, on the average, 2.9 advantages of having children, whereas those with less than 10 years of education gave only 2.1 advantages. Thus, with this measure, the less educated respondent would appear to place less value on having children than would the more educated respondent. Yet on the structured questions, less educated respondents receive higher value scores. The authors suggest that responses to the structured questions may be influenced by an overall response set or "halo" effect operating more strongly among less educated subjects. To alleviate some of the difficulty caused by a possible halo effect, Hoffman et al. (1978) suggest that, when the structured approach is used, respondents also be requested to rank-order which values are most important to them.

7. There is some lack of clarity in the instructions to the subjects rating the values of having children measures. The structured item asks the individual to rate the importance of each value as a reason for having children. For an individual who already has a child, it is unclear whether she or he is being asked to respond about reasons that might apply generally to all previous and future children, or whether the instructions apply to reasons for wanting another child. Different values may apply in each situation.

Theoretical issues and future research directions

Considerable research effort must continue to be directed toward identifying the salient values and costs of having children and determining whether the empirically derived dimensions apply to various groups. It is possible that the value dimensions will prove to change over the course of adult development. Investigation of this possibility will require research beginning with the assessment of values of having children during adolescence and following the development of these values across all stages of marriage and parenthood.

One of the major goals of the values of having children approach has been to develop a conceptual framework for predicting fertility behavior internationally and ultimately addressing the issue of world overpopulation. At this stage, such a goal is probably overambitious. The results of the research reviewed in this chapter can be best described as demonstrating moderate relationships between values of having children and the fertility attitudes and behaviors that have been investigated. Yet this should not be taken as a cause for discouragement. It is likely that values of having children will be found to be an important component of a *group* of psychosocial factors that mediate or influence fertility behavior. Values of having children need not be the primary psychological component of fertility behavior in order for such values to be a crucial component. In the future, researchers must begin to construct more complex models in which values of having children will be seen as interacting with the other psychological variables that have been hypothesized to influence fertility.

As mentioned briefly in the preceding section, values of having children must also be seen to take their place within the individual's overall value system, which includes many other non-child-oriented values that may be powerful motivators of goal-directed behavior. It is somewhat surprising that there has been little attempt to integrate values of having children into an overall value schema such as Rokeach's (1973) instrumental and terminal value hierarchies, since both models follow a similar rational decision-making approach. Within a broader value framework one can see that having a child might satisfy particular values of having children but could also frustrate other non-child-related values in the value hierarchy – for example, such Rokeach values as "ambitious," "independent," "freedom," and "an exciting life." An individual's decision about whether to have children may then depend on the place that the values of having children hold within his or her overall value hierarchy.

It should be stressed that it would be a mistake to limit our interest in values of having children to the possibility of predicting fertility behavior, because understanding parenthood motivation is an important goal in its own right. This suggests the continuation of a research approach wherein values of having children are also seen as the dependent, rather than only as the independent, variable in planned studies. The developing understanding that parenthood motivation is not a unitary construct represents an important step beyond both the early psychoanalytic theoretical writings that referred to a single parenthood drive and the early biological and more recent sociobiological theories that ignore altogether the psycho-

logical experience of what is presumed to be an innate motivation to promote evolutionary survival. With parenthood becoming more and more
a choice rather than an expectation, there is an important need to clarify
the ways in which having children can add meaning to life, on the one
hand, or prevent the achievement of a fulfilling lifestyle, on the other.
Furthermore, once important dimensions of parenthood motivation have
been identified, researchers can begin the process of investigating the development of each of these motivations – for example, how the motivation
is learned, what factors influence its importance, and how subject it is to
change.

One of the enduring and most interesting questions for future study is
whether there are any values of having children for which there are no
sources of alternative need satisfaction, that is, whether some part of satisfaction or meaning from life can be obtained only through parenting.
One possible candidate is the idea of ensuring some form of immortality
by passing on part of oneself through one's children. This meaning of
parenthood is often raised in discussions of voluntary childlessness as an
area where the childless couple inevitably experiences something missing
in life. But the uniqueness of childbearing as a means of satisfying this
value has been questioned. Erikson's (1950) concept of generativity as a
primary motive of adulthood, for example, holds that, although the needs
underlying generativity may be universal and in part innate, the means of
expressing them in a way that brings fulfillment may differ. The motive
of generativity can be expressed through helping others, teaching the next
generation, or creating an artistic or scholarly work that will be appreciated
by others. However, Erikson (1964) writes that the first, and for many
people the primary, generative encounter is that of parenthood, and it is
in the attainment of parenthood that the human virtue of "caring" has its
roots:

Only man can and must extend his solicitude over the long, parallel, and over-
lapping childhoods of numerous offspring united in households and communities.
As he transmits the rudiments of hope, will, purpose and skill, he imparts meaning
to the child's bodily experiences, he conveys a logic much beyond the literal
meaning of the words he teaches, and he gradually outlines a particular world
image and style of citizenship. . . . Once we have grasped this interlocking of the
human life-stages, we understood that adult man is so constituted as to need to
be needed lest he suffer this mental deformation of self-absorption, in which he
becomes his own infant and pet. (p. 10)

In part, the question of whether having children is integral to finding
fulfillment in life is being answered by researchers studying the life satisfaction of individuals and couples who are voluntarily childless. The
research to date suggests that these couples may be as satisfied, or even

more satisfied, with their lives than couples who have children (Rempel, 1985).

This chapter also points out the need for future research on the process by which an individual chooses between two sources of need satisfaction. For example, we need to learn more about what compels one woman to seek gratification of the value "achievement and creativity" primarily through her children and through family life, and what compels another woman to fulfill this need through involvement in a career. Variations in individual socialization and cultural influences certainly play an important role in the direction taken to satisfy these needs, but other psychological factors may be important.

In a historical and sociological vein, it is worthwhile to ask whether the values of having children perspective can help account for the decrease in U.S. family size that has occurred since the late 1960s. Hoffman (1975) suggests three possible explanations based on the values of having children model. One is that the basic desire to have children has not changed but that current obstacles or barriers are causing couples to settle for having fewer children. If this explanation were correct, the removal of the obstacles would lead to increases in family size. A second possibility is that people who want fewer children are now achieving satisfaction of values in other areas. Hoffman (1975) specifically cites the increased acceptability of jobs and careers for women, which may fulfill some of the satisfactions formerly obtained primarily from having children. Women would then need to have fewer children in order to feel that they were having a fulfilling life. A third possibility may have to do with the costs of having children. The lower birthrate may be due to greater costs in addition to a greater number of alternatives.

Couples feel more free today than they did in the past to weigh the benefits and costs of having each additional child. Future research may help couples make such decisions by addressing the question of which values of having children can be satisfied by raising one child versus a larger family and to what extent increased value satisfaction occurs with each additional child. Similarly, research should address whether the costs or negative values of having children increase linearly with the number of children in the family.

Many middle-class parents appear to be attempting to resolve the problem of the increased negative values or costs of having additional children by pouring great amounts of energy and resources into raising only one or two children in order to attain as much value satisfaction as possible. There is a new cultural stereotype of the yuppie parent pushing an infant or toddler in a $150 stroller and dressing him or her in designer clothes. From a values of having children perspective this may not necessarily be an ostentatious display of wealth, because underlying this type of behavior may be a great deal of emotional intensity and need. It remains to be answered whether this feverish focus of attention on a small number of children brings with it, for this generation of parents, an increased likelihood of disappointment because (1) it may not be possible to satisfy enough of the values of having children without a larger family since each child has unique traits or characteristics and invariably lacks others; (2) there is a possibility that the one or two children will be an unusual and unexpected disappointment; or (3) the time period during which parents can enjoy the satisfactions of parenthood with one or two children is much more limited than was true for previous generations of parents with larger families. Parents with one or two children may be left with the feeling that the years of parenting have passed too quickly, which may be a problem in the case of recurrent needs that are not quickly met. For example, many parents describe a hunger for a baby that emerges when their youngest child starts to become more autonomous and there is less physical contact with the child.

It is useful to consider that the potential satisfactions provided by a child themselves change systematically and dramatically as the child grows older. Different types of satisfactions are gained at different developmental stages – during the pregnancy, during infancy, from a school-aged child, from an adolescent, from an adult child, and so on. Up to now the values of having children model has been used mainly in a static way to assess overall reasons for wanting or not wanting children. It might be more useful to assess the satisfactions anticipated both currently and in the future and, again, to attempt to integrate values of having children with other life values that also have different degrees of saliency at different points in the life cycle. Taking into account the developmental nature of value satisfaction may increase the utility of the values of having children model for predicting fertility behavior since an individual decision about whether to have another child may be influenced by the combination of value satisfactions available from one's existing children at their particular developmental stages. Furthermore, identification of the values and costs generated by children at each developmental stage may provide a basis for evaluating parenting and family adjustment problems. If parents search for types of satisfaction that are unattainable from children of a particular age, this may cause considerable frustration, disappointment, and family stress.

The values of having children model, with its emphasis on a rational weighing of satisfaction versus costs of having children, along with the assessment of possible alternative means of value satisfaction, lends itself

rather well to the development of therapeutic interventions aimed at helping couples decide whether they should have, or are ready to have, children. Consistent with the value clarification approach that has been used
extensively in educational settings, a number of books are appearing in
the psychology or self-help shelves of bookstores with such titles as *The
Baby Decision* (Bombardieri, 1981) and *Pre-parenting* (Fournier & Fournier, 1980). These books ask couples to list the pros and cons of having
children at a particular time in their life trajectories and to map out for
themselves how having children fits into their overall life plans. Such value
clarification approaches also provide an opportunity for spouses to work
out the differences in their values. Interventions based on value clarification might also be helpful to couples with fertility problems who are
considering the adoption of a child. However, here research will have to
determine whether value satisfaction typically differs when a child is
adopted.

As a final comment on the possible use of intervention strategies for
helping couples decide whether and when to have children, it is important
to point out that motivation for parenthood may itself be influenced qualitatively and quantitatively once the child is born and the process of bonding and attachment to the newborn begins. In discussion groups that this
author conducted for expectant couples and new parents, the participants,
especially the new fathers, frequently reported that they were surprised
by the strength of their attachment to their baby, which they described
as almost a visceral feeling that made separation from the infant (e.g.,
because of a business trip) psychologically very painful. It seems possible,
then, that some values of having children cannot be known or predicted
in the abstract by individuals when they are not yet parents, and this may
place some limitations on the utility of the value clarification approach,
unless perhaps a group leader is present who can help the couple anticipate
such changes.

In the beginning of this chapter it was pointed out that the values of
having children approach focuses primarily on overt or conscious satisfactions and costs that children bring. Nowhere is there represented the
indirect, unconscious motives that were at the forefront of discussion by
the early psychoanalytic writers in their attempts to explain motivation
for parenthood. Though some of these psychoanalytically derived motivations should probably be relegated to a brief citation in the history of
motivation for parenthood research, it is clear to this author that reasons
for wanting to have a child frequently exist outside the individual's awareness, and that these unconscious reasons or motivations are of a nature
that makes them unlikely to appear in any values of having children in-

ventory. Examples from this author's own clinical experience include a
woman in her twenties who wanted a baby chiefly to compete with her
sister, who was pregnant, and a woman in her thirties for whom a major
motivation for having a baby was the hope of acceptance by her parents,
who had rejected her during her adolescence and college years. The values
of having children categories do include ideas that overlap with such concerns. For example, the categories "primary group ties and affection"
and "adult status and social identity" certainly include some of the issues
of the woman in the second example. Yet missing from the questionnaire
items and structured interview are the specificity and intensity of the
women's motives in the examples just cited. Furthermore, it is very
doubtful whether the women in these examples would recognize, on the
one hand, the strong competitive wish or, on the other, the desire for
parental acceptance that underly their desire for a child, and so it is doubtful that these women would report such motivations to an interviewer or
on a questionnaire. The question, then, concerns how these less visible
components of motivation for parenthood can be incorporated into the
values of having children framework. The measurement of unconscious
or indirect motivations presents a serious problem. For the present, the
problem has no clear solution, and researchers might be advised to consider
using clinical instruments and projective approaches in conjunction with
the more psychometrically developed values of having children measures.

References

Alan Guttmacher Institute (1981). *Teenage pregnancy: The problem that hasn't changed.*
    New York: Author.
Bailey, K. P. (1974). Interpreting smallest space analysis. *Sociological Methods and Research,*
    3, 3–29.
Barash, D. (1977). *Sociobiology and behavior.* New York: Elsevier.
Beach, L. R., Campbell, F. L., & Townes, B. D. (1979). Subjective expected utility and
    the prediction of birth planning decisions. *Organizational Behavior and Human Per-
    formance, 24,* 18–28.
Beach, L. R., Townes, B. D., Campbell, F. L., & Keating, G. W. (1976). Developing and
    testing a decision aid for birth planning decisions. *Organizational Behavior and Human
    Performance, 15,* 99–116.
Beckman, L. J. (1978). The relative rewards and costs of parenthood and employment for
    employed women. *Psychology of Women Quarterly, 2,* 215–34.
Beckman, L. J. (1982). Measuring the process of fertility decision-making. In G. L. Fox
    (Ed.), *The childbearing decision* (pp. 73–5). Beverly Hills, CA: Sage.
Beckman, L. J., & Houser, B. B. (1979). Perceived satisfactions and costs of motherhood
    and employment among married women. *Journal of Population, 2,* 306–27.
Bem, S. L. (1974). The measurement of psychological androgyny. *Journal of Consulting
    and Clinical Psychology, 42,* 155–62.
Benedek, T. (1959). Parenthood as a developmental phase. *Journal of the American Psy-
    choanalytic Association, 7,* 398–417.

Benedek, T. (1960). The origin of the reproductive drive. *International Journal of Psychoanalysis, 41,* 1–15.

Blake, R. R., Insko, C. A., Cialdini, R. B., & Chaikin, A. L. (1969). *Beliefs and attitudes about contraception among the poor.* Chapel Hill: University of North Carolina, Carolina Population Center.

Boehm, F. (1930). The femininity complex in men. *International Journal of Psychoanalysis, 11,* 444–69.

Bombardieri, M. (1981). *The baby decision.* New York: Rauson, Wade.

Bram, S. (1974). To have or have not: A social-psychological study of voluntary childless couples, parents, and to-be parents. *Dissertation Abstracts International,* 1975, *35,* 4250B–4251B (University Microfilms No. 75, 639).

Campbell, F. L., Townes, B. D., & Beach, L. R. (1982). Motivational bases of childbearing decisions. In G. L. Fox (Ed.), *The childbearing decision* (pp. 145–59). Beverly Hills, CA: Sage.

Crawford, T. J. (1973). Beliefs about birth control: A consistency theory analysis. *Representative Research in Social Psychology, 4,* 53–65.

Davidson, A. R., & Jaccard, J. J. (1976). Social-psychological determinants of fertility intentions. In S. H. Newman & V. D. Thompson (Eds.), *Population psychology: Research and educational issues.* Bethesda, MD: Department of Health, Education, and Welfare.

Deutsch, H. (1945). *Psychology of women: Vol. 2. Motherhood.* New York: Grune & Stratton.

Edwards, W., Lindmann, H., & Phillips, L. D. (1965). Emerging technologies for making decisions. In *New directions in psychology II* (pp. 259–325). New York: Holt, Rinehart, & Winston.

Erikson, E. H. (1950). *Childhood and society.* New York: Norton.

Erikson, E. (1964). *Insight and responsibility.* New York: Norton.

Flügel, J. C. (1947a). *Population, psychology, and peace.* London: Watts.

Flügel, J. C. (1947b). The psychology of birth control. In *Men and their motives* (pp. 1–43). New York: International Universities Press.

Fournier, B. E., & Fournier, G. (1980). *Pre-parenting.* Englewood Cliffs, NJ: Prentice-Hall.

Freud, S. (1955a). Analysis of phobia in a five year old boy. In J. Strachey (Ed. & Trans.), *The standard edition of the complete psychological works of Sigmund Freud.* London: Hogarth. (Original work published 1909.)

Freud, S. (1955b). From the history of an infantile neurosis. In J. Strachey (Ed. & Trans.), *The standard edition of the complete psychological works of Sigmund Freud.* London: Hogarth. (Original work published 1918.)

Freud, S. (1958). Psycho-analytic notes on an autobiographical account of a case of paranoia. In J. Strachey (Ed. & Trans.), *The standard edition of the complete psychological works of Sigmund Freud.* London: Hogarth. (Original work published 1911.)

Freud, S. (1961). The ego and id. In J. Strachey (Ed. & Trans.), *The standard edition of the complete psychological works of Sigmund Freud.* London: Hogarth. (Original work published 1923.)

Gerson, M. (1980). The lure of motherhood. *Psychology of Women Quarterly, 5*(2), 207–18.

Goldberg, W. A., Michaels, G. Y., & Lamb, M. (1985). Husbands' and wives' adjustment to pregnancy and first parenthood. *Journal of Family Issues, 6*(4), 483–503.

Hoffman, L. W. (1972). A psychological perspective on the value of children to parents. In J. T. Fawcett (Ed.), *The satisfactions and costs of children: Theories, concepts, methods.* Honolulu: The East–West Population Institute.

Hoffman, L. W. (1975). The value of children to parents and the decrease in family size. *Proceedings of the American Philosophical Society, 119*(6), 430–8.

Hoffman, L. W., & Hoffman, M. (1973). The value of children to parents. In J. T. Fawcett (Ed.), *Psychological perspectives on population* (pp. 19–76). New York: Basic Books.

Hoffman, L. W., & Manis, J. D. (1979). The value of children in the United States. *Journal of Marriage and the Family, 41*(3), 583–96.

Hoffman, L. W., Thornton A., & Manis, J. D. (1978). The value of children to parents in the United States. *Journal of Population 1*(2), 91–131.

Hoffman, L. W., & Wyatt, F. (1960). Social change and motivations for having larger families: Some theoretical considerations. *Merrill–Palmer Quarterly, 6*, 235–44.

Inazu, J., Langmeyer, D., & Lundgren, D. (1974, August). *Personal beliefs and normative beliefs about intended family size.* Paper presented at the Eighty-Second Annual Meeting of the American Psychological Association, New Orleans, LA.

Jaccard, J. J., & Davidson, A. R. (1976). The relation of psychological, social and economic variables to fertility-related decisions. *Demography, 13*, 329–38.

Jones, E. (1961a). The early development of female sexuality. In *Papers on psychoanalysis.* Boston: Beacon Press. (Original work published 1927.)

Jones, E. (1961b). The phallic phase. In *Papers on psychoanalysis.* Boston: Beacon Press. (Original work published 1933.)

Kirchner, E. P. (1973). *Reasons for wanting children: Factors and correlates* (Final Report, Grant No. 1-RO-1-HD-06258-01 NICH and HD). University Park, Pennsylvania State University, NIH Institute for Research on Human Resources.

Kirchner, E. P., & Seaver, W. B. (1977). *Developing measures of parenthood motivation* (final report). University Park: Pennsylvania State University, Institute for Research on Human Resources.

Kothandapani, V. (1971). Validation of feeling, belief, and intention to act as three components of attitude and their contribution to prediction of contraceptive behavior. *Journal of Personality and Social Psychology, 19*, 321–33.

Lingoes, J. C. (1973). *The Guttman–Lingoes nonmetric program series.* Ann Arbor, MI: Mathesis Press.

Lott, B. E. (1973). Who wants children? Some relationships among attitudes toward children, parents, and the liberation of women. *American Psychologist, 28*, 573–82.

Maslow, A. H. (1959). *New knowledge in human values.* New York: Harper & Row.

Maslow, A. H. (1962). *Towards a psychology of being.* New York: Van Nostrand.

Michaels, G. Y., & Brown, R. (1987). *Values of children in adolescent mothers.* Manuscript submitted for publication.

Miller, W. B. (1983). Chance, choice, and the future of reproduction. *American Psychologist, 38*, 1198–1205.

Osgood, C. E., Suci, G. J., & Tannenbaum, P. H. (1975). *The measurement of meaning.* Urbana: University of Illinois Press.

Pohlman, E. (1973). *The psychology of birth planning.* Cambridge, MA: Schenkman.

Rainwater, L. (1965). *Family design: Marital sexuality, family size, and family planning.* Chicago: Aldine.

Rempel, J. (1985). Childless elderly: What are they missing? *Journal of Marriage and the Family, 47*(2), 343–8.

Rokeach, M. (1973). *The nature of human values.* New York: Free Press.

Russell, C. S. (1980). Unscheduled parenthood: Transition to "parent" for the teenager. *Journal of Social Issues, 36*(1), 45–63.

Siegelman, M. (1965). College student personality correlates of early parent–child relationships. *Journal of Consulting Psychology, 29*, 558–64.

Smetana, J. G., & Adler, N. E. (1979). Decision-making regarding abortion: A value X expectancy analysis. *Journal of Population, 2*, 339–57.

Soddy, J. (1964). The unwanted child. *Journal of Family Welfare, 11*(2), 39–52.

Three's a crowd. (1986, Sept. 1). *Newsweek*, pp. 68–76.

Townes, B. D., Beach, L. R., Campbell, F. L., & Wood, R. L. (1980). Family building: A social psychological study of fertility decisions. *Population and Environment, 3*(3–4), 210–20.

Vinokur-Kaplan, D. (1977). Family planning decision-making: A comparison and analysis of parents' considerations. *Journal of Comparative Family Studies, 8*(1), 79–88.

Wengraf, F. (1953). *Psychosomatic approach to gynecology and obstetrics.* Springfield, IL: Thomas.

Werner, P. D., Middlestadt-Carter, S. E., & Crawford, T. J. (1975). Having a third child: Predicting behavioral intentions. *Journal of Marriage and the Family, 37,* 348–58.

Wyatt, F. (1967). Clinical notes on the motives of reproduction. *Journal of Social Issues, 23,* 29–55.

2 The power of parenthood: personality and attitudinal changes during the transition to parenthood

Toni C. Antonucci and Karen Mikus

This chapter examines the effects of the transition to parenthood on the individual's personality and attitudes. The chapter reviews what is known about the impact of parenthood on adult personality development. A brief discussion of adulthood as a time of continuing growth and development is followed by an analysis of the characteristics of the transition to parenthood and the parental role that contribute to its effect on adult development. Factors that may mediate the impact of parenthood are identified, and two possible processes by which change occurs in parenthood are presented. Finally, changes that have been documented or might be expected are examined.

Although a rich tradition of theory and research has examined the impact of parents on children and child development, the significance of the transition to parenthood for ongoing development in adulthood has been studied only recently and by only a small group of researchers (Belsky, 1981). Yet parents' personal accounts clearly reveal that becoming a parent changes and shapes adults in dramatic ways. For instance, mother-author Carol Kort (1981) emphatically states: "Becoming a mother changed every fiber, every feeling, and every relationship for me. I am constantly in the process of evaluating, recognizing, and repudiating the upheaval of motherhood" (p. 127). "Be prepared," Phyllis Chesler (1979) tells a pregnant friend, "to have your life turned upside down in unpredictable ways. Probably forever" (p. 191). If parenthood is powerful enough to function as a major agent of change in adulthood, we must ask, Who changes in what directions as a result of which conditions? Does becoming, and then being, a parent alter the experience, self-concept, world view, traits and styles, values and attitudes of the adults involved? The purpose of this chapter is to consider these issues.

62

Personality change as a function of new adult roles

There is increasing support for the proposition that throughout adulthood new situations, new role partners, and new demands elicit different behaviors while providing new rewards and negative sanctions (Baltes, Reese, & Lipsett, 1980; Brim & Wheeler, 1966). Not only do new behaviors emerge, but the personality as a whole may change as well (Sarbin & Allen, 1968). Turner (1978) addresses this issue in his theory of person–role merger. According to Turner, roles that become deeply merged with a person have an impact on personality formation. For instance, Turner specifies that roles requiring the greatest investment to acquire or maintain are likely to be merged with the person. Investment, in his terms, increases when substantial amounts of time and energy are contributed, sacrifices are made, and/or a high rate of public visibility or justification for a role is involved. He postulates that individuals will merge critical aspects of those roles into their personality when investment has been very high or when adequate return from investment has not been realized (Turner, 1978). These criteria certainly apply to the transition to parenthood.

Turner (1978), like others (e.g., Burr, 1972), observes that transitions in roles with pervasive significance for personal behavior are often "stressful and tumultuous." This point of view corresponds with those presented in critical life-events frameworks (Dohrenwend & Dohrenwend, 1981) and in crisis intervention theory (Caplan, 1964). According to these perspectives, upheaval and change in adults' external environment often lead to internal change as well.

The birth of the first child ushers in a period of disequilibrium and reorganization; it is a period that includes disengagement from selected roles and relationships as well as the definition, creation, and integration of new roles and relationships. Whether one shares the crisis view or the role transition–critical life-events approach to the birth of the first child, one can probably agree with Lopata (1972) that the birth of a child is "not just a crisis which is resolved by a return to previous roles and relations but an event marking a complete change in life approach" (pp. 200–1). There does appear to be a consensus that assumption of the parental role represents an important phenomenon and a significant change in the lives of the adults involved. Crises and role transitions can be viewed as opportunities to regress, to become rigidly entrenched in current though dysfunctional patterns, or to develop new coping strategies along with new dimensions of the self.

A number of characteristics make parenthood a role with the potential to create change in adulthood, and research has begun to document this power. Parenthood is often valued as the key to adulthood; that is, the birth of a child makes the parent not only a mother or a father but simultaneously an adult (Fawcett, 1978; Hoffman, 1978). For women, childbearing has also been seen as proof of femininity, and childrearing quite often has been regarded as the primary means to a fulfilling and rewarding life. For men, the birth of children has served to affirm virility. In addition, the generative function of parenthood for families and individuals heightens the role's significance. Without parenthood, one's impact on the world may be perceived as quite transitory. Since the survival of our species and culture depends on successful reproduction and child-rearing, the parental role is truly an essential role both societally and culturally. At the individual level, also, parenthood's generative function (Erikson, 1959) is important in enabling a person to continue biologically beyond his or her life span. In addition, a sense of psychological continuation beyond one's own life span is afforded to the extent that parental values and world view are shared and implemented by one's offspring.

For these reasons, one might assume that parenthood occupies a significant place in people's lives and role hierarchies. Indeed, research has shown that family life, including parenthood, is highly valued. Chilman (1980) reported that 62% of the mothers in her middle-class sample identified parenthood as the most important aspect of their life. Looking at a hierarchy of family roles and values, Nye (1976) found that good care and training of children (i.e., parenting) ranked ahead of other family roles, including the sexual, therapeutic, recreational, provider, and housekeeper roles. Parenthood provided a source of high satisfaction for the women in Hoffman and Manis's (1978) national survey. Campbell, Converse, and Rodgers (1976) observed that satisfaction in the family domain was one of the most effective predictors of a sense of general well-being and that a good family life was very important to the people they interviewed. Benedek (1970) maintained that parenthood is important to a person's identity and self-concept.

Nonetheless, parenthood has been found to correlate with increased strain in both men and women (Veroff, Douvan, & Kulka, 1981). Early parenthood, in particular, appears to be a time of satisfaction coupled with stress and worry (Hoffman & Manis, 1978). It may be that the problems and pains of being a parent serve to increase the parent's commitment to his or her children and to the role of parent (Veroff et al., 1981). In other words, the struggles and worries inherent in childrearing may heighten the salience of the role rather than diminish its significance. This is directly related to the concept of investment that Turner (1978) has proposed is operative in instances of a person–role merger. He reports that "undergoing and coping with strain in a role is a way of investing in that role, making it more difficult . . . to shed it" (Turner, 1978, p. 16) and, therefore, providing a significant opportunity for personality change.

The labor-intensive nature of caring for young children means that people devote enormous amounts of physical time, energy, and effort to enacting the parental role; parents are parents 24 hours per day, seven days per week, year after year, and for most people, the parental role is irrevocable and continuous. At the same time, this physical intensity is paralleled, or exceeded, by the emotional intensity of parenthood. Being a parent engages people emotionally in ways that few other roles can match. Research has shown that, although people often feel competent, adequate, and/or satisfied with their parental role performance, they also experience problems with their children and deep concerns about their parenting (Campbell et al., 1976; Douvan, 1978; Hoffman, 1978; Lowenthal, Thurnher, Chiriboga, & Associates, 1976; Veroff & Feld, 1970). A great deal of worry, conflict, and strain have often been found to characterize the parental role (Chilman, 1980; Nye, 1976).

The parental role is uniquely and emotionally evocative in part because old feelings and concerns about developmental issues such as dependence, control, autonomy, intimacy, sexuality, and aggression are reawakened daily in people as they experience pregnancy and early parenthood (Colman & Colman, 1971). Although the particular issues and conflicts called forth by parenthood will vary depending on the adult involved, the characteristics of the baby, and the context in which baby and parent exist, certain generalized issues are likely to be associated with early parenthood. Loss of control is an issue that surfaces in late pregnancy and at the time of the birth (Colman & Colman, 1971; Galinsky, 1981). Issues of dependence and independence, nurturing, deprivation, autonomy, separateness, anger, and aggression may emerge as highly salient in the pregnancy and early parenthood periods. Reactivation of old issues may be accompanied by a strongly regressive pull (Cohen & Weissman, 1984; Coleman, Kris, & Provence, n.d.), which can cause parents to behave childishly, that is, at a much less developmentally sophisticated level.

The possibilities for regression and difficulties are offset, however, by opportunities for change and growth. Dealing with a conflict or issue again, but as an adult with more psychological resources than one had as a child, may enable a parent to rework and resolve old issues. Experiencing events and developmental issues as an adult but through the eyes of one's own child can further extend a parent's perceptions and can, perhaps, facilitate the resolution of old themes and issues. Thus, parenthood offers people opportunities for growth and development in their adult years (Cowan,

Cowan, Coie, & Coie, 1978; Group for the Advancement of Psychiatry [GAP], 1973; Rapoport, Rapoport, Strelitz, & Kew, 1977).

At the same time, however, repeated encounters with unresolved developmental and emotional issues can be distressing and unsettling. Tolerance for such arousal and the capacity to reprocess prior developmental concerns may vary from individual to individual. The sensitivity and involvement of one's social network may be a powerful factor in the occurrence of the reactivation process and its outcome. An intervention such as a couples' group (Cowan et al., 1985; see also Duncan & Markman, Chapter 9, this volume) may also provide a secure context in which to surface, acknowledge, and develop alternative resolutions to the psychologically difficult issues that parenthood may trigger. The complexity of this process and its impact on adult personality development clearly require extensive further study.

Parenthood is both intense and emotionally demanding in other ways. Most mothers and fathers are unprepared for the extremes of affect that they inevitably experience at various points during parenthood (Lopata, 1972). The helpless screaming of a sick or colicky infant, for instance, can trigger jolting and frightening feelings of rage, helplessness, or inadequacy in a parent who has never before encountered these emotions with such strength. Parents may also be surprised and emotionally drained by a "lack of fit" between the parents' style or temperament and the baby's. Unlike other major adult roles, parenthood offers its occupants little opportunity for choosing the kind of role partner with whom a smooth fit will be most likely (Rossi, 1968). In addition, the norms and laws pertaining to parenthood prohibit changing role partners in the event that a lack of fit between partners (parent and child) emerges. Thus, a spouse can be divorced, jobs changed, new friends made, new neighbors acquired, but our children are our children forever (Rossi, 1968). Facing such challenges offers revelations about the self that, when dealt with adequately, can lead to the development of new strategies and competencies.

Continuing transactions between parent and child involve mutual adjustments in which each is altered by the other and each controls and changes the other (Chess & Thomas, 1977; Osofsky, 1970; Parke & Sawin, 1977; Rheingold, 1969; Sameroff, 1975). Currently, therefore, a more interactive, at least bidirectional, approach to the study of parent–child growth and development is being pursued (Bell, 1971, 1974, 1979; Walters & Walters, 1980). This approach highlights the need to examine the effects of parenthood on adults as well as the results of parenting on children.

The power of the parenthood role also stems from the fact that it provides an opportunity for involvement in a nurturing and intimate relationship with a significant nonadult other. Parenthood allows its actors to develop and express a warm, caring, selfless side of themselves, which may go undiscovered or untapped in other adult roles and settings. The opportunity to view the world through the eyes of one's child and to be childlike (as distinguished from childish) are two of the rich rewards parenthood offers. For many, no arena outside of the family offers quite the same avenues for loving expressiveness and intimacy. Long left primarily to mothers, parenthood's joys, pains, and opportunities for growth are now actively being sought and experienced by fathers as well (Fein, 1978; Greene, 1984; Gronseth, 1972; Lamb, 1978; Levine, 1976; Steinberg, 1977).

In summary, there is support for the proposition that the parenthood role has the power to be a significant force for personality change in the adult years. Research on the mutual socialization process between parent and child supports the idea that parenthood affects adult as well as child development (Bell, 1971, 1974, 1979; Walters & Walters, 1980). The reciprocal nature of the parent–child relationship means that parents and children serve as change agents, regulating and shaping each other's behaviors (Ahammer, 1973; Bell, 1974; Harper, 1971). Factors that mediate the individual differences in the response to the parenthood role are considered next.

Factors that mediate the impact of parenthood on personality

Just as a range of factors serve as mediators of a parent's influence on his or her child (Belsky, 1981), a range of factors cause parenthood to have a differential impact on its occupants. Research has shown that parenthood is not a unitary experience and that people react in different ways to the parental role. A host of factors may affect the intensity and quality of the parental role. Although this has not yet been studied, we can take some direction from the types of variables that influence other aspects of the transition to parenthood.

Parenthood and responses to parental role assumption and enactment vary with social class (Lopata, 1972; Russell, 1974; Veroff et al., 1981; Veroff & Feld, 1970) and gender (Chilman, 1980; Cowan et al., 1985; Hobbs & Cole, 1976; Russell, 1974; Steffensmeier & Steffensmeier, 1975; Veroff et al., 1981). Family of origin and past experiences (Benedek, 1970; Cox et al., 1985; Fraiberg, Adelson, & Shapiro, 1975), infant temperament (Shereshefsky & Yarrow, 1973; Sirignano & Lachman, 1985), the marital relationship (Belsky, 1981; Goldberg, Michaels, & Lamb, 1985; Shereshefsky & Yarrow, 1973), and the parenting alliance (Cohen & Weissman, 1984) have been identified as factors that influence not only the ways in which people parent but also the ways in which people adjust to parenthood. More recently, work–family interface has been implicated as an influential factor during the transition to parenthood (Belsky, Perry-Jenkins, & Crouter, 1985), and prebirth personality factors have long been cited as key variables shaping one's adjustment to and enactment of the parental role (Anthony, 1984; Oates & Heinicke, 1985).

Such factors as the timing of the birth in the adult's life cycle and the nature of the pregnancy and delivery must be considered. For instance, long awaited parenthood that was nearly lost to infertility may affect parenthood's influence on adult development. Negative or ambivalent feelings about parenthood may be denied, thereby constricting the growth that often evolves when the pain and frustration of parenthood are acknowledged. Characteristics of the infant (gender, health, and temperament) as well as characteristics of the adult (gender, age, and socioeconomic, work, and marital status) are expected to make parental role occupants differentially receptive to significant change throughout the transition and early stages of parenthood.

It is clear that the adult's prebirth personality characteristics play a large role in shaping his or her receptivity to parenthood. Tolerance for ambiguity, flexibility and adaptability, capacity for relationships, and needs and motives of the individual are examples of variables that might influence personality change during the transition to parenthood (Oates & Heinicke, 1985; Veroff & Feld, 1970). The portion of overall identity devoted to "parent" varies from person to person, as does the level of parenthood in one's role hierarchy and the salience of the parental role. It might be hypothesized that the portion of the overall self-concept (Cowan et al., 1985) devoted to parenthood must reach a certain size before being a parent can significantly alter an adult's personality. However, too large a portion of one's self-concept devoted to the parenting self might block parental influence due to defensiveness and a lack of perspective.

Interpersonal factors can also serve as mediators of parenthood's influence on personality and attitudinal change. These include the marital relationship; the availability of social support from friends, neighbors, relatives, co-workers, and spouse; and the presence of formal helping resources such as individual or group therapy. Cohen and Weissman (1984) argue persuasively for the existence of the parenting alliance, which is distinct from the marital relationship and "provides a substrate for the psychological growth and development of the parents" (p. 39). All of these factors cannot be considered extensively in this chapter. However, it is important to note that any investigation of the effect of parenthood on adult personality must examine these mediating factors if an accurate picture of the formative nature of parenthood is to be obtained.

Process models of personality change

The processes by which adult personality is expanded or altered by parenthood have received little scientific attention. This section focuses on two avenues by which the initiation of the parenthood role may have an impact on the adult self-concept and personality. A discussion of the phenomenon of possible selves (Markus & Nurius, 1986, 1987) is followed by an application of the act-frequency approach to personality (Buss & Craik, 1986) to parenthood.

Possible selves

There is a long tradition of psychological research that focuses on the self (Markus & Wurf, 1987). This includes work on self-concept, self-image, and self-esteem (Gecas, 1982; Gordon, 1968; Rosenberg, 1965, 1979; Wylie, 1979). A more recent research effort in this area has focused on the development and identification of self-schemata (Markus, 1977, 1983; Markus & Sentis, 1982). One unique and potentially quite relevant development suggests that in addition to the more traditional conceptualizations of the self, individuals may also maintain a separate conceptualization about themselves, which Markus and Nurius (1986, 1987) call "possible selves." This concept is meant to represent individuals' conceptions of themselves as they might become and as they would like to become. Possible selves can be positive or negative. In other words, one might have a conception of oneself as one hopes to develop or grow or as one fears one might become. Thus, this notion of possible selves has both positive and negative implications. Markus and Nurius (1986) describe possible selves as a critical domain of self-knowledge that thus far remains unexplored by psychologists. They describe one's repertoire of possible selves as "the cognitive manifestation of enduring goals, aspirations, motives, fears and threats" (p. 158; see also Markus & Nurius, 1987). Because they are so central to one's view of oneself, possible selves are hypothesized to represent some important ways in which motivation and affect are represented within an individual's self-concept.

Although the possible-selves idea is still in an early developmental phase, there is empirical evidence that individuals do maintain a sense of self or self-concept that includes both the current self with characteristics that are actually now present, as well as a future-oriented self, which includes one's conceptualization of things that are, as Markus and Nurius put it, "possible for you." In their study of more than 200 college students, most people were able to conceptualize goals, characteristics, general descriptors, or adjectives that could possibly describe themselves. Thus, despite the fact that much empirical work remains to be done, there is evidence that the notion of possible selves is a viable one.

The concept of possible selves can be readily applied to the transition to parenthood. It seems likely that in Markus and Nurius's terms, people maintain a "possible self" as parent. What shapes that concept is unclear, but again Markus and Nurius offer several possibilities. They argue that possible selves develop from a conceptualization of self in the past and include aspirations for the future. Possible selves are defined as different from the now self, and may be a representation of what one hopes to become in the future. Possible selves, Markus and Nurius tell us, are often views of the self that have not been verified or confirmed by our social experience but provide incentives for engaging in certain behaviors. They can also provide a context within which to evaluate one's current views of self.

It seems clear that individuals who are not yet parents are likely to have a "possible self" of parenthood. Indeed, a number of authors exploring the transition to parenthood have postulated the presence of a possible parental self without so naming it. Galinsky (1981) refers to the first stage of parenthood as the "Image-Making" period, during which the pregnant woman and father-to-be develop an image of themselves as parents. Similarly, Colman and Colman (1971) report that the key task of pregnancy is the development of a mothering identity unique to the parent-to-be. Cowan et al. (1978; see also Chapter 4, this volume) refer to the increasingly larger part of the self that is allocated to the parental self. Shereshefsky and Yarrow (1973) discuss the possible parental self in terms of a pregnant woman's ability to "visualize" herself as a mother.

Pregnancy seems to be the most salient time for a full-blown possible parental self to emerge. It is reasonable to speculate, however, that each person who considers parenthood a possibility quietly and slowly develops a possible parental self from childhood to adolescence and throughout adulthood. Psychodynamic theorists would argue that the possible parental self is grounded in one's early years, when identification with one's own parents occurs (Anthony, 1984; Sadow, 1984). Thus, the parenting a person receives as a child not only influences the way he or she parents but also contributes to the development of the possible self and thereby to ongoing personality development in adulthood. Colman and Colman (1971) identify the need for prospective parents to develop a parental identity that is differentiated and separate from that of their own parents. Thus, the possible parental self could be expected to contain elements that match one's own parents, whereas other aspects of the possible parental self might represent a conceptualization of one's self as parent that diverges from that of one's own parents.

It might be hypothesized that the possible self influences or generates changes in adult personality. It is proposed that the active, expanded possible parental self that most fully emerges during pregnancy is itself a change in the self-concept of the adult. The birth of the first child ushers in a "test period" of the possible parental self. The actual parenting self is evaluated against the possible parental self and revisions are, most likely, bidirectional. That is, the adult probably changes some aspect of his or her actual parenting self in order to match the possible parental self, and changes are made in the possible self that more accurately reflect reality. There is some evidence (Breen, 1975; Cowan et al., 1978; Leifer, 1977) that the ideal–real contrast is an important area for future research with regard to the self and early parenthood. The gap between the ideal and real selves and a person's ability to reduce what dissonance exists may influence the parent's role experience and sense of self-worth (Lawton & Coleman, 1983). It should be understood that the origin and evolution of the possible parental self and its impact on adult development are empirical questions that can and should be examined experimentally. Some of the issues that should be investigated are considered below.

The rapidly changing demands of infancy and early childhood require differential parenting behaviors and may require corresponding changes in the possible parental self. As revisions in possible and actual parenting selves take place, various traits or dimensions of the adult's personality may also be expanded or restricted. The possible parental self, then, may have a developmental trajectory of its own.

A second point for consideration is the impact of parenthood's multiple role senders on the possible parental self. Multiple role senders are those "experts" in the field who help define a role by imposing or sharing their expectation of the role with the role occupant. The presence and activity of multiple role senders for parenthood have been documented (Mikus, 1981). The influences of professional childrearing experts (psychologists, educators, authors, pediatricians, nurses, and social workers) on the development and revision of the possible parental self should be studied. Nor should the impact of informal everyday parenting experts such as grandparents, neighbors, friends, cereal box designers, media professionals, and grocery store cashiers be underestimated.

A third important consideration is the role of the possible self in shaping, determining, and evaluating one's current behavior and one's transition to parenthood. For example, although one thinks of the parent possible self as being an ideal parent – having and raising children in some pre-conceived idyllic manner – the opposite may in fact be true. One may have a view of oneself as a terrible parent with a parental possible self that actually has a negative influence because of an assumed or feared inability to raise a child adequately. Very little knowledge or conceptual basis is available on which to speculate how possible selves affect behavior or how they might be modified, extended, or developed on the basis of actual events.

In the case of parenting, the possible-selves notion suggests several important issues that could elucidate those factors thought to contribute to personality change during this transition and to successful adjustment to parenthood. It would be important to assess the role of possible self in the assumption of the parenting role. Thus, one might predict, especially in light of increased family planning capabilities, that individuals for whom the possible self of parent is negative would be much less likely to become parents than individuals with a positive possible self of parent. Unfortunately, if these adults have unplanned children or plan children they feel obligated to have but inadequate to parent, they are less likely to make a successful transition to parenting. However, individuals who have a positive possible self of parenthood, even when the family addition is not planned, may be more likely to make choices and decisions that will maximize the successful transition to parenthood. Thus, many "unplanned parents" may make very good parents and successfully meet the challenges of this transition period.

A final factor should be considered in this conceptualization of the role of possible selves in the adaptation to parenthood. Although conception generally involves two people, parenthood does not necessarily do so. It is important to emphasize the effect of two possible selves, not one, on both the decision and experience of becoming a parent. The ideal parenting experience, especially in our culture, includes two people. It is preferable for both of these people to have a positive possible self as parent as they think about, consider, plan, and experience the transition to parenthood. But it may also be important that these two possible selves not be too rigidly in place so that there is room for blending, adaptation, concession, and complementarity. Other permutations are, of course, possible. For example, both new parents might have negative parental possible selves; the new mother might have a positive parental possible self; the new father a negative one; or vice versa. Each combination suggests special difficulties that might ensue as the couple become parents. Similarly, one might have a certain possible self as part of a couple but quite a different one as a single parent. Thus, different parental possible selves would dominate depending on various practical and actual conditions.

The act-frequency approach to personality

Another recent development in personality theory may be relevant to understanding individuals' experience of the transition to parenthood. Buss and Craik (1986) have suggested a unique and relatively novel conceptualization of personality. They assume that the goal of personality theory is to describe and organize the regularities of personality that individuals exhibit. Personality, they suggest, is best understood in terms of the frequency of acts that can be organized into the numerous dispositions or constructs of which personality is composed. Thus, such personality dispositions as dominance, altruism, and extraversion are described in terms of the frequency with which acts representing these dispositions occur. They acknowledge that not all acts are equally illustrative or representative of any particular personality disposition. Some acts are more prototypical of the personality disposition than others, and thus their frequency has a more serious impact on the presence of or conceptualization of a particular personality characteristic. Buss and Craik have been exploring this notion of act frequency both empirically and theoretically. A brief representation of their work is presented below and is followed by a consideration of its applicability to our understanding of the transition to parenthood.

Buss and Craik (1985) have delineated several distinct and conceptually interrelated criteria for assessing and ordering personality dispositions. The disposition should represent a clear, meaningful, and reasonably broad category of acts: It must be distinctive, and it should be possible to reach a consensus about the representativeness and prototypicality of specific acts to specific dispositions. Buss and Craik assume the following: There is some stability in the multiple-act composites of prototypical acts that represent a personality disposition; individual differences exist in act frequencies for specific dispositions; and there are reasonable frequency rates for diverse acts from a dispositional category. Buss and Craik have applied these criteria empirically using such personality dispositions as dominance and calculatedness. Their work incorporates a cognitive component to the conception and development of personality, which has initiated an exciting and new approach to the study of personality. Although this brief introduction to their work is meant only to be suggestive, several interesting aspects of both their empirical work and their recent theoretical writings will be considered.

As noted above, people appear to be successful in both assessing and ordering personality dispositions using the act-frequency notion. An interesting line of inquiry undertaken by Buss and Barnes (1986) focused on human mate selection. In a series of studies these investigators demonstrated that there are mate characteristics that are consensually considered desirable; that there are distinct gender differences in the preferred value of various mate characteristics; and that married couples show an assortment of mate characteristic preferences that are related to the actual characteristics of their mate. Judging from Buss and Barnes's empirical work, individuals both have a concept of the characteristics they would like to see in their mate and, at least to some degree, manage to choose a mate who possesses a fair representation of these characteristics.

This work seems especially relevant to the current focus on personality changes that take place during the transition to parenthood. In particular, it is interesting that there appears to be some consensus about the personality characteristics of an ideal mate. Buss and Barnes's work on mate selection might be extended to the adaptation and transition to parenthood. Although no data are available, it seems likely, judging from cultural norms, personal perception, and the like, that as in the case of mate characteristics, there is a clear broad-based view of what characteristics a parent should possess. These are likely to vary according to gender, ethnicity, and socioeconomic class.

The relationship between one's broad-based view of being a parent and the actual characteristics of the specific mother and father is not clear. Unlike mate selection, in which case a partner's characteristics can be assessed prospectively before the actual mate selection takes place, actual parenting characteristics cannot be assessed before the individual becomes a parent. It is not clear from Buss and Barnes's work, however, whether even the mate choice is made because the characteristics of a desirable mate are already present in that mate or if there is something about the interaction between mates that affects the presence or maintenance of specific acts. For example, acts the partner considers positive would be positively reinforced, whereas those perceived to be negative would be negatively reinforced. Buss and Barnes would probably agree that it is a combination of both, *a priori* selection and selective reinforcement, that best accounts for the data.

In the case of parenting, however, except in unusual cases, there are almost no *a priori* data available on the parenting characteristics of a partner. Although each partner probably possesses some hypothesized notion of what personality characteristic a parent should have, they have rarely had the opportunity to assess those characteristics in their partners. In this case, the expectations about the spouse as a parent are likely to be managed from the post hoc perspective, perhaps through selective reinforcement. That is, after becoming a parent, each partner attempts to positively reinforce the valued or expected behaviors in their partner and negatively reinforce behaviors that are not valued.

The work of Buss and his colleagues suggests a somewhat different approach to understanding the process through which the transition to parenthood is experienced. By exploring the transition through an interpersonal perspective and by using Buss's act-frequency notion, one might best conceive the transition to parenthood as the achievement of a goal or role about which there are prescribed, accepted, and expected personality characteristics held by each of the two parents or between the parent and significant others in the case of single parents. The work on mate selection indicates that there are gender differences in that arena, and there is little reason to believe that the same would not be true in the parenting role. In addition to the aforementioned view of what a parent should be like, the individual and the partner can be assumed to engage in those acts and be reinforced by their partner for those acts that are considered appropriate. The act-frequency approach might be helpful for understanding the types of problems that develop, the kinds of behaviors that emerge, and the kinds of problem-solving strategies that might be profitable during the transition to parenthood.

Areas of change in adult personality development

Having discussed theoretical models for the change that parenthood brings, we shall consider the aspects of adult development that are altered by the parental experience. Most of the research on the impact of early parenthood has focused on behavioral changes in roles and environmental structures and patterns. Little study has been devoted to the effects of parenthood on the psychological development of adults (Belsky, 1981). This section includes a review of available data and suggestions for future investigation. Findings regarding changes in adult self-perceptions, personal efficacy, affective states, personal maturity, and values are examined.

Self-perceptions

Although limited in number, studies of the influence of parenthood on adult development have included a focus on modifications of, or additions to, adults' self-perceptions. It may be that self-concept and self-perceptions are aspects of adult personality that are most likely to register change. Or it may be that changes here are more readily reported. Nonetheless, self-perceptions appear to be affected by the transition to parenthood. Psychodynamic theorists have long alluded to the role of parenthood in the ongoing evolution of the self-concept (Benedek, 1970; Elson, 1984; GAP, 1973; Schwartz, 1984). Shereshesky and Yarrow (1973) found heightened self-awareness and new developments in adults' sense of self during the transition to parenthood. Cohen and Weissman (1984) maintain that "changes and expansions in the self are continuous for both parent and child" (p. 37).

It is not just women who experience changes in self-perception. Men's affective postpartum adjustment has been related to the development of a coherent parenting role, which itself may be part of a coherent parental identification (Fein, 1978). In their study of couples during the transition to parenthood, Cowan et al. (1985) found that being a parent became a larger part of the psychological self, whereas partner/lover grew smaller for both spouses, with an additional decline in psychological involvement in work outside the home for women. The possible-self idea discussed earlier is relevant here. Initially, there may be the possible parental self, which is later joined with (and compared with) the actual parental self. Identity and self-concept development seem to be key areas for further exploration: What factors comprise the parental self-concept? How does it develop and change? How does the extent to which one has developed a coherent, realistic parental self affect adjustment to parenthood?

Self-esteem as an important by-product of self-expansion has also received attention. Improvements in self-esteem (Leifer, 1977), increases in feeling valuable (Fawcett, 1978), and a positive shift in feelings of self-confidence for mothers and fathers (Wandersman, 1978) have been noted. Close to 34% of the men and 44% of the women with children younger than 5 years of age reported positive changes in the self and in self-perceptions in Hoffman and Manis's (1978) study of parenthood. New mothers have registered an increase in confidence in parenting, and new fathers have displayed an increase in feeling of global efficacy (Sirignano & Lachman, 1985). Other studies have shown no differences between parents and nonparents in self-esteem (Cowan et al., 1985; Mikus, 1981).

As a time of intensity and paradoxes (Hoffman & Manis, 1978), early parenthood can be expected to yield both increases and decreases in self-esteem. Distress with body image (Russell, 1974) may be one factor that leads to lowered self-esteem. It seems logical to expect that the uneven nature of the first year of parenthood and the complexities of parental role enactment would be reflected in a range of changes and a fluctuation in the valences attached to these shifts. The permanence of revisions in one's view of self cannot be gauged from investigations during the first year only. In-depth longitudinal studies employing a number of different measures of self-concept and self-esteem are needed.

It is reasonable to expect that the influence of parenthood on self-concept extends beyond the addition of a parental self and fluctuations in self-esteem. Different conceptions of the self may be challenged, while new dimensions may be added. For instance, the experience of parenthood may heighten one's perception of oneself as nurturing, patient, tolerant, anxious, or angry. Father-authors (Greene, 1984; Levine, 1976; Steinberg, 1977) and other investigators of early parenthood (Feldman & Aschenbrenner, 1983; Schwartz, 1984) have discussed the opportunities parenthood offers to expand otherwise undeveloped aspects of the self, such as "motherliness" for men. Whether parenthood actually adds a new dimension or merely unlocks and expands existing dimensions is not clear.

The mediating influence of the baby must be remembered when one is exploring personality dimensions that emerge at the transition to parenthood. Since each baby shapes the parenting he or she receives, one baby may elicit certain adult behaviors and personality dimensions that would lie dormant in interactions with a different baby.

Personal efficacy

Changes in one's sense of personal efficacy is another area of personality functioning that has begun to receive attention. McLaughlin and Micklin (1983) found a decrease in feelings of personal efficacy in mothers versus nonmothers of the same socioeconomic or educational background if the first child's birth occurred before the mother's 18th birthday. In their study of personality change during the transition to parenthood, Sirignano and Lachman (1985) found that changes in feelings of personal control were related to the infant's temperament as perceived by parents. Mothers who perceived their babies as difficult temperamentally reported a loss of perceived control, whereas mothers who perceived their infants' temperaments as easy attributed successful outcomes to luck, an external source, rather than to more internal, self-centered sources.

In her study of early motherhood, Mikus (1981) found that mothers of young children felt less in control of their lives than women without children. It is important to note that the mothers in this study did not evidence significantly less self-esteem, more depression, or more negative opinions of themselves. Perhaps, the mothers' responses had less to do with di-

minished views of themselves as effective agents in the world and more
to do with the realities of worlds that include young children. Further
examination revealed that sense of efficacy was a significant predicator
of reported parental experience. The relationship found between a sense
of control over one's life and one's response to parenthood was an intriguing one: A strong sense of being able to run one's life as desired was
correlated with a negative response to motherhood (Mikus, 1981). A moderate, rather than strong, sense of efficacy among mothers with young
children may be the most adaptive response to the demands of parenthood.
The permanence of this sense of efficacy has not been examined. Perhaps
a stronger sense of personal effectiveness returns as children grow older.
Perhaps, early parenthood has a lasting impact on one's personality by
increasing one's adaptability.

Affective states

Changes in affective states during the transition to parenthood have long
been investigated with various results. Although some researchers (Dyer,
1963; Feldman, 1974; LeMasters, 1957) have found significant levels of
crisis and stress associated with the birth of the first child, others (Hobbs
& Cole, 1976; Raush, Barry, Hertel & Swain, 1974; Rossi, 1968; and Russell, 1974) have not. The data on depression is similarly inconsistent.
Brown and Harris (1978) consider having a preschool child a risk factor
for depression among women, and Campbell et al. (1976) concluded

that the situation of young parenthood is a time of many dissatisfactions and psychological stresses. Women and men both describe their lives at this stage of the
life cycle in relatively negative terms. . . . It is the young mothers, however, with
their frequent thoughts of escaping from their marital roles and their fears of a
nervous breakdown who appear to feel this pressure most acutely. (p. 409)

Haynes, Feinleid, Levine, Scotch, and Cannel (1978) found that having
a preschool child is a risk factor for heart disease among women. In contrast, Sirignano and Lachman (1985) found that depression levels did not
change in either mothers or fathers with the birth of a child, and Mikus
(1981) found no differences in measures of depression between mothers
of young children and childless women. Shereshefsky and Yarrow's (1973)
respondents reported depression and anxious feelings in early pregnancy
but an enhancement of well-being by the seventh month of pregnancy. In
Sirignano and Lachman's study (1985), no relationship between perceptions of infant temperament and anxiety was found for mothers; "fathers'
trait anxiety levels, however, were related to perceived temperament, with

fathers of babies noted as easily adaptable and as having a predominantly positive mood experiencing a decrease in anxiety'' (p. 565).

Once again, the need to consider mediating variables and to take a differentiated look at the transition to parenthood seems to be indicated. Complex questions must be addressed to understand the constellation of variables that are predictive of depression and/or anxiety in early parenthood; that is, which adults are most susceptible to negative affective states and to what extent? (An extensive review of depression states associated with pregnancy and early parenthood is presented by Fedele and colleagues, Chapter 3, this volume.)

Personal maturity

Increased maturity is popularly cited as a personality outcome of parenthood. However, maturity has not been consistently or clearly defined or investigated with regard to parenthood. Dyer (1963), Elson (1984), Gutmann (1975), and Heath (1978) interpret their findings as support for a link between parenthood and maturity. Shereshefsky & Yarrow (1973) observed that "psychological integration" increased following the birth of a child, and Hoffman (1978) noted a decrease in egocentrism and an increase in responsibility associated with early motherhood. Increased empathy and role-taking skills have been specified as outcomes derived from parental role entry and enactment (Galinsky, 1981; Heath, 1978). Clearly, the relationship between maturity and parenthood requires further examination.

Values

As a time of reevaluation and psychological activity, early parenthood may well stimulate an appraisal of one's deeply held values and beliefs. Heath's (1978) sample of fathers reported an increase in examining and confronting their values, but little research has been done on the impact of parenthood on adults' social and moral values (see Michaels, Chapter 1, this volume, for a review of the research). An increased sensitivity to social and political issues might develop as a result of parental concern for the current and future safety and well-being of the children. Conversely, new parents might turn inward in an effort to consolidate and nurture the new family. Energy, caring, and concern previously directed toward social issues might then be rechanneled to focus on the child.

Michaels (1981) found some evidence for an "ideological turning away from concern with welfare of people not in one's own family or circle of friends . . . [a] turning inward [and a] lessening of interest in values which relate to social justice, equality, community duty" (p. 145). At the same time, however, the parents in his study registered an increase in empathy and caring for the people with whom they had contact in their immediate social environment. Hoffman and Manis (1978) found that parents with young children displayed less concern than childless couples about the "troubled world"; parents were more likely to voice concerns about the world in terms of the potential of world problems and dangers to harm their children. Perhaps a parent's orientations to the external world shifts as the baby grows into childhood and slowly moves out into the world beyond the family. Values about education, childcare, work, religion, drug and substance abuse, sex, and legal and political issues may be determined, at least in part, by parental status.

Summary

The extent and range of the impact of parenthood on adult personality has yet to be thoroughly investigated. The question of permanent versus transient shifts and changes as a function of the transition to parenthood pervades all areas of study with respect to the impact of parenthood. In this chapter the power of the parenthood role in facilitating adult development has been recognized. Two conceptualizations that focus on ways of predicting and explaining personality change have been offered: the notion of possible parental selves and its potential for influencing one's experience of self as parent; and the act-frequency approach to personality change and development, which provides a perspective on the shaping of parental behaviors. Potential areas of change have been suggested in light of available literature, and areas needing additional research have been noted.

References

Ahammer, I. (1973). Social learning theory as a framework for the study of adult personality development. In P. B. Baltes & K. W. Schaie (Eds.), *Lifespan developmental psychology* (pp. 253–84). New York: Academic Press.

Anthony, J. E. (1984). Creative parenthood. In R. S. Cohen, B. J. Cohler, & S. H. Weissman (Eds.), *Parenthood: A psychodynamic perspective* (pp. 24–32). New York: Guilford Press.

Baltes, P. B., Reese, H. W., & Lipsett, L. P. (1980). Life-span developmental psychology. *Annual Review of Psychology, 31,* 65–110.

Bell, R. Q. (1971). Stimulus control of parent or caretaker behavior by offspring. *Developmental Psychology, 4,* 63–72.

Bell, R. Q. (1974). Contributions of human infants to caregiving and social interaction. In M. Lewis & L. A. Rosenblum (Eds.), *The effect of the infant on its caretaker* (pp. 1–19). New York: Wiley-Interscience.

Bell, R. Q. (1979). Parent, child, and reciprocal influences. *American Psychologist, 34,* 821–6.

Belsky, J. (1981). Early human experience: A family perspective. *Developmental Psychology, 17*(1), 3–23.

Belsky, J., Perry-Jenkins, M., & Crouter, A. C. (1985). The work–family interface and marital change across the transition to parenthood. *Journal of Family Issues, 6*(2), 205–20.

Benedek, T. (1970). Parenthood during the life cycle. In E. J. Anthony & T. Benedek (Eds.), *Parenthood: Its psychology and psychopathology* (pp. 185–206). Boston: Little, Brown.

Breen, D. (1975). *The Birth of a first child: Towards an understanding of femininity.* London: Tavistock.

Brim, O. G., & Wheeler, S. (1966). *Socialization after childhood: Two essays.* New York: Wiley.

Brown, G., & Harris, T. (1978). *Social origins of depression: A study of psychiatric disorder in women.* New York: Free Press.

Burr, W. (1972). Role transition: A reformation of theory. *Journal of Marriage and the Family, 34,* 407–16.

Buss, D. M., & Barnes, M. (1986). Preferences in human mate selection. *Journal of Personality and Social Psychology, 50,* 559–70.

Buss, D. M., & Craik, K. H. (1985). Why *not* measure that trait? *Journal of Personality and Social Psychology, 48,* 934–46.

Buss, D. M., & Craik, K. H. (1986). The act frequency approach and the construction of personality. In A. Angleitner, G. L. M. van Heck, & A. Furnham (Eds.), *Personality psychology in Europe: Theoretical and empirical developments* (Vol. 2). Lisse, Switzerland: Swets & Zeitlinger.

Campbell, A., Converse, P., & Rodgers, W. (1976). *The quality of American life: Perceptions, evaluations, and satisfactions.* New York: Russell Sage.

Caplan, G. (1964). *Principles of preventive psychiatry.* New York: Basic Books.

Chesler, P. (1979). *With child.* New York: Crowell.

Chess, S., & Thomas, A. (1977). *Temperament and development.* New York: Brunner/Mazel.

Chilman, C. S. (1980). Parent satisfactions, concerns, and goals for their children. *Family Relations, 29,* 339–45.

Cohen, R. S., & Weissman, S. H. (1984). The parenting alliance. In R. S. Cohen, B. J. Cohler, & S. H. Weissman (Eds.), *Parenthood: A psychodynamic perspective.* New York: Guilford Press.

Coleman, R. W., Kris, E., & Provence, S. (n.d.). *The study of variations of early parental attitudes: A preliminary report.* New Haven, CN: Yale University School of Medicine, Child Study Center.

Colman, A., & Colman, L. (1971). *Pregnancy: The psychological experience.* New York: Bantam Books.

Cowan, C. P., Cowan, P. A., Coie, L., & Coie, J. D. (1978). Becoming a family: The impact of a first child's birth on the couple's relationship. In W. B. Miller & L. F. Newman (Eds.), *The first child and family formation* (pp. 296–324). Chapel Hill: University of North Carolina, Carolina Population Center.

Cowan, C. P., Cowan, P. A., Heming, G., Garrett, E., Coysh, W. S., Curtis-Boles, H. K., & Boles, A. J., III. (1985). Transitions to parenthood: His, hers, & theirs. *Journal of Family Issues, 6*(4), 523–42.

Cox, M. J., Owen, M. J., Lewis, J. M., Riedel, C., Scalf-McIver, L., & Suster, A. (1985). Intergenerational influences on the parent–infant relationship in the transition to parenthood. *Journal of Family Issues 6*(4), 523–42.

Dohrenwend, B. S., & Dohrenwend, B. P. (1981). *Stressful life events and their contexts.* New York: Prodist.

Douvan, E. (1978, April). *Family roles in a twenty year perspective*. Paper presented at the Pre-Centennial Conference on New Directions for an Era, Radcliffe College, Cambridge, MA.

Dyer, E. D. (1963). Parenthood as crisis: A re-study. *Marriage and Family Living, 25,* 196–201.

Elson, M. (1984). Parenthood and the transformation of narcissism. In R. S. Cohen, B. J. Cohler, & S. H. Weissman (Eds.), *Parenthood: A psychodynamic perspective* (pp. 297–314). New York: Guilford Press.

Erikson, E. H. (1959). Identity and the life cycle: Selected papers. *Psychological Issues, 1,* 50–100.

Fawcett, J. T. (1978). The value and cost of the first child. In W. B. Miller & L. F. Newman (Eds.), *The first child and family formation* (pp. 244–65). Chapel Hill: University of North Carolina, Carolina Population Center.

Fein, R. A. (1978). Consideration of men's experiences and the birth of a first child. In W. B. Miller & L. F. Newman (Eds.), *The first child and family formation* (pp. 327–39). Chapel Hill: University of North Carolina, Carolina Population Center.

Feldman, H. (1974). Changes in marriage and parenthood: A methodological design. In E. Peck & J. Senderowitz (Eds.), *Pronatalism: The myth of mom and apple pie* (pp. 206–26). New York: Crowell.

Feldman, S. S., & Aschenbrenner, B. (1983). Impact of parenthood on various aspects of masculinity & feminity: A short-term longitudinal study. *Developmental Psychology 19*(2), 278–89.

Fraiberg, S., Adelson, E., & Shapiro, V. (1975). Ghosts in the nursery: A psychoanalytic approach to the problems of impaired infant–mother relationships. *Journal of Child Psychiatry, 14*(3), 387–421.

Galinsky, E. (1981). *Between generations: The stages of parenthood*. New York: Berkley Books.

Gecas, V. (1982). The self-concept. *Annual Review of Sociology, 8,* 1–33.

Goldberg, W. A., Michaels, G. Y., & Lamb, M. E. (1985). Husbands' and wives' adjustment to pregnancy and first parenthood. *Journal of Family Issues, 6*(4), 483–503.

Gordon, C. (1968). Self-conceptions: Configurations of content. In C. Gordon & K. Gergen (Eds.), *The self in social interaction* (pp. 115–36). New York: Wiley.

Greene, B. (1984). *Good morning, merry sunshine*. New York: Atheneum.

Gronseth, E. (1972). The breadwinner trap. In L. K. Howe (Ed.), *The future of the family* (pp. 175–91). New York: Simon & Schuster.

Group for the Advancement of Psychiatry. (1973). *The joys and sorrows of parenthood*. New York: Scribner's.

Gutmann, D. (1975). Parenthood: A key to the comparative study of the life cycle. In N. Datan & L. H. Ginsberg (Eds.), *Life-span developmental psychology*. (pp. 167–84). New York: Academic Press.

Harper, L. V. (1971). The young as a source of stimuli controlling caretaker behavior. *Developmental Psychology, 4,* 73–88.

Haynes, S. G., Feinleid, M., Levine, S., Scotch, N., & Cannel, W. B. (1978). The relationship of psychosocial factors to coronary heart disease in the Framingham Study II, Prevalence of Coronary Heart Disease. *American Journal of Epidemiology, 107,* 304–402.

Heath, D. H. (1978). What meaning and effects does fatherhood have for the maturing of professional men? *Merrill–Palmer Quarterly, 24*(4), 265–78.

Hobbs, D. F., Jr., & Cole, S. P. (1976). Transition to parenthood: A decade replication. *Journal of Marriage and the Family, 38,* 723–31.

Hoffman, L. W. (1978). Effects of the first child on the woman's role. In W. B. Miller & L. F. Newman (Eds.), *The first child and family formation* (pp. 340–67). Chapel Hill: University of North Carolina, Carolina Population Center.

Hoffman, L. W., & Manis, J. (1978). Influences of children on marital interaction and parental satisfactions and dissatisfactions. In R. M. Lerner & G. W. Spanier (Eds.), *Child influences on marital and family interaction: A life-span perspective* (pp. 165–213). New York: Academic Press.

Kort, C. (1981). Primal bond versus marriage bond. In R. Friedland & C. Kort (Eds.), *The mother's book: Shared experiences.* (pp. 123–7). Boston: Houghton Mifflin.

Lamb, M. (1978). Influence of the child on marital quality and family interaction during the prenatal, perinatal, and infancy periods. In R. M. Lerner & G. B. Spanier (Eds.), *Child influences on marital and family interaction: A life-span perspective* (pp. 137–63). New York: Academic Press.

Lawton, J. T., & Coleman, M. (1983). Parents' perceptions of parenting. *Infant Mental Health Journal, 4*(4), 352–61.

Leifer, M. (1977). Psychological changes accompanying pregnancy and motherhood. *Genetic Psychology Monographs, 95*, 55–96.

LeMasters, E. E. (1957). Parenthood as crisis. *Marriage and Family Living, 19*, 352–5.

Levine, J. (1976). *Who will raise the children? New options for fathers (and mothers).* Philadelphia: Lippincott.

Lopata, H. (1972). *Occupation: Housewife.* New York: Oxford University Press.

Lowenthal, M. F., Thurnher, M., Chiriboga, D., & Associates (1976). *Four stages of life.* San Francisco: Jossey-Bass.

Markus, H. (1977). Self-schemata and processing information about the self. *Journal of Personality and Social Psychology, 35*(2), 63–78.

Markus, H. (1983). Self-knowledge: An expanded view. *Journal of Personality and Social Psychology, 51*(3), 543–65.

Markus, H., & Nurius, P. (1986). Possible selves. *American Psychologist, 41*(9), 954–69.

Markus, H., & Nurius, P. (1987). Possible selves: The interface between motivation and the self-concept. In K. M. Yardley & T. M. Honess (Eds.), *Self and identity: psychosocial perspectives* (pp. 157–72). New York: Wiley.

Markus, H., & Sentis, K. (1982). The self in social information processing. In J. Suls (Ed.), *Psychological perspectives on the self.* Hillsdale, NJ: Erlbaum.

Markus, H., & Wurf, E. (1987). The dynamic self-concept: A social psychological perspective. In M. R. Rosenszweig & L. W. Porter (Eds.), *Annual Review of Psychology, 38*, 299–337.

McLaughlin, S. D., & Micklin, M. (1983). The timing of the first birth and changes in personal efficacy. *Journal of Marriage and the Family, 45*(1), 47–55.

Michaels, G. Y. (1981). *Transition to parenthood: Impact on moral, personal values, attitudes and life goals.* Unpublished doctoral dissertation, University of Michigan, Ann Arbor.

Mikus, K. (1981). *Paradoxes of early parenthood.* Ann Arbor, MI: University Microfilms.

Nye, F. I. (1976). *Role structure and analysis of the family.* Beverly Hills, CA: Sage.

Oates, D. S., & Heinicke, C. M. (1985). Prebirth prediction of the quality of the mother–infant interaction. *Journal of Family Issues, 6*(4), 523–42.

Osofsky, J. D. (1970). The shaping of mother's behavior by children. *Journal of Marriage and the Family, 32*, 400–5.

Parke, R. D., & Sawin, D. B. (1977, March). *The family in early infancy: Social interactional and attitudinal analyses.* Paper presented at a symposium, "The Family System: Networks of Interactions Among Mother, Father, and Infant," at the Society for Research in Child Development meeting, New Orleans, LA.

Rapoport, R., Rapoport, R. N., Strelitz, Z., & Kew, S. (1977). *Fathers, mothers, and society: Towards new alliances.* New York: Basic Books.

Raush, H., Barry, W., Hertel, R., & Swain, M. A. (1974). *Communication, conflict, and marriage.* San Francisco: Jossey-Bass.

Rheingold, H. L. (1969). The social and socializing infant. In D. Goslin (Ed.), *The handbook of socialization theory and research* (pp. 779–90). Chicago: Rand McNally.

Rosenberg, M. (1965). *Society and the adolescent self-image.* Princeton, NJ: Princeton University Press.

Rosenberg, M. (1979). *Conceiving the self.* New York: Basic Books.

Rossi, A. S. (1968). Transition to parenthood. *Journal of Marriage and the Family, 30,* 26–39.

Russell, C. S. (1974). Transition to parenthood: Problems and gratifications. *Journal of Marriage and the Family, 36*(2), 294–301.

Sadow, L. (1984). The psychological origins of parenthood. In R. S. Cohen, B. J. Cohler, & S. H. Weissman (Eds.), *Parenthood: A psychodynamic perspective* (pp. 285–96). New York: Guilford Press.

Sameroff, A. (1975). Transactional models in early social relations. *Human Development, 18,* 65–79.

Sarbin, T. R., & Allen, V. L. (1968). Role theory. In G. Lindzey & E. Aronson (Eds.), *The handbook of social psychology* (2nd ed., Vol. 1, pp. 488–567). Reading, MA: Addison-Wesley.

Schwartz, B. (1984). Psychoanalytic developmental perspectives on parenthood. In R. S. Cohen, B. J. Cohler, & S. H. Weissman (Eds.), *Parenthood: A psychodynamic perspective* (pp. 356–72). New York: Guilford Press.

Shereshefsky, P. M., & Yarrow, L. J. (1973). *Psychological aspects of a first pregnancy and early postnatal adaptation.* New York: Raven Press.

Sirignano, S. W., & Lachman, M. E. (1985). Personality change during the transition to parenthood: The role of perceived infant temperament. *Developmental Psychologist, 21*(3), 558–67.

Steffensmeier, R. H., & Steffensmeier, D. J. (1975, April). *An empirical test of a causal model of the transition to parenthood.* Paper presented at the Southern Sociological Society, Washington, DC.

Steinberg, D. (1977). *fatherjournal: Five years of awakening to fatherhood.* New York: Times Change Press.

Turner, R. H. (1978). The role and the person. *American Journal of Sociology, 84*(1), 1–23.

Veroff, J., Douvan, E., & Kulka, R. (1981). *The inner American: A self-portrait from 1957 to 1976.* New York: Basic Books.

Veroff, J., & Feld, S. (1970). *Marriage and work in America: A study of motives and roles.* New York: Van Nostrand Reinhold.

Walters, J., & Walters, L. H. (1980). Parent–child relationships: A review: 1970–1979. *Journal of Marriage and the Family, 42,* 807–822.

Wandersman, L. P. (1978). *Longitudinal changes in the adjustment to parenthood.* Paper presented at the meeting of the American Psychological Association, Toronto.

Wylie, R. C. (1979). *The self-concept* (rev. ed., Vols. 1 & 2). Lincoln: University of Nebraska Press.

3   Psychological issues in adjustment to first parenthood

Nicolina M. Fedele, Ellen R. Golding,
Frances K. Grossman, and William S. Pollack

Introduction

The prospective birth of a child has profound psychological significance
when the baby is still a gleam in the parents' eye. From that point
throughout parenthood, there are major shifts in the lives of adults, the
equilibria of marriages, and the contexts of families. Determining the major
contributors and facilitators of adaptation and growth in this transition is
central to our attempts to understand both individual and family development.

Historically, the clinical literature on the transition to parenthood began
with a focus on women and psychopathology, whereas sociologists were
struggling with the question of whether the transition to parenthood is a
period of serious crisis or merely one of stressful transition in normal
families. The focus of the clinical literature expanded to include fathers'
and couples' responses to this transition. Gradually, clinical theory evolved
to consider normal adaptation of all members of the family system, as
well as the system itself.

As clinicians doing research on the development of families, we bring
to a systems perspective the clinical object relations framework, that is,
recent developments in psychoanalytic theory that emphasize the centrality
of relationships in early ego development. In addition, current object relations theory posits that each individual is engaged in ongoing negotiations
of the tension between separateness and relatedness. A systems approach
to parenting provides a unique and complex view because it proposes that
each individual involved in the family unit – the mother, the father, and
each child – is involved in mutually interactive transactions. In combining
these points of view into a relational systems approach, we suggest that
family researchers must regard the tension between simultaneous strivings
for affiliation and for autonomy as a salient issue for both the individual
in negotiating the evolution from one life stage to another and the family

as a unit in its own development. The addition of a child to a couple causes a shift in the number and quality of relationships that each adult experiences, resulting in various affiliations and attachments. Although the ongoing dialectic between an individual's tendency toward autonomy and an individual's tendency toward affiliation is prevalent throughout the life span of an adult, it is of particular salience during transitional periods, such as the birth of the first child, when changes in the life cycle of the family directly influence the ongoing individual development of a parent.

The chapter begins with a review of relevant literature addressing a number of areas. Consistent with the historical development of the research on the transition to parenthood, we begin by focusing on women and psychopathology, and then broaden our perspective to include men. Next, we turn to the more recent literature on women's and men's normative development, with its increasingly complex, systemic view. This analysis will demonstrate the range of responses to the pressures of the transition, from the dysfunctional response seen in severe psychopathology to more normative adaptive struggles.

Throughout the literature, there is widespread recognition of the interplay between individual psychological and family relationship factors. The second section of this chapter includes research data supporting the hypothesis that the tension between autonomy and affiliation is an important dimension of psychological development that critically affects the individual and the family system. The chapter concludes with a discussion of the clinical and psychological implications, both for the individual and for the family, of the adjustment to first parenthood.

Early research on psychopathological responses

Research on women

Recent research has designated three classes of postpartum psychiatric disorders: postpartum psychoses, nonpsychotic postpartum depression, and postpartum blues. The three postpartum disorders are selectively reviewed below in terms of symptomatology, prevalence, and course. This review is followed by a discussion of the known predictors and correlates of postpartum depression focusing primarily on psychological and relationship factors (see comprehensive reviews by Cutrona, 1982, and Hopkins, Marcus, & Campbell, 1984).

Postpartum psychoses. Postpartum psychosis, the most severe of the postpartum disorders, has been compared to other acute nonpuerperal psychoses that may be either affective or schizophrenic (Herzog & Detre, 1976). Delusions in postpartum psychosis may reflect concerns about childbearing, childcare, or coping with family demands. Women with postpartum psychosis may be delirious, restless, tearful, and depressed (Notman & Nadelson, 1978). The onset of psychosis usually occurs within 6 weeks of delivery, prevalence estimates ranging from 0.01 to 0.02% of deliveries (Cutrona, 1982; Kaij & Nilsson, 1972). Approximately 15 to 20% of women who become psychotic after delivery have had a prior psychotic episode (Protheroe, 1969). One-third of women who experience postpartum psychosis develop similar difficulties in later pregnancies (Notman & Nadelson, 1978). The data summarized by Cutrona (1982) and Herzog and Detre (1976) indicate that puerperal schizophrenia and non-puerperal schizophrenia are fundamentally the same illness, as are puerperal and nonpuerperal affective disorders. More empirical research is needed to clarify the relationship between postpartum psychosis and previous as well as subsequent nonpostpartum psychotic episodes in order to evaluate subtle characteristics of this relatively rare disorder.

Nonpsychotic postpartum depression. Postpartum depression, moderate in severity between postpartum psychosis and the maternity blues, is beginning to be recognized as a separate syndrome (Cutrona, 1982). However, no formal diagnostic criteria have yet been developed to distinguish postpartum depression from depression not associated with pregnancy and birth. In fact, Hopkins et al. (1984) argue convincingly that the normative data are not sufficient to distinguish accurately between normal distress and pathological reactions following pregnancy. In their review it is evident that there is no consensus and very little empirical data on the duration of a postpartum depression, although there is some agreement that symptoms must persist beyond the first postpartum week and may persist throughout the first year.

The frequency of nonpsychotic postpartum depression varies according to measures used to define or diagnose it. Cutrona (1982) reviewed 11 studies that demonstrate a range of incidence rates between 3 and 33%, emphasizing how little is known about this disorder. Very low prevalence (less than 8%) was found when case status was assigned only to women who sought psychiatric treatment for postpartum depression. Somewhat higher estimates (10–17%) were found in studies using standard measures of depression including cognitive, motivational, and/or physiological symptoms of depression. Studies utilizing less rigorous diagnostic procedures such as symptom checklists or global depression ratings without specific diagnostic criteria reported inflated prevalence estimates (25–30%).

Methodological inadequacies, inconsistencies in diagnostic criteria, and a paucity of studies, in general, make it difficult to draw conclusions, and major differences across studies complicate comparison of data (Cutrona, 1982). However, Hopkins et al. (1984) conclude that data from recent studies using more rigorous assessment strategies suggest that about 20% of women experience a clinical depression in the postpartum period (O'Hara, 1980; Paykel, Emms, Fletcher, & Rassaby, 1980).

Several researchers have compared depression that occurs during pregnancy with that which occurs in the postpartum period. Using a nonclinical sample, Grossman et al. (1980) found that the level of anxiety and depression in the first trimester was comparable to that in a normal sample of adult women. The individual levels of anxiety and depression in early pregnancy strongly predicted anxiety and depression in the 2-month postpartum period. However, at 1 year postpartum, the women in the sample were generally less anxious and depressed than they had been at any point since the beginning of the pregnancy.

O'Hara, Neunaber, and Zekoski (1984) also found a decrease in depressive symptomatology from the pregnancy (second trimester) to postpartum (9 weeks). They found no differences between 9-week and 6-month follow-ups. This seems to indicate that depression in pregnancy may predict depression in the early postpartum period but that the overall rate of nonpsychotic depression decreases from early pregnancy to the end of the first postpartum year. Conversely, O'Hara et al. (1984) found most women in their sample who were depressed postpartum not to be depressed during pregnancy. Notman and Nadelson (1978) also found no association between serious nonpsychotic depressive disorder pre- and postpartum in the same woman. Further detailed research on specific symptom patterns is necessary in order to define nonpsychotic postpartum depression as a psychological entity.

Postpartum blues. Many women experience postpartum blues, which Cutrona (1982) defined as tearfulness, crying spells, and confusion in the early postpartum period. The importance and prevalence of this common problem have recently been recognized (Leifer, 1977). Cutrona (1982) reviewed six studies that reveal that 50 to 70% of women experience at least transitory symptoms of depression in the week following childbirth (e.g., Ballinger, Buckley, Naylor, & Stansfield, 1979). However, Cutrona found that more stringent criteria, requiring that depressive symptoms be at least moderately severe, cause the prevalence figure to drop to about 33% in the first week postpartum. In approximately one-third of a sample of 62 women, Shereshefsky and Yarrow (1973) noted feelings of anxiety and depression about the ability to mother, overreaction to realistic problems, and hostile attitudes toward the infant. Adjustment to new parenthood may be a factor in this disturbance, since blues have been described more frequently in first-time mothers (Hopkins et al., 1984). At this point, it is unclear whether postpartum depression is caused by a failure to recover from initial blues or whether postpartum blues and postpartum depression are actually two independent syndromes. These issues must be clarified by future research.

Predictors of psychological responses in women. Most researchers agree that all degrees of postpartum depression from psychosis to the blues are associated with multiple factors. Psychological changes during and after pregnancy, demographic variables such as socioeconomic status, stress, and previous psychiatric and genetic predisposition have been implicated as causes in postpartum psychiatric disorders. Social supports, relationships, and individual psychological characteristics are also widely viewed as significant etiological factors (reviewed in Cutrona, 1982; Grossman et al., 1980; Hopkins et al., 1984).

Individual psychological variables associated with postpartum depression have included low motivation for the pregnancy and low level of psychological health, the latter especially among first-time mothers (Grossman et al., 1980). Women who have strong internal conflicts vis-à-vis motherhood or feminine identification are also at risk for the development of postpartum depression (Hopkins et al., 1984). Anxiety, hostility, and self-critical thought patterns have been implicated in the development of postpartum psychopathology (Hayworth et al., 1980).

Looking at relationship or systems variables reviewed by Cutrona (1982) and Hopkins et al. (1984), there is a relatively clear relationship between lack of social support, marital difficulties (Ballinger et al., 1979), or lack of support in the marriage (Paykel et al., 1980) and postpartum depression. In fact, Hopkins et al. (1984) suggest that evaluating the interaction of external stress and deficits in social supports is necessary in order to understand postpartum depression. Infant characteristics, such as medical risk status and difficult temperament, may also be associated with the development of postpartum depression.

Psychopathological responses in men

Although there has been recent writing on adaptive responses of men as fathers, there has been very little recent literature on serious psychopathology in men in the initial postpartum period (Cath, Gurwitt, & Ross,

1982). Several early clinical studies reported the psychopathological responses of men attendant on the adult-to-parent transition (Freeman, 1951; Reitterstol, 1968; Wainwright, 1966; Zilboorg, 1931; cited in LaCoursiere, 1972). These studies focused on men who had developed serious psychological problems, in most instances a psychosis, after the birth of their first child. This is reminiscent of the full-blown male couvade described by Cavenar & Weddington (1978), which entailed physically disabling symptoms.

However, the phenomenon of expectant fathers experiencing couvade-like physical symptoms, including loss of appetite, toothaches, and nausea or sickness, is commonly seen in our culture (Coleman & Coleman, 1971). These symptoms may be interpreted as a man's normative way of participating in the pregnancy and birth. LaCoursiere (1972) described the process of becoming a father as a stressful experience and emphasized issues of dependency that are accentuated during the wife's pregnancy and the first weeks postpartum. LaCoursiere posits that dependency needs are aroused during this time, in part because the husband often receives less attention from his wife while she deals with her own physical and psychological needs. If the husband has a history of unresolved issues of dependency, he might become depressed by the change in his wife's ability to nurture him. LaCoursiere views fatherhood as a period requiring the recapitulation and new resolution of earlier life-span developmental conflicts. This is similar to Benedek's view (discussed below) of parenthood for men and women (Benedek, 1970). If issues from these earlier phases have been resolved inadequately, the successful adaptation to pregnancy, birth, and early parenting may also be in jeopardy.

Conceptual models of adaptation to parenthood

Benedek (1959, 1970) was an important forerunner of current thinking about families. She considered parenthood to be a stage of adult development and characterized it as an experience that activates and maintains a developmental process in the parent. She suggested that each critical period of a child's development revives in the parent her or his own developmental conflicts. The resolution of this conflict provides the opportunity for a new level of integration for the parent. While parents deliberately monitor and modify their child's behavior and their ongoing relationship with their child, they also unconsciously modify their own intrapsychic processes such as repressed memories, emotions, conflicts, and disappointments. As an example, while fathers consciously attempt to shape their children's behavior according to social values and norms, their children's behaviors, in turn, stir up repressed memories in the fathers. This supports a spiral model of development throughout the life span (Vaillant & Milofsky, 1980).

This process of development has an impact on the parent's parenting and the child's functioning. The parent's response to the needs and behavior of a child depends, in some part, on the parent's internalized developmental experience. Benedek's model highlights the reciprocal effects that adult development, parenting, and child development have on one another. It also demonstrates the importance of examining how life-span development and family systems theories are complementary and provide a fuller understanding of human development throughout the life span.

Belsky (1981), in reviewing the implications of recent transition-to-parenthood research, stresses the absence of a conceptual framework for considering factors that might mediate the quality of normative adjustment to parenthood. He suggests the value of a life-span perspective. Using this conceptual scheme, he views the timing and sequencing of parenthood as important factors (Belsky, 1981, 1984). Specifically, for example, the transition is less severe when the parents are older (Hobbs & Wimbish, 1977). It is also less difficult when the parents have been married for a longer period of time before conception (Dyer, 1963; Russell, 1974). In addition, the transition is affected by whether conception takes place before or after marriage (Russell, 1974). A life-span developmental perspective on parenthood, then, provides a useful framework for viewing family systems involving the marital relationship, the family of origin, and the parent–child relationship.

In recent years, a number of researchers have begun to reexamine the adult-to-parent transition from this life-span perspective. It has increasingly been viewed as a normative process of adaptation (Cowan, Cowan, Coie, & Coie, 1983; Feldman & Nash, 1984; Grossman et al., 1980). When regarded in this manner, there are four important domains of individual and family functioning that can be affected: (1) the internal psychological, (2) the sociocultural, (3) the marital, and (4) the parental (Grossman et al., 1980). Research that focuses on one or more of these domains is discussed below.

On the basis of their longitudinal study of couples, Cowan et al. (1983; see also Chapter 4, this volume) stress the marital domain, viewing the key to adaptation during the transition as the quality of the couple's relationship before and after they become parents. Their research suggests that intrapsychic and marital difficulties may manifest as stress in the parent–child relationship. Furthermore, they found male–female differences in adaptation to parenthood. For men, internal issues of high life stress and low self-esteem seem to be predictors of parental stress and marital dissatisfaction. For women, low self-esteem and marital dissatisfaction seem to be predictors of parental stress. The authors conclude that becoming a parent may be a qualitatively different experience for women and men. The stress associated with early parenthood may have different antecedents and different consequences, depending on the parent's gender.

Feldman and Nash (1984) also conclude that gender is an important factor in determining predictors of parenting. They examined three sets of predictors of adaptation to parenting: (1) the parent's characteristics (i.e., age, personality, and mood states); (2) adjustment to, and psychological preparation for, pregnancy; and (3) relationships with significant others (i.e., social networks and occupational experience). They found molar personality antecedents such as integrity and strength of ego functioning to be the most adequate predictors of later maternal functioning. There was, however, no conclusive evidence establishing the effectiveness of men's personality characteristics as predictors of fathering behavior. The quality of the marriage was a stronger predictor of parental functioning for men than for women.

Recently, a number of family researchers have stressed the importance of indirect as well as direct patterns of influence (Belsky, 1981; Fedele, 1984; Feldman & Aschenbrenner, 1983; Feldman & Nash, 1984; Grossman, 1982; Pedersen, Andersen, & Cain, 1980; Pollack, 1981; reviewed in Pollack & Grossman, 1985). Feldman and Nash (1984), for example, predicted parenting behavior from a spouse's feelings and attitudes during expectancy. Feldman, Nash, & Aschenbrenner (1983) also demonstrated gender differences in indirect (i.e., cross-parent) effects. They found that a woman experienced more strain in parenting when her husband was older, when he experienced the marriage and the expectancy as more stressful, and when he was more preoccupied with his job. A man's strain was less when his wife was less anxious and happier with the marriage. They were able to predict men's behavior with their 6-month-old from their wives' characteristics as well as from the characteristics of the men measured during the pregnancy. Dickie and Gerber (1980) found that an increase in fathers' interactions with their 4- and 12-month-olds caused a decrease in mothers' interactions with those children. Although these researchers have examined indirect effects on parenting, they have not looked at indirect effects in the adult-to-parent transition. This question was one focus of interest in our own research, which we present later in this chapter.

One very interesting recent formulation that integrates the sociological and clinical perspectives on the family is that of Shapiro (1978, in press).

She represents the current thinking on the family life cycle from a systems interactional perspective. Points of transition such as that from adult to parent require role changes in order to meet the new demands of interacting with family members. Concurrently, they require reassessment of the self within numerous family relationships. Shapiro, then, views family role transitions as crucial phases of the life cycle in which the individual self is challenged to develop novel responses to others and novel views of the self.

The adult-to-parent transition, viewed from this perspective, provides the opportunity for expansion as well as restriction of an individual's identity (autonomy) and interpersonal relationships (affiliation). We propose that the psychological development of an individual's autonomy and affiliation is usually accomplished within the social network of the family system and, hence, must be sensitive to family life-cycle transitions. The study of parenting as a process that necessitates an individual's negotiation between separateness (autonomy) and membership (affiliation) in the family system is crucial to the understanding of both adult development and the family life cycle.

Previous psychological models of the transition to parenthood (e.g., Hobbs, 1968; Hobbs & Wimbish, 1977; Russell, 1974) have not adequately described the complexity of an individual's evolution as a parent because they have not attended to the interactive elements of development within a family system. We now present our model of adaptation to parenthood, based on motives of autonomy and affiliation as crucial dimensions of development that are especially relevant during family life-cycle transitions. This model (Grossman, 1984; Grossman, Pollack, Golding, & Fedele, 1985) integrates the individual psychological and family system focuses, drawing on recent object relations theory.

New model of adaptation to parenthood: autonomy and affiliation

Recent literature examines the significance of concepts related to affiliation and autonomy in both individual and family development (see Grossman, 1984). Some of these concepts include agency and communion (Bakan, 1966), inclusion and differentiation (Kegan, 1982), and allocentric and autocentric (Guttman, 1970). Our understanding of autonomy and affiliation derives primarily from a combination of object relations, self-psychological, and developmental perspectives. This is augmented by our unique position as clinicians familiar with psychological processes in adjustment and as researchers who integrate developmental and family systems perspectives. Literature on adult development (particularly recent work on women) and family development illuminates the importance of autonomy and affiliation in the adult-to-parent transition. Although it is not possible to review this literature in its entirety, we will highlight the relevant theory.

The classical psychoanalytic view as expressed, for example, by Mahler (1968) posits a single line of development from symbiosis to autonomy. In contrast, Stechler and Kaplan (1980) and Pollack (1981), following Kohut's self-psychological framework (Kohut, 1971, 1977), propose the existence of two separate, parallel lines of development representing the need of the self for separateness and relatedness. Research in child development provides support for these parallel developmental lines. Stechler and Kaplan (1980) and Pollack (1981), for example, suggest that even infants alternate the need for separateness with the need for relatedness.

Both women and men require autonomy and affiliation for healthy adaptation. Recent psychological theory regarding female development has highlighted sex differences in the development, process, and meaning of these two capacities. Gilligan (1977, 1979, 1982) contrasts two differing approaches to the world: one involving a focus on relationships and the other focusing on a separate identity. On the basis of her data, she argues that women tend to experience themselves as essentially connected but are more fearful of, and less competent at, experiencing themselves as separate from their context of relationships. Men, however, tend to focus on their separate selves, which she refers to as their identity, but experience difficulty in relationships.

Chodorow (1978) outlines a developmental basis for understanding sex differences in intimacy and identity. Because women are most often the primary caretakers of children, boys and girls form their identities in relation to women. Girls, in identifying with their mother, form their sexual identification through attachment to the same-sex parent. Boys, however, must separate themselves from their mother to define themselves as masculine. This involves a greater stress on boundaries and separateness. Through these differential developmental processes, men's gender identity is threatened by intimacy, whereas women tend to have problems with individuation.

The work of both Gilligan and Chodorow adds a new perspective to previous research regarding adult development, which had focused primarily on men. Research and theory on development in men (e.g., Erikson, 1959, 1963; Levinson, 1978) has overemphasized the development of autonomy, failing to give adequate attention to the concomitant development of affiliation or intimacy. Nonetheless, recent literature on men also suggests the importance of relatedness in addition to or along with autonomy. For instance, Fasteau (1974) has described the difficulties men face when they are focused on independent, separate, usually career-related activities to the exclusion of affiliation. In a similar vein, Biller (1982) views the quality of a man's relationship with his children as significant to his life satisfaction.

Although writers interested in early parenting have not addressed the specific concepts of affiliation and autonomy, related concepts have been considered. In particular, Feldman and Nash (1984) discuss the tendency of men to become less expressive and women to become less instrumental under the stress of the tasks of early parenting. Grossman (1984) describes the importance, to men and to their families, of fathers' balancing the emphasis on autonomous activities with more affiliative connections at this time.

Balance is an important issue for couples who must negotiate both "individuality" and "coupleness" (Cowen et al., 1983), as well as all other aspects of family life (Rapaport, Rapaport, & Strelitz, 1977). A similar emphasis on balance has been described in literature on role conflict in women who commit themselves both to parenting and to a career (see Fedele, 1983).

We see achieving a balance between autonomy and affiliation as a central task of young adults in the adult-to-parent transition. We define autonomy as a view of oneself as separate or distinct from others; a participation in and enjoyment of activities carried out alone, or at least separate from important personal relationships; and a valuing of that individual part of oneself as important to one's development. Autonomy, then, is related to but not defined entirely by participation in "separate" activities (Grossman, 1984).

Affiliation refers to a view of oneself as connected in an important way to others; to participation in, and enjoyment of, empathic and responsive relationships in which one retains a sense of a separate self; and to valuing that part of oneself as important to one's development. Affiliation is related to but not solely defined by participation and investment in relationships (Grossman, 1984).

The concepts of autonomy and affiliation have been touched upon in a number of developmental models. Erikson (1959, 1963) describes a specific progression from identity, that is, the development of an autonomous self, to intimacy, that is, the development of an affiliative self in relationship. Sullivan (in Goethals, 1976), in contrast, emphasizes identity formation resulting from the experience of interpersonal intimacy. Chodorow (1978) in an interesting theoretical discussion asserts that differentiation is not equivalent to separateness; it also involves a relationship to, and perception of, another person. In her view, autonomy itself grows out of the early relatedness to the parent and may never be entirely apart from this sense of relatedness. Jean Baker Miller and her colleagues at the Wellesley College Stone Center have written a number of theoretical papers on the psychology of women that focus on the issues involved in the ongoing development of a relational self (Jordan, 1984; Jordan, Surrey, & Kaplan, 1983; Kaplan, 1984; Miller, 1984; Surrey, 1983).

Whatever the sequence of development or congruence between autonomy and affiliation – and we are not yet prepared to take a position on this theoretical question – it is clear that there is a lifelong negotiation and counterpoint between the two (Erikson, 1959, 1963; reviewed in Fedele, 1983). Since parenthood involves negotiating commitments to self and to others, the dialectic between autonomy and affiliation becomes highlighted around the transition to parenthood. The search for the balance between self and other affects the marital relationship and the parent–child relationship (discussed in Fedele, 1983). Parenting provides a unique and complex interaction of affiliation and autonomy since each individual in the family unit – mother, father, and child – is in some way negotiating the dilemma, but in reference to one another.

Literature on early parenthood stresses the complexity of a three-person system with multiple levels of effect (Dickie & Gerber, 1980). A mother or father negotiating autonomy and affiliation will affect his or her spouse and child. The negotiation will also influence self-esteem (Grossman, 1984), which in turn will influence the individual's capacity to relate to the other individuals in the system.

Within the field of multiple determinants of successful adaptation to early parenthood, we find parental balancing of affiliation and autonomy to be a crucial area for study. The balance of investment in self- and other-related activities is put to a test at this transition time, and successful negotiation of these conflicting demands can augur well for adaptation to early family life.

Autonomy and affiliation: research findings

The Boston University Pregnancy and Parenthood Project has examined the adult-to-parent transition in a longitudinal study of family functioning (described in detail in Grossman et al., 1980). Data were first gathered for the project early in the woman's pregnancy, and the most recent data collection took place at the child's fifth birthday. For the purposes of this chapter, the focus is on the adult-to-parent transition at the birth of the first child. The findings through the first year have been reported in Grossman et al. (1980). The recently defined variables of autonomy and affiliation are here described fully for the first time as they relate to the earlier variables (see also Grossman, 1984).

In this longitudinal study, for primiparous women and their husbands, pregnancy and early parenthood was indeed a transition of considerable proportions wherein many of the couple's resources – psychological, sociocultural, physiological, and marital – were called into play. Couples with significant problems in any of these areas seemed handicapped in their capacity to navigate successfully the complex tasks involved in introducing a first child into the couple's structure. For them, the transition may, in fact, have become a crisis with less than optimal resolution in terms of their feelings about themselves, their marriage, or their relationship to their new baby. Grossman (1984) has noted some tendency for men to become less affiliative and more extremely focused on independent activities around the birth of a child at the same time as their wives are becoming less autonomous and more caught up in intimate and empathic relationship. This was also reported by Feldman and Nash (1984).

The Pregnancy and Parenthood Project found that the imminent birth of a first child arouses anxieties in men about their capacity to provide. Many begin to put in more hours at work in order to bring home more money or to be a better father-provider. Women, however, tend to submerge within the family boundaries when they have babies. Some, particularly with a first child, are inclined to become completely immersed in the world of mother and infant and greatly reduce their involvement with their husband, as with the rest of the world, at least for a period of time. Some more actively exclude their husband from involvement with the infant (Grossman et al., 1980).

The early data from the longitudinal study suggest that how adults deal with closeness and separateness during early expectancy, as well as how they feel about themselves, is an important factor in later relationships with their child and their spouse. The following brief report describes our efforts to study these issues in a more systematic way.

Method

Sample

The sample consisted of mothers and fathers who were part of the Boston University Pregnancy and Parenthood Project during the pregnancy and early parenthood of their first child. For the purposes of this chapter, the focus is on the data collected early in pregnancy, at 2 months and at 1 year postpartum. Several scores from the 5-year follow-up are also considered. Thirty families were included in the sample. They ranged from working class to upper middle class. Most of the marriages were relatively traditional, the husband being considered the primary breadwinner and the wife primarily responsible for childcare. Approximately half of the couples had boys and half girls.

Procedures and measures

The data presented in this paper were collected by the researchers from the families in their own homes. For the postpartum visits, research contacts were made within 2 weeks of the child's 2-month, 1-year, and 5-year birthday. The sample and procedures are described in detail in Grossman et al. (1980). The variables included measures scored from semistructured interviews, paper-and-pencil scales, as well as standardized clinical ratings derived from dyadic interaction observations. For the purposes of this discussion, relevant variables from the longitudinal study are representative of three dimensions: psychological, marital, and parental.

Psychological dimension. The scales for affiliation and autonomy were developed for this project and consisted of two 6-point scales, one for each concept (Tables 3.1 and 3.2). Trained scorers listened to tape recordings of the initial semistructured interviews conducted with each

Table 3.1. *Affiliation scoring*

1. No mutual sharing; isolated from others; or totally merged
2.
3. Some activities engaged in together but not fully enjoyed or valued; or somewhat more merged than one would find in a mutual relationship; no sense that relationships are valued or contribute to one's self-development
4. Beginning sense that mutual activities are valued or contribute to the development of the sense of self; matter-of-fact description of oneself as part of a relationship
5.
6. Well-developed involvement in at least one relationship; highly valued involvement without loss of separate identity; clarity of view of other person and his or her needs and commitment to mutual responsiveness

Note: See text for definition of "affiliation." If the person's children are used in scoring, in general greater elaboration of both the importance of the relationship and the respect for the separateness of the child are necessary to receive the same score an adult relationship would receive.

Table 3.2. *Autonomy scoring*

1. No apparent ability to make independent choices or pursue independent activities, decisions, or ideas; experiences extreme dependency on another; communicates sense that cannot function on own; no awareness of sense of self as a separate person

2.

3. Some activities, decisions, etc., done separately from another person, but seem to be due to other's unavailability or to necessity (e.g., classes or separate job); or somewhat more isolated than would be expected in "healthy" autonomy; no sense of personal efficacy or valuing separateness

4. Beginning sense that separate activities, ideas, etc., can be pleasurable and important to one's own development; and/or clear sense of self as separate from important others, reflected in clarity about own opinions

5.

6. Well-developed involvement with activities outside relationships, e.g., commitment to a career or field of study; and/or communicates sense of self-reliance with personal fulfillment or pleasure in individualized activities, decisions, etc.; individually motivated goals enhance a sense of self-esteem

Note: See text for definition of "autonomy." Involvement with one's own child is never by itself considered evidence of autonomy.

member of the couple individually during the pregnancy research visit. Scorers listened to and rated the first five consecutive 5-minute segments of the interview, assigning them a score for affiliation and a score for autonomy based on the definitions and the code book developed for the study. Each individual's scores were the average of scores across the five time periods for each dimension.

The interscorer reliabilities were based on Pearson correlations between the total averaged score on each dimension for independent raters. Reliability for men on autonomy ($N = 12$) was .84 and that on affiliation was .73; reliability for women ($N = 7$) was .5 for autonomy and .8 for affiliation. The range of scores for affiliation for women was 2.32 with a variance of 0.43; for men it was 1.95 with a variance of 0.29. The range of scores for autonomy for women was 2.75 with a variance of 0.56; for men it was 2.0 with a variance of 0.34. Grossman et al. (1984) describes the scoring in detail.

The level of anxiety was measured at 2 months and 1 year by the State Anxiety Scale (Spielberger, Gorsuch, & Lushene, 1968), a 20-item self-report paper-and-pencil measure. It was normed on a wide variety of populations, has good internal consistency, and correlates well with other anxiety scales currently in use. The level of depression was measured at

2 months and 1 year by a 24-item questionnaire designed to reflect depression during pregnancy (Pitt, 1968).

Emotional well-being is a measure developed for the longitudinal project and scored from the semistructured interviews conducted at 2 months and 1 year (Grossman et al., 1980). It includes four subscales: parent's anxiety about coping with the infant, acceptance of the parent's own needs, parent's physical condition, and parent's mood. Each of these is scored on a 6-point scale. Interscorer reliability of two raters for $N = 12$ on the average score for the four subscales was .86.

Marital dimension. Locke and Wallace's (1959) Marital Adjustment Inventory is a 23-item, self-administered, paper-and-pencil measure of marital satisfaction, which was collected at 2 months. It has been demonstrated to have good internal consistency (Cronbach's alphas range from .82 to .93). It correlates highly with similar measures of freedom from conflict and satisfaction with a marriage such as the Dyadic Adjustment Scale described below.

Marital adjustment was measured at 1 year by the Dyadic Adjustment Scale (Spanier, 1976), which is a 32-item, self-administered, paper-and-pencil scale. Spanier (1976; Spanier & Thompson, 1982) reports evidence for content, criterion-related, concurrent, and construct validity.

Sexual importance and activity, a scale developed for this project (Grossman et al., 1980), was administered at the 1-year visit. The scores on this variable come from a self-report paper-and-pencil form that asks for the rating of the frequency and the importance of marital sex.

Parental dimension. Observed adaptation was a variable developed for the project on the basis of the work of Shereshefsky and Yarrow (1973). The scale was designed to measure the adequacy of the parent's interaction with his or her infant, based on observational ratings of four separate dimensions: the quality of physical contact, the degree of expression and of affection, parental sensitivity and responsiveness, and acceptance of the infant. The observations were scored at 2 months. Interscorer reliability of the mean score across the scales for 28 observations was .69 (Grossman et al., 1980).

Reciprocity (Price, 1975) is a measure that reflects the degree of reciprocal relatedness between mother and infant. The score is based on ratings in 10 categories of behavior from observations at 2 months. Interscorer reliability on the basis of 12 observations was .86.

Parental adaptation (interview) was measured at 1 year by a scale designed for the project (Grossman et al., 1980). The scale reflects the adequacy of the parent's interactions with his or her infant based on our judgments from the taped interview of the parent's descriptions of the infant and the relationship between them. Each parent was rated on 14 dimensions. The interscorer reliability for the mean score for the mothers and fathers from 12 tapes was .91.

Parental support for child's affiliation and parental support for child's autonomy are measures developed by Pollack and other members of the longitudinal project (Pollack, 1981). The scores involve semistructured dyadic interactions at the fifth-year research visit. Mother–child and father–child dyads were each asked to perform two tasks. First, the parent was instructed to help the child carry out a moderately difficult physical activity – for example, balancing a box of marbles on her or his head; and second, parent and child played store, using props we provided. The order of parents was counterbalanced, as was the match between parent and child gender. Each part of the interactions was observed and scored in six 50-second-observe, 50-second-score intervals.

Subscales of the support for child's affiliation included warmth, attention, appropriate mirroring, and responsiveness, each scored on 5-point scales by trained raters. Pollack (1981) found that intercorrelations among subscales for the mothers ranged from .60 to .79, with an average of .69. For the fathers, the intercorrelations ranged from .69 to .84, with an average of .78. Interscorer reliability for the mothers was .75; that for the fathers was .87.

Subscales of support for child's autonomy were toleration of child's distress and allowing self-direction, scored on 5-point scales. Pollack (1981) reported that intercorrelations between the subscales was .50 for the fathers. Interscorer reliability for the mothers was .76; that for the fathers, based on the sum of the subscales, was .81.

Results and discussion

In this section we look at affiliation and autonomy rated from the interview obtained from the parents individually early in pregnancy. We examine how these psychological measures predicted aspects of parental adaptation in the postpartum period. First, we examine the women's intrapsychic, marital, and parental adaptation as these are predicted directly by scores obtained from the women during their pregnancy and indirectly by scores obtained by the men during the expectancy. Then we look at these direct and indirect (cross-parent) effects predicting men's adaptation.

Women's autonomy and affiliation

Turning to the women's scores, the first postpartum dimension we considered was the intrapsychic one: the health of the woman's psychological sense of self reflected in her anxiety level, her sense of emotional well-being, and her level of depression, at 2 months and 1 year postpartum (Table 3.3). The higher the woman's affiliation during early pregnancy, that is, the more she values and is involved in important relationships, the lower her anxiety and the greater her sense of well-being at 2 months but not 1 year. Higher affiliation in pregnancy also predicted lower depression scores at 2 months but not at 1 year postpartum. Women who were more autonomous in pregnancy felt a greater sense of emotional well-being in that postpartum year at 2 months and 1 year and were less anxious at 1 year.

The internal dimensions of affiliation and autonomy seem to be significantly relevant to the psychological task of mothering a first child during the first postpartum year. In these data, affiliation seemed particularly important in the early postpartum months since women beginning the tasks of childrearing in these traditional families felt better about themselves and more comfortable if they were more affiliative. In contrast, the capacity to be autonomous may be more salient for women during the latter part of the first year, at least in part sparked by their growing awareness of their child's ongoing development of a sense of self (Stechler & Kaplan, 1980).

We posit that both affiliation and autonomy appear to be relevent to

Table 3.3. *Direct and indirect effects of affiliation and automony on women's individual psychological adaptation*

Psychological adaptation	Women's			Men's		
	Affiliation	Autonomy	N	Affiliation	Autonomy	N
At 2 months						
Emotional well-being	.63***	.35*	30	.31	−.10	28
Anxiety	−.67***	−.25	31	−.18	−.11	29
Depression	−.65***	−.31*	30	−.27	.09	27
At 1 year						
Emotional well-being	.30	.31*	29	.11	.26	27
Anxiety	−.22	−.58***	28	−.40*	−.45**	25
Depression	−.12	−.31	24	−.37*	−.20	20

***$p < .001$, 2-tailed.   **$p < .01$, 2-tailed.   *$p < .05$, 2-tailed.

various degrees and at different points for women during the adult-to-parent transition. One task of this period involves a woman's coming to terms with her changing role. Another is finding and accepting the degree of motherliness in herself and the limitations of that motherliness. A third involves reevaluating her relationship to her own mother and the extent to which that does, or does not, leave her with a model for parenting. And finally, a mother begins to get a glimmer of the extent to which she is going to be left on her own to rear this new member of the family or to have assistance from her husband or others.

We hypothesize that the first postpartum period, extending at least to, and probably beyond, 2 months postpartum, finds new mothers very much in what might be called an adaptational crisis as they struggle with these psychological tasks and the day-to-day care of a newborn. Thus, one can make substantial predictions from women's affiliation early in pregnancy about how they will function psychologically near the end of the same process. By 1 year, new issues are salient. We believe that understanding the psychological mechanisms women and their families use to deal with these new issues is quite important and can be addressed to a significant degree by measuring her autonomy in early pregnancy.

When we looked at the indirect effects of the men's personality characteristics as predictors of the women's intrapsychic adaptation during this period (Table 3.3), we found that men's affiliation and autonomy during the expectancy were unrelated to the intrapsychic adaptation of these primiparous women at 2 months but were strongly related by 1 year postpartum. The more affiliative the man, the less the woman's anxiety and depression at 1 year; and the more autonomous the man, the lower her anxiety at 1 year. At 2 months we see these new mothers as engrossed with their infant and relatively oblivious to their husbands. By 1 year, however, the marital system reasserts its centrality as husbands and wives influence each other's sense of well-being.

Looking next at the woman's marital adaptation in the first postpartum year (Table 3.4), we find that the more affiliative the woman during the pregnancy, the more satisfied she was with the marriage at 2 months and 1 year. There was no significant relationship between a woman's autonomy in pregnancy and aspects of her marital adaptation. Affiliation in pregnancy did not predict her sexuality in her first postpartum year. This lack of connection is not striking since marital sexuality seems to be linked to other aspects of personal and marital adaptation in complicated and surprising ways (Grossman et al., 1980).

In the marital domain, there was one indirect effect of the men's personality characteristics as a predictor of the women's marital adjustment

Table 3.4. *Direct and indirect effects of affiliation and autonomy on women's marital adaptation*

Marital adaptation	Women's			Men's		
	Affiliation	Autonomy	N	Affiliation	Autonomy	N
At 2 months						
Marital adjustment	.64***	.16	31	.39*	−.03	29
At 1 year						
Marital adjustment	.41*	.26	28	.25	.23	25
Sexual activity and satisfaction	−.13	−.21	24	−.08	−.22	20

***$p < .001$, 2-tailed.   *$p < .05$, 2-tailed.

(Table 3.4). The more affiliative the man during expectancy, the higher was his wife's marital adjustment at 2 months postpartum. Within the marital domain, then, it is the women's and men's affiliation and not their autonomy that can successfully predict women's adjustment to the marriage in the first postpartum year.

Finally, we looked at parenting (Table 3.5), measured by observed adaptation, reciprocity, and maternal adaptation. Women who were more affiliative during pregnancy were rated as responding more skillfully with their 2-month-olds and 1-year-olds on all measures. More autonomous women also received higher maternal adaptation scores from the interview at 1 year. We also looked at two observational interactional measures of parenting from the 5-year follow-up: support for child's affiliation and support for child's autonomy (what Pollack, 1981, called "I"'ness and "We"'ness). For these primiparous women, there was no relationship between their own autonomy and affiliation scores at pregnancy and their parenting at 5 years (Table 3.5).

Once again, as the traditional literature suggested, one sees the centrality of affiliation in carrying out the traditional tasks of women: maintaining a good marriage and parenting an infant. We are struck with several things about this reaffirmation of the conventional view. First, we are looking at a relatively traditional group of women, most of whom have, with their husbands, chosen the traditional route of full-time homemaking at this stage in their families' lives. Second, we are looking at these women at a time in their lives when affiliation is central; their tasks are to nurture, to maintain ties, and to provide warmth. Thus, their capacity to do these things is central to the success of their lives at this point. Our data suggest

Table 3.5. *Direct and indirect effects of affiliation and autonomy on women's parental adaptation*

Parental adaptation	Women's			Men's		
	Affiliation	Autonomy	N	Affiliation	Autonomy	N
At 2 months						
Observed maternal adaptation	.55**	.11	26	−.37*	−.22	25
Reciprocity	.37*	.27	28	−.28	−.02	25
At 1 year						
Maternal adaptation from interview	.51**	.36*	29	.25	.23	27
At 5 years						
Support for affiliation	−.03	.27	23	−.23	−.14	21
Support for autonomy	−.09	.18	23	.01	.19	21

**$p < .01$, 2-tailed.   *$p < .05$, 2-tailed.

that, when children are beginning to develop more independence and need support for their own developing autonomy, their mother's autonomy, as measured earlier during her pregnancy, becomes important in her capacity to parent. Concurrent measures of mother's autonomy during this postpartum period would also provide useful information but are not available from this study.

One intriguing indirect effect (Table 3.5) is that, the more affiliative the husband in expectancy, the lower is the mother's observed maternal adaptation with her 2-month-old. It seems as if the very affiliative first-time father tends to reduce the intensity of his wife's exclusive, intimate ties with the infant by maintaining a close relationship with his wife and by meeting some of the infant's needs for closeness and nurturance.

Men's autonomy and affiliation

Men's affiliation during expectancy had no relationship with their intrapsychic adaptation during the first postpartum year, as reflected in their anxiety level or their comfort with themselves (Table 3.6).[1] The higher their measured autonomy, the greater was their emotional well-being at 1 year. This again supports the conventional view found in the research

---

[1] With the exception of depression and reciprocity scores, which we have only for the women, the measures for intrapsychic, marital, and parental adaptation are the same for the women and men in the sample.

Table 3.6. *Direct and indirect effects of affiliation and autonomy on men's individual psychological adaptation*

Psychological adaptation	Men's			Women's		
	Affiliation	Autonomy	N	Affiliation	Autonomy	N
At 2 months						
Emotional well-being	.30	.08	27	−.17	−.10	28
Anxiety	−.21	−.20	28	−.44*	−.28	30
At 1 year						
Emotional well-being	.31	.37*	25	.10	.34*	26
Anxiety	.06	−.19	24	−.50**	.13	26

**$p < .01$, 2-tailed.   *$p < .05$, 2-tailed.

literature that men's separate selfhood is very important for their general well-being. In these families, the tasks of the men have been defined by the families: first, as earning a good living and, second, as being responsive to their wives and children. Autonomy is central to the former, whereas affiliation is crucial for the latter.

Turning to the indirect effects (Table 3.6) we find that the higher the women's affiliation during pregnancy, the less anxious were the men at 2 months and 1 year; and the more autonomous the women, the greater was the men's emotional well-being at 1 year. Again, although we are not able to argue causality directly, the interconnectedness of the marital system at this point is clearly evidenced.

In the marital domain (Table 3.7), men's affiliation during pregnancy had no relationship to their marital adaptation during the first postpartum year. In contrast, women's affiliation during pregnancy predicted significantly men's marital adjustment during that period. Autonomy had one significant correlate: The more autonomous the men were judged to be from the interview during their wife's pregnancy, the lower was their own estimate of their marital adjustment at 1 year.

Clearly, the task of the women in these families at this stage in the families' careers is to keep, by their own affiliative responsiveness, the marriage salient and satisfying for both themselves and their husbands. The men in these families seem to fulfill their tasks in this endeavor by providing economically. Their emotional contribution has yet to be understood.

Looking at men's parenting (Table 3.8) at 2 months, 1 year, and 5 years, the more affiliative the men were in expectancy, the better was their pa-

Table 3.7. *Direct and indirect effects of affiliation and autonomy on men's marital adaptation*

Marital adaptation	Men's			Women's		
	Affiliation	Autonomy	N	Affiliation	Autonomy	N
At 2 months						
Marital adjustment	.21	.11	27	.48**	−.05	29
At 1 year						
Marital adjustment	−.28	−.36*	23	.11	.06	24
Sexual activity and satisfaction	−.01	−.36	16	.03	−.32	19

**$p < .01$, 2-tailed.   *$p < .05$, 2-tailed.

ternal adaptation at 1 year (with a trend in that direction at 2 months) and, impressively, the greater was their support for their 5-year-old's autonomy. The men's autonomy in expectancy predicted only these 5-year measures: The more autonomous the man during his wife's pregnancy, the more support he provided for his 5-year-old's affiliation and autonomy.

With regard to indirect effects (Table 3.8), the more autonomous we judged the wife to be, the more skillful her husband appeared in our observations of his parenting when his child was 2 months old and the more support he provided for autonomy when his child was 5 years old.

Once again, it appears as if the woman's affiliation has strong reper-

Table 3.8. *Direct and indirect effects of affiliation and autonomy on men's parental adaptation*

Parental adaptation	Men's			Women's		
	Affiliation	Autonomy	N	Affiliation	Autonomy	N
At 2 months						
Observed paternal adaptation	.35	.27	16	.37	.56**	16
At 1 year						
Paternal adaptation from interview	.50**	−.32	25	.00	.15	26
At 5 years						
Support for affiliation	.31	.39*	21	−.32	.32	23
Support for autonomy	.40*	.53**	21	−.18	.43*	23

**$p < .01$, 2-tailed.   *$p < .05$, 2-tailed.

cussions on the marital system, whereas her autonomy has repercussions primarily on her husband's parenting. Possibly her autonomy allows him more space to interact with the child. Alternatively, it allows the child the awareness that the mother will tolerate the child's attachment to the father, despite the intensity of the mother–child tie with a firstborn. This raises a provocative question: What is the difference between this healthy space given by a well-functioning mother out of her own sense of autonomy and the vacuum left by a depressed or otherwise incapacitated mother?

Clinical implications

On the basis of the literature and the findings of our study, we have begun to understand some of the clinical implications of the adult-to-parent transition. We suggest the following formulations as possible extensions of this research on normal families to the clinical world – a world that we as clinicians also inhabit.

Perhaps an overriding impression is that, in families, things are often not what they seem. A mother who is completely devoted to her firstborn infant, who is always warm and empathic, who never seems to miss a cue from the baby is satisfying to observe but is probably a mixed blessing for her family. It is probably mixed for her infant because, on the one hand, it provides the empathic bond that allows the baby to thrive, but on the other hand, it may cement that bond in a way that will make it much harder for the baby to develop an early important attachment to his or her father. Most fathers of middle-class firstborns may be better able to become substantially involved and attached if the mother leaves space, that is, if she is depressed, is more autonomous herself, or has a cesarean section and is unable to provide for the child (Grossman et al., 1980). A lack of involvement costs the father, in depriving him of the special experience and impetus to the growth of an intense tie to an infant.

Things are again not what they first seem in families when one looks at the effect of a parent's pathology. Although it is always troubling to see a seriously disturbed adult in a family, we suggest that it is not psychopathology in one parent alone that necessarily harms a child's development. A serious problem in one parent coupled with the inability of the other parent to step in and fill the void can disrupt family functioning considerably and can jeopardize the children in the family system. One must look at the family system and its flexibility, as well as the health of each parent, in evaluating whether a family is likely to have difficulty making the adult-to-parent transition or dealing with other stressful points of family development.

One of the most striking characteristics of adaptive families is their flexibility and reciprocity. Usually, in the families that we have seen and that others have studied, each adult serves a function in the family, whether it be as the emotional caretaker, as the representative to the outside world, or as the primary nurturer of the infant. This role is not rigidly fixed since it does not seem important who does it. What does seem important is the idea that, if the usually designated parent does not do it – cannot do it, cannot do it just now, wants or needs to stop doing it – the other can step in. This reciprocal flexibility, always within the context of a midrange of organizational capacity, seems to operate at both micro and macro levels of family functioning and may be the hallmark of adaptive families.

With regard to autonomy and affiliation, in these relatively traditional families a marked division of these characteristics appears to work well at the time in the family's life when they have a young infant. The men can be primarily autonomous and go out and confront the world, as long as they have sufficient affiliative capacity to provide some support for their wives. The women can be essentially involved in affiliative tasks and still be, by and large, appropriately responsive to the needs of a young infant. Our preliminary findings suggest that this marked division of autonomy and affiliation rapidly becomes less adaptive even for these families as the parents experience limitations of the division in their own development and as the child begins to require more separate space from the mother and more intimacy with the father. At this point, again, the flexibility of each parent's psychological system, as well as the family system, is of crucial importance.

In accord with clinicians' experiences, the enduring psychological characteristics of the parents play a continuing role in the functioning of the newly developing family over time. The relationship between parental personality characteristics during pregnancy and observed parenting at 5 years is quite dramatic. Overall, our data suggest that coping in early expectancy is most predictive of how the parents will negotiate the adult-to-parent transition, which ultimately has ramifications for the entire family system.

Implications for future research on families

An important issue in examining individuals and families in transition is simplifying family process sufficiently in order to study it with reliable and interpretable measures while preserving the richness of a dynamic, interactive system with multiple levels of effect. We have found it essential to use multiple measures from many sources in our research efforts. Interview data and observational measures provide clinical richness; paper-and-pencil and self-report scales have added to the data base. As Cowan and Cowan have described (see Chapter 4, this volume), complex interactive processes cannot be understood with single variables, and researchers must increasingly develop systemic measures.

The Boston University Pregnancy and Parenthood Project's emphasis on multiple and systemic perspectives is further demonstrated by the dimensions of individual, marital, parental, and contextual contributors to family functioning. We believe that an essential area of future research involves looking at the dimensions of affiliation and autonomy in each family member at different phases of family development. This will be useful for understanding the process of adaptation in individuals and families. It is essential to examine direct and indirect effects of family members within the family system. We also support concern for individual development within the network of family relationships. The systemic interactive view appreciates the necessary changes that childbirth causes both in individuals and in the family system as a unit.

Finally, in understanding the family in transition, we stress the importance of a longitudinal approach. The experience of the Boston University Pregnancy and Parenthood Project and other research groups has repeatedly suggested that family development can be understood only if we examine influences over time. The longitudinal approach reflects a view of the family as a system in perpetual development, highlighted at transitional phases such as the birth of a first child.

Acknowledgment

We thank Abigail Stewart, Anne Copeland, Henry Grossman, and Don Chase for their helpful comments.

References

Bakan, D. (1966). *Duality of human existence*. Chicago: Rand McNally.

Ballinger, C. G., Buckley, D. E., Naylor, G. J., & Stansfield, D. A. (1979). Emotional disturbance following childbirth: Clinical findings and urinary excretion of cyclic AMP. *Psychological Medicine, 9,* 293–300.

Belsky, J. (1981). Early human experience: A family perspective. *Developmental Psychology, 17,* 3–23.

Belsky, J. (1984). The determinants of parenting: A process model. *Child Development, 55,* 83–96.

Benedek, T. (1959). Parenthood as a developmental phase. *Journal of Psychoanalysis, 7,* 377–407.

Benedek, T. (1970). Parenthood during the life cycle. In E. J. Anthony & T. Benedek (Eds.), *Parenthood, its psychology and psychopathology* (pp. 185–206). Boston: Little, Brown.

Biller, H. B. (1982). Fatherhood: Implications for child and adult development. In B. B. Wolman, & G. Stricker (Eds.), *Handbook of developmental psychology*. Englewood Cliffs, NJ: Prentice Hall.

Cath, S. H., Gurwitt, A. R., & Ross, J. M. (1982). *Father and child*. Boston: Little, Brown.

Caverna, J. O., & Weddington, W. W. (1978). Abdominal pain in expectant fathers. *Psychosomatics, 19*, 761–8.

Chodorow, N. (1978). *The reproduction of mothering*. Berkeley and Los Angeles: University of California Press.

Coleman, A., & Coleman, L. (1971). *Pregnancy: The psychological experience*. New York: Seabury Press.

Cowan, C. P., Cowan, P. A., Coie, L., & Coie, J. D. (1983). Becoming a family: The impact of a first child's birth on the couple's relationship. In W. Miller & L. Newman (Eds.), *The first child and family formation* (pp. 45–63). Chapel Hill: University of North Carolina, Carolina Population Center.

Cutrona, C. E. (1982). Nonpsychotic postpartum depression: A review of recent research. *Clinical Psychology Review, 2*, 487–503.

Dickie, J. R., & Gerber, S. C. (1980). Training in social competence: The effect on mothers, fathers and infants. *Child Development, 51*, 1248–51.

Dyer, E. (1963). Parenthood as crisis: A restudy. *Marriage and Family Living, 25*, 488–96.

Erikson, E. H. (1959). Identity and the life cycle. *Psychological Issues, 1*, 1–164.

Erikson, E. H. (1963). *Childhood and society*. New York: Norton.

Fasteau, M. F. (1974). *The male machine*. New York: McGraw-Hill.

Fedele, N. M. (1983). *The developing parent: The impact of life span upon the quality of parenting*. Unpublished doctoral dissertation, Boston University.

Fedele, N. M. (1984, October). *The developing parent: Development within a family context*. Paper presented at National Council on Family Relations Conference, San Francisco.

Feldman, S. S., & Aschenbrenner, B. (1983). Impact of parenthood on various aspects of masculinity and feminity: A short-term longitudinal study. *Developmental Psychology, 19*(2), 278–89.

Feldman, S. S., & Nash, S. C. (1984). Antecedents of parenting. In A. D. Fogel & G. F. Melson (Eds.), *Origins of nurturance* (pp. 209–32). Hillsdale, NJ: Earlbaum.

Feldman, S. S., Nash, S. C., & Aschenbrenner, B. (1983). Antecedents of fathering. *Child Development, 54*, 1628–36.

Freeman, T. (1951). Pregnancy as a precipitant of mental illness in men. *British Journal of Medical Psychology, 24*, 49–54.

Gilligan, C. (1977). In a different voice: Woman's conception of self and morality. *Harvard Educational Review, 49*, 365–78.

Gilligan, C. (1979). Woman's place in man's life cycle. *Harvard Educational Review, 49*, 365–78.

Gilligan, C. (1982). *In a different voice*. Cambridge, MA: Harvard University Press.

Goethals, G. (1976). The evolution of sexual and genital intimacy: A comparison of the views of Erik Erikson and Harry Stack Sullivan. *Journal of the American Academy of Psychoanalysis 4*, 529–44.

Grossman, F. K. (1982, April). *A look at two and five year olds: Longitudinal predictions from pregnancy*. Paper presented at the Society for Research in Child Development, Detroit, MI.

Grossman, F. K. (1984, May–June). *Separate and together: Men's autonomy and affiliation in the transition to parenthood*. Paper presented at NICHD Conference, Bethesda, MD.

Grossman, F. K., Eichler, L. S., Winickoff, L. S., with Anzalone, M. K., Gotseyeff, M., & Sargent, S. D. (1980). *Pregnancy, birth and parenthood*. San Francisco: Jossey-Bass.

Guttman, D. (1970). Female ego styles and generational conflict. In E. Walker (Ed.), *Feminine personality and conflict* (pp. 77–96). Belmont, CA: Brookes/Cole.

Hayworth, J., Little, B. C., Bonham Carter, S., Raptopoulos, P., Priest, Z. G., & Sandler, M. (1980). A predictive study of postpartum depression: Some predisposing characteristics. *British Journal of Medical Psychology, 53,* 161–7.

Herzog, A., & Detre, T. (1976). Psychotic reactions associated with childbirth. *Diseases of the Nervous System, 37,* 229–35.

Hobbs, D. F., Jr. (1968). Transition to parenthood: A replication and extension. *Journal of Marriage and the Family, 30,* 413–17.

Hobbs, D., & Wimbish, J. (1977). Transition to parenthood by black couples. *Journal of Marriage and the Family, 39,* 677–89.

Hopkins, J., Marcus, M., & Campbell, S. B. (1984). Postpartum depression: A critical review. *Psychological Bulletin, 45*(3), 498–515.

Jordan, J. V. (1984). Empathy and self boundaries. *Work in Progress.* Wellesley, MA: Stone Center Working Papers Series.

Jordan, J. V., Surrey, J. L., & Kaplan, A. G. (1983). Women and empathy. *Work in Progress.* Wellesley, MA: Stone Center Working Papers Series.

Kaij, L., & Nilsson, A. (1972). Emotional and psychotic illness following childbirth. In J. Howells (Ed.), *Modern perspectives in psychoobstetrics* (pp. 364–82). New York: Brunner/Mazel.

Kaplan, A. G. (1984). The "self-in-relation": Implications for depression in women. *Work in Progress.* Wellesley, MA: Stone Center Working Papers Series.

Kegan, R. (1982). *The evolving self: Problem and process in human development.* Cambridge, MA: Harvard University Press.

Kohut, H. (1971). *The analysis of the self.* New York: International Universities Press.

Kohut, H. (1977). *The restoration of the self.* New York: International Universities Press.

LaCoursiere, R. (1972). Fatherhood and mental illness: A review and new material. *Psychiatric Quarterly, 46,* 109–24.

Leifer, M. (1977). Psychological changes accompanying pregnancy and motherhood. *Genetic Psychological Monographs, 95*(1), 55–96.

Levinson, D. J. (1978). *Seasons of a man's life.* New York: Knopf.

Locke, H. J., & Wallace, K. M. (1959). Short marital-adjustment and prediction tests: Their reliability and validity. *Marriage and Family Living, 21,* 251–5.

Mahler, M. S. (1968). *On human symbiosis and the vicissitudes of individuation.* New York: International Universities Press.

Miller, J. B. (1984). The development of a woman's sense of self. *Work in Progress.* Wellesley, MA: Stone Center Working Papers Series.

Notman, M. T., & Nadelson, C. C. (1978). *The woman patient: Medical and psychological interfaces.* New York: Plenum.

O'Hara, M. W. (1980). *A prospective study of postpartum depression: A test of cognitive and behavioral theories.* Unpublished doctoral dissertation, University of Pittsburgh.

O'Hara, M. W., Neunaber, D. J., & Zekoski, E. M. (1984). Prospective study of postpartum depression: Prevalence, course, and predictive factors. *Journal of Abnormal Psychology, 93*(2), 158–71.

Paykel, E. S., Emms, E. M., Fletcher, J., & Rassaby, E. S. (1980). Life events and social support in puerperal depression. *British Journal of Psychiatry, 136,* 339–46.

Pedersen, F. A., Andersen, B. J., & Cain, R. L. (1980). Parent–infant and husband–wife interactions observed at age 5 months. In F. A. Pedersen (Ed.), *The father–infant relationship: Observational studies in the family setting* (pp. 71–86). New York: Praeger.

Pitt, B. (1968). "Atypical" depression following childbirth. *British Journal of Psychiatry, 114,* 1325–35.

Pollack, W. S. (1981). *"I"ness and "We"ness: Parallel lives of development.* Unpublished doctoral dissertation, Boston University.

Pollack, W. S., & Grossman, F. K. (1985). Parent–child interaction. In L. L'Abate (Ed.), *Handbook of family psychology* (pp. 586–622). New York: Wiley.

Price, G. M. (1975). *Influencing maternal care through discussion of videotapes of maternal–infant feeding interaction.* Unpublished doctoral dissertation, Boston University.

Protheroe, C. (1969). Puerperal psychoses: A long-term study 1927–1961. *British Journal of Psychiatry, 115,* 9–30.

Rapaport, R., Rapaport, R. N., & Strelitz, Z. (1977). *Fathers, mothers, and society.* New York: Basic Books.

Reitterstol, N. (1968). Paranoid psychosis associated with impending or newly established fatherhood. *Acta Psychiatrica Scandinavia, 44*(1), 51–61.

Russell, C. (1974). Transition to parenthood: Problems and gratifications. *Journal of Marriage and the Family, 36,* 294–301.

Shapiro, E. R. (1978, August). *Transition to parenthood in adult and family development.* Paper presented at the American Psychological Association Conference, Toronto.

Shapiro, E. R. (in press). Individual change and family development: Individuation as a family process. In C. Falicov (Ed.), *Family transitions, continuity and change over the life cycle.* New York: Guilford.

Shereshefsky, P. M., & Yarrow, L. J. (1973). *Psychological aspect of a first pregnancy and early postnatal adaptation.* New York: Raven Press.

Spanier, G. B. (1976). Measuring dyadic adjustment: New scale for assessing the quality of marriage and similar dyads. *Journal of Marriage and the Family, 38,* 15–28.

Spanier, G. B., & Thompson, C. A. (1982). A confirmatory analysis of the Dyadic Adjustment Scale. *Journal of Marriage and the Family, 44,* 731–8.

Spielberger, C., Gorsuch, R., & Lushene, R. (1968). *The State-Trait and Anxiety Inventory.* Palo Alto, CA: Consulting Psychologist Press.

Stechler, G., & Kaplan, S. (1980). The development of the self: A psychoanalytic perspective. *Psychoanalytic Study of the Child, 35,* 85–106.

Surrey, J. (1983). The "self-in-relation": A theory of women's development. *Work in Progress.* Wellesley, MA: Stone Center Working Papers Series.

Vaillant, G., & Milofsky, E. (1980). Natural history of male psychological health: IX. Empirical evidence for Erikson's model of the life cycle. *American Journal of Psychiatry, 137,* 1348–59.

Wainwright, W. (1966). Fatherhood as a precipitant of mental illness. *American Journal of Psychiatry, 123,* 40–4.

Zilboorg, G. (1931). Depressive reactions related to parenthood. *American Journal of Psychiatry, 10,* 927–62.

4   Changes in marriage during the transition to parenthood: must we blame the baby?

Philip A. Cowan and Carolyn Pape Cowan

Until the mid-1950s, the prevailing mythology seemed to be that, for couples who had planned the event, the arrival of a first child would bring joy and a sense of fulfillment. Becoming a parent meant taking on a major adult role and continuing one's family line linking the past with the future. It offered the opportunity to see the world anew through a child's eyes and to contribute to the formation of the next generation. Most of all, it signaled an opportunity for husband and wife to grow emotionally closer as they shared the excitement and the challenge of bringing *their* child into the family. A look at more recent popular and professional writings suggests that the romantic glow of becoming a family has been fading. Two related sets of research findings, initially based on cross-sectional or retrospective studies, have led researchers to portray babies as potential disrupters of marital intimacy.

The first line of research has produced a group of studies describing the transition to parenthood as a crisis for couples. The second area of study has shown that marital satisfaction declines as partners become parents and continues to decline throughout the childrearing years.

Our review of this research raises questions about methodological shortcomings and unanswered questions. We do not mean to imply that partners becoming parents can expect relatively smooth sailing. Data from newer longitudinal studies, including our own, make two things clear: (1) More negative than positive changes occur in parents' lives during the early postpartum period; and (2) the transition to parenthood is disequilibrating for men, for women, and for their relationship as a couple. We do take issue, however, with the tendency to blame the baby for *causing* distress in the marriage. More differentiated questions must be raised about this major adult transition. It is no longer necessary to ask *whether* change occurs in the marriages of new parents; we must begin to understand the process of change in order to determine *how* some couples cope well and others experience substantial distress as they move from couple to family life.

114

Despite the fact that many studies of becoming a parent mention its impact on marriage, the relationship between new parents has not been directly studied until recently. In this chapter we present a five-domain structural model of marital and family adaptation to examine complex changes in partners becoming parents. We then suggest a dynamic model of couple process to show how structural changes affect marital quality. In the last section of the chapter, we touch on some of the issues involved in conceptualizing transitions as crises for relationships rather than for individuals.

Adaptation to parenthood

Transition as crisis: LeMasters versus Hobbs

In his landmark book *Families under Stress* (1949), Hill suggested that the arrival of a first child could be expected to set the stage for a crisis for couples. His use of the term "crisis" did not in itself imply catastrophe but rather "any sharp or decisive change for which the old patterns are inadequate. . . . the usual behavior patterns are found unrewarding, and new ones are called for immediately." Consistent with developmental theories such as Erikson's (1950, 1968), Hill speculated that crisis could be a force for growth as well as dysfunction. The positive or negative outcome for each couple, he reasoned, should depend on several factors in the history of their relationship: (1) the state of organization or disorganization of the family when the major change occurs, (2) the resources of the family to adapt to change, and (3) family members' interpretations of the stressful event.

Unfortunately, empirical work on the transition to parenthood has increasingly strayed from Hill's initial complex formulation and focused instead on a single, narrowly defined question: How frequently does crisis, defined negatively, occur for couples after the birth of a first child? In the premier study in this series, LeMasters (1957) interviewed 57 married couples who had become parents during the previous 5 years. According to ratings made retrospectively and in collaboration with the participants, 83% of the couples had experienced extensive or severe crisis within the first year after giving birth. This must have been shocking news, judging from eight major studies and countless dissertations on the same topic over the following two decades (Beauchamp, 1969; Dyer, 1963; Hobbs, 1965, 1968; Hobbs & Cole, 1976; Hobbs & Wimbish, 1977; Meyerowitz & Feldman, 1966; Russell, 1974). These researchers described a lower incidence of crisis than LeMasters had reported, with all but Meyerowitz and Feldman using similar measuring instruments.

In 1976, after reviewing 20 years of research on the transition to parenthood, Hobbs and Cole (1976) concluded: "Initiating parenthood may be slightly difficult, but not sufficiently difficult to warrant calling it a crisis experience for parents whose first child is still an infant" (p. 729). In an attempt to provide an index of crisis more "objective" than an open-ended interview, Hobbs (1965) used a 23-item checklist based on responses obtained by both LeMasters (1957) and Dyer (1963). Each partner indicated whether an item was a "bothersome event" (e.g., increased money problems, meals off schedule, decreased sexual responsiveness), and the responses were summed to produce a single global index of crisis in the individual. Scores were then averaged to obtain an index of crisis in the couple. In our view there are serious difficulties with this scale and the research based on it. Jacoby (1969) presented an excellent critique of this work, but it apparently has not been heeded. Virtually every study and textbook chapter discussing the impact of parenthood still quotes the research as if Hobbs's approach provides valid information about the transition to parenthood and about marital crisis. Because the results have had such a pervasive influence on sociologists' and psychologists' descriptions of couples' transition to parenthood, we list and elaborate four of Jacoby's points and add five cautions of our own:

1. Hill's definition of crisis refers not to bothersome events per se but to discrepancies between external challenges and individual or couple resources for coping with them. Hobbs's items fail to distinguish between simple descriptions of events and parents' evaluations of the difficulty they create.

2. With the exception of Russell's study (1974), the checklist approach fails to assess positive outcomes of the transition.

3. Jacoby (1969) points out that, whereas LeMasters included parents of children up to 5 years of age in his sample, Hobbs and his colleagues focused on parents' adaptation in the first few postpartum months. Hobbs's conclusions about minimal impact may stem from the occurrence of an early "baby honeymoon" for some families. We also wonder whether couples who experience great strain in becoming parents might find it easier to acknowledge the stress of new parenthood after it has been at least partially resolved. In either case, later interviews with Hobbs's couples might have produced higher current and retrospective estimates of crisis.

4. Both Jacoby (1969) and Russell (1974) suggested that the reported incidence of crisis may be affected by the method of gathering data. Hobbs (1968) had argued against this possibility, citing his finding that self-report checklist scores and ratings made by observers from audiotapes of couple

interviews were significantly correlated. Since neither method revealed more than 20% of the sample experiencing extreme or severe crisis, he reiterated his conclusion that beginning parenthood was not the stressful experience that LeMasters had implied. But whereas checklist data showed no couples in the extensive or severe category, ratings from interviews with the same couples described 4% of the men and 19% of the women as experiencing severe crisis when their babies were about 24 weeks old. It would appear that the checklist method minimizes reports of the intensity of the experience of becoming a new parent. We believe that in the extensive debate over percentages, a critical issue has been glossed over. If 19% of the women in a nonclinic sample of parents can be rated as experiencing severe crisis on the basis of an interview and 26% as experiencing moderate crisis on the basis of a checklist, the proportion of spouses in difficulty raises serious concerns about the well-being of parents during the period of family formation.

5. Individuals are classified on the basis of equal score intervals on the checklist. In our view, there is no *a priori* reason to suppose that the dividing lines between "slight," "moderate," or "severe" crisis occur every 9.5 points on Hobbs's scale. In addition, there are no empirical studies validating the correspondence between checklist categories and couples' or researchers' assessments of severity of distress.

6. The research on transition as crisis does not provide valid information about *couples*. Despite the fact that husbands' and wives' responses were not significantly correlated in the early studies and only moderately correlated in later ones, couple crisis scores were derived by combining partners' individual scores. Since our data and those of other researchers cited above show that women have consistently higher scores than men on variables that suggest distress, a combined score does not accurately represent a *couple's* response to the transition. We shall discuss the implications of spouses having different experiences of the transition or of the marriage later in the chapter.

7. We believe that cohort effects cannot be ignored in the interpretation of research on becoming a family. One telling example of cohort differences comes from Hobbs's own work: In 1965, when he asked new parents directly about the impact of having a first child, 91% of the men and 71% of the women endorsed the statement: "Since the birth of the baby my marriage is more happy and satisfying than before." Ten years later, in a new sample (Hobbs & Wimbish, 1977), only 45% of the men and 39% of the women believed that having a baby had increased their marital happiness.

8. Almost all of the studies of transition as crisis have been retrospective

and thus subject to both positive and negative biases of recall and attribution. In our experience, parents try to avoid viewing their infants as a source of stress, but as they try to make sense of what has happened to them, they often attribute much of their chaotic state as a couple to the presence of the child. It seems clear that only with prospective studies examining the state of the parents and the marriage before women give birth can we assess the impact of becoming a parent on the marriage. Only longitudinal studies will enable us to describe individual differences in the pathways to marital adaptation or distress.

9. We have been surprised to note that sociologists' discussions of crisis in transition to parenthood omit any reference to the psychiatric literature suggesting that women, and possibly men, are at increased risk for postpartum psychosis, depression, and the "blues" (e.g. Brockington et al., 1981; Davenport, Adland, Gold & Goodwin, 1979; Hamilton, 1962; Osofsky, 1982; Paffenbarger & McCabe, 1966; Yalom, Lunde, Moos, & Hamburg, 1968; Zaslow et al., 1981; see also Fedele, Golding, & Grossman, Chapter 3, this volume). There is no consensus about the etiology of postpartum distress or the extent to which it is triggered by childbirth (Weiner, 1982). Nevertheless, the fact that the birth of a child may be accompanied by psychosis or depression in a small proportion of families constitutes another reason to question Hobbs's dismissal of the transition to parenthood as a period of potential crisis for parents and for their relationship as a couple.

Marital satisfaction and the life cycle

An extensive body of research attempts to assess what happens to marital satisfaction as partners have and rear children.

Cross-sectional studies. Assessing samples ranging from newlyweds to couples who have been together for more than 25 years, cross-sectional studies converge on a consistent set of findings: Couple satisfaction appears to decline over the first 15 years of marriage (Blood & Wolfe, 1960; Bradburn & Caplovitz, 1965; Gurin, Veroff, & Feld, 1960; Hicks & Platt, 1971; Lewis & Spanier, 1979; Luckey & Bain, 1970; Spanier & Lewis, 1980). Similar curves are found for parents and nonparents, but childless spouses tend to describe themselves as closer to their partners, more companionate, and more satisfied with marriage than do couples with children (Campbell, Converse, & Rodgers, 1976; H. Feldman, 1971; Glenn, 1975; Glenn & McLanahan, 1982; Miller, 1976; Renee, 1970). This difference does not appear to be affected by whether the couples without children are childless due to choice or to circumstance (Houseknecht, 1979).

Some investigators claim to find a U-shaped pattern in which marital satisfaction begins to rise again in couples who maintain their relationship for more than 15 years (Glenn & Weaver, 1978; Rollins & Feldman, 1970). Spanier, Lewis, and Cole (1975) and Hudson and Murphy (1980) argue, however, that with adequate controls and appropriate statistical tests, the upward trend would not reach statistical significance. Nevertheless, the U-curve has been accepted as an accurate description of changes in marital satisfaction over the family life span. The later upswing in marital satisfaction is usually attributed to the positive impact on the couple of children beginning to leave home (Rossi, 1968). There is no doubt about who is being blamed for parents' marital distress. "The negative effects [of having a child] are quite pervasive, very likely outweighing positive effects among spouses of both sexes and all races, major religious preferences, educational levels and employment status" (Glenn & McLanahan, 1982, p. 62).

Despite the unanimity of findings, there is much to question in the cross-sectional research on marital satisfaction. The usual difficulties in inferring change over time from comparisons of groups at different points in the life cycle are compounded by the fact that some of the least satisfied couples have divorced and are no longer available for inclusion in studies of intact marriages. Almost all cross-sectional comparisons of parents and childless couples fail to control carefully for differences in length of relationship: The parent samples tend to be older and to have been married longer (Heming, 1985). It is also risky to assume from comparisons of couples with and without children that childrearing *causes* marital distress. It is possible that choices about childrearing follow from preexisting qualities in the marital relationship. Finally, the decline in marital satisfaction does not mean that having children increases the probability of marital dissolution. In fact, Cherlin (1977) shows that preschool children in the home are a *deterrent* to marital separation and divorce.

Longitudinal studies. Research designs following couples from before to after the birth of the first child can help to answer some of our criticisms of cross-sectional studies. Fortunately, a longitudinal perspective on marital satisfaction has begun to emerge. Of 20 longitudinal studies we were able to locate that commented on the state of the marriage, five provided no pre- and postbirth measures of the marital relationship. In only one of the five (Meyerowitz & Feldman, 1966) was a significant *increase* in marital satisfaction reported from pregnancy to 5 months after birth. Each interview assessment was based on partners' retrospective comparison with an earlier point in their married life. Entwisle and Doering's (1981) otherwise detailed study of the first birth did not examine the marital relationship. Their impression from interviews at 2 to 3 and 4 to 8 weeks postpartum was that there were few effects on the marriage so far, but they acknowledged that this was very early in the postpartum period for the impact of the transition to be felt by the couple. By contrast, three careful interview studies from psychodynamic (H. Osofsky & J. Osofsky, 1980; Wenner et al., 1969) and sociological (LaRossa & LaRossa, 1981) perspectives describe both individual and couple stress and upheaval during pregnancy and at 6 months postpartum.

Almost all of the studies using prebaby and postbaby marital measures support the conclusion that marital satisfaction declines after the birth of a first child. Two showed *nonsignificant declines,* in satisfaction with marriage (Ryder, 1973) or with marital problems and disagreements (White & Booth, 1985). Thirteen longitudinal studies reported *significant declines:* in observer-rated marital adjustment (Shereshefsky & Yarrow, 1974), in researcher-created marital quality questionnaires (H. Feldman, 1971; S. Feldman & S. Nash, 1984; McHale & Huston, 1985; Miller & Sollie, 1980), and in the Locke–Wallace or Dyadic Adjustment Scale (Awalt, Snowden, & Schott, in press; Belsky, Lang, & Rovine, 1985; Belsky, Spanier, & Rovine, 1983; Blum, 1983; Cowan et al., 1985; Grossman, Eichler, & Winickoff, 1980; Waldron & Routh, 1981; see also Duncan & Markman, Chapter 9 this volume).

Even when the change in mean marital satisfaction is statistically significant, it is not very large. In studies using the Locke–Wallace (Locke & Wallace, 1959) or Dyadic Adjustment Scale (Spanier, 1976), the average decline ranged between 4 and 10 points, usually from about 125 to 115, with most new parents remaining above the means according to the norms proposed by the developers of the scales.

When we were planning our own study, we were surprised by the fact that very few longitudinal investigations included a comparison sample of childless couples. All of the pre–post change in marital satisfaction was attributed to the transition to parenthood, despite clear suggestions from cross-sectional research that time affects the perceived quality of all marital relationships. In their review of the impact of becoming a family on marriage, Belsky and Pensky (in press) also note the need for childless couple comparison groups assessed over the same period as new parents; they conclude on the basis of the few existing studies using comparison samples that time and the transition to parenthood, separately and together, take their toll on couple relationships. They also note the tendency for women to show the impact of this transition more than men. We shall return to this point later in the chapter.

Individual differences. Miller and Sollie (1980) have pointed out that group averages showing slight declines in marital satisfaction not only hide the couples for whom the transition was extremely difficult, but also obscure the fact that individual life and marital life sometimes improve. Of the couples in our study who did not participate in an intervention and were assessed in late pregnancy and at 6 and 18 months postpartum, 17% of the women and 22% of the men had higher Locke–Wallace marital satisfaction scores 18 months after the child was born. There have been some (largely unsuccessful) efforts in cross-sectional studies to discover what makes the difference between couples who adapt well and those who experience marital distress during the transition to parenthood; such inquiries in longitudinal studies are just beginning.

Belsky et al. (1983) argue that an important question concerning the consistency of marital satisfaction over time has been omitted from most previous research. Even if average scores change after a baby is born, it is important to know whether couples remain in the same rank order. In fact, recent evidence shows that they do (e.g., Belsky et al., 1983; Heinicke, 1984). Belsky and his colleagues (1983) report across-time correlations of marital satisfaction ranging from .52 to .79 over three assessment periods (pregnancy, 3, and 9 months postpartum). Grossman et al. (1980) found similar predictability from the first trimester of pregnancy to 2 months and 1 year postpartum. Feldman and her colleagues have also reported consistency in various aspects of mood and personality (S. Feldman & B. Aschenbrenner, 1983; S. Feldman & S. Nash, 1984). The data from our study are comparable, showing even higher correlations from pregnancy to 18 months than from pregnancy to 6 months postpartum. The fact that correlations are higher over the longer test–retest period suggests to us that, after a period of disorganization and change in the early postpartum months, couples may reestablish some sense of equilibrium in the marriage.

A simple but important conclusion can be drawn from the fact that, despite their drop in marital satisfaction, there is continuity in the quality of new parents' marriages over time. Babies do not appear to create severe marital distress where it was not present before, nor do they tend to bring already maritally distressed couples closer together. Especially when dissatisfaction is evident before the birth of the child, we cannot blame the baby for parents' continuing marital distress. Nevertheless, we must account for the average decline in marital satisfaction and understand what role, if any, the baby plays in producing this change in the marriage.

A five-domain structural model of marital and family adaptation

Regardless of their specific measuring techniques, most investigators of the transition to parenthood rely on a single global index of satisfaction to describe the quality of a marriage. This strategy assumes that satisfaction with one's mate is a unidimensional construct that can be ordered on a continuum from positive to negative. In our view, marital satisfaction is necessarily multidimensional. Partners' views of marriage are affected not only by what goes on within the relationship but also by what is happening to each partner inside and outside the family.

In his call for an ecological perspective on the family, Bronfenbrenner (1979) argues that a multilevel analysis is necessary to account for the development of both psychopathology and competence in its members. The recent work of several researchers reflects this more complex view of development. Belsky (1984) has proposed a three-domain model of the determinants of parenting that includes personal resources of the parents, characteristics of the child, and contextual sources of stress and supports. Heinicke's model (1984) focuses on four similar dimensions: characteristics of the parents, the quality of their marriage, the parent–child relationship, and the characteristics of the child. In their research on at-risk infants, Parke and Tinsley (1982) described four levels of social organization that help to determine the status of the child, including formal and informal support systems, the wider culture, and each of the relationships within the family (mother–child, father–child, mother–father, mother–father–child). In more recent work on the child's social network, the same authors (Tinsley & Parke, 1984) add both maternal and paternal grandparents to the list of major influences on child development.

We have become concerned that central aspects of the couple relationship have been hidden within the general category of "mothers' social support." Similarly, the unique influences of grandparents have been combined with very different aspects of "social networks." Our own research (C. Cowan & P. Cowan, 1987c; C. Cowan et al., 1985) focuses on the structural connections among five domains:

1. The characteristics of each individual in the family, with special emphasis on self-concept and self-esteem
2. The husband–wife relationship, with special emphasis on their division of labor and patterns of communication
3. The relationship between each parent and the child

4. The connection between patterns in the new family and the two families of origin
5. The balance between parents' external sources of stress and support, with special emphasis on social networks and jobs or careers

We propose that these five domains form the elements of a structural model of marital and family adaptation in two ways. First, each domain describes a different level of system organization – individual, dyad, triad, three-generations, and the relation between the nuclear family and other social systems. Second, the focus is not only on the content within domains but on their pattern of interconnection. Our model suggests that what happens in each of the domains combines to influence satisfaction or dis- satisfaction and adaptation or distress for the individuals, the marriage, or the family as a whole. For example, a decline in one parent's self- esteem can affect the quality of his or her relationship with the child; this, in turn, may exacerbate tensions between parents and grandparents and stimulate conflict in the couple relationship. Starting at another point in the system, we can see that job stress may intensify parent–child and parent–grandparent discord; this in turn could result in a lowering of the parent's self-esteem and adversely affect the couple's interaction.

As we present current research on the impact of becoming a parent, one domain at a time, we include a brief description of our own longitudinal study, the Becoming a Family Project. More detailed reports of various aspects of the study appear elsewhere: gender differences in the transition to parenthood (C. Cowan et al., 1985); the effects of a couples group in- tervention (C. Cowan & P. Cowan, 1987a; C. Cowan, 1987); antecedents and correlates of fathers' involvement (C. Cowan & P. Cowan, 1987b).

Methods and methodological issues

We followed 72 expectant parents, beginning in pregnancy and continuing over a period of 2 years. Our goals in this first phase of the project were to assess the impact of a first child on the marriage and to examine the effects of a preventive intervention designed to strengthen couple rela- tionships during the transition to parenthood. Couples were interviewed and assessed with an extensive set of questionnaire instruments in late pregnancy and again at 6 and 18 months after childbirth. In the second phase of our study, we followed the families again when the children were 3½, focusing on the impact of couple relationship quality on the child's development and mental health. In a third part of the study, now underway, we are investigating the impact of family factors on the first child's entrance into kindergarten and the impact of the transition to elementary school on the family. In this chapter, we report data from the first phase of the study.

Because we expected that all couple relationships would show change over time, we included a comparison group of couples who were not becoming parents. Twenty-four couples were recruited before they had made a decision about whether to have a first baby and followed over a comparable period. The total sample of 96 couples ranged widely in socioeconomic and ethnic background, 85% of the participants being white and 15% black, Asian-American, or Hispanic.

Because so much previous research suggests that becoming a parent affects a marriage, we developed a preventive intervention to work with both partners, focusing on the relationship between them. One-third of the expectant couples, randomly selected, were offered the opportunity to participate in a couples group conducted by trained co-leaders and meeting weekly for 6 months. When we interviewed each couple assigned to the intervention, we spoke of our concern about the growing distress in marriages today and noted that childbirth preparation and other forms of support end just when the challenge of building a *family* begins. We offered couples a chance to participate with other expectant couples in a group that would (1) bridge the transition from before to after the birth of the child and (2) focus not primarily on parenting but on men and women as individuals and as couples. Since the staffing of the project was supported by a grant, there was no charge for the intervention groups.

In general, women were more enthusiastic than men about participating in a couples group. Some women had friends they could talk to, but they welcomed the opportunity to talk more with their husbands and to hear the views of other expectant fathers and mothers. Although some men could imagine positive benefits for themselves, others agreed to participate primarily because it seemed to be important to their wives. We recruited the intervention participants from a sample of couples who had already expressed interest in participating in a study of couples becoming families. Almost all of the men and women who initially agreed to participate in the study mentioned concern about what would happen to their marriage once the child became part of their family. Most knew few other couples going through this life change, and many lived far from their extended families. Of the random subsample offered the intervention, 85% agreed to participate. We continued to recruit couples until there were 24 couples who had agreed to join one of six groups. Each group had four expectant couples and one co-leader couple.

The three teams who interviewed couples and led groups, including the present authors, were married couples. Five of the six partners were clinical psychologists or doctoral candidates in clinical psychology (Philip

Cowan, Carolyn Pape Cowan, Abner Boles, Harriett Curtis-Boles, and William Coysh); the sixth (Ellen Garrett) is a businesswoman. After the initial interviews and before the group discussions began, the couples were asked to fill out a set of questionnaires assessing the five domains of family life that we described above. Each group then began meeting weekly for 6 months, from late pregnancy through the early months of parenthood. Our 2½-hour discussions focused on participants' responses to the questionnaires and on any questions or concerns they had about their lives as partners and parents. We have used the audiotapes of each session for generating hypotheses and providing a qualitative context for our interpretations of the quantitative analyses.

A second set of 24 couples was invited to participate in the interviews and questionnaire assessments during pregnancy and again at 6 and 18 months postpartum, but they were not offered an intervention. Many couples viewed the interviews and questionnaires as an opportunity to review and discuss their lives as individuals and couples. Because our pilot work (Cowan, Cowan, Coie, & Coie, 1978) had suggested that the prepartum assessment had an impact on the couples' experience of becoming parents, we included a third randomly assigned subsample of 24 couples who were interviewed but not given questionnaires to fill out until the postpartum follow-ups.

All 23 of the couples who participated in the intervention and all 24 of those who participated in the full pretest–posttest design remained in the study until at least the 18-month follow-ups, even if they moved away from the area. Of the 24 couples interviewed during pregnancy but not assessed until 6 months postpartum, 9 did not complete the 18-month assessment. In retrospect, it seemed to us that, when couples came to know us during late pregnancy and filled out questionnaires that allowed them to share their view of this important time in their lives, they developed a commitment to the study that transcended the disequilibration of the hectic months of becoming a family. By contrast, couples asked to fill out questionnaires for the first time after becoming parents seemed less motivated to focus on their relationship or to do the work that participation in the project required. This seems consistent with the suggestion by Laslett and Rapoport (1975) that true collaborative work between researchers and participants often leads to more self-revelation as time goes on.

Change in the five domains of family life

In this section we use our five-domain model to describe the changes that we and other researchers have found in couples who are welcoming their first child into the family.

1. The psychological sense of self. Explorations of change in the inner dynamics of self, identity, and adjustment over the transition to parenthood come primarily from psychoanalytically oriented researchers using a retrospective case study approach (e.g., Benedek, 1959, 1970). Early papers focused on severe distress in patients who had become disturbed shortly before or after childbirth (see Weiner, 1982, for a review). Later researchers turned to nonclinic samples (e.g., Herzog, 1979), some investigators following couples through the transition to parenthood (Leifer, 1979; H. Osofsky & J. Osofsky, 1980; see also Antonucci and Mikus, Chapter 2, and Fedele et al., Chapter 4, this volume). A comprehensive review of psychodynamic approaches to men's and women's transition to parenthood has been published by J. Osofsky and H. Osofsky (1985).

The emphasis in most of these studies is on negative change. Both men and women report considerable stress and upheaval during pregnancy, as well as increased stress after childbirth (H. Osofsky & J. Osofsky, 1980). Many women and some men report concerns about their bodies; psychosomatic symptoms extend from isolated gastrointestinal tension described by both partners to a full-blown physically disabling male couvade (Cavenar & Weddington, 1978). Increasing emotional difficulties, moodiness, and dependency are noted in women (Wenner et al., 1969), and feelings of neediness, anxiety, and rivalry in men (H. Osofsky & J. Osofsky, 1980), as they become parents. Having a baby tends to alter the meaning of sexuality for both husbands and wives, although not always in the same direction. Some spouses describe an increase in desire, others note a decrease, and some describe fluctuations over the period of transition (J. Osofsky & H. Osofsky, 1985). Finally, as we have already noted, the transition to parenthood increases the risk of severe, hospitalizable psychiatric disturbance for women, and possibly for men.

There is a brighter side to this gloomy picture. Benedek (1959, 1970), Parens (1975), and the Osofskys argue strongly that "for the wife and husband – as individuals and as a couple – expectant and new parenthood represents a crisis and a developmental opportunity for maturation and new growth" (H. Osofsky & J. Osofsky, 1980, p. 45). Partners' worries and sense of increased responsibility may be accompanied by a growing sense of personality integration and of being an adult. Initial evidence suggests that positive outcomes are generally associated with more positive prior levels of ego development (e.g., Grossman, 1987). We have begun to describe dimensions of maturity in adulthood that could be used to assess increases or decreases in level of maturity after the birth of a child (P. Cowan, 1987).

In the Becoming a Family Project study, one method we used to conceptualize change in partners' sense of self was a graphic representation of the way important aspects of self fit together. On an instrument we call "The Pie" (Cowan et al., 1978), expectant parents described the way they see themselves. Given a circle 4 inches in diameter, each partner divided "The Pie" to show the main roles in his or her life right now, based not on the amount of time spent, but on how large or salient each aspect of self felt. The "parent" aspect of self increased markedly from pregnancy to 6 months postpartum, especially for women, but the size of "partner" or "lover" declined sharply. Whereas the "worker" or "student" aspects of self remained stable over the transition to parenthood for men, women described marked declines in their involvement in work outside the family, with less severe declines in mothers who had participated in the intervention groups.

As we have noted, adding "mother" or "father" to one's identity can be a positive experience, conferring "grown up" status on men and women. Nevertheless, changes as seen on "The Pie" illustrate graphically how alterations in partners' self-concept can be linked inextricably with shifts in the relationship domains of family life. The question of how to fit "parent" into an already full sense of self and how to reconcile the loss of the lover or worker aspects of one's identity is a challenge faced by most contemporary spouses, with potential spillover into the marriage. The psychodynamic studies we have cited also remind us that becoming a parent stimulates insecurities and reworking of feelings about relationships in the family of origin (Benedek, 1970; J. Osofsky & H. Osofsky, 1985), and these internal disequilibrations are often played out in relationships in the new family (cf. Clulow, 1982, 1985; Dicks, 1967).

There have not been many systematic studies of self-esteem during the transition to parenthood, but inferences have been drawn from results of cross-sectional studies. Earlier data suggest that, for mothers, self-evaluation and self-esteem decline over the childrearing years, whereas fathers' self-esteem remains stable (Bradburn & Caplovitz, 1965; Gurin et al., 1960; Rossi, 1968). Most recent longitudinal studies of the transition to parenthood have not measured self-esteem. Of three that did, one found the expected downward shift for women (Entwisle & Doering, 1981), whereas our own (Cowan et al., 1985) and Liefer's (1979) found self-esteem to be remarkably stable. It is not clear whether this inconsistency is due to differences between cross-sectional and longitudinal methods, cohort effects, differences in measures of self-esteem, or sample differences, including the age of the child when the parents were studied. Some support for the hypothesis that timing of assessment makes a difference comes from Reilly, Entwisle, and Doering's (1987) report that women's average ratings of themselves dropped from pregnancy to the first few weeks after birth, but returned to their original levels by 1 year postpartum.

2. Marital interaction: roles and communication. Prior research and theory and our pilot work with couples becoming parents (C. Cowan et al., 1978) led us to expect partners' role arrangements and communication styles to be primary contributors to their satisfaction with marriage.

Partners' mutual role arrangements. Data from our own study correspond with findings from large cross-sectional American samples (Hoffman, 1978; Hoffman & Manis, 1979). Regardless of where couples were located on the egalitarian to traditional continuum in late pregnancy, they shifted toward a more traditional division of household tasks in the first year and one-half after having a child. It is important to note that, in our sample, the division of *overall* responsibility for household and family tasks remained stable; at all times women took more responsibility than men. But once partners became parents, there was less sharing of each individual task and a more gender-stereotypic allocation of tasks. Our data show that families become much more mother-centered in child-care than either fathers or mothers had *predicted* in late pregnancy. One consequence of less than predicted father involvement may be seen in studies by Garrett (1983) and Belsky et al. (1983) finding that unfulfilled expectations during the transition to parenthood are associated with men's and women's dissatisfaction with marriage.

Goldberg, Michaels, and Lamb (1985) make the important point that the magnitude of the shift toward more traditional roles may depend in part on when couples are assessed. In their study, men and women described their household task arrangements in early pregnancy (3–4 months gestation), late pregnancy (7–8 months gestation), and early parenthood (3–4 months after the child's birth). Goldberg et al. found a U-shaped curve, with a tendency for adopting gender-stereotyped divisions of household tasks occurring *least* in late pregnancy. Since this is the single pregnancy assessment point chosen by most of the longitudinal studies of transition, and it appears to be a time of more egalitarian division of labor, Goldberg et al. argue that the reported shift to traditional postpartum roles for new parents may have been exaggerated. Our impression is that, because many husbands take an active role in family tasks until their wives recover from the delivery and the disequilibrium of the first postpartum weeks, 4-month postpartum follow-ups may be *underestimating* the extent of traditional role shifts.

Certainly, research exploring change over short segments of time, extending through the early years of family life, is needed to determine the shape of the curve showing changes in the roles each partner plays. It may not be possible to categorize behavioral and psychological changes in family roles as moving unequivocally in traditional or egalitarian directions during the transition to parenthood. For example, we found that men decreased their participation in household tasks but increased their involvement in childcare from 6 to 18 months postpartum (C. Cowan & P. Cowan, 1987c). We also need clearer definitions of "traditional" roles. In the Goldberg et al. (1985) study, "traditionality" was defined as increased participation in gender-stereotyped tasks. In ours, it was defined as the shift from shared to sole responsibility for tasks, along with increased gender differentiation of tasks.

Do traditional or nontraditional divisions of labor have implications for marital satisfaction? This answer, too, may depend on when the connections between family work and marital satisfaction are assessed. Our account here combines our results with those of Goldberg and her colleagues (1985). In our study, there was no correlation between household task division and marital satisfaction in late pregnancy either for men or for women. At 4 months postpartum, only one of the Goldberg et al. household task measures was correlated with marital satisfaction, and that only for men ($r = -.35$ between men's participation in feminine tasks and their marital satisfaction). Returning to our study, husbands' participation in household tasks at 6 months postpartum was beginning to be positively correlated with their *wives'* marital satisfaction ($r = .30$). By 18 months postpartum, issues concerning the allocation of family tasks were becoming more important to men's experience of the marriage. Men's participation in household tasks was now positively correlated with both their own ($r = .21$) and their wives' ($r = .40$) marital satisfaction. Similarly, when their husbands were more involved in caring for the children, wives were more satisfied with the marriage ($r = .37$). Men's participation in household and childcare tasks may have different implications at different points in the process of becoming a family.

We should note that at both the 6- and 18-month postpartum assessments, *satisfaction* with the division of household and childcare tasks was consistently correlated with marital satisfaction for both men (r values ranging from .27 to .64) and women (r values ranging from .47 to .62). That is, even more important for the marriage than the fact of sharing tasks was each partner's feelings about how the tasks were divided. Some spouses are reasonably content with what would be regarded as fairly traditional divisions of labor, whereas others are dissatisfied with divisions that approach the egalitarian end of the continuum.

Marital communication. Here we refer to overt and covert patterns of communication in which partners exchange information and expectations in order to share tasks, convey feelings, make decisions, resolve conflicts, and show their caring. There is reasonably convincing evidence from both self-report and observational studies that amount of communication (Navran, 1967) and style of communication (Gottman, 1979; Gottman, Markman, & Notarius, 1977) are highly correlated with self-reported marital satisfaction. Gottman's observational research demonstrates that happily married spouses do not necessarily emit more positive responses to each other, but in more maritally satisfied couples one partner, usually the wife, manages not to escalate conflict when negative feelings are expressed.

Having established a connection between communication and relationship satisfaction, let us proceed to examine the very few studies that investigate communication between partners who are in the process of family formation. Meyerowitz and Feldman (1966) reported a decline in the quantity of communication from midpregnancy to 6 months after the birth of a first child. Spending less time as a couple is a common lament during this period. In a study by McHale and Huston (1985), couples with both "companionate" and "parallel" relationships showed a significant reduction in dyadic activities from pregnancy to the first year after birth, although the companionate couples tended to reestablish their earlier level of shared activities after becoming parents.

The quality of marital communication may also change when partners become parents. Raush, Barry, Hertel, and Swain (1974) found an increase between early marriage and pregnancy in husbands' "cognitive and conciliatory communication," assessed in a laboratory conflict task. Cognitive acts included suggestions and rational arguments, whereas conciliatory acts, such as attempting to "make up" or compromise, were aimed at reducing the emotional tension. When the same couples were observed 4 months after the birth of their first child, men's cognitive and conciliatory communication had declined. "If this finding reflects their actual practice at home," Raush et al. commented, "these husbands may be failing wives just when support is needed" (p. 191).

In our study, new mothers and fathers reported no significant change in the *closeness* they felt as a couple during the transition, but they tended ($p < .11$) to perceive an increase in *distance* after the birth of their babies. By contrast, our childless couples tended to perceive less distance over a comparable period of time. Nonparents and new mothers reported more positive change in their sexual relationship over the first two years of the study, but new fathers reported more negative change in this aspect of intimate communication.

During the 2-year period from late pregnancy to 18 months postpartum, more than 90% of the parents reported an increase in conflict and disagreement – from an initially low amount to somewhat higher. Not surprisingly, the number one issue leading to conflict – as seen by husbands and wives – was division of labor in the family. During interviews with each couple before and after birth, and during our months of meeting with the couples in the intervention subsample, we heard over and over that satisfaction with role arrangements depended on how the couples negotiated their new division of family labor. That is, above and beyond issues of equity and fairness in the actual division, partners' satisfaction was related to whether and how family tasks were discussed. Neither partner liked to be nagged about doing a task or criticized for the style in which the task was done, and both felt badly when their contributions to the family were unrecognized or unacknowledged.

Not all of the changes in communication after childbirth were negative. In our postbirth interviews, many couples noted that, with more issues to disagree about and less time available, they had become more efficient and effective problem solvers. As one mother reported with amusement, "We simply don't have all week to spend on a disagreement any more!"

3. The parent–child relationship. We have been discussing the impact of the child on the marriage without considering the nature of the child or the quality of the parent–child relationship. Our model suggests that what happens in the parent–child domain affects and is affected by the marital relationship in circular fashion. We know from our interviews with new parents that, when things are going well in their relationships with the baby, the couple relationship often benefits. Conversely, when partners are feeling good about the marriage, they may have more energy and warmth to bring to the relationship with their child (cf. Pedersen, Anderson, & Cain, 1977). In follow-ups with our families 42 months after birth, preliminary findings (P. Cowan & C. Cowan, 1987) suggest that maritally satisfied mothers and fathers show different parenting styles with their preschoolers than do maritally dissatisfied spouses. Thus, in trying to understand the impact of parents on their children, or of children on their parents, we need data from both marital and parent–child domains of the family system.

Findings of several longitudinal studies illustrate how individual, marital, and parent–child domains of family life may be interconnected. Shereshefsky and Yarrow (1973) found links between marital quality and adaptation to pregnancy and parenthood. Similarly, Grossman and her colleagues (1980) found that marital satisfaction during the first trimester of pregnancy was the highest correlate of first-time mothers' adaptation to labor and

delivery. Women's experience of labor and delivery, in turn, was related
to mothers' adaptation to parenthood at 2 months and 1 year postpartum
and to some aspects of psychological and physiological functioning in the
children at 2 and 12 months of age. Completing the circle, women's adaptation to labor and delivery predicted their satisfaction with marriage
1 year later. Labor and delivery complications and marital quality at each
assessment period were also correlated with *fathers'* adaptation to parenthood.

Because mothers and fathers do not always agree in their beliefs about
the nature of children or how they should be raised, there is an important
link between parenting attitudes and the state of the marriage. Roberts,
Block, and Block (1984) found that differences between partners in ideas
and attitudes about raising their 3-year-olds predicted parental divorce
when the children were 11 years old. In our study, partners who described
greater husband–wife differences in ideas about how to raise a child *before*
their baby was born experienced greater parenting stress 2 years later
(Heming, 1985). As we describe below, the more husbands and wives in
our study differed, the more dissatisfied they were with the *marriage*. In
other words, it seems clear that what occurs in the parent–child domain
is related to the state of things in the individual domain, on one hand,
and the marital domain, on the other.

Important reviews by Belsky (1984) and Heinicke (1984), along with
research by Goldberg and Easterbrooks (1984), also demonstrate strong
connections between marital quality and parents' interactions with their
young children. From our longitudinal data, we have tentatively proposed
a "path" model (P. Cowan & C. Cowan, 1987):

| prebirth parent individual and marital qualities | → | postbirth parent individual and marital qualities | ↔ | parenting style | ↔ | child outcome |

The model suggests that parent characteristics and parent–child interaction
styles play separate but interconnected roles in the developmental course
of the child. Our very preliminary findings show strong connections between individual, couple, and parenting style "risk" indices obtained when
the child is 3½ and the child's adaptation to elementary school 2 years
later, as assessed by achievement tests and teacher ratings.

Of course, the direction of influence does not only extend from parent
to child. Childrearing authorities imply that "difficult" and "easy" babies
have quite different effects on their parents. Evidence concerning the
contribution of the child's characteristics to parents' well-being is surprisingly sketchy, there being only rare instances in which infant tem-

perament has been assessed independently of parent reports. It seems reasonable to assume that parents react differently to infants with different levels of irritability and responsiveness. A full model of parent–child relationships, then, must include contributions from each of the family participants to both dyadic and whole-family interaction.

4. The three-generational perspective. The quality of men's and women's relationships with their parents appears to be correlated with adaptation to both pregnancy and parenthood. Gladieux (1978) found that "fathers seem to play a more important role in their daughters' pregnancy experience than has previously been documented . . . [A] positive relationship with their fathers 'assured' a satisfying beginning and end to the pregnancy experience" (p. 293). The more positive a woman's relationship with her father, the greater is her tendency to have a more affectionate, expressive, and satisfying relationship with her husband. Shereshefsky and Yarrow (1973) found that, when women reported more positive relationships with their mothers, observers tended to rate the women as more confident in the maternal role and as having better functioning marriages and infants who were more individuated. Barry (1979) reported that husbands with better marital adjustment described closer relationships with their fathers and greater satisfaction in their parents' marriage.

Like middle children caught between "privileged" older siblings and "indulged" younger ones, new parents often feel sandwiched between the needs of their parents and their children. Immersed in the task of figuring out how to look after a totally dependent being whose demands cannot be put off, new parents are also caught up in trying to maintain or reestablish links with their own parents, especially if they live far away. This three-generation squeeze faced by many contemporary couples has implications for the new parents' relationship as a couple. Some partners want to re-create the kind of family they grew up in, whereas others are determined to do the opposite in order to avoid repeating patterns that left them feeling unhappy or insecure. We have not completed analyses of our data on this domain of family life, but one area shows clear connections between the families of origin and the present nuclear family. Men who described their families of origin as more cohesive, more expressive, and lower in conflict on the Family Environment Scale (Moos, 1974) tended to become more involved in the care of their 18-month-old children and to experience lower parenting stress (C. Cowan & P. Cowan, 1987b).

The Moos Family Environment Scale describes characteristics of the family as a whole; it does not differentiate between mother and father.

In the Becoming a Family Project we administered a Family Relationship Questionnaire adapted from Grossman et al. (1980) to assess men's and women's memories of their early relationships with *each* parent and the parents' relationship with each other (Cowan, Cowan, & Heming, 1985). Correlations between positive relationships with parents and marital satisfaction showed much stronger cross-gender than same-gender effects. The more positively *women* described their past relationship with their fathers ($r = .47$), the greater was their own marital satisfaction when their babies were 6 months old. There was no significant correlation between marital satisfaction and women's description of the past relationship with their mothers. The more positively *men* described their past relationship with their mothers, the greater was their own marital satisfaction when their babies were 18 months old ($r = .36$). There was no systematic link between men's marital happiness and their descriptions of their relationships with their fathers.

The links from past to present family life are determined not only by mother–child and father–child relationships, but also by the quality of the parents' marriage. For both men and women, current marital satisfaction was correlated with the remembered positive quality of their parents' marriage when they were growing up.

In other domains, we have been describing changes in average scores over time. Data from the three-generational perspective illustrate the possibility that major life transitions affect the "hooking together" or "unhooking" of important cross-domain correlations. Marital satisfaction scores in pregnancy were not linked in a systematic way with scores on the Family Relationship Questionnaire or the Family Environment Scale. That is, parents' family of origin data and current marital satisfaction did not begin to be correlated until after the birth of the first child. Furthermore, correlations were stronger for mothers at 6 months postpartum and for fathers at 18 months postpartum. It is not yet clear whether experiences in past family relationships color the present marriage or whether changes in one's own marriage alter memories of past relationships. What the data do suggest is that the functional connections between past and present family life shift in the course of becoming a family.

So far, we have been discussing the links between two generations of adults – the parents and grandparents. It is also true that grandparents have an ongoing impact on their grandchildren, and young children an often unappreciated effect on their grandparents (Tinsley & Parke, 1984). Though viewing the family in a three-generational perspective has become a cornerstone of some schools of family therapy (cf. Framo, 1981; Schultz, 1984), three-generational data are surprisingly sparse in the study of nonclinic families (cf. Walsh, 1982). In our opinion, this omission has led to a critical gap in our understanding of individual and marital adaptation during the transition to parenthood.

5. *Life stress–social support balance.* Recent research has devoted increasing attention to the possibility that an individual's social support network can buffer or protect him or her from many of the negative effects of life stress events (Cobb, 1976; M. Lieberman, 1981), including childbirth (Nuckolls, Cassel, & Kaplan, 1972).

There are problems associated with the conception and measurement of both life stress and social support. Life stress is often assessed with checklists of weighted life events (Dohrenwend & Dohrenwend, 1974) that are described as if they have an impact on passive victims. But as Mitchell, Billings, and Moos (1982) remind us, life events do not just "happen" to people. They tend to follow from characteristics of individuals and families. Lazarus and his colleagues (Lazarus, 1980; Lazarus, Kanner, & Folkman, 1980) are critical of the use of large-scale, infrequent events as indices of life stress. Because they believe that they have a stronger connection to psychological adaptation and physical health, these researchers suggest that we measure daily "hassles" and "uplifts" instead. So far, their scales have not been used in assessing the impact of a major life transition.

Measures of social support also tend to lack specificity and differentiation. The studies of Nuckolls et al. (1972) and Crockenberg (1981) combined social supports from father, kin, and other outside-the-family sources into one general category. Richardson and Kagan (1979) suggest that the impact of social support varies with the category of people in the support network (family, friends who are parents, friends who are not parents), the kind of support (socializing, emotional, encouragement, cognitive guidance), and the gender of the recipient. They, too, lumped husbands and parents together in a family support concept. On the basis of interviews with couples in our longitudinal study, we suspect that especially at times of critical family changes, support from a spouse has a different meaning than support from others and should be kept separate until we understand more about how these supports function for women and men and how social support is connected with events in each of the other domains of family life.

Using a measure of life stress events adapted from Horowitz and his colleagues (Horowitz, Schaefer, Hiroto, Wilner, & Levin, 1977), we found no statistically significant changes in the level of general life stress from pregnancy to 18 months postpartum. The Lazarus et al. hassles measure (1980) might have been more sensitive to change during this disequilibrating period. We found an initial increase and then a decrease in perceived social support for most new parents in our study. For mothers who had participated in our intervention groups there was a slight increase in the positive balance between social support and life stress, whereas for mothers without the intervention and for all fathers the balance between support and stress did not change.

Tensions and satisfactions from work outside the family are two ingredients of social support and life stress. In the last months of pregnancy, women often reduce their time at work; most stay home for some time after birth, although we know of instances in which the time was as short as 1 week. Though work has not been treated as central to women's identity, as it has in the case of men, we assume that changes in women's work lives have an impact on their sense of themselves and possibly on their satisfaction with marriage.

Many men's work lives change too during the transition to parenthood. Fathers in our pilot study described a substantial amount of unexpected job change, loss, or insecurity (Cowan et al., 1978). Data from interviews in our current study suggest that partners' work decisions affect the couple's relationship. Certainly when one partner stops bringing in an income, the couple is affected. Many couples reported income losses of as much as 50% of the total family earnings during the first year or two of becoming a family. Although some new fathers increase their involvement in their jobs as a way of playing a more central family role, their wives may experience this as a retreat from involvement with the baby and the whole family enterprise. As partners' changes in outside-the-family work move in opposite directions, with women decreasing their involvement as men increase theirs, many new parents report that they feel ''like ships passing in the night.''

In sum, our review of the data has shown that, for partners becoming parents, there are critical changes in each of the five domains of family life we have outlined: individual, couple, parent–child, three-generation, and outside-the-family.

Consistency over time and across domains

With all the emphasis on change, it is important to consider the fact that there is also a great deal of predictability from before to after having a baby, and impressive consistency in adaptation across domains.

Cross-time consistency. We have discussed the general finding that marital satisfaction scores are consistent and predictable across time, simple cor-

relations between pre- and postpartum marital satisfaction ranging between
.5 and .7 (Belsky et al., 1983; C. Cowan et al., 1985; S. Feldman & S.
Nash, 1984; Grossman et al., 1980; Heinicke, 1984). In our study, many
other measures showed similar predictability (e.g., role satisfaction: .56
for men, .62 for women; self-esteem: .75 for men, .76 for women). We
have noted above that these data suggest the possibility of early identification of individuals and couples at risk for distress in the early period
of family formation. They also argue strongly against blaming the baby
for new parents' marital distress.

Cross-domain consistency. Satisfaction and adaptation tend to generalize
across domains. The studies cited in the preceding paragraph indicate that
individual, marital, parent–child, family-of-origin, and outside-the-family
measures tend to covary. In our study, stepwise and hierarchical multiple
regressions indicate that from 35 to 75% of the variance in 18-month postpartum marital satisfaction, depression, father involvement, and parenting
stress could be explained by a *combination* of prebirth variables from
different domains of the model. In addition, cross-domain combinations
functioned as better predictors than measures taken from single domains
(Heming, 1985). It seems clear that we are dealing with a network of interrelated aspects of family life. These findings lend credence to our five-
domain model and suggest that adaptation and dysfunction during the
transition to parenthood are complex products of reciprocal connections
among multiple aspects of family life.

Gender differences

We have suggested that men and women experience the transition to parenthood in different ways (C. Cowan et al., 1985). There were many "main-
effect" differences between men's and women's responses in each domain.
Women, for example, tended to show less satisfaction with themselves
and their mutual role arrangements than men did. Mothers' more negative
experiences of these aspects of the transition may be partly explained by
the fact that, in addition to having more of the responsibility for managing
the household and caring for the child, they were much more likely than
fathers were to put aside their work or studies after giving birth.

Regardless of the reasons for these gender differences, what we want
to focus on here is the transition's potential for *increasing* differences
between husbands and wives once they become parents. Feldman and
her colleagues (S. Feldman, 1987; S. Feldman & B. Aschenbrenner, 1983)
have shown that women described more positive *and* more negative

changes over the transition to parenthood than men did. The couples in our study who were *not* having a baby showed many of the husband–wife differences we have described, but the extent of difference between spouses tended to remain constant over the three assessment periods. By contrast, the spouses who had babies became increasingly different from one another in every domain (see C. Cowan et al., 1985). Sometimes we saw differences in *amount* of change: Women's sense of self as "parent" increased and their satisfaction with their role arrangements decreased significantly more than men's. Sometimes there were differences in the *direction* of change, as in partners' differing reports of change in the sexual relationship or in their involvement in work outside the home.

The structural model helps us to examine the relationships among the variables, but we are interested mainly in understanding the relationship between husbands and wives. We believe that a more dynamic process model can explain how these structural changes in the family lead partners to experience a change in the way the marriage *feels:* Why does parents' satisfaction with their couple relationship decline and why is the decline, on the average, as small as it is?

A process model of marital change

We are using the concept of process in a slightly different sense than Belsky (1984) does in his "process view" of parenting. By describing the multiple influences on parenting behavior of individual, marital, work, and social network sources, Belsky has been focusing on the structural connections among different parts of the family system. In this section, we are concerned with describing the system of transactions by which one part of the system has an effect on the others. We focus on the couple dynamics that set the transactions in motion and contribute to the trend toward marital satisfaction decline.

Individuality and mutuality

In the theories of family systems developed from work with both clinic and nonclinic families, the overarching task for adult couples is described as finding a way to balance individuality and mutuality (cf. Bowen, 1978; Framo, 1981; Minuchin, 1974; Satir, 1972; see also Fedele et al., Chapter 3, this volume). Each partner must be able to satisfy at least some of his or her own needs, hopes, and dreams. Yet both partners must find ways to coordinate separate life paths into a mutually satisfying journey. Both tasks require a high degree of skill in resolving both intrapersonal and interpersonal conflicts among competing choices and possibilities.

Over our years of meeting with couples in groups and conducting interviews with individual couples over time, we have noticed that a small proportion of couples seem well established as individuals; their challenge appears to lie in discovering how to work together at the mutual aspects of their lives. These partners often comment that the baby has done wonders for their relationship because it is the first major enterprise they have undertaken together. But in a larger proportion of the couples, we notice that spouses began their family venture with one or both partners emphasizing a strong ideology of togetherness. During this major life change from couple to family, they discover that they are really quite different people: They have different pictures of "their" family, different ideas about how to raise "their" child, different notions of who will do what, and so on. What we are suggesting is that the transition to first-time parenthood highlights existing differences between spouses and introduces some new ones, in both cases increasing opportunities for disagreement and conflict in their relationship as a couple.

Multiple regression analyses (C. Cowan et al., 1985) indicate that a composite index of *increasing difference* between spouses from pregnancy to 6 months postpartum and a single index of *increased conflict* in the marriage contribute significantly to the decline in men's and women's marital satisfaction from pretest to 18 months after the birth of their first child. Parents' interview responses seem to support the questionnaire data. As it becomes clear that their individual ideas and feelings are diverging, partners begin to feel more distant from one another. Especially when time for individual interests and needs is at an all-time low, this feeling of distance makes cooperative problem solving increasingly difficult. Husbands and wives who used to gloss over their different ideas about childrearing must now decide what to *do* when their baby cries in the middle of the night. Both struggle to maintain ongoing relationships with parents, friends, co-workers – and one another – at the same time developing a new relationship with the most recent family addition. The greatest challenge for two excited and usually exhausted spouses making this major life transition, then, is to work out a way to maintain a sense of individuality *and* mutuality while becoming a family.

Antagonists or partners?

Jessica Ball (1983, 1984) conducted an observational study of couple problem solving in a subset of our sample. Her findings shed light on why partner differences may add to marital distance and distress. In an important contrast to the focus of many problem-solving studies, Ball showed that the *outcome* of partners' problem-solving discussions was not related to their satisfaction with problem solving or to their feelings of distance in the relationship. Rather, it was the feeling of not "being on the same side" during their attempts to resolve differences that led to partners' negative feelings about their problem-solving strategies and about the overall marriage.

As new fathers and mothers recognize these differences in their experience of becoming a family, they report that they feel more like parents and less like lovers. When their differences generate conflict that they cannot resolve successfully, partners may lose the feeling of "being on the same side" and begin to experience distance in the marriage. We believe that this pattern, coupled with the natural vulnerability and exhaustion of the first months of parenthood, sets the stage for some increase in dissatisfaction with the overall marriage. Although this process may not be unique to the parenthood transition, it is clear that it becomes salient at this time of life because shifts in so many aspects of life require mutually arrived at solutions if equilibrium in the family is to be regained.

Most family theorists and therapists have emphasized the importance of communication and problem solving in understanding marital distress (e.g., Jacobson, 1981; Margolin, 1981). Our research suggests that a naturally occurring outcome of the transition to parenthood makes mutuality in communication more difficult at this time. Gottman and Levenson's studies of psychophysiology and marriage add a poignant twist to our analysis (Gottman & Levenson, 1984; Levenson & Gottman, 1983). They are amassing evidence that male–female differences in managing the arousal associated with negative affect leads to different styles of behavior in men and women during couple conflict; in maritally distressed couples, women tend to "open up" issues, whereas men tend to "stonewall." On the basis of these findings, we have speculated (C. Cowan et al., 1985) that, when new fathers and mothers come together in an attempt to reconcile their different points of view, their stylistic differences may exacerbate rather than relieve the tensions that led to the discussion in the first place.

So far, our discussion of the process model has focused primarily on the instrumental tasks of solving problems or resolving conflicts. But the highs and lows of couple relationships often lie in the realm of sharing feelings. Here, too, growing differences between partners apparently interfere with the comfort of the relationship. Wile (1981) observes that one of the primary difficulties in couple relationships arises when one or both partners believe that they are not *entitled* to have the feelings they are experiencing. This leads to indirect, confusing, and often hostile communication. As men and women travel different pathways toward parenthood, trying to cope with new and unexpected events and emotions, they often wonder whether what they are feeling is "normal." They look to their partner for validation, but as we have seen, the partner may be having a different experience. Especially with the vulnerability of feeling more "parent" and less "lover," spouses may hesitate to give voice to their anxieties and doubts. Many find it easier to say what they "ought" to feel and attempt to put the more unacceptable feelings aside. Thus, communication between the parents can become tense, stilted, and unsatisfying, as the research of Rausch et al. (1974) suggested. In both instrumental and expressive realms, then, the transition to parenthood holds the potential for drawing parents into more separate worlds at a time when they dreamed of making a world together.

Why is the decline in satisfaction with marriage so small?

Let us remind readers here that, although a decline in marital satisfaction is reported in almost every study of new parents, the decline is generally not very large. When Heming (1985) compared new parents at 18 months postpartum with nonparent couples in our study, she found that only 8% of the variance in posttest marital satisfaction could be accounted for by parenthood status. By contrast, 17 to 50% of the variance in marital satisfaction could be explained by pretest measures in several family domains. It may be as important to understand the relatively small size of the impact of the transition on marriage as it is to account for the prevalence of the negative effects.

Stability and positive change. Elaborating the changes in new parents' lives, as we have done here, can obscure the fact that a number of important aspects of individual and marital life remain stable during family formation. Perhaps the most critical of these unchanging aspects of life comes from our data on self-esteem and personality characteristics in new mothers and fathers: Both look remarkably stable during spouses' transition to first-time parenthood. It may be this stability in core aspects of the self that buffers the effects of negative or unexpected change in other domains.

At each of our follow-up interviews, after asking what had been the hardest part of becoming a family, we asked parents, "What has been the best part of becoming a family for each of you?" Almost every man and woman first named their child. Some talked about how enthralled they were as they watched their son or daughter develop. Others spoke of rediscovering the world around them by viewing it from their toddler's vantage point. A number of men and women said that they felt more respected in the community "now that we're a real family." Thus, even though there was sometimes a feeling of more distance between spouses, for most, talking about or spending time with their baby led to feelings of pride and closeness. A number of couples reported more efficient problem solving, and a few said that the quality of their sexual relationship had improved. In some cases, parents' felt more positive connections with their own parents than ever before, partly because their parents included them in the "adult" part of the extended family circle at family gatherings and partly because the new parents themselves had begun to appreciate what their parents had been through in raising them. Although work outside the family often exhausted already tired parents, many reported a renewed sense of purpose both in their work and in their links to the community. Few parents in our study adopted an explicit exchange-theory approach to their evaluations of life satisfaction, yet most volunteered that the "rewards" of being parents far outweighed the "costs." In many cases, parents said that these positive changes provided a balance that helped make the more negative and stressful changes seem temporary and bearable. These interview impressions correspond with other researchers' comments that, *when asked,* parents are as eager to describe the positive as the negative aspects of having children (Bradburn & Caplovitz, 1965; Hoffman & Hoffman, 1973; Luckey & Bain, 1970; Russell, 1974).

Parents' understanding of the transition. The couples in our study usually attempted to put their disequilibration into a meaningful perspective. The cognitive theory of stress and emotion developed by Lazarus and his colleagues (Lazarus, 1984; Lazarus, et al., 1980) suggests that individuals' *appraisal* of both external and internal events is one of the key determinants of the stress they experience. We think that the effects of our couples group intervention (C. Cowan, 1987; C. Cowan & P. Cowan, 1987a) suggest how parents' understanding of the changes they have undergone while becoming a family may affect their feelings about their marriage. When randomly selected intervention and control couples were compared, it became clear that the intervention had not prevented the shifts in sense of self, role arrangements, or marital conflict that we have described above. Nevertheless, participation in the intervention did seem to help keep couples from generalizing these negative changes to their evaluation of the marriage.

To illustrate this effect, consider that the marital satisfaction of men and women who were in a couples group declined slightly from pregnancy to 6 months after birth and then leveled off over the next year – despite the decline in their role satisfaction and the increases in marital distance and conflict. Couples who were not in the intervention showed a sharp decline in marital satisfaction from pregnancy to 6 months postpartum and another even sharper drop from 6 to 18 months after birth. It is as if the 6 months of discussion with other new parents and trained co-leader couples helped "unhook" the usual links between dissatisfaction or distress in each domain and unhappiness with the overall marriage. That is, the intervention may interfere with the difference–distance–conflict dynamic that often translates structural family change into a process that ends with dissatisfaction with the *marriage*.

We are speculating that the couples groups provided a safe setting in which parents could feel and normalize the changes they were experiencing. Because the groups were designed to help parents explore their anxiety or distress rather than ignore it as unexpected or unwelcome, it was possible for many to move to the next step of thinking about how to reconcile the discrepancy between their expectations and their reality of life as a family. The intervention effects suggest that, when there is a supportive context for appraising the structural changes of a transition period, parents' understanding of change can act as a moderator of distress with the overall couple relationship. That 12.5% of the nonintervention parents were separated or divorced when their babies were 18 months old, whereas all of the parents in the intervention subsample remained in intact marriages, lends support to the idea that the spouses from the intervention felt more optimistic about working out marital differences or difficulties.

In interviews with couples not in the intervention groups, we noticed the reactions of the more optimistic spouses. They believed that the chaos of their lives would eventually settle down; once again they would have time to think a complete thought or spend a few uninterrupted hours as a couple. These couples seemed able to step back, to take a look at their situation and feel encouraged by the positive things that were happening, and to tolerate the sleeplessness and chaotic feelings that normally accompany new parenthood. In other words, with or without the help of an intervention, couples' interpretation of the changes of the transition seemed to affect their level of distress. When couples' distress stayed at manageable levels or felt temporary, they did not seem to suffer negative effects on the marriage beyond the average 10-point decline on the Locke–Wallace Short Marital Adjustment Test.

This discussion of the intervention underscores a point about research design in studies of the transition to parenthood. The inclusion of an intervention has theoretical as well as practical payoffs. It introduces an experiment into an otherwise correlational study, allowing us to distinguish between sets of variables that are merely associated with each other and variables that are inextricably interrelated.

Blaming the baby

We return to a discussion of parents and researchers who imply that children are the cause of their parents' marital distress. Couples with new babies do appear to have become more dissatisfied with some aspects of their lives in the first year and one-half of family making than do comparable childless spouses. We have tried to show that becoming a family introduces a challenge to the individuality–mutuality balance that most partners seem to be working toward. Even so, the data suggest several arguments against blaming the babies for their parents' distress with the marriage.

First, marital satisfaction before the baby enters the family is highly related to the state of the postbirth marriage. Those spouses in least distress before becoming a family tended to experience the most marital satisfaction in the first two years of becoming a family. This argues against the notion that babies come along to disrupt perfectly satisfying relationships. Second, as many of us know from our own lives, children are a source of immense satisfaction – for fathers and mothers as individuals and for their relationship as a couple. Finally, the issues that seem to cause new parents difficulty are not *inevitable* consequences of childbirth. Although there are extensive individual, familial, and societal barriers to adopting nontraditional role arrangements (C. Cowan & P. Cowan, 1987b), couples showed some range along a continuum of gender-specific divisions of labor. The couples in our study who bucked the general trend and arranged greater sharing of housework and childcare were those most satisfied with their role arrangements and with the overall marriage. It seems clear to us that it is not babies who are responsible for the dilemmas about self, roles, and communication that new parenthood poses for men and women. Rather, contemporary spouses who decide to move from couple to family life must confront conflicting individual and couple needs at a time in history when male–female and work–family arrangements are lagging behind the new *ideology*. Our concern about what these dilemmas mean for the marriages of new parents mirror those expressed by the Rapoports a decade ago when they reviewed the literature on family formation (Rapoport, Rapoport, & Streilitz, 1977): "Many ordinary families are in trouble . . . partly because they have inherited conceptions of family life that are inadequate to cope with the requirements of modern living."

With little support from business and government, individual spouses are on their own to resolve serious conflicts between the needs of adults, children, marriages, and families. We believe that, as long as it is up to each man and woman to work out these difficult gender role and work–family issues, the relationship between the spouses will be vulnerable to strain during the transition to parenthood. These issues, rather than the baby, seem to be responsible for partners' dissatisfaction with marriage during this critical family transition.

A note on measures and concepts in the study of families

Choosing and interpreting measures of individual and marital functioning

A recurring theme in the research we have reviewed and discussed is the importance of obtaining measures that allow respondents to describe *and* evaluate what is happening in each of the family domains. Even when we ask about conflict and disagreement, we do not assume that conflict is inevitably negative. Some respondents, admittedly in the minority, would rather have *more* conflict and disagreement than they now do. They are usually partners who feel that they cover up their disagreements because they have not learned how to work out their differences in a constructive manner.

We have been impressed with how central the division of household and childcare tasks is to men's and women's feelings about their relationship as a couple. Still the staple of situation comedies and comic novels, decisions about who does the dishes, takes out the garbage, or cares for the children are no laughing matter for couples navigating the early years of life as a family. Our "Who Does What?" measure seems to work well in our sample and in other samples of both heterosexual (Awalt et al., in press; V. Lieberman, 1982) and homosexual couples (Picciotto, 1984), giving a sense of partners' *relative* share of the family work and their satisfaction with their mutual role arrangements.

We have also been impressed with both the quantitative and qualitative utility of "The Pie" for assessing the intersection between the self as individual and the self in relationship. The shifting sizes of parent, partner, and worker neatly sum up the key dilemmas men and women face as they create new families. Although it allows respondents to label and quantify as many or as few parts of themselves as they wish, a common coding system has facilitated comparisons among individuals. Participants in the study also find it useful. Some of them adopt it as a central metaphor, saying, "You should see what's happening to my 'Pie' this time," or "I just don't know how to fit space for *me* into my 'Pie.' "

After all of our focus on marital satisfaction, we are still uneasy about the use of a single measure to describe the quality of a marriage. Though Spanier's Dyadic Adjustment Scale (1976) is more psychometrically elegant than the traditional Locke–Wallace (1959), the correlation between the two scales is a hefty .92, and the Locke–Wallace has the advantage of being substantially shorter. Any self-report instrument has the possibility of eliciting socially desirable or self-deceptive answers, and we expect that the Locke–Wallace is no exception. Our clinical impression and some preliminary data (Heming, 1983) suggest that the scores correspond fairly well with observer ratings of the couple and that the Locke–Wallace is especially accurate at the low end; people who say that they are very unhappy in their marriage usually show other signs of being in a strained or dysfunctional relationship.

Our central concern, however, is not the scale's global validity. We worry about the fact that, despite decades of research, the *meaning* of marital satisfaction is not entirely clear. We have described the fact that some couples who are experiencing a great deal of stress in their marital interactions manage somehow to take the long view and evaluate their marriage as solid; others who seem to be doing well from our point of view are expressing serious discontent. We believe that, even when the focus is on the quality of marriage, investigations should assume that each partner's evaluation of the marriage includes satisfaction in all five domains of family life. The goal should not be to create a new "superindex" but rather to provide a multidimensional assessment of individual and relationship functioning in the family.

Our concern about the meaning of marital satisfaction raises a general issue about measures and methods in the study of becoming a family. We believe that systematic, quantitative data from multiple sources are essential for describing and understanding the complex nature of a family life transition. We also believe that a more qualitative "clinical" approach is necessary, to make certain that we do justice to the issues as couples experience them in their daily lives. We have found that our extensive interviews and group meetings establish a context for interpreting quantitative data *and* provide a rich source for forming and validating hypotheses about the way family structures and processes are interrelated.

The concept of crisis for couples

Most of the research we have been discussing was stimulated by the notion that the transition to parenthood presents a potential crisis for the marriage of new parents. The initial definition of crisis as a function of normative developmental events was formulated by Erikson (1950) and Caplan (1964) as it applied to individual development. Hill (1949) explored the meaning of life crises for *families*. Unfortunately, almost every theorist and clinician has a different definition of the term, although all incorporate elements of Hill's ABCX formulation (1949; Hansen & Johnson, 1979): The gap between what the new situation demands (A), the current resources of the family (B), and the family's definition of the event (C) combine to produce a crisis (X).

Articles by Felner, Farber, and Primavera (1983), Hansen and Johnson (1979), and Patterson (1983) agree that crisis should not be interpreted as a short-term response to a defined stimulus. It seems more realistic to think of crisis as a chain of events in a complex *process* in which individual personalities, relationships, and external events constantly interact (see Mitchell, Billings, & Moos, 1982). This point is particularly apropos for couples who decide to begin a family. The level of development men and women have reached as individuals and as a couple when they decide to have a child has implications for their adaptation or distress during the transition from couple to family, and their management of the transition has obvious connections to their satisfaction with the "outcome."

One consequence of considering crisis as an ongoing process is that it becomes very difficult to define "the transition to parenthood" – when it begins and how long it lasts. When their children are 3½ years old, our parents vary extensively in their interpretation of when, or *whether*, they have completed the transition from couple to family. Perhaps, as Offer and Sabshin suggest (1984), crisis and transition can be defined only in retrospect, or by observers, since participants in the midst of life's flux do not have a clearly demarcated concept of their own.

This more process-oriented view of crisis corresponds very closely to the model of marital and family functioning we have presented here. Major life-change events stimulate change in individual, couple, parent–child, three-generational, and outside-the-family domains. Since husbands and wives appear to be traveling separate paths toward their family goals, they experience increasing differences, distance, and conflict. Though it is possible to define this state of affairs operationally as a crisis, the concept of crisis does not seem to have contributed to our understanding of what happens to parents and the marriage during this adult life transition. "Crisis" has had too many negative connotations and has implied a subjective feeling of distress. How partners make sense of and handle this difference–distance–conflict pattern determines whether the disequilibration becomes a danger or an opportunity for the partners and the marriage.

Although Hill and others have defined "crisis" in terms of the family rather than the individuals, the bulk of research and theory on the transition to parenthood has focused on individual partners. This problem has been endemic in family research. What can we say about *couple* distress or dissatisfaction when one partner is satisfied while the other is approaching despair? Average scores do not tell the story. Statistical analyses, including ours so far, tend to report men's and women's data separately; it is time for us to look at *relationship* patterns that are associated with his, her, and their adaptation.

Although researchers have tended to focus on individuals, clinicians have focused on family systems. In our view the two approaches are not mutually exclusive. Rather, the understanding of families in transition requires a synthesis of individual, dyadic, triadic, three-generational, and societal perspectives to provide a differentiated portrait of families' adaptation to life change. We do not yet have the data to show it, but we expect that the couple relationship will be "first among equals" in accounting for different pathways to individual and family adaptation.

In our opinion, the transition to parenthood is not a crisis for couple relationships in the sense that one or both partners will necessarily experience severe or disabling distress or that the marriage will become dysfunctional. It is clear, however, that if one partner experiences marked shifts in any of the major domains of family life we have described, it is likely that the change will have an impact on his or her relationship with the child, with the grandparents, with colleagues at work – and with the spouse. This, our longitudinal data suggest, will inevitably lead to some disequilibration in the marriage. At that point, we must be careful to pay attention to how each partner *evaluates* the state of affairs and to how the combination of their evaluations affects both partners' satisfaction with the overall marriage. Only then can we know whether a couple may in fact experience the more negative aspects of crisis that have been written about for so long. Often, when the entire transition is examined, couples find that becoming a family has been a more positive experience for them than the media and researchers have led us to believe.

References

Awalt, S. J., Snowden, L. R., & Schott, T. L. (in press). Personal and marital adjustment in the transition to parenthood. *Journal of Marriage and the Family.*

Ball, F. L. J. (1983, August). *Understanding problem solving in couple relationships.* Paper presented at a symposium, "Individual and Couple Satisfaction During the Transition to Parenthood," at the meetings of the American Psychological Association, Anaheim, CA.

Ball, F. L. J. (1984). *Understanding and satisfaction in marital problem solving: A hermeneutic inquiry.* Unpublished doctoral dissertation, University of California, Berkeley.

Beauchamp, D. (1969). Parenthood as crisis: An additional study. Reported in Arthur P. Jacoby, Transition to parenthood: A reassessment. *Journal of Marriage and the Family, 31*, 720–7.

Belsky, J. (1984). The determinants of parenting: A process model. *Child Development, 55*, 83–96.

Belsky, J., & Pensky, E. (in press). Marital change across the transition to parenthood. *Marriage and Family Review*.

Belsky, J., Lang, M. E., & Rovine, M. (1985). Stability and change in marriage across the transition to parenthood: A second study. *Journal of Marriage and the Family, 47*, 855–65.

Belsky, J., Spanier, G. B., & Rovine, M. (1983). Stability and change in marriage across the transition to parenthood. *Journal of Marriage and the Family, 45*, 567–77.

Benedek, T. (1959). Parenthood as a developmental phase. *Journal of the American Psychoanalytic Association, 7*, 389–417.

Benedek, T. (1970). Parenthood during the life cycle. In E. J. Anthony & T. Benedek (Eds.), *Parenthood: Its psychology and psychopathology* (pp. 185–209). Boston: Little, Brown.

Blood, R. O., & Wolfe, D. M. (1960). *Husbands and wives: The dynamics of married living*. Glencoe, IL: Free Press.

Blum, M. E. (1983, August). *A longitudinal study of transition to parenthood in primiparous couples*. Paper presented at the meeting of the American Psychological Association, Anaheim, CA.

Bowen, M. (1978). *Family therapy in clinical practice*. New York: Aranson.

Bradburn, N., & Caplovitz, D. (1965). *Reports on happiness*. Chicago: Aldine.

Brockington, F., Crnik, K. F., Schonfield, E. M., Downing, A. R., Francis, A. F., & Keelan, C. (1981, July). Puerperal psychosis: Phenomena and diagnosis. *Archives of General Psychiatry, 38*, 829–33.

Brockington, I. F., Winokur, G., & Dean, C. (1982). Puerperal psychosis. In I. F. Brockington & R. Kumar (Eds.), *Motherhood and mental illness* (pp. 207–35). New York: Academic Press.

Bronfenbrenner, U. (1979). *The ecology of human development*. Cambridge, MA: Harvard University Press.

Caplan, S. (1964). *Principles of preventive psychiatry*. New York: Basic Books.

Cavenar, J. O., & Weddington, W. W. (1978). Abdominal pain in expectant fathers. *Psychosomatics, 19*, 761–8.

Campbell, A., Converse, P. E., & Rodgers, W. L. (1976). *The quality of American life*. New York: Russell Sage Foundation.

Cherlin, A. (1977). The effect of children on marital dissolution. *Demography, 14*, 264–72.

Clulow, C. F. (1982). *To have and to hold: Marriage, the first baby, and preparing couples for parenthood*. Aberdeen, Scotland: University of Aberdeen Press.

Clulow, C. F. (1985). *Marital therapy: An inside view*. Aberdeen, Scotland: University of Aberdeen Press.

Cobb, S. (1976). Social support as a moderator of life stress. *Psychosomatic Medicine, 38*, 300–14.

Cowan, C. P. (1987). Working with men becoming fathers: The impact of couples group intervention. In P. Bronstein & C. P. Cowan (Eds.), *Fatherhood today: Men's changing role in the family*. New York: Wiley.

Cowan, C. P., & Cowan, P. A. (1987a). A preventive intervention for couples becoming parents. In C. F. Z. Boukydis (Ed.), *Research on support for parents and infants in the postnatal period*. Norwood, NJ: Ablex.

Cowan, C. P. & Cowan, P. A. (1987b). Men's involvement in parenthood: Identifying the antecedents and understanding the barriers. In P. Berman & F. Pedersen (Eds.), *Men's transition to parenthood*. Hillsdale, NJ: Erlbaum.

Cowan, C. P., & Cowan, P. A. (1987c). Who does what when partners become parents: Men's involvement in the family. *Marriage and Family Review*.

Cowan, C. P., Cowan, P. A., Coie, L., & Coie, J. D. (1978). Becoming a family: The impact of a first child's birth on the couple's relationship. In W. B. Miller & L. F. Newman (Eds.), *The first child and family formation* (pp. 296–324). Chapel Hill: University of North Carolina, Carolina Population Center.

Cowan, C. P., Cowan, P. A., Heming, G., Garrett, E., Coysh, W., Curtis-Boles, H., & Boles, A. (1985). Transitions to parenthood: His, hers, and theirs. *Journal of Family Issues, 6*, 451–81.

Cowan, P. A. (1987). Becoming a father: A time of change, an opportunity for development. In P. Bronstein & C. P. Cowan (Eds.), *Fatherhood today: Men's changing role in the family*. New York: Wiley.

Cowan, P. A., & Cowan, C. P. (1987, April). *Couple relationships, parenting styles, and the child's development at three*. Paper presented at a symposium, "The transition to parenthood," at the meetings of the Society for Research in Child Development, Baltimore, MD.

Cowan, P. A., Cowan, C. P., & Heming, G. (1985). *The changing role of past and present family of origin in marital satisfaction*. Unpublished manuscript, University of California, Berkeley.

Crockenberg, S. (1981). Infant irritability, mother responsiveness, and social support influences in the security of infant–mother attachment. *Child Development, 52*, 857–65.

Davenport, Y., Adland, M. L., Gold, P. W., & Goodwin, F. K. (1979). Manic-depressive illness: Psychodynamic features of multigenerational families. *American Journal of Orthopsychiatry, 49*, 24–35.

Dicks, H. V. (1967). *Marital tensions: Clinical studies toward a psychological theory of interaction*. New York: Basic Books.

Dohrenwend, B. S., & Dohrenwend, B. F. (Eds.). (1974). *Stressful life events: Their nature and effects*. New York: Wiley.

Dyer, E. (1963). Parenthood as crisis: A re-study. *Marriage and Family Living, 25*, 196–201.

Entwisle, S., & Doering, S. (1981). *The first birth: A family turning point*. Baltimore, MD: Johns Hopkins University Press.

Erikson, E. (1950). *Childhood and society*. New York: Norton.

Erikson, E. (1968). *Identity, youth and crisis*. New York: Norton.

Feldman, H. (1971). The effects of children on the family. In A. Michel (Ed.), *Family issues of employed women in Europe and America* (pp. 104–25). Lieden: Brill.

Feldman, S. S. (1987). Predicting strain in mothers and fathers of six-month-olds: A short-term longitudinal study. In P. Berman & F. A. Pedersen (Eds.), *Men's transitions to parenthood*. Hillsdale, NJ: Erlbaum.

Feldman, S. S., & Aschenbrenner, B. (1983). Impact of parenthood on various aspects of masculinity and femininity: A short-term longitudinal study. *Developmental Psychology, 19*, 278–89.

Feldman, S. S., & Nash, S. C. (1984). The transition from expectancy to parenthood: Impact of the firstborn child on men and women. *Sex Roles, 11*, 84–96.

Felner, R. D., Farber, S. S., & Primavera, J. (1983). Transitions and stressful life events: A model for primary prevention. In R. D. Felner, L. A. Jason, J. N. Moritsugu, & S. S. Farber (Eds.), *Preventive psychology: Theory, research, and practice*. New York: Pergamon.

Framo, J. L. (1981). The integration of marital therapy with sessions with family of origin. In A. S. Gurman & D. P. Kniskern (Eds.), *Handbook of family therapy* (pp. 133–58). New York: Brunner/Mazel.

Garrett, E. T. (1983, August). *Women's experiences of early parenthood: Expectation vs. reality*. Paper presented at the American Psychological Association Meetings, Anaheim, CA.

Gladieux, J. (1978). The transition to parenthood: Satisfaction with the pregnancy experience as a function of sex role conceptions, the marital relationship and the social network. In W. Miller & L. Newman (Eds.), *The first child and family formation* (pp. 275–95). Chapel Hill: University of North Carolina, Carolina Population Center.

Glenn, N. D. (1975). Psychological well-being in the postparental stage: Some evidence from national surveys. *Journal of Marriage and the Family, 37,* 105–10.

Glenn, N. D., & McLanahan, S. (1982). Children and marital happiness: A further specification of the relationship. *Journal of Marriage and the Family, 44,* 63–72.

Glenn, N. D., & Weaver, C. N. (1978). A multivariate multisurvey study of marital happiness. *Journal of Marriage and the Family, 40,* 269–82.

Goldberg, W. A., & Easterbrooks, M. A. (1984). Role of marital quality in toddler development. *Developmental Psychology, 20,* 504–14.

Goldberg, W. A., Michaels, G. Y., & Lamb, M. E. (1985). Husbands' and wives' adjustment to pregnancy and first parenthood. *Family Issues, 6,* 485–503.

Gottman, J. M. (1979). *Marital interaction: Experimental investigations*. New York: Academic Press.

Gottman, J. M., & Levinson, R. W. (in press). The social psychophysiology of marriage. In P. Noller & M. A. Fitzpatrick (Eds.), *Perspectives on marital interaction*. San Diego, CA: College Hill Press.

Gottman, J., Markman, H., & Notarius, C. (1977). The topography of marital conflict: A sequential analysis of verbal and nonverbal behavior. *Journal of Marriage and the Family, 39,* 461–77.

Grossman, F. (1987). New fatherhood: An optional developmental crisis. In P. Berman & F. A. Pedersen (Eds.), *Men's transition to parenthood*. Hillsdale, NJ: Erlbaum.

Grossman, F., Eichler, L., & Winickoff, S. (1980). *Pregnancy, birth, and parenthood*. San Francisco: Jossey-Bass.

Gurin, G., Veroff, J., & Feld, S. (1960). *Americans view their mental health*. New York: Basic Books.

Gurwitt, A. R. (1976). Aspects of prospective fatherhood: A case report. *Psychoanalytic study of the child, 31,* 237–71.

Hamilton, J. A. (1962). *Postpartum psychiatric problems*. Saint Louis, MO: Mosby.

Hansen, D., & Johnson, V. (1979). Rethinking family stress theory: Definitional aspects. In W. R. Burr, R. Hill, F. I. Nye, & I. L. Reiss (Eds.), *Contemporary theories about the family: Research-based theories* (Vol. 1). New York: Free Press, 582–603.

Heinicke, C. (1984). Impact of prebirth parent personality and marital functioning on family development: A framework and suggestions for further study. *Developmental Psychology, 20,* 1044–53.

Heming, G. (1983, August). *Predicting adaptation and stress*. Paper presented at a symposium, "Individual and Marital Satisfaction During the Transition to Parenthood," at the meetings of the American Psychological Association, Anaheim, CA.

Heming, G. (1985). *Predicting adaptation in the transition to parenthood*. Unpublished doctoral dissertation, University of California, Berkeley.

Herzog, J. M. (1979). Disturbances in parenting high-risk infants: Clinical impressions and hypotheses. In T. F. Field (Ed.), *Infants born at risk* (pp. 357–63). New York: Spectrum, 357–363.

Hicks, M., & Platt, M. (1971). Marital happiness and stability: A review of research in the sixties. *Journal of Marriage and the Family, 32,* 553–73.

Hill, R. (1949). (Ed.). *Families under stress*. New York: Harper.

Hobbs, D. F., Jr. (1965). Parenthood as crisis: A third study. *Journal of Marriage and the Family, 27,* 367–72.

Hobbs, D. F., Jr. (1968). Transition to parenthood: A replication and an extension. *Journal of Marriage and the Family, 30,* 413–17.

Hobbs, D., & Cole, S. (1976). Transition to parenthood: A decade replication. *Journal of Marriage and the Family, 38,* 723–31.

Hobbs, D. F., & Wimbish, J. M. (1977). Transition to parenthood by black couples. *Journal of Marriage and the Family, 39,* 677–89.

Hoffman, L. W. (1978). Effects of a first child on women's social role development. In W. Miller & L. Newman (Eds.), *The first child and family formation* (pp. 340–67). Chapel Hill: University of North Carolina, Carolina Population Center.

Hoffman, L. W., & Hoffman, M. L. (1973). The value of children to parents. In J. T. Fawcett (Ed.), *Psychological perspectives on fertility* (pp. 462–91). New York: Basic Books.

Hoffman, L. W., & Manis, J. D. (1979). The value of children in the United States: A new approach to the study of fertility. *Journal of Marriage and the Family, 42,* 583–96.

Horowitz, M., Schaefer, C., Hiroto, D., Wilner, N., & Levin, B. (1977). Life Event Questionnaire for measuring presumptive stress. *Psychosomatic Medicine, 39,* 413–31.

Houseknecht, S. K. (1979). Childlessness and marital adjustment. *Journal of Marriage and the Family, 41,* 259–65.

Hudson, W. W., & Murphy, G. J. (1980). The non-linear relationship between marital satisfaction and stages of the family life cycle: An artifact of Type I errors? *Journal of Marriage and the Family, 42,* 263–7.

Jacobson, N. (1981). Behavioral marital therapy. In A. S. Gurman & D. Kniskern (Eds.), *Handbook of family therapy.* New York: Brunner/Mazel.

Jacoby, A. P. (1969). Transition to parenthood: A reassessment. *Journal of Marriage and the Family, 31,* 720–7.

LaRossa, R., & LaRossa, M. M. (1981). *Transition to parenthood: How infants change families.* Beverly Hills, CA: Sage.

Laslett, B., & Rapoport, R. (1975). Collaborative interviewing and interactive research. *Journal of Marriage and the Family, 37,* 968–77.

Lazarus, R. S. (1980). The stress and coping paradigm. In C. Eisdorfer, D. Coehn, A. Kleinman, & P. Maxim (Eds.), *Theoretical bases for psychopathology.* New York: Spectrum.

Lazarus, R. (1984). On the primacy of cognition. *American Psychologist, 39,* 124–9.

Lazarus, R. S., Kanner, A. D., & Folkman, S. (1980). Emotions: A cognitive-phenomenological analysis. In R. Plutchik & H. Kellerman (Eds.), *Theories of emotion.* New York: Academic Press.

LeMasters, E. E. (1957). Parenthood as crisis. *Marriage and Family Living, 19,* 352–5.

Levenson, R. W., & Gottman, J. M. (1983). Marital interaction: Physiological linkage and affective exchange. *Journal of Personality and Social Psychology, 45,* 587–97.

Lewis, R. A., & Spanier, G. B. (1979). Theorizing about the quality and stability of marriage. In W. R. Burr, R. Hill, F. I. Nye, & I. L. Reiss (Eds.), *Contemporary theories about the family* (Vol. 1, pp. 269–94). New York: Free Press.

Lieberman, M. A. (1981). The effects of social support on responses to stress. In L. Goldberger & S. Breznitz (Eds.), *Handbook of stress* (pp. 764–81). New York: Free Press.

Lieberman, V. (1982). *Sex-role organization and sex differences in depression: A study of heterosexual couples.* Unpublished doctoral dissertation, University of California, Berkeley.

Liefer, M. (1980). *Psychological effects of motherhood: A study of first pregnancy.* New York: Praeger.

Locke, H., & Wallace, K. (1959). Short marital adjustment and prediction tests: Their reliability and validity. *Marriage and Family Living, 21,* 251–5.

Luckey, E., & Bain, J. (1970). Children: A factor in marital satisfaction. *Journal of Marriage and the Family, 32,* 43–54.

Margolin, G. (1981). Behavior exchange in distressed and nondistressed marriages: A family life cycle perspective. *Behavior Therapy, 12,* 329–43.

McHale, S. M., & Huston, T. L. (1985). The effect of the transition to parenthood on the marriage relationship. *Journal of Family Issues, 6,* 409–33.

Meyerowitz, J. H., & Feldman, H. (1966). Transition to parenthood. *Psychiatric Research Reports, 20,* 78–84.

Miller, B. (1976). A multivariable developmental model of marital satisfaction. *Journal of Marriage and the Family, 38,* 643–57.

Miller, B., & Sollie, D. (1980). Normal stresses during the transition to parenthood. *Family Relations, 29,* 459–65.

Minuchin, S. (1974). *Families and family therapy.* Cambridge, MA: Harvard University Press.

Mitchell, R. E., Billings, A. G., & Moos, R. H. (1982). Social support and well-being: Implications for prevention programs. *Journal of Primary Prevention, 3,* 77–98.

Moos, R. H. (1974). *Family Environment Scale.* Palo Alto: Consulting Psychologists Press.

Navran, L. (1967). Communication and adjustment in marriage. *Family Process, 6,* 173–84.

Nuckolls, K. B., Cassel, J., & Kaplan, B. H. (1972). Psychological assets, life crises and the prognosis of pregnancy. *American Journal of Epidemiology, 95,* 431–41.

Offer, D., & Sabshin, M. (1984). *Normality and the life cycle.* New York: Basic Books.

Osofsky, H. (1982). Expectant and new fatherhood as a developmental crisis. *Bulletin of the Menninger Clinic, 46,* 209–30.

Osofsky, H. J., & Osofsky, J. D. (1980). Normal adaptation to pregnancy and new parenthood. In P. M. Taylor (Ed.), *Parent–infant relationships.* New York: Grune & Stratton.

Osofsky, J. D., & Osofsky, H. J. (1985). Psychological and developmental perspectives on expectant and new parenthood. In R. D. Parke (Ed.), *Review of child development research. Vol. 7: The family.* University of Chicago Press.

Paffenbarger, R. S., Jr., & McCabe, L. J., Jr. (1966). The effect of obstetric and perinatal events on risk of mental illness in women of childbearing age. *American Journal of Public Health, 56,* 400–7.

Parens, H. (1975). Parenthood as a developmental phase. *Journal of the American Psychoanalytic Association, 23,* 154–65.

Parke, R. D., & Tinsley, B. R. (1982). The early environment of the at-risk infant: Expanding the social context. In D. Bricker (Ed.), *Intervention with at-risk and handicapped infants: From research to application.* Baltimore, MD: University Park.

Patterson, G. (1983). Stress: A change agent for family process. In N. Garmezy & M. Rutter (Eds.), *Stress, coping, and development in children* (pp. 235–64). New York: McGraw-Hill.

Pedersen, F. A., Anderson, B. J., & Cain, R. L. (1977, March). *An approach to understanding linkages between the parent–infant and spouse relationships.* Paper presented at the Society for Research in Child Development, New Orleans, LA.

Picciotto, S. (1984). *Marital satisfaction in stable gay male couples.* Unpublished doctoral dissertation, University of California, Berkeley.

Raport, R., Rapoport, R., & Streilitz, Z. (1977). *Mothers, fathers, and society: Towards new alliances.* New York: Basic Books.

Raush, H. L., Barry, W. A., Hertel, R. K., & Swain, M. A. (1974). *Communication, conflict and marriage.* San Francisco: Jossey-Bass.

Reilly, T. W., Entwisle, D. R., & Doering, S. G. (1987). Socialization into parenthood: A longitudinal study of the development of self-evaluations. *Journal of Marriage and the Family, 49,* 295–308.

Renee, K. (1970). Correlates of dissatisfaction in marriage. *Journal of Marriage and the Family, 32,* 54–66.

Richardson, M. S., & Kagan, L. (1979, September). *Social support and the transition to parenthood.* Paper presented at the Meetings of the American Psychological Association, New York.

Roberts, G., Block, J. H., & Block, J. (1984). Continuity and change in parents' child-rearing practices. *Child Development, 55,* 586–97.

Rollins, B., & Feldman, H. (1970). Marital satisfaction over the family life cycle. *Journal of Marriage and the Family, 32,* 20–8.

Rossi, A. (1968). Transition to parenthood. *Journal of Marriage and the Family, 30,* 26–39.

Russell, C. (1974). Transition to parenthood: Problems and gratifications. *Journal of Marriage and the Family, 36,* 294–302.

Ryder, R. (1973). Longitudinal data relating marital satisfaction and having a child. *Journal of Marriage and the Family, 35,* 604–6.

Satir, V. (1972). *Peoplemaking.* Palo Alto, CA: Science and Behavior Books.

Schultz, S. (1984). *Family systems therapy: An integration.* New York: Aronson.

Shereshefsky, P. M., & Yarrow, L. J. (1973). *Psychological aspects of a first pregnancy.* New York: Raven Press.

Spanier, G. B. (1976). Measuring dyadic adjustment: New scales for assessing the quality of marriage and similar dyads. *Journal of Marriage and the Family, 38,* 15–28.

Spanier, G., & Lewis, R. (1980). Marital quality: A review of the seventies. *Journal of Marriage and the Family, 42,* 825–39.

Spanier, G., Lewis, R., & Cole, C. L. (1975). Marital adjustment over the family life cycle: The issue of curvilinearity. *Journal of Marriage and the Family, 37,* 263–75.

Tinsley, B. R., & Parke, R. D. (1984). Grandparents as support and socialization agents. In M. Lewis (Ed.), *Beyond the dyad.* New York: Plenum.

Waldron, H., & Routh, D. (1981). The effect of the first child on the marital relationship. *Journal of Marriage and the Family, 43,* 785–8.

Walsh, F. (Ed.). (1982). *Normal family processes.* New York: Guilford Press.

Weiner, A. (1982). Childbirth-related psychiatric illness. *Comprehensive Psychiatry, 23,* 143–54.

Wenner, N. K., Cohen, M. B., Weigert, E. V., Kvarnes, R. G., Ohaneson, E. M., & Fearing, J. M. (1969). Emotional problems in pregnancy. *Psychiatry, 32,* 389–410.

White, L. K., & Booth, A. (1985). The transition to parenthood and marital quality. *Journal of Family Issues, 6,* 435–50.

Wile, D. B. (1981). *Couples therapy: A nontraditional approach.* New York: Wiley.

Yalom, I. D., Lunde, D. T., Moos, R. H., & Hamburg, D. A. (1968). "Postpartum blues" syndrome. *Archives of General Psychiatry, 18,* 17–27.

Zaslow, M., Pedersen, F., Kramer, E., Cain, R., Suwalsky, J., & Fivel, M. I. (1981, April). *Depressed mood in new fathers: Interview and behavioral correlates.* Paper presented at the Society for Research in Child Development, Boston.

Part II

**The transition to parenthood under
conditions of risk**

5 Medical perspectives on pregnancy and birth: biological risks and technological advances

Linda Hughey Holt

Pregnancy is a time of extensive interaction with the medical system. In contrast to occasional visits to the doctor for actual illnesses or routine checkups, prenatal care involves many visits. Rapid and confusing physical changes are occurring in a woman's body while equally rapid emotional changes take place in her mind. This may be the first time she has interacted so closely with the medical professional.

In the first part of this chapter, we review the physical changes taking place during pregnancy and discuss how these changes affect women's and men's transition to parenthood. We then discuss how changing medical technology is affecting modern pregnancy and parenting. Obstetrical care is heavily patterned into the "disease model" of medicine, whereas many parents-to-be are striving for a "natural" pregnancy and birthing experience. These two models are at times in conflict. The challenge to the health care provider is to deal concurrently with a host of potential physical complications of pregnancy and at the same time offer emotional insight into and support during the rapid psychosocial changes that are occurring.

Getting pregnant: the decision

Despite assumptions otherwise, sometimes getting pregnant is a nondecision. Although there are many couples who contracept effectively for years, then plan a pregnancy, promptly conceive, and nine months later have a baby, many people at some point in their lives either face an unplanned pregnancy or fail to achieve or to carry to term a desired pregnancy. Of 6,000,000 pregnancies in the United States annually, it has been estimated that only 2,700,000 are "intended" (Ory, 1983). Almost half of the unintended pregnancies end in abortion, resulting in 1,500,000 abortions annually (Ory, 1983). Approximately 15% of couples will experience infertility of more than one year's duration, and this figure may be on the

157

rise, especially among the current crop of baby boomers who are intentionally holding off on starting families until they are in their thirties. One study suggested a decrease in fertility of 8 to 10% every five years after a couple's late twenties (Schwartz & Mayanx, 1982). Another study showed that only 52% of women attempting a pregnancy from age 35 to 39 became pregnant in 1 year (Vessey, Meissler, Flavell, & Yates, 1979). Women having babies obviously then range from women who became pregnant unintentionally and at least consciously did not want to become pregnant to women who may have tried for many years and undergone costly and invasive medical procedures in an effort to become pregnant.

One would expect to find great differences in parental attitudes and outcomes of planned pregnancies and unplanned pregnancies – but in fact they are hard to distinguish (Goshen-Gottstein, 1966; Hall & Mohr, 1933). Ambivalent feelings are common during early pregnancy, whether the pregnancy is planned or unplanned; a supportive social network that reinforces pregnancy will encourage positive attitudes (Caplan, 1954; Gladieux, 1978). Some ambivalent feelings result from lack of knowledge about pregnancy and parenting in technological societies (Newton, 1973). Cross-cultural studies indicate that social expectations have an impact on whether pregnancy is welcomed (Brody, 1978; Goshen-Gottstein, 1966; Hubert, 1974). The almost universal social pressures to have children in a wide variety of cultures make most women at least a little excited upon learning of a pregnancy.

What has changed over the past two generations is a reduction in the time allotted for "wanted" pregnancies. The current trend toward later marriages and delaying childbirth for several years after marriage (Thornton & Freedman, 1982) has resulted in an increasing maternal age at first birth (National Center for Health Statistics, 1982). Increases in the divorce rate have also led to many couples embarking on second marriages relatively late in their reproductive years. Since older couples run a higher risk of infertility problems (Vessey et al., 1979) and simply have a shorter time period for exposure to pregnancy than do younger couples, there has been a reduction in the time allotted to conception and childbearing. As a result, couples feel pressured to conceive quickly, and pregnancy complications or loss have a more devastating effect because there may be no time left for a "next time." Fortunately, improved antenatal and neonatal care and the availability of genetic screening have made women more willing to plan pregnancies at later ages (Roghmann & Doherty, 1983), allowing a small time extension at the far end of a woman's reproductive life span.

The pregnancy: obstetrical perspectives

Couples often seek medical advice before conception. This is an excellent idea, because it allows the obstetrician to screen for health problems that should be corrected, advise the elimination of such toxins as cigarettes and alcohol, and initiate proper nutrition. It should offer a wonderful opportunity to talk to parents-to-be about transitional issues, but few obstetricians have the time or training to explore these issues, and few couples have any interest in the subtler issues of parenting when parenting is an abstraction. What interests most couples at this time is the question, "How do we guarantee a healthy baby?" Aside from the standard advice about not smoking, not drinking, and eating well, the obstetrician must try to communicate the rather frightening truth that we are unable to control the bulk of the unknown hereditary and environmental factors that produce defects. The few medical inroads we have made are mainly in the realm of counseling couples that they are at increased risk (e.g., advanced age) and offering them early detection of the few defects that are detectable. Many couples have difficulty accepting this uncertainty, preferring to think that, by some magic formula, if they do everything right they should be able to mold nature – even choose their child's sex!

First trimester

The first trimester is initially a time of adjustment to the idea of pregnancy and then a time of coping with the physical and emotional changes that occur. Before the availability of early and rapid pregnancy tests, the suspicion of pregnancy had a chance to sink in gradually. Now women can find out within a few days of conception if they are pregnant. For most women, a late menstrual period is the first warning sign of pregnancy, followed by tiredness, often nausea, and at times a sense of bloating or abdominal discomfort. Women anxious about getting pregnant quickly or with a known infertility problem often feel a wave of depression with each menses. Women who experience few early symptoms of pregnancy worry that there is something wrong, not an unreasonable fear since most of the early signs and symptoms of pregnancy are related to high levels in early pregnancy of human chorionic gonadotropin (HCG), progesterone, and estrogen. With the current availability of early pregnancy tests, many women seek testing within days of conception. Both "at-home" pregnancy tests and commercially available urine or blood tests will detect normal pregnancy within days of implantation (although the accuracy of the at-

home tests varies). There are disadvantages to this: Many very early mis-
carriages (sometimes called "chemical" pregnancies) are of questionable
clinical significance, and identifying them as pregnancies may cause emotional trauma. Also, abnormal pregnancies such as tubal pregnancies may
have lower than normal HCG levels. Since at-home pregnancy tests are
comparable in cost to the testing offered by many medical facilities, some
women prefer to have the testing done in a clinic or doctor's office; other
women prefer the privacy of their homes. The concern has been raised
that at-home testing might distance women from the support network of
the medical establishment and might delay medical care for abnormal
pregnancies, but there is no evidence that this is the case. The warnings
about abnormal pregnancies and false negatives contained in the at-home
testing kits may on occasion facilitate entry into the medical system.

Symptoms of early pregnancy have commonly been attributed to psychogenic factors, although the bulk of evidence points to a physiological
basis (Lennane & Lennane, 1973). Women frequently feel tired, bloated,
and nauseated much of the time and may not yet be ready to share the
news with friends and family in order to obtain much needed social reinforcement. Trying to involve the male partner may be difficult at this
stage. Many men react to the news of early pregnancy by increased involvement in work or by retreat into hobbies (Colman & Colman, 1971).
The male partner may not visualize a baby until well into pregnancy,
whereas the woman necessarily must quickly make adjustments in her
life. The divergence of the impact of parenting on husbands' and wives'
social roles may make its first appearance in the wife's physical adaptation
to pregnancy.

Second trimester

A number of physical and psychosocial landmarks occur during second
trimester. A woman first feels movement and starts to "show"; she now
wears maternity clothes, adopts a new social role, and adjusts to a changing
body image. In recent years this has become a time in which prenatal
genetic studies and ultrasounds may occur, topics discussed later in the
chapter. Quickening, or the first perceived fetal movement, usually occurs
approximately 19 weeks after the last menstrual period. Quickening has
assumed a major role in many cultures and in psychoanalytic thought.
Historically, it was the first definite sign a woman might have that she
was pregnant. In early Catholic doctrine, a woman was not considered
pregnant until quickening occurred; any termination of a pregnancy before
quickening was not considered an abortion (Mohr, 1978).

As the pregnancy becomes physically obvious, women start to wear maternity clothes. Most women worry about their changing body shape and the often conflicting advice they receive on weight gain. Obstetrical advice in years past has been contradictory; for a time in the 1950s and 1960s women were pressured by obstetricians to diet and use diuretics to keep their gain under 15 pounds. The medical evidence actually has pointed consistently to an optimal gain of 20 to 30 pounds for women of normal weight; this gain is due to the combined weight of fetus, placenta, amniotic fluid, increased maternal blood volume, and small normal maternal fat stores (Naeye, 1979). Underweight women should gain more, women with twins should gain more, and overweight women should gain less (Naeye, 1979). Despite social pressure and medical advice, however, a large number of pregnant women gain too much or too little weight. Little research has been done on the psychological reasons for excessive or inadequate prenatal weight gain.

As a woman's pregnancy becomes apparent, she may resent the sense that her personal life seems to have become public property. Many women report annoyance at the fact that co-workers, casual acquaintances, and strangers feel free to pat their abdomen and make comments about subjects ranging from sex to diet to body size. In one sense this interest reflects a healthy involvement by the larger social network in issues of parenting and family life. But the woman who has tried to separate her personal life from her public image may find this intrusion highly irritating. Even an otherwise minor act such as drinking an alcoholic beverage, smoking a cigarette, or having a cup of coffee may get disapproving stares from friends and strangers. Men are not immune to social pressures at this time. Even though wives increasingly continue to work after childbearing and the prebaby two-income family remains that way, men report feeling that their role as "breadwinner" comes under scrutiny. They may feel pressured by their wives and extended family to cut down on all-male social activities in recognition of upcoming family responsibilities (Colman & Colman, 1971).

Third trimester

By the third trimester, the physical discomforts as well as the emotional impact of pregnancy intensify. In a normal pregnancy, the mother may experience normal discomforts such as tiredness, heartburn, muscle aches in the pelvic area, and disturbed sleep due to discomfort and anxiety. Concrete plans must be made for supplies and space for the newborn. Working women must make arrangements for time off from work, and often try to make major career decisions at the same time. Many couples take childbirth education classes, which serve the dual role of educating them about the birth process and providing a peer group of prospective parents – a support system that may be particularly important for the father, who until now may have had little extended social recognition of his role. Since the childbirth education network in many locales is independent of the medical care system, couples may get mixed or even contradictory messages from the two sources. Although it is healthy to some extent for couples to recognize that there are variations in ways of managing delivery, at times they may be more anxious if the childbirth classes undermine trust in the medical system.

A major fear of the third trimester is that something will be wrong with the baby. This almost universal fear may occupy various levels of conscious and subconscious thought. Nightmares are common during this period; Deutsch (1945) attributed these to an attempt to deal with separation conflicts. Many women have nightmares about labor itself. Women commonly also describe nightmares about deformed or dead infants. Although a number of rituals, including baby showers and room preparation, occur at this time, many women are fearful during these preparations and superstitious that such concrete plans could be too presumptuous and bring on tragedy. Many women, as well, during the third trimester experience more intense ambivalence about having a baby (Colman & Colman, 1971). Working women and women with small children may fare better psychologically even though they may feel exhausted physically during their final weeks, since the simple mechanics of keeping busy with familiar activity defuses some anxiety. Participation in childbirth education classes also diminishes couples' anxiety by increasing their sense of knowledge about and control over the delivery process (Beck et al., 1980).

The obstetrician–patient relationship

A number of popular books have outlined consumer frustration with certain aspects of American obstetrical practice (Arms, 1975; Haire, 1974; Harrison, 1982; Kitzinger, 1972). One of the most commonly used obstetrical texts admits the following in the first chapter:

There is no question that some individuals who collaborate in the effort to provide in-hospital care for the mother and the fetus-infant have not necessarily been as considerate of the pregnant mother and her family as they should have been. The expectant mother has been commonly treated as if she were seriously ill, even when she was quite healthy. All too often she has been forced to conform to a common pathway of care that stripped her of most of her individuality and much of her dignity. . . .

. . . In recent years, obstetricians, for many good reasons, have worked mostly in groups; as a consequence, about the time of delivery – the ultimate event in the minds of mother and her family – there may have been either a "changing of the obstetric guard" or the obstetrician created the appearance of wanting to hurry up the labor and delivery since he or she would soon be "going off." . . . Too often the expectant mother has felt that her fate and the fate of her baby were dependent not so much on skilled personnel but upon a mysterious electronic gadget that appeared to possess inherently some great power that prevailed above all others. (Pritchard, MacDonald, & Gant, 1985)

This passage summarizes some of the consumer's concerns about contemporary obstetrical practices. Obstetricians have been accused of being brusque, insensitive, hurried, and above all more interested in the dollar than in the patient. As a result, some women have turned to home deliveries, midwife deliveries, and/or alternative birthing centers to avoid the perceived inflexibility of hospital "routines" and to avoid the high cesarean rates associated with hospital care.

At the root of this problem is the inherent vulnerability of a woman seeking obstetrical care. Despite the fact that they are not basically "sick," few first-time mothers have any idea of what to expect during pregnancy and delivery, and that lack of knowledge can lead to great dependence on the obstetrician as a source of knowledge and reassurance. At the same time, widespread public perception of delivery as a "natural" process has led couples to expect a "good" experience during pregnancy and delivery; often if there are complications they blame the obstetrician.

One way of avoiding conflicts is the careful choice of an obstetrician. Some women gravitate toward female obstetricians with the perception that they may be more empathetic; there are few data to support this assumption. A small minority of patients choose home births or alternative birthing centers as a way of avoiding the interventions associated with hospital procedures. Gradually hospitals have been changing these procedures and creating birthing rooms and family-centered maternity care to give couples a more relaxing environment.

As an obstetrician, I think many obstetricians feel caught in a crunch of conflicting demands. Obstetrical training focuses on utilizing high technology. The courts generally have held obstetricians liable for failing to use available technologies such as fetal monitoring or cesarean section if a baby suffers birth trauma. Although in most cases the needs of mother and baby coincide, in many instances choices must be made between procedures that trade off increased maternal risk for decreased fetal risk. In many cases, the wishes of the parents, hospital protocols, concerns about potential liability for a "bad baby," and the needs of other waiting patients are in conflict.

The pressures and economic demands (i.e., office overhead and high malpractice premiums) in obstetrics have led the majority of obstetricians into group practice. Although patients can accept on a conscious level that obstetricians have a need for time with their families, on a subconscious level they may feel that the obstetrician should be available for their particular delivery. However, being on call 7 days per week leads to the very burnout and brusqueness that so many women complain about! Female obstetricians may feel this crunch the most, since they have been socialized to put a high priority on family time and are less likely to have a homebound caretaker for their own children.

The hallmark of the obstetrician–patient relationship is probably its intensity. In almost no other circumstance is an otherwise healthy individual seeing a doctor so often at such a critical time in her life. In some ways, she is putting both her own life and that of her child in the obstetrician's hands. The irony of the relationship is that in most instances mother and baby will do fine regardless of any interventions or lack thereof, but when things do go wrong they are catastrophic emotionally, physically, and financially. This intense relationship is stressful for both the patient and the obstetrician; when needs are met the rewards are great, but when needs are not met much anger is generated. As one obstetrician put it, "You get thanked for things that are not your doing and blamed for things that are not your fault."

Birth

Birth itself is, of course, one of the most basic and moving of human experiences. Virtually every culture has built up elaborate rituals around the birth process; our own culture is no exception. What has been unfortunate in this culture, however, is the fact that, in recent generations, the informal "handing down" of birth stories and experiences to succeeding generations has broken down, first in the Victorian era, when such matters were never discussed, then by the preempting of the firsthand experience of birth by the introduction of obstetrical anesthesia (Arms, 1975). An entire generation of American women have little recall of their birth experiences owing to the heavily medicated deliveries of the 1950s and 1960s (Arms, 1975). However, many women welcomed the advent of medications that would promote a painless labor, and many physicians and women felt that they were being "modern" and were acting in women's best interest. It was only over time that a number of adverse affects of heavily medicated deliveries became apparent, ranging from possibly adverse affects on the infant (Brackbill et al., 1974) to the anger women experienced in later years over their lost experience (Arms, 1975) to the later realization that the first hour of life is an important time for early mother–infant and father–infant interaction (Curry, 1982; Greenberg & Brenner, 1977; Klaus et al., 1970). With the advent of natural childbirth preparation classes, there has been an increasing demand for very minimal amounts of labor analgesia; obstetrical practice has reflected these changing demands, and new techniques of labor anesthesia such as epidural anesthesia (a nonsedating "regional block" anesthetic) have been developed in an attempt to offer the best of both worlds.

Two sometimes conflicting trends have become apparent in birthing practices in recent decades. There is increasing consumer demand for "natural," unmedicated, noninterventive births; at the same time obstetrical technology has advanced rapidly, with increasing dependence on a variety of equipment for ensuring healthy babies. A number of feminist writers have interpreted medical intervention in the childbirth process as a means for a male-dominated medical profession to wrest control of a natural, safe process out of the hands of women themselves; this effort to control the childbirth process is attributed to a combination of economic and sexist issues. There is enough support for this line of thinking to have resulted in a number of widely read books and articles (Arms, 1975; Haire, 1974; Harrison, 1982; Kitzinger, 1972; Rich, 1976). A beneficial effect of pressure from such feminist writers has been some willingness on the part of the obstetrical profession to reconsider "routine" procedures and a relaxing of rigid hospital routines. As a result, many hospitals offer "homelike birthing rooms" rather than sterile operating-room-like settings for labor and delivery; such "routines" as enemas, shaving of perineal hair, separation of infants from their parents, and others that women found dehumanizing are being dispensed with in many hospitals. In recognition of women's desires for a family-centered experience, many hospitals now allow husbands, friends, and family members to be present during labor, delivery, and even cesarean sections. Obstetricians and delivery room nurses are likelier to be knowledgeable about and supportive of natural childbirth techniques. Although these changes may seem trivial, it has taken years of consumer pressure to bring them about; even now physicians in obstetrical training programs are likely to have relatively little exposure to feminist thinking about childbirth routines or techniques for noninterventive birth. Despite predictions of early feminist writers that there would be a massive movement toward home births and alternative birth settings, these continue to represent only a tiny fraction of American births. The acknowledgment by virtually all of the free-standing birth centers of the need for careful patient screening and immediate hospital backup lends credence to the medical profession's claim that there can indeed be problems during delivery that may require rapid medical intervention.

The birth process itself is a complex integration of natural forces, parental expectations, and medical interventions aimed at meeting varied goals. At times the goals – healthy baby, healthy mother, happy experience, natural process – may have conflicting meanings. The process may assume an undue importance in the minds of couples planning to have an infant, perhaps because they assume a good outcome. In the meantime, the medical professionals may fixate on the outcome and pay relatively little attention to the process. Although the majority of people have positive feelings about the birth experience, a bad experience can result in a sense of failure and/or anger, which can negatively affect parenting ability (Marut & Mercer, 1979; Sugarman, 1977).

Despite the stresses of pregnancy and childbirth, suicide and psychiatric hospitalization rates are low during pregnancy (Kane et al., 1969; Paffenbarger, 1964; Rosenberg & Silver, 1965) but high postpartum (Butts, 1969; Pugh, Jerath, Schmidt, & Reed, 1963). Whereas pregnancy and birth are important processes, the early weeks and months of new parenting may be a critical time for medical surveillance and intervention as meticulous as that given to pregnancy and birth.

Thus far, we have looked at traditional transitional issues in pregnancy. But modern technology has introduced a number of wrinkles into the traditional process. The following section deals with some of these technological advances and how they may affect the process of parenting.

Technological considerations

Several technologies have affected the pregnancy and parenting process. Ultrasound enables parents to visualize fetal parts and a beating heart as early as the first trimester. Antenatal genetic testing can screen for an increasingly large number of defects, and screening tests such as the AFP (alpha-fetoprotein) blood test may provide useful but sometimes confusing and unsought information. Later in pregnancy, fetal monitoring can identify babies at risk for problems during labor, but may lead to unnecessary intervention and increased maternal risk. Obstetricians often feel squeezed between court decisions that demand that every technology available be used and parents who demand that costs be kept low and intervention minimal. We could look at many different technologies but will use ultrasound, amniocentesis, AFP testing, and fetal monitoring as examples of the ways that new technologies are changing the pregnancy and parenting process.

Ultrasonography is a technique in which high-frequency sound waves are transmitted through human tissues. As some of the sound waves bounce off of tissues of differing densities, the refracted sound waves are integrated by computer circuitry into a "picture" of the internal structures. Since ultrasound can identify soft-tissue planes and lacks the now well-known risks of radiation exposure, it is particularly well adapted to in utero examinations. It has become increasingly useful in obstetrics for determining fetal position and size, localizing the placenta, dating pregnancies, diagnosing multiple gestations, and even diagnosing certain fetal abnormalities (Sabbagha, 1980).

Concerns have been raised about the safety of ultrasound. In an extensive literature review, Abdulla (1980) cites scores of studies that fail to demonstrate any harmful effects of ultrasound in both in vitro cell cultures and a wide variety of animal and human studies (Sabbagha, 1980). However, he also cites a scattering of studies showing increases in growth retardation, death, and paraplegia in rodents and some gonadal damage in animal gonads subjected to high-intensity sound waves. Thus far, no human epidemiological evidence suggests any increase in defects in children exposed in utero to ultrasound, and since the technique has been widely used for more than 20 years it seems less and less likely that any ill effects will be found. But the memory of diethylstilbestrol (Holt & Herbst, 1981) and the dangers of early x-ray exposure still hang over any new technique. Parents, therefore, are sometimes in the difficult position of having a technique recommended by their physician but not being entirely sure of its safety. Meanwhile, physicians are reluctant not to use ultrasound to confirm dating or detect multiple gestation or major anomalies for fear of being liable legally for failing to detect problems.

Virtually no research has been conducted regarding the emotional impact of visualizing a fetus on ultrasound. Many couples comment that they feel more bonded to a developing fetus after seeing its image on the ultrasound; it is not unusual for a woman to decide against a late abortion after ultrasonography. (Many institutions require ultrasound dating for late abortion to avoid terminating gestations that are too advanced.) Since amniocentesis for genetic testing is done with ultrasonographic guidance, the visualization of the fetus may make the decision to terminate if an abnormality is found considerably more wrenching psychologically. Advance notice about twins is usually considered advantageous to parents, because it allows for appropriate high-risk medical care and logistical preparation for two infants. But what of the parents who learn of a fetal anomaly? If a lethal anomaly is identified in the early months of pregnancy, some parents will find a termination less devastating emotionally than the full-term delivery of a baby who dies soon thereafter. But many of the abnormalities that are found, such as cystic kidneys or hydrocephalus, may not be detected until it is too late to terminate a pregnancy and may carry uncertain prognoses anyway, leaving parents agonizing over unanswered questions before the birth.

Genetic screening

Amniocentesis and chorionic villus sampling are techniques for collecting cells that contain fetal genetic material, allowing for the detection of gross genetic defects and certain other types of inherited defects at a time when abortion is still possible. In amniocentesis, the physician collects a small sample of amniotic fluid by sticking a long needle through the abdominal wall; cell cultures of fetal cells floating in the amniotic fluid are set up. The procedure cannot be done until there is sufficient amniotic fluid to allow safe removal (usually approximately 16 weeks from the last menses), and cell cultures may take as long as 3 to 4 weeks to grow, necessitating very rapid counseling and decision making if a couple decides to terminate a pregnancy with a defect. The procedure is relatively low risk but seems to carry an increased risk of fetal loss of a little less than 0.05%, while maternal risk is almost negligible; accuracy is greater than 99% (Milunsky, 1975).

Chorionic villus sampling (CVS) involves inserting a small catheter up the vagina through the cervix and taking a sample of placental tissue. Its major advantage is that it is generally done at approximately 10 weeks' gestation, and the results are obtained within days since direct karyotyping (genetic analysis) can be performed on the tissue obtained. Thus, women obtain the results early enough for a safer first-trimester abortion, a procedure that in addition to its greater maternal safety most women find considerably easier to accept psychologically and ethically. The disadvantages of CVS sampling are that the risks are not as well known as those of amniocentesis but seem to run a bit higher, including a few cases of serious maternal infection (Ward, Modell, Petron, Karagozlu, & Douratsos, 1983). In addition, rates of abnormalities detected by CVS are higher than expected, leading to speculation that the test may have a higher false positive rate than does amniocentesis, although it is more likely that CVS is simply detecting abnormalities that might have led to miscarriage anyway.

The combination of genetic screening and availability of legal abortion have introduced a new level of decision making into the process of becoming a parent. Becoming a parent has always been a risky business, even more so in the past when both infant mortality and maternal mortality were high. In most cultures, couples are expected to follow certain behaviors, either dietary and lifestyle behaviors or ritualistic behaviors, to ensure the birth of a healthy baby (Newton & Mead, 1967). Recently, increased medical appreciation of the risks of exposure to teratogens during pregnancy has led to even more restrictions on the use of medications and abuse substances such as alcohol and tobacco. But the addition of an invasive test that can detect fetal defects and the implicit concept that parents might well abort an abnormal baby are more recent phenomena. Whereas abortion itself is an ancient procedure (Mohr, 1978), aborting a wanted pregnancy because of a tragic defect is a recent phenomenon. As more and more defects become detectable through screening, this will be an issue couples will increasingly have to confront.

There is a very thin line between having a test available and being pressured to have the test done. In general, parents garner much sympathy when a defective infant is born. Will parents feel less support and sympathy when an infant is born with a detectable defect for which they failed to screen? Doctors have been held liable for failing to counsel parents that a test is available; can holding the parents responsible for failing to have the test done be far behind?

Another antenatal test that involves complex issues is the AFP blood test. AFP is a protein made in the fetal central nervous system. It is used obstetrically mainly to detect fetuses with open neural tube defects (in which the spinal canal and/or brainstem have failed to close completely). There are significant problems with the AFP test: It has a large false positive rate (elevated values for reasons other than neural tube defects), and even for true positive tests, careful assessment by an experienced ultrasonographer may reveal defects ranging from very serious to fairly minor problems. Some babies with neural tube defects can lead almost normal lives; some will be significantly handicapped and severely retarded (Allen et al., 1982; Pritchard et al., 1985).

Testing antenatally for AFP raises some complicated issues. Since it is a simple blood test for the mother, it may at times be part of "routine" testing; however, an abnormal result is an indication for rather elaborate follow-up examinations and counseling. The issues raised with parents are not nearly as clear-cut as they are in the case of many genetic abnormalities, since it may be difficult to predict what the baby's functional level will be. In contrast to amniocentesis or CVS, in which the parents have made a conscious decision to seek the information provided by the test, AFP screening often does not require that conscious effort because it is often routine. In addition, low AFP levels have been associated with a number of fetal anomalies including Down syndrome (Davenport & Macri, 1983), which can again provide unsought information that may require additional and sometimes unnecessary testing.

Fetal monitoring: whose rights prevail?

Another area where technology is changing the pregnancy and birthing process is that of electronic fetal monitoring (EFM). EFM is a means of recording both a fetus's heartbeat and uterine contractions continuously. EFM can be done externally by means of an ultrasound transducer for the baby's heart rate and a pressure transducer on a belt attached to the mother's abdomen, or internally by means of a metal electrode attached to the baby's head and a fluid-filled tube inside the uterus attached to a pressure gauge. In general, there are distinctive differences in heart rate patterns between healthy babies and compromised babies.

Since it has come into widescale use, EFM has been controversial. During the 1960s and 1970s, hospitals used fetal monitors first on high-risk but then eventually on almost all patients (Hughey, LaPata, & Lussky, 1977; Ingermarssen, Ingermarssen, & Svenningsen, 1981). Monitoring is prone to a high number of false positives (healthy babies with a distressed-appearing monitor tracing) and, rarely, false negatives (distressed infants with reassuring tracings). Most obstetricians feel that monitoring gives them a minute-by-minute update on the status of the baby and that, by continuously monitoring most women in labor, they can deliver better babies. In defense of this claim, supporters of EFM point to the consistent decline in infant mortality and morbidity observed over the years that EFM has come into widescale use (Pritchard et al., 1985) and to specific studies showing improvement in outcome when fetal monitoring is used routinely (Hughey et al., 1977; Ingemarssen et al., 1981).

Critics of EFM feel that it diverts personal attention and caregiving from the mother (Arms, 1975; Haire, 1974). Critics also blame much of the dramatic increase in cesarean section on EFM "false positives" (Gleicher, 1984). In addition, the handful of small, randomized studies comparing EFM to idealized bedside one-on-one clinical auscultation of fetal heart tones generally have failed to demonstrate any statistically significant benefit from EFM (Haverkamp, Thompson, McFee, & Cetrulo, 1976). Advocates of EFM are quick to point out that such studies bear little resemblance to real-life delivery situations in which such staffing would be impossible to maintain at all times.

Perhaps sadly, the issue that determines whether mothers will be monitored in labor may well be the U.S. legal system. Obstetricians fear that, if they deliver a compromised infant, they will be held liable for failing to monitor the baby. They also believe that, if they have a monitor tracing, it will help to defend their actions either on the grounds that they had evidence of fetal well-being before delivery or on the grounds that a fetal injury was preexisting and not preventable.

At the heart of the controversy over interventionistic obstetrics is the issue of cesarean section. The U.S. cesarean rate has risen dramatically, approaching 20% (Placek & Taffel, 1983). It seems ironic that at the same time that the "natural" childbirth movement is leading to an increased demand for noninterventionistic births, the push to minimize infant morbidity and mortality is leading to one in five deliveries requiring major surgery. This trend is tied very closely to both high-technology obstetrics and the medical malpractice arena. There are certain obstetrical situations (prolonged labor, large babies, twins, breech [feet-first] presentations) in which fetal injury is a little more likely to occur in a difficult vaginal delivery. Fearful of both lawsuits and of feeling responsible for a fetal injury, obstetricians are increasingly likely to perform a cesarean when fetal injury seems even remotely possible. Unfortunately, cesarean section is riskier for the mother than is vaginal birth (Pritchard et al., 1985), so the issue becomes one of increased fetal risk versus increased maternal risk.

Unfortunately, many couples invest a great deal in the normal birthing process and feel a sense of failure when a cesarean is performed (Marut & Mercer, 1979; Sugarman, 1977). Clearly, the rise in cesarean rates is due to technological, legal, and social trends that are outside the control of the individual parent, but the attitudes that many couples carry into the labor room are forged out of an earlier time. Also unfortunately, recent feminist works that rightly challenge the frequency of cesareans may add to the "blaming the victim" mentality, making women feel that, if only they had been more relaxed, more assertive, "better," they could have avoided cesarean section (Arms, 1975; Haire, 1974).

Conclusions

Pregnancy and birth are times of both crisis and growth for individuals and couples. Demographic trends indicate that pregnancy is occupying a relatively short time span in the adult life cycle. Many people who have prepared for a wide variety of careers and adult activities may be poorly prepared for parenting. In our highly mobile society, many expectant parents also lack the extended family and social support network that has traditionally helped to ease the transition into parenthood.

Changing medical technology is rapidly and drastically changing the transition to parenthood. Recent advances in the fields of infertility, antenatal diagnosis of defects, and care of sick newborns are resulting in benefits to couples who previously would not have had surviving children, but at the same time are creating some agonizing decisions for parents, health professionals, and the courts.

This is a challenging but often frustrating time to practice obstetrics. On the one hand, couples are demanding noninterventionistic, "natural" childbirth experiences. On the other hand, a trained obstetrician is expected to make use of available technology to ensure the best possible outcome. I often yearn for an era (which probably never existed) when babies simply came out, and if they were ill it was considered an act of God, not a lapse on the part of the obstetrician. In many areas of the country, a substantial proportion of obstetrician-gynecologists are dropping obstetrics from their practices, in large part because of the huge insurance premiums and high jury awards that result from the "blame the obstetrician" mentality whenever a birth injury occurs.

The trend toward low birthrates and later childbearing may be aggravating the pressure on parents and obstetricians alike to make every baby a perfect baby. Older women face a variety of increased risks during pregnancy and childbirth, and are often more dependent on the medical system for care. With many parents planning only one or two babies, the pressure is enormous on all concerned to ensure that their offspring are normal.

In the immediate future, the conflict between high-technology fetal surveillance and the naturalistic expectations of parents is likely to get worse before it gets better. Rapid advances in technology will lead to more prenatal screening tests being available; greater availability will gradually give way to pressure on parents to have screening tests done and the expectation that they will prevent the birth of a child with defects. The increasing unwillingness of obstetricians to risk delivering a "bad baby" will result in cesarean sections whenever there is a question of fetal compromise. In the long run, social expectations likely will change to mesh with the new technologies, but those changes may be slow and fraught with conflicts.

A final challenge to obstetrical practice in easing the transition to parenthood will arise in the arena of improving the transition of medical care from obstetrician to pediatrician. As mentioned previously, parents often express a sense of letdown from the very close dependency relationship that may develop with an obstetrician to an often casual relationship with a pediatrician for well-baby care. The advantages of a close interaction between obstetrical perinatologists and pediatric neonatologists has already been demonstrated in the area of high-risk obstetrics (Lee & Paneth, 1980).

Ideally, this model of teamwork could be incorporated into the area of routine antenatal and well-baby care as well. The necessary contact between parents-to-be and health care professionals represents an exciting opportunity for the recognition of problems and early intervention; one would hope that the problems facing the field of obstetrics will not interfere with the opportunity to help parents make a successful adaptation to their parental role.

References

Abdulla, U. (1980). Biological effects of ultrasound. In R. Sabbagha (Ed.), *Diagnostic ultrasound applied to obstetrics and gynecology* (pp. 10–25). New York; Harper & Row.

Allen, L. C., Doran, T, A., Miskin, M., Rudd, N. L., Benzie, R. J., & Sheffield, L. J. (1982). Ultrasound and amniotic fluid alpha-fetoprotein in the prenatal diagnosis of spina bifida. *Obstetrics and Gynecology, 60,* 169–73.

Arms, S. (1975). *Immaculate deception: A new look at childbirth in America.* Boston: Houghton Mifflin.

Beck, N. C., Siegel, L., Davidson, N., Kormeier, S., Breitenstein, A., & Hall, D. (1980). The prediction of pregnancy outcome: Maternal preparation, anxiety, and attitudinal sets. *Journal of Psychosomatic Research, 24,* 343–51.

Brackbill, Y., Kane, J., Manniello, R., & Abramson, D. (1974). Obstetric meperidine usage and assessment of neonatal status. *Anesthesiology, 40,* 116–20.

Brenner, P., & Greenberg, M. (1977, July). The impact of pregnancy on marriage. *Medical Aspects of Human Sexuality,* pp. 15–21.

Brody, E. B. (1978). The meaning of the first pregnancy for working class Jamaican women. In W. B. Miller & L. F. Newman (Eds.), *The first child and family formation.* Chapel Hill: University of North Carolina, Carolina Population Center.

Butts, H. F. (1969). Postpartum psychiatric problems: A review of the literature dealing with etiologic theories. *Journal of the National Medical Association, 61,* 136–9.

Caplan, G. (1954). Psychological aspects of maternity care. *American Journal of Public Health, 47,* 25–9.

Colman, A., & Colman, L. (1971). *Pregnancy: The psychological experience.* New York: Herder & Herder.

Curry, M. A. (1982). Maternal attachment behavior and the mother's self-concept: The effect of early skin-to-skin contact. *Nursing Research, 31,* 73–8.

Davenport, D. M., & Macri, J. N. (1983). The clinical significance of low maternal serum alpha-fetoprotein. *American Journal of Obstetrics and Gynecology, 146,* 657–61.

Deutsch, H. (1945). *The psychology of women.* New York: Grune & Stratton.

Gladieux, J. D. (1978). Pregnancy and the transition to parenthood. In W. B. Miller & L. F. Newman (Eds.), *The first child and family formation.* Chapel Hill: University of North Carolina, Carolina Population Center.

Gleicher, N. (1984). Cesarean section rates in the U.S. *Journal of the American Medical Association, 252,* 3273–6.

Goshen-Gottstein, E. (1966). *Marriage and first pregnancy: Cultural influences and attitudes of Israeli women.* London: Tavistock.

Greenberg, M., & Brenner, P. (1977, August). The newborn's impact on parents' marital and sexual relationship. *Medical Aspects of Human Sexuality,* pp. 16–22.

Haire, D. (1974). *The cultural warping of childbirth.* Seattle: Internation Childbirth Association.

Hall, D. E., & Mohr, G. J. (1933). Prenatal attitudes of primiparae. *Mental Hygiene, 17,* 226–34.

Harrison, M. (1982). *A woman in residence.* New York: Random House.

Haverkamp, A. D., Thompson, H. E., McFee, J. G., & Cetrulo, C. (1976). The evaluation of continuous fetal heart rate monitoring in high-risk pregnancy. *American Journal of Obstetrics and Gynecology, 125,* 310–15.

Holt, L. H., & Herbst, A. L. (1981). DES: Thirty years later. *Perinatology–Neonatology, 5,* 14–21.

Hubert, J. (1974). Belief and reality: Social factors in pregnancy and childbirth. In M. P. Richard (Ed.), *The integration of a child into a social world.* Cambridge University Press.

Hughey, M., LaPata, R. E., & Lussky, R. (1977). The effect of fetal monitoring on the incidence of Cesarean section. *Obstetrics and Gynecology, 49,* 513–19.

Ingemarsson, E., Ingemarsson, I., & Svenningsen, N. W. (1981). Impact of routine fetal monitoring on fetal outcome with long-term followup. *American Journal of Obstetrics and Gynecology, 141*(1), 29–36.

Kane, F., Jr., Lipton, M. A., & Ewing, J. A. (1969). Hormonal influences in female sexual response. *Archives of General Psychiatry, 20,* 202–9.

Kitzinger, S. (1972). *The experience of childbirth.* New York: Taplinger.

Klaus, M., Kennell, J., Plumb, N., & Zuehlke, S. (1970). Human maternal behavior at first contact with her young. *Pediatrics, 46,* 187–92.

Lee, K. S., & Paneth, N. (1980). Neonatal mortality: An analysis of the recent improvement in the United States. *American Journal of Public Health, 70,* 15–21.

Lennane, K. J., & Lennane, R. J. (1973). Alleged psychogenic disorders in women: A possible manifestation of sexual prejudice. *New England Journal of Medicine, 288,* 288–92.

Marut, J. S., & Mercer, R. T. (1979). Comparison of primiparas' perceptions of vaginal and Cesarean births. *Nursing Research, 28,* 260–6.

Milunsky, A. (1975). Risk of amniocentesis for prenatal diagnosis (editorial). *New England Journal of Medicine, 293,* 932–3.

Mohr, James C. (1978). *Abortion in America: The origins and evolution of national policy 1800–1900.* New York: Oxford University Press.

Naeye, R. L. (1979). Weight gain and the outcome of pregnancy. *American Journal of Obstetrics and Gynecology, 135,* 3–9.

National Center for Health Statistics. (1982). Advance report of final natality statistics, 1980. *Monthly Vital Statistics Report, 31* (Suppl.), 8.

Newton, N. (1973). Interrelationships between sexual responsiveness, birth, and breast feeding. In J. E. Zubin & M. Money (Eds.), *Contemporary sexual behavior: Critical issues in the 1970s.* Baltimore, MD: Johns Hopkins University Press.

Newton, N., & Mead, M. (1967). Cultural patterning of perinatal behavior. In S. Richardson & A. Guttmacher (Eds.), *Contemporary sexual behavior: Critical issues in the 1970s.* Baltimore, MD: Williams & Wilkins.

Ory, H. W. (1983). Mortality associated with fertility and fertility control: 1983. *Family Planning Perspectives, 15,* 57–63.

Paffenbarger, R. S. (1964). Epidemiologic aspects of parapartum mental illness. *British Journal of Preventive and Social Medicine, 18,* 189–95.

Placek, P. J., & Taffel, S. M. (1983). The frequency of complications in cesarean and non-cesarean deliveries, 1970 and 1978. *Public Health Reports, 98,* 396–400.

Pritchard, J. A., MacDonald, P. C., & Gant, N. F. (1985). *Williams' Obstetrics* (17th Ed.). Norwalk, CN: Appleton-Century-Crofts.

Pugh, T. F., Jerath, B. K., Schmidt, W. M., & Reed, R. B. (1963). Rates of mental disease related to childbearing. *New England Journal of Medicine, 268,* 1224–8.

Roghmann, K., & Doherty, R. (1983). Reassurance through prenatal diagnosis and willingness to bear children after age 35. *American Journal of Public Health, 73,* 760–2.

Rosenberg, A. J., & Silver, E. (1965). The psychiatrist and therapeutic abortion. *California Medicine, 143,* 407–11.

Sabbagha, R. E. (1980). Congenital anomalies. In R. E. Sabbagha (Ed.), *Diagnostic ultrasound applied to obstetrics and gynecology.* New York: Harper & Row.

Schwartz, D., & Mayaux, M. J. (1982). Female fecundity as a function of age. *New England Journal of Medicine, 306,* 373–4.

Sugarman, M. (1977). Paranatal influences on maternal–infant attachment. *American Journal of Orthopsychiatry, 47,* 407–21.

Thornton, A., Freedman, D. (1982). Changing attitudes towards marriage and single life. *Family Planning Perspectives, 14,* 297–9.

Vessey, M. P., Meisler, R., Flavell, R., & Yates, D. (1979). Outcome of pregnancy in women using different methods of contraception. *British Journal of Obstetrics and Gynecology, 86,* 548–55.

Ward, R. H., Modell, B., Petrou, M., Karogozlu, F., & Douratsos, E. (1983). Method of sampling chorionic villi in first trimester of pregnancy under guidance of real time ultrasound. *British Medical Journal, 286,* 1542–4.

6 Effects of infant risk status on the transition to parenthood

M. Ann Easterbrooks

Normative stressors and crises refer to those changes or life cycle transitions that are expected and predictable, which most, or even all, families will experience over the life cycle and which require adjustment and adaptation.

H. McCubbin and C. Figley, *Stress and the Family*

The chapters of this volume suggest that the successful negotiation of the transition to parenthood is an important family life event for the couple (as individuals, marital partners, and parents) and for their child. This transition period is thought to be a focal point of psychological development or regression for the individual and the relationship between the couple (Wynne, 1984). Most new parents meet the challenges of this developmental period successfully, although some degree of stress during the transition is normative (Cowan & Cowan, 1983). Viewed from different theoretical perspectives, the transition to parenthood has been alternately called a life crisis (Hobbs, 1965; Russell, 1974) and a normative development event (Belsky, Spanier, & Rovine, 1983). Whether one assumes the "crisis" or "normative life event" orientation, discussion of the transition to parenthood has been based on the model of a low-risk pregnancy and the birth of a normal infant. Most research studies, in fact, eliminate risk factors (e.g., medical, social, psychological) in order to reduce the "noise in the data." By doing so, theory and research on the transition to parenthood have failed to consider whether this model "fits" for couples who experience a high-risk pregnancy or the birth of a high-risk infant. For these couples, the transition to parenthood may differ in process or outcome at the level of the individual, the dyad (marital, parent–child), and the family triad.

In this chapter I discuss the effects of infant risk status on the transition to parenthood. The term "infant risk status" itself encompasses a broad collection of medical and biological factors, ranging from medical risk factors during the pregnancy (e.g., gestational diabetes, toxemia, fetal alcohol syndrome) to preterm birth and congenital infant conditions such as Down syndrome, spina bifida, and cleft palate. These differing conditions vary on a number of dimensions, including chronicity, severity or degree to which they are life threatening, and the extent to which parents anticipated the birth of a preterm or damaged infant. Though biological or medical risk is not a unified category in itself, the scope of the problem is increased if one considers how biological risk interacts with other risk factors, namely, social risk (low socioeconomic status, teenage parenthood, single parenthood) and general psychological risk (emotional or marital difficulties, history of pregnancy complications or loss). A full discussion of the intersection of these factors is beyond the scope of the present chapter; however, those important issues are discussed in Chapters 3, 5, and 7 of this volume. Several other chapters provide the context for comparing the "normative" transition to parenthood with the case of high-risk birth.

With the birth of a child, parents enter a new phase of the transition to parenthood. Most commonly, the birth of a healthy infant is greeted by both mother and father as a positive, moving occasion, a "peak" experience (Greenberg, 1973; Greenberg & Morris, 1974; Klaus & Kennell, 1976). Some researchers report a "baby honeymoon" period (Hobbs, 1965), roughly the first 6 months postdelivery, during which marital satisfaction is enhanced when compared with that during pregnancy, although this notion has not been confirmed by other research (Wente & Crockenberg, 1976). On the contrary, most studies report that a decline in marital satisfaction is accompanied by the arrival of the first child, particularly for women (Belsky et al., 1983; Feldman, 1971; Hobbs, 1965; Hobbs & Cole, 1976; Ryder, 1973).

The entrance of a third individual into a dyadic marital system creates new possibilities for interactions and demands the creation of new roles. First-time mothers and fathers must construct new behavior patterns in interaction with each other as well as with their infant. Research grounded in family and social systems models has identified a number of variables that contribute to parents' success in developing and integrating new family roles. Salient among these variables are marital quality, parental personality characteristics, and social network support. Positive marital quality influences both parental behavior with the child and aspects of the child's socioemotional development (Belsky, 1986; Goldberg & Easterbrooks, 1984; Pedersen, Anderson, & Cain, 1977). The importance of parents' own childbearing history is noted in clinical statements emphasizing the remembrance "of the past in order to prepare for the future" (Lieberman, 1983, p. 104) and in parents' reports of increased reflection on their own parents (Leifer, 1977). Finally, a large number of studies have documented the influence of social networks and other forms of social support on adaptation to pregnancy and new parenthood (Belsky, 1983; Caplan, 1974; Cassell, 1974; Cowan & Cowan, 1983; Parke & Tinsley, 1983; Power & Parke, 1984; Shereshefsky & Yarrow, 1973). These data demonstrate that both formal (e.g., childbirth and parenting groups) and informal (family and friends) sources of practical, ideological, and emotional support influence mothers' and fathers' adaptation to new parenthood. All of this research, however, has focused on the typical low-risk case.

Infant risk and the transition to parenthood

In the preceding pages, I have briefly outlined some characteristics that set the stage for understanding the transition to parenthood for most couples. For some prospective parents, however, the transition to parenthood is clouded by a high-risk pregnancy or the birth of a high-risk infant.

A high-risk pregnancy has been defined broadly as one in which the physical or psychological health of the mother or infant may be compromised (Jones, 1979). The outcome of a high-risk pregnancy may be an infant with a congenital handicap, or a preterm birth, but the outlook is not always dim – healthy infants are frequently born following high-risk pregnancies in which the mother is hospitalized or on complete bed rest. At the same time, the outcome of uncomplicated, nonrisk pregnancies may be preterm delivery or the birth of a handicapped child. In comparing the transition to parenthood in situations of high-risk pregnancy versus the birth of a high-risk infant, it seems logical that one of the defining factors is the degree of parental anticipation of an uncomplicated pregnancy and the birth of a healthy full-term infant. I know of no studies that have explicitly compared the transition to parenthood for these two groups, and my review of the literature, which ranges widely in degree of methodological sophistication, suggests that, although variations may be influenced by expectations, planning, and anticipatory grief, there are many similarities in emotional responses. A similar conclusion may be advanced regarding different infant risk conditions. Although there are differences in severity, chronicity, treatment potential, and chances for long-term survival in such conditions as Down syndrome, preterm birth, or physical limb malformations, the early phases of the transition reveal many striking concordances.

During the past thirty years, improvements in prenatal care and perinatal medical technology have resulted in decreases in infant mortality and morbidity (Chase, 1977; Reed & Stanley, 1977; Usher, 1977). Despite these advances, in the past decade, approximately half of all high-risk pregnancies were associated with perinatal adversity of some nature (Kopp, 1983; Vaughn & McKay, 1975). Infant risk encompasses a broad spectrum. Kopp's (1983) comprehensive review chapter outlined types of prenatal (conception to the seventh month of pregnancy) and perinatal (seventh month of pregnancy through first month of life) risk. Prenatal factors, responsible for 85 to 90% of severe handicapping conditions in infants, include both genetic and environmental factors (chemicals, nutrition, maternal virus). Prenatal risk factors are also associated with such chromosomal aberrations as Down syndrome, congenital malformations (e.g., spina bifida, cleft palate), and enzyme or protein deficiencies (e.g., Tay Sachs). These prenatal conditions are often less easily detected and prevented than are perinatal risk factors – for example, hypoxia or other traumas around the time of birth, growth retardation, or preterm birth.

A note must be inserted regarding the empirical data base from which conclusions about infant risk status and the transition to parenthood may be drawn. First, these data represent many disciplines of inquiry (psychology, sociology, psychiatry, social work), with accompanying differences in perspectives and methods of collecting and reporting data. Many studies are clinical reports of interviews with parents of handicapped infants and often lack comparison control groups. In addition, many clinical reports of handicapped infants have focused on those parents who experience extended or severe problems in adaptation (for a discussion of this problem see Darling, 1983; Darling & Darling, 1982). The infant risk condition that has been studied with the greatest methodological sophistication is preterm birth. With this in mind, my discussion will focus heavily on the case of preterm birth.

Preterm birth is a major infant risk factor; it is related to severe problems in perinatal medicine and is the leading cause of infant perinatal death (fetal death after 20 weeks' gestation or when the weight of the fetus is greater than 500 grams) (Borg & Lasker, 1981; Callahan, Brasted, & Granados, 1983). The term "prematurity," or "preterm birth" as used here, refers to infants born before 37 weeks of gestational age and/or whose weight is 2,500 grams (5½ lb). The "causes" of preterm birth, or factors associated with increased risk, are diverse, including maternal health and nutrition before and during the pregnancy (chronic conditions such as diabetes and hypertension are included), low weight gain during pregnancy, alcohol and tobacco use during pregnancy, structural conditions of the uterus, and low socioeconomic status.

Since preterm birth is relatively more common than other types of infant risk conditions, it is cited as the most pressing issue in perinatal medicine and is represented by a number of well-controlled investigations. Although it is a factor that places the survival and healthy development of infants in jeopardy, the rate of survival and the long-term developmental course have improved in the past two decades. According to medical studies, 25 years ago, 40% of surviving preterm infants were found to exhibit neurological and intellectual deficits (Drillien, 1961), whereas the figures cited in more recent reports range from 10 to 30% for the very low birth weight or ill neonate (Ciba Foundation, 1978).

Effects on parents

Ordinarily, the resolution of the "crisis" of pregnancy is facilitated by the birth of a healthy, full-term infant. Though the transition to parenthood is experienced by some couples as a normative developmental event rather than a crisis (Belsky et al., 1983; Cowan & Cowan, 1983), those parents who are not able to meet the goals of a healthy full-term pregnancy "successfully" undoubtedly experience more stress (Borg & Lasker, 1981). For these couples, different psychological tasks join different practical tasks of parenting. Adaptation varies with the resources available to the parent: internal psychological and social support. On the basis of interviews with parents of seriously ill newborns, Penticuff (1980) states: "Coping mechanisms are mobilized. The family whose internal and external sources of support are great will deal constructively and realistically with the problems encountered. The family whose supports are weak has a high probability of failure in coping realistically . . . denial or distortion of the complications and serious illness in the newborn may impair realistic problem-solving approaches" (p. 171). As noted above, however, the dearth of well-controlled empirical investigations focused on these questions makes comparison with the normative case difficult. In the absence of convincing data, then, parents, professionals, and researchers may assume that the course should be similar. According to Friedlander (1980) this assumption is not without problems, since it places high demands on the parents of high-risk and disabled infants to follow "a regimen of attachment, self-sacrifice, self-denial, and repression" (p. 192).

Although the effects of risk status on parents are not well researched, clinical studies mention a host of emotional and psychological reactions of new parents. Some responses to a high-risk pregnancy or birth (such as fear and ambivalence) are found in the nonrisk case as well, differing only in degree (Comfort, 1980), whereas others may be more specific to risk status (e.g., grief and guilt). In order to facilitate understanding of the feelings encountered upon the birth of a risk infant, a brief example of a birth experience is provided below.

Scenario of a preterm birth

In the 30th week of her uncomplicated pregnancy, Betty awakens with some discomfort, which she attributes to "gas." She does not realize that she is beginning to enter labor until her water breaks, and even then what is happening seems like a dream. Her husband, Bill, cannot immediately understand that their child, due in 2½ months, is about to arrive. Both parents are unprepared for the early birth of the child, psychologically as well as practically. Planning for a natural childbirth experience, with as little medication as possible, Bill and Betty were soon to begin attending childbirth preparation classes. A room of their home was in the process of being made into a nursery, and neither furnishings nor clothing for the baby had been purchased. Betty had been planning the first 2 weeks of her maternity leave before the baby's due date in order to get everything in order. Betty and Bill were looking forward to the birth and enjoying their last months as a couple before the baby arrived. Suddenly, all of their plans and hopes changed as the arrival of their child became a crisis. The hospital was an unfamiliar setting; they had planned to tour the facilities 6 weeks before the due date. As is often the case in high-risk situations, the delivery took place by cesarean section instead of the unmedicated vaginal delivery they had hoped for. Though Bill was present at the birth, neither he nor Betty was able to hold the 2-pound baby, because she was rushed from the room before they had had more than a brief glance at her. Since the hospital did not have a special neonatal intensive care nursery, their daughter was transferred to a regional hospital 30 miles away. Bill accompanied his daughter in the ambulance, leaving Betty in the recovery room. Betty was transferred to a bed in the maternity ward, in a room with two other mothers of healthy, full-term infants. As Betty awaits word on her daughter, the other mothers and their husbands feed and play with their babies.

This brief scenario captures some of the events that may occur when an infant is born before his or her due date, at risk for respiratory and neurological problems. The question to be addressed is: What impact do these events have on parents' adaptation – their feelings and behaviors?

Parental emotions

Since it is likely that different individuals respond to this crisis in different ways, my approach here is to describe the variety of emotions that parents experience, rather than the typical case, particularly since these emotions are common to a variety of risk conditions. Although for all new parents there may be discrepancies in the images of a real and fantasized baby, for parents of a preterm, chronically ill infant or infant with special needs these discrepancies are great, based not only on the appearance of the baby but on the entire birth experience. Thus, denial ("This isn't really happening to me" or "What they are telling me isn't true") is a common early response. Taken to an extreme, denial can be maladaptive in preventing parents from developing active coping strategies, but a limited degree of denial as an immediate response has been reported to serve a protective function against forthcoming problems (Howard, 1978).

According to the model proposed by Klaus and Kennell (1976, 1982), as parents accept the reality of their situation, *grief and mourning* responses follow. Frequently, anticipatory grief develops during the course of a high-risk pregnancy or immediately at the birth of a high-risk infant. Grief is elicited by the violation of the hopes and expectations that developed for the child and the family during the pregnancy and even before conception in many cases. Depression accompanying the grief response is the most common reaction to the birth of a damaged infant; this depression may be similar to the mourning that occurs at the death of a child, which is less acute and longer lasting (D'Arcy, 1968; Solnit & Stark, 1961). When an infant is born prematurely, critically ill, or severely damaged, early anticipatory grief (Kaplan & Mason, 1960) may help with the resolution of a possible neonatal loss. In this case, feelings of love or investment are withheld to protect the parent from grief should the infant die. A recent study of reports of pediatricians and neonatologists to mothers of critically ill newborns concluded that physicians consistently underestimated the infant's chances of survival based on statistical data from their own hospital records and conveyed these impressions to mothers (Clyman, Snidermen, Ballard, & Roth, 1979). In this way, physicians may instigate anticipatory grief and expectations of infant death in parents. If the infant survives, parents may have difficulty making the transition from withdrawal and depression to an active and ongoing emotional relationship with the child. Taken further, the results of several studies suggest that failure to resolve grief or the continued expectation that the child may die can lead to the "vulnerable child syndrome," in which parents persist in their concerns about minor acute illnesses or abnormalities or act in an overprotective manner despite the fact that the child is no longer at medical risk (Crnic, Ragozin, Greenberg, Robinson, & Basham, 1983; Harmon, 1980; Klaus & Kennell, 1982; Korn, Chess, & Fernandez, 1978). These characteristics of parent–infant interaction will be discussed later in this chapter.

Feelings of *ambivalence* toward the baby, a mixture of anger and distress, are also common. When faced with a child who may have a variety of lasting handicaps (auditory, visual, neurological), new parents, who probably feel helpless and hopeless, experience anger directed toward the newborn as the cause of their distress. According to clinical reports, in the strongest case parents may sometimes wish for the child's death (Heisler, 1972). Since this response is not socially sanctioned, the new father and mother may not be comfortable discussing these negative feelings with each other or other family members, friends, or professionals. Lack of communication, coupled with guilt feelings, may prevent parents from realizing that these emotions are not atypical (Friedlander, 1980). These feelings are in turn associated with problems in spousal communication if new parents feel that their partners will not accept the expression of negative feelings about the baby. Ambivalence toward the infant may deepen if either parent feels that the baby had endangered the health of the mother or had created marital tension, especially if there had been strong ambivalence about the pregnancy. Further ambivalence may arise as some mothers, accustomed to receiving extra attention and support during the pregnancy, suddenly feel uncared for when all the attention is diverted to the infant at risk. These feelings may be especially acute if the infant is transferred to a hospital apart from the mother and she is unable to visit the newborn, whereas the father is able to spend time with his baby – attention that takes time away from his wife. The father, too, may resent the demands of balancing employment and family care during this time, especially if he desires the attention and support of others, yet feels unimportant and helpless.

Most parents of high-risk or damaged infants experience feelings of *guilt*, as though they were responsible for the outcome of the pregnancy (Callahan et al., 1983; Prugh, 1953). Introspection and concern that the outcome would have been different had they taken more care (e.g., eliminating trips, intercourse, alcohol, stress) is common. Some fathers and mothers feel as though the birth of a high-risk infant is punishment for their ambivalence about the pregnancy or for other events in their lives (Howard, 1978).

In combination, the range of emotions experienced by parents with a high-risk pregnancy or a high-risk infant can lead to a significant *loss of self-esteem*. Many parents experience failure, particularly if they equate successful childbearing with success as an individual or as a couple (Caplan, Mason, & Kaplan, 1965; Howard, 1978; Seashore, Leifer, Barnett, & Leiderman, 1973). The failure to fulfill what some consider the fundamentally human act of producing a healthy child may, in turn, lead to feelings of losing one's sense of adulthood or having one's sexuality challenged (Borg & Lasker, 1981). Others may interpret the birth of a high-risk child as a sign of their own mortality. A loss of self-esteem need not be permanent, however. Darling (1983) suggests that as parents of infants with special needs observe the ways in which their infant responds to them, self-esteem increases. She also indicates that, in most cases, feelings of helplessness should subside as parents develop adaptive strategies by the time their child is 1 year old.

Summary

In this section, I have attempted to outline some of the emotions that parents may encounter when the transition to parenthood is coupled with the birth of an infant who may sustain severe handicaps, may experience developmental delays, or is seriously ill. The unpredictability of the baby's medical and psychological status during the first days and weeks of extrauterine life complicates the emotional responses to childbirth (Call, 1958; Heisler, 1972). One complex and critical issue, which is beyond the scope of this chapter, encompasses ethical decisions regarding medical care. Even when the baby's medical crises have stabilized and the infant enters the home environment, emotions can remain in flux. Resolution of the birth experience and early weeks may not be immediate. With each developmental milestone, parents' hopes and expectations for their child are raised. Comparisons of their children with those of their friends or neighbors are salient. If the meeting of these milestones is delayed or if they are not reached, mothers and fathers may reexperience the earlier feelings of sadness, failure, and loss of self-esteem. Simon (1985), integrating interviews with parents of handicapped (Down syndrome, deaf, cerebral palsied) infants, states that parents often recycle through the grief process at the time of significant events (anticipated or actual) – such as birthdays, holidays, observations of friends' children, and missed milestones.

Influences on the quality of parental adaptation

A host of factors may influence adaptation to new parenthood with a high-risk infant. Several important variables that are commonly encountered are parent–infant separation, financial strain, and the support perceived to be available from family and friends.

Infant–parent separation

It is commonplace for parents of a healthy, full-term infant to be allowed time alone with their newborn immediately after the delivery. Often the infant will be given to the parents nude and placed on the mother's abdomen and chest for skin-to-skin contact. The potential influences of this early contact have been both heralded as facilitating mother– and father–infant bonding (Klaus & Kennell, 1976, 1982) and criticized as overstated (Goldberg, 1978; Pannabecker & Emde, 1977). Regardless of the controversial nature of the findings regarding early and extended contact, the experience is enjoyable for most parents.

In high-risk cases, however, both the parents and the infant are deprived of these early contact experiences. Because of the high-risk medical nature of their birth, preterm infants are typically taken immediately from the delivery room to the neonatal intensive care unit before their parents have been able to touch them – often before they have seen them. Transport of the neonate to a different hospital with intensive care facilities frequently follows. Thus, the mother will often not see her baby for the first few days of the baby's life. The facility in which the baby is receiving care may be a great distance from the maternal hospital and the parents' home. The new father may divide his available time between visiting his wife and visiting his baby or may wait to see the infant until the mother is able to travel also. Once they are able to see their infant, this couple, who have become parents too soon, are confronted by the frightening strangeness of the intensive care unit, a fragile-looking baby, and the message that their infant needs very special care that they cannot provide. Although many hospitals do encourage some forms of maternal (or parental) caregiving, parents cannot be responsible for the critical medical care their infant needs to survive (Harmon, 1980). It is not surprising, then, that many parents report feeling inadequate, as though the baby really belongs to the medical staff, not to themselves (Borg & Lasker, 1981; Howard, 1978; Pizzo, 1983). In one study of preterm and full-term infants (Jeffcoate, Humphrey, & Lloyd, 1979) it was found that nearly all (91%) of the parents of preterm infants felt ill-prepared for caring for their infants upon hospital discharge, compared with half (50%) of the parents of full-term infants. This pattern existed despite the fact that the infants were now healthy and, because they were older, their parents had experienced more time observing and learning about the infant's characteristics.

This separation of infant and parents complicates the host of emotions already aroused by the high-risk birth. In this light, parents wonder, consciously or unconsciously, how close emotionally they should allow themselves to become to their infant. Should they protect themselves from extended grief, or should they give the infant all they can emotionally and feel better about themselves if the baby dies (Borg & Lasker, 1981)? Although there are no data on this issue for fathers, two studies that included interviews of mothers of very low birth weight preterm infants during the first year of life (Harmon & Culp, 1981; Jeffcoate et al., 1979) found that half of these mothers experienced delays of several weeks or months in developing feelings of warmth or love for their child. All had experienced separation from their infant for various lengths of time, at least in the Harmon and Culp study, though the newborns were not transported to a different hospital from their mothers. The physical separation of infant and mother complicates parents' intended caregiving plans also. Plans to breastfeed may be altered, because the baby may not initially be able to receive this kind of nourishment. Expressing breast milk for bottle feedings may become an alternative at some point in the infant's hospital course – an alternative that may be disappointing to mothers who strongly desired to breastfeed.

The data addressing links between infant–parent separation and maternal attachment to the infant are not consistent across studies (Klaus & Kennell, 1970, 1976, 1982; Pannabecker & Emde, 1977). Some research suggests that, with the birth of a high-risk infant, the dyadic relationship is already put at risk and that separation and lack of early contact increases the probability of later maternal attachment and mothering disorders (Penti- cuff, 1980). Another study suggests that feelings of maternal depression, dissatisfaction, and incompetence mediate the relationship between ma- ternal attachment and interaction with the infant (eye-to-eye contact, han- dling) (Howard, 1978). Still another study reveals that the entire family system may be influenced by contact between preterm infant and parents (Leifer, Leiderman, Barnett, & Williams, 1972), since in this study there were more divorces and relinquishment of the infant for adoption among families in which contact between infant and parents was delayed for 3 to 12 weeks.

A longitudinal study (Seashore et al., 1973) of separated and nonsep- arated preterm mother–infant dyads revealed differential effects of sep- aration on various aspects of parent–child interactions. During early in- fancy, mothers who had been separated from their babies engaged in less caregiving and touched their infants less frequently than other mothers, though there were no differences in playful interactions. By 1 year, most of the effects of early separation on maternal attitudes and behavior had dissipated. An unexpected finding emerged at a 21-month (postdischarge) follow-up, however. In the early-separation group there were more marital separations and divorces than in the nonseparation group. The authors explained that the early separation was a "stress that created disequili- brium in the nuclear family system" (Seashore et al., 1973, p. 230). Firm conclusions regarding the role of separation in the adaptation of these high-risk infants and parents await further research. However, some of the present data are likely to be confounded by changes in hospital policy over the past decade and infant health status. Research is needed that addresses the role of parental personality characteristics, individual differences among infants, and other mediating or process variables, as well as studies that specifically examine the role of fathers in these family systems.

Financial concerns

The monetary costs of special prenatal care for high-risk pregnancies and of perinatal care for high-risk infants are high. Couples frequently do not have insurance policies that assume the entire financial burden of extended intensive care for the newborn, which may last weeks or months, resulting in bills of many thousands of dollars. Additional costs of transportation and lodging are encountered if the baby has been transferred and the parents must travel great distances (frequently out of state) to visit their child. In high-risk pregnancies, the financial concerns may be increased if the prospective mother is advised by her physician to terminate her employment and remain on bed rest for the course of the pregnancy. Thus, a loss of income may result months before the baby's birth. An interview study of parents of critically ill or handicapped infants revealed that financial concerns are rarely discussed openly between the couple or with medical staff (because concern about the monetary aspect of the crisis is not sanctioned while the baby's life hangs in the balance; Borg & Lasker, 1981). Parents do wonder, however, how they will pay and may feel bitter when the bills arrive, particularly if the child has sustained severe illness or permanent handicap (Borg & Lasker, 1981). Other research suggests that, if the new father perceives that his role in the family is one of economic provider, his inability to meet the financial costs and to fulfill his role successfully may damage an already shaken self-esteem (Benson, 1967). Though this may be the case in families who have traditional role arrangements, these data were collected 20 years ago, and we do not know whether similar dynamics would operate in families in which maternal and paternal employment is characteristic.

Social support

Informal social support by family and friends can be important at the time of a high-risk birth and during the postnatal period. Often, however, others are not clear how they should respond to the birth of an atypical or high-risk preterm infant, especially if survival is uncertain. Parents, too, may be uncertain whether to engage in the typical activities of new parents, such as contacting their friends or sending out birth announcements, in light of their child's unpredictable health status at birth and during the first few weeks. Several clinical studies indicate that telling family and friends about an ill or handicapped child's condition and the initial ventures into public places with a handicapped child are critical junctures for parents (Darling, 1983). Similarly, parents who had lost a child to sudden infant death syndrome (SIDS) claimed that interacting with family, friends, and co-workers was one of the most difficult aspects of life following their loss (DeFrain & Ernst, 1978; Helmrath & Sternitz, 1978). Some clinicians believe that long delays in informing others of an infant's status are indicative of the parents' failure to accept the infant's condition themselves (Darling, 1983).

The discomfort of some friends and family members may lead them to withdraw from contact with the new parents at a time when their support is critical. Having not personally had a similar experience, friends and relatives may not be able to comprehend the depth of grief and the range of emotions felt by most parents of a high-risk infant. Some attempt to minimize the crisis, saying, "Look on the bright side"; others withdraw or exhibit anger at the parents' responses. The failure to understand fully and empathize with the issues these parents are struggling with may damage family or friendship ties, since social support is crucial for family adjustment (Parke & Tinsley, 1983; Power & Parke, 1984). One study demonstrated that mothers of preterm infants who felt they had a good relationship with their spouse and their own mother were more active in caregiving and interaction with their baby, both in the hospital nursery and at home upon discharge (Minde, Marton, Manning, & Hines, 1980).

Social support may come from sources other than established networks of family and friends (see also Gottlieb & Pancer, Chapter 8, this volume). A common form of support is that of other parents who have undergone similar experiences with their own pregnancies and infants. Both informal support (conversations and interactions with other parents in the intensive care nursery) and formal support (organized groups of "graduate parents") may be available. Formal support groups can serve multiple functions, offering information, practical services, relaxation, and a source of belief systems (Caplan & Kililea, 1976). An interesting clinical study of separate discussion groups for mothers and fathers of Down syndrome infants found that mothers and fathers often had unique concerns about life with a Down syndrome child that differed from their spouse's concerns (Erickson, 1974). Sharing ideas and concerns with other mothers and fathers with a similar perspective may aid the family's adaptation. The validation and reaffirmation that parents receive from supportive contact with others (family, friends, other parents of high-risk infants, and formal support groups) can fuel their self-confidence and self-esteem to promote adaptive coping with the tasks before them.

Impact of infant risk status on the couple relationship

What impact does the experience of preterm or high-risk birth have on the couple's relationship as they undergo the transition to parenthood? One might predict that the developmental course of this transition would be altered by virtue of the emotions and crises discussed earlier. To illustrate, it was noted earlier that a traditionalizing effect of pregnancy on family roles was the norm. In a high-risk pregnancy in which the prospective mother is on bed rest, the husband may, in fact, need to assume more responsibility for household care, not supporting these stereotypes.

Clinical research suggests that there is no single path that these couples take as they become new parents (Berezin, 1982; Borg & Lasker, 1981). For some couples (and at some times), the grief and stress experienced as a couple enhances the strength of the marital dyad, as the parents share their sadness, fear, and shattered dreams (Korn et al., 1978). At other times, and for other couples, this pattern of mutual support does not always exist, for each individual's personal grief may leave little psychological energy available to support the spouse. Failures in communication between husband and wife can create a barrier, deepening the existing crisis around their baby (Pawl & Petarsky, 1983). For many couples facing their first major crisis together, a lack of understanding of the different ways of expressing grief and coping with stress may create tension in the relationship. There are a variety of ways in which grief is expressed; what may be comforting to one individual may indicate an uncaring attitude to another. Whereas one individual may find solace in sexual intimacy or leisure and recreational activities, this may be interpreted as callousness by the spouse. Gender differences in the expression of emotion may be associated with failure to communicate feelings. Men may be more reticent to express sadness because of their discomfort and efforts to protect their distressed wives, and women may find it more difficult to express anger (Berezin, 1982; Borg & Lasker, 1981; Callahan et al., 1983; Simon, 1985); both are common reactions to high-risk birth.

When spousal communication is functioning poorly, the sexual relationship can be affected for a variety of reasons. The association between sexual intercourse and childbearing may reinforce parents' feelings of their failure to produce a healthy, "normal" child, the most fundamental and natural of human acts. Blaming the spouse or self for the failure to carry the pregnancy to a successful, healthy, or term date can be damaging to each individual's self-esteem, sexually and otherwise. Fortunately, in most cases sexual difficulties are not long term (Berezin, 1982).

Some interview studies have demonstrated that a high-risk pregnancy or birth results in dramatic changes in the life plans of many couples. Changes in values and lifestyle are frequently reported – beyond what might be expected with the birth of a first child (Berezin, 1982; Harmon, 1980). Parents report placing less value on material possessions and less selfishness. In Harmon's study, mothers of preterm infants but not full-term infants frequently reported altering their prebirth plans to return to their employment, in order to stay at home with their infant. Because of the lack of well-controlled longitudinal studies, we do not know whether these changes in values or plans are relatively transient or long lasting. Although all new parents experience stress associated with the additional demands of childrearing, parents of a nonrisk, nonhandicapped child are able to look to the future, secure that each difficult period will pass as "a phase the child is going through." Parents of atypical infants often have no such assurance (Korn et al., 1978).

The vast majority of research on high-risk infants has focused on patterns of mother–infant interaction and infant cognitive developmental outcome. Several studies, however, shed light on the transition to parenthood and the marital relationship among couples with high-risk infants. Herzog (1977, 1979), after interviewing parents of critically ill preterm infants, suggested that in some cases fathers may develop particularly strong attachments to the baby; if the mother feels "left out" or unsupported in her maternal role by her husband, parental competition may ensue, resulting in marital discord. According to Herzog, the risk of this phenomenon increases if the infant is transported to another hospital and the husband feels pulled between his concern for his child and support for his wife. Herzog (1979) suggests, then, that the father's initial task is to nurture his wife so that she can care for the newborn. Though he suggests that fathers of high-risk infants should not assume a primary caregiving role with the infant, we should not prematurely conclude that high father involvement is the source of marital stress. On the basis of her data showing a positive correlation between reports of father involvement at 4 months and later developmental problems in high-risk infants, Barnard (1980) suggests that high levels of father involvement *reflect* maternal or family stress instead of being the instigating factor. Though the direction of effects is not always clear, we do know that the quality of a marriage serves an important role in the initial transition and interactions with the preterm baby. In studies of parents of ill preterms, marital quality was positively associated with the frequency of maternal visitation of the hospitalized preterm infant (Minde et al., 1980) and was the best predictor of maternal coping behavior. We know little about influences on paternal behavior. For both parents, the idea that preoccupation with the infant "steals" time from the spousal relationship (Simon, 1985), which then initiates a cycle of withdrawal from the marital relationship, may provide some insight into one process that links risk status and marital quality.

Other studies support the idea that these families are at an increased risk for marital distress, including a higher percentage of couple separations and divorces in families of high-risk preterm infants (Caplan et al., 1965; Leiderman, Leifer, Seashore, Barnett, & Grobstein, 1973; Leifer et al., 1972; Korn et al., 1978; McIntyre, 1977), although Harmon (1980) failed to find support for this hypothesis in his study of very low birth weight preterm infants. In fact, 50% of the mothers in his study reported a closer marital relationship since the birth of their child. The reasons for these divergent findings are not yet clear, except that in some studies mothers were interviewed, whereas in others separation and divorce statistics were used. In our own ongoing work comparing families of very low birth weight preterm infants and full-term infants (Easterbrooks & Harmon, 1986), mothers' and fathers' questionnaire reports of marital quality when their infants are 1 year (corrected age for preterms) do not differ by birth status. This is one of the very few studies to assess fathers' as well as mothers' reports of the marital relationship. One mediating factor in this study may be that mothers of preterms frequently reported that the father had been the greatest source of help and support since the birth.

The degree to which the birth of a high-risk infant has a disorganizing and negative impact on the marital relationship likely depends on a complex interaction of variables. Factors suggested as putting the marital relationship at risk include poor quality of the prebirth marital relationship (Gath, 1978; Hewitt, 1976; Korn et al., 1978; Martin, 1975), lower socioeconomic status (Leiderman, 1982), a lack of support networks, dysfunctional parental personality characteristics, separation from the infant during the hospitalization period (Leifer et al., 1972), and the increased demands associated with the rigors of parenting a high-risk infant at home. When the infant leaves the hospital for the home environment, parents may encounter a lack of spontaneity in daily life, constrained by the extra caregiving needs of their special infant – perhaps physical therapy, speech and hearing therapy, or the use of oxygen (Comfort, 1980). Leisure activities the parents enjoyed individually and as a couple before the baby's birth may be curtailed drastically, because the couple may be reluctant to leave their child or unable to find a babysitter competent to meet the baby's special caregiving needs (Korn et al., 1978).

Infant characteristics

In addition to a delivery experience that differed from their expectations, mothers and fathers of a high-risk preterm baby encounter an infant who is different in many ways from his or her full-term counterpart and from parental expectations. Similarly, a handicapped infant does not fit parents' expectations of the "perfect baby." These differences involve appearance and behavior patterns, including characteristics of infant cries, positive affect, motor behavior, and sensitivity to stimulation.

Appearance

The extent to which handicapping conditions affect the appearance of the newborn ranges broadly, encompassing severe limb malformations, cleft palate, mental retardation, and respiratory conditions. Some subtle conditions are revealed fully only as the baby develops in the first months or years. These variations in appearance affect, in turn, the parents' acceptance of and adjustment to their child's condition. To illustrate, several studies of parents of Down syndrome infants revealed that parents initially hope their child will develop normally since they do not strongly violate norms of infant appearance and behavior in the early months (Darling, 1983; Emde & Brown, 1978). There has been a considerable amount of research on the appearance and effects of the appearance and behavior of preterm infants. The data on physical appearance demonstrate that even when their size is appropriate for gestational age, preterm infants appear small, underdeveloped, fragile, perhaps emaciated – lacking fat pads (Johnson, 1979) and having facial differences (concavity of face, height of eyes) – which are responded to discriminatingly by adults (Brooks & Hockberg, 1960). Preterm infants are rated less attractive, less likable, and more irritating than full-term infants, and adults indicate less willingness to engage in social interaction with them than with full-term infants (Frodi, Lamb, Leavitt, & Donovan, 1978; Reich, Maier, Klein, & Gyurke, 1984; Stern & Hildebrandt, 1984).

Negative and positive affect

Different characteristics of the cries and smiles of preterm infants accompany differences in physical appearance. Deviations in cry patterns are common with a variety of medical syndromes, including Down syndrome (shorter, less active and differentiated cry bursts with longer latencies), hyperbilirubinemia (higher fundamental frequency), and preterm infants (higher-pitched) (Lester & Zeskind, 1979). These cries are rated by adults as being, on the one hand, more sickly and urgent and on the other, aversive, eliciting greater signs of physiological arousal (Frodi et al., 1978). Although it has been suggested that the cry of the high-risk infant is biologically programmed to be different in order to elicit special caregiving, it is thought, too, that the aversiveness of the cries may violate caregiver nurturance behavior and "suppress the optimal caregiving pattern necessary" (Lester & Zeskind, 1979). The possible outcomes of this pattern in parent–child interaction will be discussed later in this chapter.

Differences in the affective domain attributable to birth status are evident in positive affect as well. A number of studies of preterm birth, Down syndrome, and physical handicaps have documented both delays and decreases in smiling and positive affect in naturalistic interaction with parents during the first year (Cicchetti & Sroufe, 1976; Emde & Brown, 1978; Field, 1979; Gallagher, Jens & O'Donnell, 1983). In sum, parents may be interacting with an infant who provides them with more negative feedback in crying and appearance, coupled with fewer or less intense demonstrations of positive affect in the early months. Differences are not circumscribed within the affective realm, but are evident in the motor realm as well.

Motor behavior

Although a portion of high-risk preterm infants have major central nervous system or structural damage, even those infants who are biologically intact demonstrate immaturity of motor systems (e.g., muscle tone, reflexes, coordination) (Friedman, Leiderman, Barnett, & Williams, 1972). Delays in motor development persist beyond the expected date of birth and were evident three months beyond term date in a study of pre- and full-term infants (Leiderman et al., 1973), suggesting delays even when the infant became medically stable. These delays may contribute to interactional differences among preterm infants and their parents, a topic discussed below.

Sensitivity to stimulation and interactive behavior

Although preterm infants have a higher threshold for stimulation, they are also easily overstimulated and difficult to console once the threshold is exceeded (Field, Dempsey, & Shuman, 1979). A fine line exists, then, between providing optimal levels of stimulation necessary to arouse and interact with these infants and, at the same time, avoiding stimulation that will exceed this optimal range.

The loud, bright environment of the neonatal intensive care unit is the antithesis of the soothing, soft stimulation to which preterm infants most readily respond (Als, Lester, & Brazelton, 1979; Lipsitt, 1979). These infants, then, because of their inability to regulate stimulation without taxing their internal organization, may withdraw from the external world, in effect shutting out stimulation. During the neonatal period and the first year of life, we know that high-risk preterm infants are less attentive, less expressive of positive affect, less cuddly, less readily engaged in game playing, and more fussy than full-term infants (DiVitto & Goldberg, 1979; Field, 1977, 1979; Harmon, 1980; Parke & Sawin, 1976). Harmon and Culp's (1981) study of preterm and full-term 1-year-olds found deficits among the preterms in both positive affect in play and in challenging cognitive tasks and less negative affect when bored with or tired of the cognitive tasks. These data suggest perhaps a higher threshold for the expression of affect in general among high-risk infants. Many of these characteristics are also seen in babies with cerebral palsy, Down syndrome, and visual deficits (Cicchetti & Sroufe, 1976; Emde, Katz, & Thorpe, 1978; Fraiberg, 1980; Vietze, Abernathy, Ashe, & Faulstich, 1978).

Thus, there is an apparent paradox for parents when faced with an infant who is less alert and attentive and more easily overstimulated than normal infants. Parents must be exquisitely sensitive to infant cues, a task made all the more difficult by infants' compromised ability to produce clear, consistent signals due to physiological, sensory, or cognitive impairments (Thoman, Becker, & Freese, 1978). In general, parents of preterm infants work harder to engage their babies in social interaction, initiating more frequently than parents of full-term infants. Infants who have difficulty in maintaining lengthy states of alertness may need to be held to facilitate social interaction and environmental responsiveness; in these ways, parents help the infants to organize and regulate their state behavior (Als et al., 1979).

Parental behavior and parent–infant interaction

Thus far, I have discussed the ways in which parents may respond emotionally to a high-risk pregnancy and birth and some of the differences between infants born at term and those born prematurely. Given the nature of these differences, we might wonder whether high-risk birth is also associated with differences in the behavioral interactions of these parent–infant dyads. The answer is a clear yes (at least in the first year of life). These data reflect empirical studies that are more well controlled than the clinical evidence that characterizes the study of parental emotions. It must be noted once again, however, that the primary source of data is mother–infant interaction; fathers are included in only a few studies. This reflects the lack of emphasis, in general, on expectant fathers and new fatherhood (Osofsky & Osofsky, 1980; Parke, Hymel, Power, & Tinsley, 1980; Parke & Tinsley, 1983).

How do parents respond to the special caregiving needs of their high-risk infants? Data suggest perhaps an evolutionarily guided interactional system, parents providing what is necessary for their infant's immediate survival in the form of increased caregiving and stimulation. Several studies have found that, in interaction with preterm infants, mothers and fathers are more active, carrying more of "the interactive burden" during the first months of infancy than are parents of full-term infants (Beckwith & Cohen, 1978; Brown & Bakeman, 1979). Parents must work harder to bring their babies to behavioral states that will facilitate feeding and social interaction (parents may need to touch and vocalize more to their infants to arouse them) (DiVitto & Goldberg, 1979). Similar patterns are reported for dyadic interaction involving infants with physical handicaps and cerebral palsy (Kogan & Tyler, 1973). These effects do not seem to be a transient adjustment to life with an infant who appears fragile and needy. Patterns of greater parental activity and stimulation in interaction continue at least through the end of the first year of life (Crnic et al., 1983; Harmon & Culp, 1981), with mothers of preterms showing a more protective and "hypervigilant" relationship with their 1-year-olds than mothers of full-terms. In the Harmon and Culp study (1981), mothers were aware that they treated their child differently than they had planned (in ways that were more protective and lenient) because of the prematurity; they left the child with alternative caregivers less often, and fewer mothers returned to their employment (even though they had planned to do so) than did mothers of full-term infants. Although the pattern of maternal compensatory behavior may be adaptive for young high-risk infants, there may be negative implications over a long period of time. Barnard (1980) suggests that there is a risk of "super-parent burnout" by the time the child is a year old, as parents become exhausted attempting to compensate for the child's special needs.

Although these data may suggest that there is more interaction among high-risk infants and their parents than among normal infants and theirs, other data indicate deficits in specific types of interaction. Research conducted during the first year of life indicates that mothers of high-risk infants spend less time holding the infants in an en face position, which would facilitate social interaction (Klaus & Kennell, 1970) and that the interactions that do occur include less talking to (DiVitto & Goldberg, 1979) and smiling at the infant, combined with less close body contact (DiVitto & Goldberg, 1979; Leifer et al., 1972). Field (1979) compared two different groups of high-risk infants (preterm infants with respiratory distress syndrome and postterm, postmature infants, all of whom had experienced separation from parents) with a healthy, full-term group in a longitudinal study from birth to 2 years of age. As newborns, the infants in both of the two high-risk groups were deficient in interactive competencies, as assessed by the Neonatal Behavioral Assessment Scale (Brazelton, 1973). At 3 to 4 months of age, the infants and mothers were observed in feeding and social interaction contexts. The mothers of full-term infants were more contingently responsive to their babies' cues in feeding than were the mothers of both groups of high-risk infants; the preterm infants, however, were especially disorganized during the feedings. During play, both types of high-risk infants (particularly the preterm males) fussed and averted their gaze from their mothers more than did full-terms, and their mothers were more active in directing the interaction. Many of these differences were observed in interactions with fathers also. That the social interactions were less pleasant for high-risk dyads was demonstrated by the greater incidence of infant gaze aversion and by physiological measures of the mother during the interaction. Infant attentiveness (which is often a problem with preterm infants) was facilitated by mothers' imitation of behavior the baby had initiated. Maternal imitative behaviors were not considered aversive, because the babies did not gaze-avert at these times, and longer episodes of reciprocal interaction could be sustained. These data indicate that, when infants were allowed to lead the interaction, the interactions were more affectively positive and extended.

The *degree of infant medical complications* may be an important factor in interactional differences. In one study, preterm infants with the most complicated obstetric and neonatal courses received more frequent caregiving from their mothers at 1 month (age corrected for gestation) (Beckwith & Cohen, 1978). However, infants with fewer medical complications are more likely to be alert and able to respond to incoming stimuli (social or nonsocial) (DiVitto & Goldberg, 1979), so parents may not need to be as active in arousing these newborns. Another study, comparing four groups of infants 8 to 12 months (healthy full-terms, healthy preterms, sick preterms, and infants of diabetic mothers), found that parents were more active while playing with the infant who had been born before his or her due date and had medical complications, whereas the healthy preterm and full-term patterns were similar to one another; infants of diabetic mothers exhibited similarities to the sick preterm group. Not all the research supports these findings, however. Although, in one study, differences favoring sick preterm infants were found in the realm of eye contact with the mother (Barrera, Bronte, & Vella, 1984), these researchers also found that the mothers of healthy preterm or full-term infants engaged in more vocal stimulation of their babies. It was proposed that the mothers of the sick preterms had taken on a passive role in interaction with their infants, perhaps as a result of their inability to act or take control during the period of hospitalization. One source of the divergent research findings may be differences among studies in the degree of medical complications and length of hospitalization. It is reasonable to think that parents of infants hospitalized for 2 weeks as opposed to 4 months differ in experience, expectations, and interactional styles.

In summary, these data suggest that there are differences in the interactive properties of high- and low-risk infants as well as their parents, highlighting the systems influences of high-risk birth. Among preterm infants, less time spent in alert states, which allow for social interaction, and less responsiveness to such interactions are commonly reported characteristics (Field, 1979; Lester & Zeskind, 1979). Furthermore, when aroused, preterm infants are less affectively positive and more difficult to soothe (DiVitto & Goldberg, 1979; Field, 1977). These data often represent summaries of group data that represent a range of infants. While group data are informative, individual differences among both infants and parents should not be overlooked.

Continuity in parental behavior

Most of the research discussed thus far has focused on the characteristics of interaction between high-risk preterm infants and their parents during the perinatal period, or the first months of infancy. Given the nature of the birth experience and the course of the infant's hospitalization, the first months of infancy might represent a period when parents and infant are adapting to the home environment and the task of interacting with one another. The data suggest differences in interaction styles between these dyads and full-term infant–parent dyads during the first year of life. The question to be addressed here is whether these styles of interaction are stable over time or are more transient characteristics of adaptation to the challenges of parenting a high-risk infant.

The claim that parental behavior demonstrates strong continuities, regardless of changes in infant behavior, has been forwarded by Minde et al. (1980). He finds that, among preterms with a complicated medical course, as the babies' health improves, parental behavior does not change; parents continue to interact with their infants as though they were ill. The transactional model of Sameroff and Chandler (1975) would predict that the parent and child would change in tandem, each responsive to the alterations in the other, together creating dynamic environments. Several longitudinal research studies support the idea of continuity in some aspects of maternal behavior with preterm infants. (Note that these findings do not necessarily refute the validity of the transactional model.) In several studies, early contact with their preterm infants was related to the mothers' confidence (Seashore et al., 1973) and more skillful physical contact with their infants (Klaus & Kennell, 1970) in the perinatal period – a relatively brief period of a few weeks. DiVitto and Goldberg (1979), however, found very weak associations between interactional behavior during the hospital period and at home during the first months postdischarge, suggesting a period of instability in the behavioral organization of the parent–child system. In a longitudinal study of high-risk preterm infants from 1 to 24 months, Beckwith and Cohen (1978) found some continuity in maternal behavior from the infancy to toddler periods (especially in vocal behavior toward the child); mothers who were responsive to their infants continued to be so over time. For mothers of infants who were the most ill, however, responsiveness declined over time, indicating that serious perinatal illness was a risk factor in the development of a consistent, well-functioning relationship. Taken together, these data suggest that certain aspects of parental behavior may demonstrate at least moderate stability in light of changing infant behavior. Alternatively, other aspects of parental behavior are more responsive to the dynamic changes in infant behavior. Future research aimed at identifying characteristics of continuity and discontinuity in the organization of parent–child interactions is called for.

The role of the father

The lack of emphasis on fathers during the transition to parenthood and early childrearing (Parke et al., 1980) extends to fathers of high-risk infants as well. However, as noted earlier, fathers of high-risk infants may have a very special role (both direct and indirect) during the first days and months of the infant's life. In a direct way, fathers may need to assume far more responsibility during these early times than they had planned. Particularly if the baby is transported to a care facility apart from the mother, the father is the link of communication between mother and child. He is the mother's eyes and ears at this time and is the only parent the neonatal medical staff know. Thus, his direct role in the infant's care may increase. In supporting his wife emotionally (which Herzog, 1979, believes is his primary role) the father also influences his child indirectly. In this regard, the data are clear for full-term nonrisk infants and families: The father's positive evaluation of the newborn is associated with positive marital adjustment and, in turn, with the mother's skill in feeding the newborn – illustrating a circular system (Pedersen et al., 1977). What we do not know is whether this pattern of influence is characteristic of new families in which a high-risk infant is born. The paths of influence in the family are a fruitful arena for future research. As noted earlier, there are data indicating that fathers of preterm infants may be more involved in caregiving (bathing, diapering) than are fathers of full-term infants (Yogman, 1981). Some data suggest that increased father involvement may be a specific response of some men to high-risk status, in that in one study half of the fathers of preterm infants reported that their involvement in childcare and household tasks was greater than they had anticipated before the birth (Jeffcoate et al., 1979). Greater involvement than expected was not reported by fathers of full-term infants. Given what was discussed earlier about the characteristics of preterm infants, perhaps these fathers attempt to relieve their wives of some of the childcare burden. With the current social trend toward encouraging paternal involvement in early childhood, the effects of infant risk status on paternal caregiving and the paternal role are important areas for further inquiry.

Developmental outcome and intervention

In the preceding pages I have noted differences as well as similarities in the transition to parenthood for families with high-risk preterm and healthy full-term infants. Differences are quite evident in the styles of interaction in parent–child dyads throughout the first year of life. Various explanations of these differences have been offered (from Goldberg, Perrotta, & Minde, 1983): (1) that the behavioral differences, such as maternal activity or infant lack of responsiveness, reflect greater levels of stress in the preterm dyad than in the full-term dyad (Goldberg, 1978); (2) that they represent a maladaptive style of maternal reaction to the infant (Field, 1977, 1979), which in turn affects the level of infant engagement in social interaction; (3) that these differences reflect a need for support and active intervention in high-risk dyads (Field, 1979; Goldberg, 1978) in order to get them back into a course typified by healthy full-term dyads; and (4) that maternal behavioral differences are appropriate adaptations to the special needs of the high-risk infant and, as such, facilitate developmental adaptation of the infant. In order to determine which of these alternatives is most useful we must examine the extant data on developmental outcome of infants.

In the discussion of developmental outcome, I shall focus on socioemotional rather than cognitive factors. Many of the studies of developmental outcome in the first 2 years of life highlight a secure infant–mother attachment relationship as a hallmark of socioemotional development and a reflection of the history of mother–infant interaction during the first year of life. Maternal sensitivity to infant signals is an integral component of the development of secure attachment (Ainsworth, Blehar, Waters, & Wall, 1978), since infants who evidence insecure attachments to their mothers were found to have mothers who lacked sensitivity during the first year (responding less contingently and appropriately to infant signals). The consensus of a number of studies comparing the security of infant–mother attachment in preterm and full-term dyads is that risk status at birth does not preclude the development of secure attachment relationships to mother in infancy (Field et al., 1978; Goldberg et al., 1983; Harmon & Culp, 1981). Our own recent work demonstrates no differences in security of attachment to either mothers or fathers among groups of very low birth weight preterm and full-term infants at 12 to 13 months (corrected age for preterms) (Easterbrooks & Harmon, 1986) or at 20 months (Easterbrooks, 1988). In another study, however, differences within the preterm group were found (Plunkett, Meisels, Stiefel, Pasick, & Roloff, 1984) according to the health status of the preterm newborns. Healthy preterm infants did not evince less security than Ainsworth's original full-term sample, whereas preterms whose medical course was complicated by respiratory illness demonstrated fewer secure attachments and more insecure-resistant attachments than expected. The authors suggest less synchronous interactions between mother and infant in the first year as the mechanism for the higher incidence of anxious-resistant attachments. In a study of infants with physical handicaps, Wasserman (1986) found no differences in infant–mother security at 12 months between the handicapped and nonhandicapped groups. They did find that maternal responsiveness and positive affect during the latter portion of the infant's first year were associated with secure attachments for both of the groups.

These data suggest, then, that differences in interactional styles between preterm infants and their parents do not necessarily imply developmental deficiencies. Sensitive parenting is possible in a range of situations, with a range of infants. This makes sense, biologically and evolutionarily, and is consistent with Sameroff and Chandler's (1975) transactional model, in which both the organism and the environment change as a result of their encounters and, more specifically, single early events (such as high-risk birth) operate in combination with the characteristics of the environment. The fourth alternative, provided by Goldberg and her colleagues (1983) – namely, that mothers are able to adapt to and compensate for these differences in their infants – is supported by these data.

Other data do not strike such a positive note. Infants born preterm are at a higher risk for several adverse developmental outcomes, including SIDS, failure to thrive, and maltreatment. The incidence of SIDS is reportedly six times greater among the high-risk preterm population, the suspected factor being problematic state regulation and control of respiration (Guilleminault, Peraita, Souquet, & Dement, 1975; Kattwinkel, 1977). Furthermore, child maltreatment may be related to failures in the development of positive child–parent interactions. "In a non-supportive environment, the behavioral repertoire of the poorly organized infant with a cry that is perceived as grating and aversive may violate the limit of caregiver control behavior and suppress the optimal caregiving pattern necessary" (Lester & Zeskind, 1979, p. 141). There are signs that high-risk preterm infants are overrepresented in populations of nonorganic failure-to-thrive and abused and neglected infants (Barnett, Leiderman, Grobstein, & Klaus, 1970; Belsky, 1978; Gil, 1970; Parke & Collmer, 1975). In one study, a ninefold increase (3.9%) in the incidence of high-risk preterms in the abused or neglected population was reported (Hunter, Kilstrom, Kraybill & Loda, 1978). In this study, the infants most likely to be abused were those born the most prematurely, with a complicated hospital course, and who were transported to a hospital at a distance from the family home.

Given these findings, it would appear that positive developmental adaptation rests in part on the supportiveness of the caregiving environment, as well as characteristics of the infant. There have been reports of *intervention programs* (working with the infants directly to increase their behavioral repertoire and with the caregivers to facilitate optimal caregiving), which may further positive development of infant–parent interaction and the family system (Lipsitt, 1979; Masi, 1979). Many interventions focus on providing stimulation to the newborn, stimulation of the sort that is not typically available in the intensive care nursery. In work with the infant, stimulating body contact has been found to foster infant weight gain, activity level, and positive developmental assessment scores at 1 year of age (Klaus & Kennell, 1976; Scarr-Salapatek & Williams, 1973; Solkoff, Jaffe, Weintraub, & Blase, 1961).

Other interventions focus on providing support and informative guidance to parents. A long-term intervention program designed to facilitate maternal understanding of infant capabilities (Rauh et al., 1984) was successful in increasing maternal confidence, role satisfaction, and perceptions of infant temperament assessed at a 6-month follow-up. Maternal confidence in the intervention group was still high at a 2-year follow-up, and Bayley developmental scores for the intervention group children were higher than those who had not received intervention. The authors propose that the support mothers perceived to have come from the intervention had allowed them to circumvent the problems associated with the high-risk birth. Factors mediating the success of intervention programs include maternal education (Rauh et al., 1984) and the home environment. In another study, in which all families received intervention, the success or failure of the intervention was also associated with the incidence of marital discord in the home (Bromwich & Parmelee, 1979).

Conclusion

The transition to parenthood is a family life-cycle period that brings challenges and rewards for all parents. Thus far, theoretical formulations of this transition have focused on nonrisk pregnancies and the birth of a nonrisk infant. Although the risk case undoubtedly exhibits many of the same characteristics as the nonrisk one, it is important to consider ways in which this experience is different, in degree or kind, for prospective and new parents who do not experience an uncomplicated pregnancy or give birth to a healthy full-term infant. Basic knowledge of the developmental course of high-risk pregnancy and birth can provide parents, clinicians, and medical personnel with reassurance of the variations in normative adaptation and with strategies to facilitate adaptive coping, which in turn fosters optimal child and family development.

Recommendations for future research highlight the need for longitudinal prospective research beginning in the prenatal period. It is crucial that studies include father–infant, as well as mother–infant, interactions and perceptions. Longitudinal work on the long-term impact of high-risk pregnancy or birth on the marital relationship, childrearing attitudes and values, and the integration of family roles and the wide social network (friendship, employment, extended family) is the next step toward understanding the transition to parenthood and infant risk status.

References

Ainsworth, M. D., Blehar, M., Waters, E., & Wall, S. (1978). *Patterns of attachment.* Hillsdale, NJ: Erlbaum.

Als, H., Lester, B. M., & Brazelton, T. B. (1979). Dynamics of the behavioral organization of the premature infant: A theoretical perspective. In T. M. Field, A. M. Sostek, S. Goldberg, & H. H. Shuman (Eds.), *Infants born at risk* (pp. 173–92). New York: Spectrum.

Barnard, K. E. (1980). An ecological approach to parent–child relations. In C. C. Brown (Ed.), *Infants at risk: Assessment and intervention* (Pediatric Round Table, Series 5). Palm Beach, FL: Johnson & Johnson Baby Products Co.

Barnett, C. R., Leiderman, R. H., Grobstein, R., & Klaus, M. (1970). Neonatal separation: The maternal side of interactional deprivation. *Pediatrics, 45,* 197–205.

Barrera, M. E., Bronte, B., & Vella, D. (1984, April). *Behavior patterns of sick and healthy preterm and fullterm mother–infant dyads.* Paper presented at the meetings of the International Conference on Infant Studies, New York.

Beckwith, L., & Cohen, S. E. (1978). Preterm birth: Hazardous obstetrical and postnatal events as related to caregiver–infant behavior. *Infant Behavior and Development, 1,* 403–11.

Belsky, J. (1978). Three theoretical models of child abuse: A critical review. *International Journal of Child Abuse and Neglect, 2,* 37–49.

Belsky, J. (1983, April). *Social network contact and the transition to parenthood.* Paper presented at the meetings of the Society for Research in Child Development, Detroit, MI.

Belsky, J. (1986, April). *Maternal, infant and social contextual determinants of attachment security.* Paper presented at the meetings of the International Conference on Infant Studies, Los Angeles.

Belsky, J., Spanier, G., & Rovine, M. (1983). Stability and change in marriage across the transition to parenthood. *Journal of Marriage and the Family, 45,* 553–66.

Benson, L. (1967). *Fatherhood: A sociological perspective.* New York: Random House.

Berezin, N. (1982). *After a loss in pregnancy.* New York: Simon & Schuster.

Borg, S., & Lasker, J. (1981). *When pregnancy fails.* Boston: Beacon Press.

Brazelton, T. B. (1973). Assessment of the infant at risk. *Clinical Obstetrics and Gynecology, 16,* 361–75.

Bromwich, R. M., & Parmelee, A. H. (1979). An intervention program for preterm infants. In T. M. Field, A. M. Sostek, S. Goldberg, & H. H. Shuman (Eds.), *Infants born at risk* (pp. 389–412). Jamaica, NY: Spectrum.

Brooks, V., & Hockberg, J. (1960). A psychological study of "cuteness." *Perceptual and Motor Skills, 11,* 205.

Brown, J., & Bakeman, R. (1979). Relationships of human mothers with their infants during the first year of life. In R. W. Bell & W. P. Smotherman (Eds.), *Maternal influences and early behavior* (pp. 353–73). Jamaica, NY: Spectrum.

Call, J. (1958, September–October). Psychological problems of the cerebral palsied child, his parents and siblings as revealed by dynamically oriented small group discussions with parents. *Cerebral Palsy Review.*

Callahan, E. J., Brasted, W. S., & Granados, J. L. (1983). Fetal loss and sudden infant death: Grieving and adjustment for families. In E. J. Callahan & K. A. McCluskey (Eds.), *Life-span developmental psychology: Nonnormative life events.* New York: Academic Press.

Caplan, G. (1974). *Support systems and community mental health.* New York: Behavioral Publications.

Caplan, G., & Kililea, M. (1976). *Support systems and mutual help.* New York: Grune & Stratton.

Caplan, G., Mason, E., & Kaplan, D. M. (1965). Four studies of crisis in parents of prematures. *Community Mental Health Journal, 1,* 149–61.

Cassell, J. (1974). Psychosocial processes and "stress": Theoretical formulation. *International Journal of Health Services, 4,* 471–82.

Chase, H. C. (1977). Time trends in low birth weight in the United States, 1950–1974. In D. M. Reed & F. J. Stanley (Eds.), *The epidemiology of prematurity* (pp. 17–37). Baltimore, MD: Urban & Schwarzenberg.

Ciba Foundation. (1978). *Major mental handicap: Methods and costs of prevention* (Ciba Foundation Symposium No. 59). Amsterdam: Elsevier.

Cicchetti, D., & Sroufe, L. A. (1976). The relationship between affective and cognitive development in Down's syndrome infants. In M. Lewis & L. A. Rosenblum (Eds.), *The development of affect* (pp. 309–50). New York: Plenum.

Clyman, R. I., Sniderman, S. H., Ballard, R. A., & Roth, R. S. (1979). What pediatricians say to mothers of sick newborns: An indirect evaluation of the counseling process. *Pediatrics, 63,* 719–23.

Comfort, R. L. (1980). *The unconventional child.* St. Louis, MO: Mosby.

Cowan, C. P., & Cowan, P. A. (1983, April). *A preventive intervention for couples during family formation.* Paper presented at the meetings of the Society for Research in Child Development, Detroit, MI.

Crnic, K. A., Ragozin, A. S., Greenberg, M. T., Robinson, N. M., & Basham, R. B. (1983). Social interaction and developmental competence of preterm and full-term infants during the first year of life. *Child Development, 54,* 1199–1210.

D'Arcy, E. (1968). Congenital defects: Mother's reaction to first information. *British Medical Journal, 3,* 796–8.

Darling, R. B. (1983). The birth defective child and the crisis of parenthood. In E. J. Callahan & K. A. McCluskey (Eds.), *Life-span developmental psychology: Nonnormative life events.* New York: Academic Press.

Darling, R. B., & Darling, J. (1982). *Children who are different: Meeting the challenge of birth defects in society.* St. Louis, MO: Mosby.

DeFrain, J. D., & Ernst, L. (1978). The psychological effects of sudden infant death syndrome on surviving family members. *Journal of Family Practice, 6,* 985–9.

DiVitto, B., & Goldberg, S. (1979). The effect of newborn medical status on early parent–infant interaction. In T. Field, A. Sostek, S. Goldberg, & H. H. Shuman (Eds.), *Infants born at risk* (pp. 311–32). Jamaica, NY: Spectrum.

Drillien, C. M. (1961). Longitudinal study of growth and development of prematurely and maturely born children. *Archives of Diseases of Childhood, 36,* 233–40.

Easterbrooks, M. A. (1988). *Quality of attachment to mother and to father: Effects of perinatal risk status.* Manuscript submitted for publication.

Easterbrooks, M. A., & Harmon, R. J. (1986, April). *Perinatal risk, attachment, and the transition to parenthood.* Paper presented at the International Conference on Infant Studies, Los Angeles.

Emde, R. N., & Brown, C. (1978). Adaptation to the birth of a Down's syndrome infant. *Journal of American Academy of Child Psychiatry, 17,* 299–323.

Emde, R. N., Katz, E. L., & Thorpe, J. K. (1978). Emotional expression in infancy: II. Early deviations in Down's syndrome. In M. Lewis & L. Rosenblum (Eds.), *The development of affect* (pp. 350–60). New York: Plenum.

Erickson, M. P. (1974, November–December). Talking with fathers of young children with Down's syndrome. *Children Today,* 22–5.

Feldman, H. (1971). Changes in marriage and parenthood: A methodological design. In A. Michel (Ed.), *Family issues of employed women in Europe and America.* Lieden: Brull.

Field, T. M. (1977). Effects of early separation, interactive deficits, and experimental manipulation on mother–infant interaction. *Child Development, 48,* 763–71.

Field, T. M. (1979). Interaction patterns of preterm and full-term infants. In T. M. Field, A. M. Sostek, S. Goldberg, & H. H. Shuman (Eds.), *Infants born at risk* (pp. 333–56). Jamaica, NY: Spectrum.

Field, T. M., Dempsey, J. R., & Shuman, H. H. (1979). Developmental assessments of infants surviving the respiratory distress syndrome. In T. M. Field, A. M. Sostek, S. Goldberg, & H. H. Shuman (Eds.), *Infants born at risk* (pp. 261–80), Jamaica, NY: Spectrum.

Field, T. M., Hallock, N., Ting, E., Dempsey, G., Dabiri, C., & Shuman, H. H. (1978). A first-year follow-up of high-risk infants: Formulation of a cumulative risk index. *Child Development, 49,* 119–31.

Fraiberg, S. (1980). *Clinical studies in infant mental health.* New York: Basic Books.

Friedlander, B. Z. (1980). Pain-filled fruit of the tree of knowledge: Problems and paradoxes in the sanctity of life. In D. B. Sawin, R. C. Hawkins, L. O. Walker, & J. H. Penticuff (Eds.), *Exceptional infant: Vol. 4. Psychosocial risks in infant–environment transactions* (pp. 190–6). New York: Brunner/Mazel.

Friedman, S. L., Leiderman, P. H., Barnett, C., & Williams, J. (1972). Effect of mother–infant separation on maternal attachment behaviors. *Child Development, 43,* 1203–18.

Frodi, A. M., Lamb, M. E., Leavitt, L., & Donovan, W. L. (1978). Fathers' and mothers' responses to infant smiles and cries. *Infant Behavior and Development, 1,* 187–98.

Gallagher, R. J., Jens, K. G., & O'Donnell, K. J. (1983). The effect of physical status on affective expression of handicapped infants. *Infant Behavior and Development, 6,* 73–7.

Gath, A. (1978). *Down's syndrome and the family: The early years.* New York: Academic Press.

Gil, D. F. (1970). *Violence against children.* Cambridge, MA: Harvard University Press.

Goldberg, S. (1978). Prematurity: Effects on parent–infant interaction. *Journal of Pediatric Psychology, 3,* 137–44.

Goldberg, S., Perrotta, M., & Minde, K. (1983). *Maternal birthweight and attachment in low birthweight twins and singletons.* Unpublished manuscript, Hospital for Sick Children, Toronto.

Goldberg, W. A., & Easterbrooks, M. A. (1984). Role of marital quality in toddler development. *Developmental Psychology, 20,* 504–14.

Greenberg, M. (1973). First mothers' rooming-in with their newborns: Its impact on the mother. *American Journal of Orthopsychiatry, 44,* 783–8.

Greenberg, M., & Morris, N. (1974). Engrossment: The newborn's impact on the father. *American Journal of Orthopsychiatry, 45,* 520–31.

Guilleminault, C., Peraita, R., Souquet, M., & Dement, W. C. (1975). Apneas during sleep in infants: Possible relationship with sudden infant death syndrome. *Science, 190,* 677–9.

Harmon, R. J. (1980). Infant behavior and family development. In L. Sonstegard, B. Jennings, & K. Kowalski (Eds.), *Primary health care of women.* New York: Duxbury Press.

Harmon, R. J., & Culp, A. M. (1981). The effects of premature birth on family functioning and infant development. In I. Berlin (Ed.), *Children and our future* (pp. 1–9). Albuquerque: University of New Mexico Press.

Heisler, V. (1972). *A handicapped child in the family.* New York: Grune & Stratton.

Helmrath, T. A., & Sternitz, E. M. (1978). Death of an infant: Parental grieving and the failure of social support. *Journal of Family Practice, 6,* 785–90.

Herzog, J. M. (1977, October). *Patterns of parenting.* Paper presented at the meetings of the American Academy of Child Psychiatry, Houston, TX.

Herzog, J. M. (1979). Disturbances in parenting high-risk infants: Clinical impressions and hypotheses. In T. M. Field (Ed.), *Infants born at risk: Behavior and development* (pp. 357–63). New York: S. P. Medical and Scientific Books.

Hewitt, D. (1976). Research on families with handicapped children – an aid or an impediment to understanding? *Birth Defects: Original Article Series, 12,* 35–46.

Hobbs, D. F. (1965). Parenthood as crisis: A third study. *Journal of Marriage and the Family, 27,* 367–72.

Hobbs, D., & Cole, S. (1976). Transition to parenthood: A decade replication. *Journal of Marriage and the Family, 38,* 723–31.

Howard, J. (1978). The influence of children's developmental dysfunctions on marital quality and family interaction. In R. Lerner & G. Spanier (Eds.), *Child influences on marital and family interaction* (pp. 275–98). New York: Academic Press.

Hunter, R. S., Kilstrom, N., Kraybill, E. N., & Loda, F. (1978). Antecedents of child abuse and neglect in premature infants: A prospective study in a newborn intensive care unit. *Pediatrics, 61,* 629–35.

Jeffcoate, J. A., Humphrey, M. E., & Lloyd, J. K. (1979). Role perception and response to stress in fathers and mothers following pre-term delivery. *Social Science and Medicine, 13A*(2), 139–45.

Johnson, S. H. (1979). *High risk parenting.* Philadelphia: Lippincott.

Jones, M. B. (1979). The high-risk pregnancy. In S. H. Johnson (Ed.), *High-risk parenting.* Philadelphia: Lippincott.

Kaplan, D., & Mason, E. A. (1960). Maternal reactions to premature birth viewed as an acute emotional disorder. *American Journal of Orthopsychiatry, 30,* 539.

Kattwinkel, J. (1977). Neonatal apnea: Pathogenesis and therapy. *Journal of Pediatrics, 90,* 342–7.

Klaus, M. H., & Kennell, J. H. (1970). Mothers separated from their newborn infants. In J. L. Schwartz & L. H. Schwartz (Eds.), *Vulnerable infants: A psychosocial dilemma.* New York: McGraw-Hill.

Klaus, M. H., & Kennell, J. H. (1976). *Maternal–infant bonding: The impact of early separation or loss on family development.* St. Louis, MO: Mosby.

Klaus, M. H., & Kennell, J. H. (1982). *Parent–infant bonding.* St. Louis, MO: Mosby.

Kogan, K., & Tyler, N. (1973). Mother–child interaction in young physically handicapped children. *American Journal of Mental Deficiency, 77,* 492–7.

Kopp, C. B. (1983). Risk factors in development. In P. H. Mussen (Ed.), *Handbook of child psychology: Vol. 2. Infancy and developmental psychobiology* (pp. 1081–8). New York: Wiley.

Korn, S. J., Chess, S., & Fernandez, P. (1978). The impact of children's physical handicaps on marital quality and family interaction. In R. Lerner & G. Spanier (Eds.), *Child influences on marital and family interaction* (pp. 299–326). New York: Academic Press.

Leiderman, P. H., Leifer, A. D., Seashore, M. J., Barnett, C. R., & Grobstein, R. (1973). Mother–infant interaction: Effects of early deprivation, prior experience, and sex of infant. *Research Publication of the Association for Research in Nervous and Mental Disease, 51,* 154–75.

Leifer, A., Leiderman, P. H., Barnett, C., & Williams, J. (1972). Effects of mother–infant separation on maternal attachment behaviors. *Child Development, 43,* 1203–18.

Leifer, M. (1977). Psychological changes accompanying pregnancy and motherhood. *Genetic Psychology Monographs, 95,* 55–96.

Lester, B. M., & Zeskind, P. S. (1979). The organization and assessment of crying in the infant at risk. In T. M. Field, A. Sostek, S. Goldberg, & H. H. Shuman (Eds.), *Infants born at risk* (pp. 121–44). Jamaica, NY: Spectrum.

Lieberman, A. F. (1983). Infant–parent psychotheraphy during pregnancy. In S. Provence (Ed.), *Infants and parents.* New York: International Universities Press.

Lipsitt, L. P. (1979). Learning assessments and interventions for the infant born at risk. In T. M. Field, A. Sostek, S. Goldberg, & H. H. Shuman (Eds.), *Infants born at risk* (pp. 145–69). Jamaica, NY: Spectrum.

Martin, P. (1975). Marital breakdown in families of patients with spina bifida cystica. *Developmental Medicine and Child Neurology, 17,* 757–65.

Masi, W. (1979). Supplemental stimulation of the premature infant. In T. M. Field, A. Sostek, S. Goldberg, & H. H. Shuman (Eds.), *Infants born at risk* (pp. 367–88). Jamaica, NY: Spectrum.

McCubbin, H. I., & Figley, C. R. (1983). *Stress and the family.* New York: Brunner/Mazel.

McIntyre, M. N. (1977). Need for supportive therapy for members of a family with a defective child. In H. A. Lubs & F. de la Crez (Eds.), *Genetic counseling* (pp. 567–72). New York: Raven Press.

Minde, K., Marton, P., Manning, D., & Hines, B. (1980). Some determinants of mother–

infant interaction in the premature nursery. *Journal of the American Academy of Child Psychiatry, 19,* 1–21.

Osofsky, H. J., & Osofsky, J. D. (1980). Normal adaptation to pregnancy and new parenthood. In P. M. Tayler (Ed.), *Parent–infant relationships* (pp. 25–48). New York: Grune & Stratton.

Pannabecker, B. J., & Emde, R. (1977, May). *The effect of extended contact on father– newborn interaction.* Paper presented at the Western Society for Research in Nursing, Denver, CO.

Parke, R. D., & Collmer, C. W. (1975). Child abuse: An interdisciplinary analysis. In E. M. Hetherington (Ed.), *Review of child development research* (Vol. 5). University of Chicago Press.

Parke, R. D., Hymel, S., Power, T. G., & Tinsley, B. R. (1980). Fathers and risk: A hospital based model of intervention. In D. B. Sawin, R. C. Hawkins, L. O. Walker, & J. H. Penticuff (Eds.), *Exceptional Infant: Vol. 4. Psychosocial risks in infant–environment transactions* (pp. 174–89). New York: Brunner/Mazel.

Parke, R. D., & Sawin, D. B. (1976). The father's role in infancy: A re-evaluation. *Family Coordinator, 25,* 365–71.

Parke, R. D., & Tinsley, B. R. (1983). The early environment of the high-risk infant: Expanding the social context. In D. Bricker (Ed.), *Application of research findings to intervention with at-risk and handicapped infants.* Baltimore, MD: University Park Press.

Pawl, J. H., & Petarsky, J. H. (1983). Infant–parent psychotherapy: A family in crisis. In S. Provence (Ed.), *Infants and parents* (pp. 39–84). New York: International Universities Press.

Pedersen, F. A., Anderson, B. J., & Cain, R. L. (1977, April). *An approach to understanding link ups between the parent–infant and spouse relationship.* Paper presented at the meetings of the Society for Research in Child Development, New Orleans, LA.

Penticuff, J. H. (1980). Disruption of attachment formation due to reproductive casualty and early separation. In D. B. Sawin, R. C. Hawkins, L. O. Walker, & J. H. Penticuff (Eds.), *Exceptional infant: Vol. 4. Psychosocial risks in infant–environment transactions* (pp. 161–73). New York: Brunner/Mazel.

Pizzo, P. (1983). *Parent to parent.* Boston: Beacon Press.

Plunkett, J. W., Meisels, S. J., Steifel, G. S., Pasick, P. L., & Roloff, D. W. (1984, April). *Patterns of attachment among preterm infants of varying biological risk.* Paper presented at the meetings of the International Conference on Infant Studies, New York.

Power, T. G., & Parke, R. (1984). Social network factors and the transition to parenthood. *Sex Roles, 10,* 949–72.

Prugh, D. G. (1953). Emotional problems of the premature infant's parents. *Nursing Outlook, 1,* 461–4.

Rauh, V. A., Nurcombe, B., Achenbach, T. M., Teti, D. M., Howell, D. C., & Ruoff, P. (1984, April). *The Vermont infant studies project: Two-year report.* Paper presented at the meetings of the International Conference on Infant Studies, New York.

Reed, D. M., & Stanley, F. J. (1977). *The epidemiology of prematurity.* Baltimore, MD: Urban Press.

Reich, J. N., Maier, R., Klein, L., & Gyurke, J. (1984, April). *Effects of infant appearance and state patterns on adult perceptions.* Paper presented at the meetings of the International Conference on Infant Studies, New York.

Ryder, R. G. (1973). Longitudinal data relating marriage satisfaction and having a child. *Journal of Marriage and the Family, 35,* 604–6.

Russell, C. (1974). Transition to parenthood: Problems and gratifications. *Journal of Marriage and the Family, 36,* 294–301.

Sameroff, A. J., & Chandler, M. J. (1975). Reproductive risk and the continuum of caretaking casualty. In F. D. Horowitz, E. M. Hetherington, S. Scarr-Salapatek, & G. Spiegel

(Eds.), *Review of child development research* (Vol. 4, pp. 187–244). University of Chicago Press.

Scarr-Salapatek, S., & Williams, M. L. (1973). The effects of early stimulation on low-birthweight infants. *Child Development, 44,* 94–101.

Seashore, M. J., Leifer, A. D., Barnett, C. R., & Leiderman, P. H. (1973). The effects of denial of early mother–infant interaction on maternal self-confidence. *Journal of Personality and Social Psychology, 27,* 369–78.

Shereshefsky, P., & Yarrow, L. (1973). *Psychological aspects of a first pregnancy and early postnatal adaptation.* New York: Raven Press.

Simon, R. (1985). *After the tears.* Denver, CO: Children's Museum of Denver.

Solkoff, N., Jaffe, S., Weintraub, D., & Blase, B. (1961). Effects of handling on the subsequent development of premature infants. *Developmental Psychology, 1,* 765–8.

Solnit, A., & Stark, M. (1961). Mourning the birth of a defective child. *Psychoanalytic Study of the Child, 16,* 523–37.

Stern, M., & Hildebrandt, K. A. (1984, April). *The behavioral implications of a prematurity stereotype: The effects of labeling on mother–infant interactions.* Paper presented at the meetings of the International Conference on Infant Studies, New York.

Thoman, E. B., Becker, P. T., & Freese, M. P. (1978). Individual patterns of mother–infant interaction. In G. P. Sackett (Ed.), *Observing behavior. Vol. 1: Theory and applications in mental retardation* (pp. 95–114). Baltimore, MD: University Park Press.

Usher, R. H. (1977). Changing mortality rates with perinatal intensive care and regionalization. *Seminars in Perinatology, 1,* 309–19.

Vaughn, V. C., III, & McKay, R. J. (1975). The field of pediatrics. In V. C. Vaughn III & R. J. McKay (Eds.), *Nelson textbook of pediatrics* (pp. 1–12). Philadelphia: Saunders.

Vietze, P., Abernathy, S., Ashe, M., & Faulstich, G. (1978). Contingency interaction between mothers and their developmentally delayed infants. In G. Sacket (Ed.), *Observing behavior: Vol. 1. Theory and applications in mental retardation.* Baltimore, MD: University Park Press.

Wasserman, G. A. (1986). Affective expression in normal and physically handicapped infants: Situational and developmental effects. *Journal of the American Academy of Child Psychiatry, 25,* 393–99.

Wente, A. S., & Crockenberg, S. (1976). Transition to fatherhood: Lamaze preparation, adjustment difficulty and the husband–wife relationship. *Family Coordinator, 25,* 351–8.

Wynne, L. C. (1984). The epigenesis of relational systems: A model for understanding family development. *Family Process, 23,* 297–318.

Yogman, M. W. (1981). Development of the father–infant relationship. In H. Fitzgerald, B. Lester, & M. W. Yogman (Eds.), *Theory and research in behavioral pediatrics* (Vol. 1). New York: Plenum.

7 The transition to parenthood: special tasks and risk factors for adolescent parents

Joy D. Osofsky, Howard J. Osofsky,
and Martha Ourieff Diamond

The transition to pregnancy and new parenthood represents a major developmental period with important implications for the parents as individuals and as a couple, for the early parent–infant relationship, and for the infant's development. Pregnancy and new parenthood have at times been described as a "crisis," especially for the mother, but also for the father and the couple in their relationship (Bibring, Dwyer, Huntington, & Valenstein, 1961; J. Osofsky & H. Osofsky, 1980, 1984). Perhaps the concept is of value in emphasizing the normative struggles and upheavals that couples experience in adapting to parenthood, especially with a first pregnancy. During pregnancy and new parenthood, expectant and new parents are required to make major adjustments. The disequilibrium and new responsibilities that exist during this time can significantly affect the individual's level of functioning, the relationship of the couple, and the patterns and adequacy of interaction with the new child. In our experience as well as that of others, pregnancy and new parenthood can contribute to significant developmental growth. At the same time, the upheavals and new responsibilities can contribute to individual difficulties, family dysfunction, and, at times, increasing disagreement and estrangement between the couple.

Adolescence, historically, has also been viewed as a "crisis" of development (Blos, 1962; Freud, 1936/1966). Although the traditional "storm and stress" model of puberty is currently being modified to incorporate the moderating role of the healthy ego (Diamond, 1983), few doubt the enormous impact of this variable and often turbulent period on a child's development. The physiological, emotional, and cognitive changes that occur during adolescence are nearly matched by the experience of pregnancy. The adolescent who is also pregnant is thus responding to and must cope with a developmental "double whammy": the "crisis" of adolescence and the "crisis" of pregnancy.

Before discussing the impact of pregnancy on the adolescent, we shall clarify the normal developmental tasks of the pubertal years, as well as the psychological experience of pregnancy among normal adult women. This will enable us to develop a multifaceted model by which to understand adolescent pregnancy, one that integrates the personal psychological resources of the parents, outside sources of support, and characteristics of the child, much as Belsky (1984) suggests.

At the outset, it must be recognized not only that adolescence is a specific and unique phase of development, but that it is subdivided into stages, each with its own psychological and cognitive tasks and problems. Though little of the research on adolescence or adolescent pregnancy takes developmental stage into account, developmental studies by Hatcher (1973) and Diamond (1983) have validated the importance of doing so.

Psychoanalytic theory, as a developmental model, provides the most comprehensive elucidation of the psychology of adolescence, incorporating, as it does, individual, social, and biological issues as the child changes over time. In the psychoanalytic literature, the stages of adolescence are discussed primarily in terms of the shifts in object relations that occur in response to the upsurge of drives and accompanying anxiety at puberty (Blos, 1962, 1970; Deutsch, 1944; Greenacre, 1950; Harley, 1961, 1970). ("Object relations" here refers to internalized views of others and fantasized images of the early relationships between the child and his or her parents.) As such, adolescence is typically divided into four phases: preadolescence (10–12); early adolescence (12–14); middle adolescence, or adolescence proper (15–18); and late adolescence (18–21). It must be emphasized that the age ranges are only estimates; adolescence is a physiological and psychological process with enormous variation in children of the same chronological age. The meaning of an adolescent girl's pregnancy will therefore reflect the specific tasks and conflicts of her psychological, physiological, and cognitive age, distinct from her chronological age. Hatcher (1973) illustrated this in her in-depth study of 13 pregnant adolescents. By dividing her subjects along developmental lines rather than chronologically, she was able to demonstrate distinct and "stage-appropriate" motivations and reactions to pregnancy in her subjects. Indeed, Hatcher points out that one explanation of the diverse and often discrepant results in past research on adolescent pregnancy is that the subjects' developmental age frequently was not taken into account so that children of widely differing stages were being compared with one another.

The stages of normal adolescence

In this section, we briefly summarize the stages of normal adolescence in order to provide a developmental framework by which to understand the numerous and often conflicting results of extant research on adolescent pregnancy. This discussion includes a brief subsection on adolescent boys as well as a summary of cognitive growth during adolescence.

Early adolescence

For current purposes, the term "early adolescence" refers to the years between latency and adolescence proper and encompasses both pre-adolescence (before the emergence of the secondary sex characteristics) and puberty (when the somatic changes actually blossom).

At the beginning of early adolescence, the girl's primary psychological task is to separate from the pre-oedipal mother in order to open the way for mature heterosexual relationships (Blos, 1962). Continued attachment represents an instinctual danger due to its homosexual nature. The ego is also at stake, however, in that its natural drive toward independence and growing up may be thwarted by continued submergence in the early, dyadic relationship with the mother (Harley, 1961). Much of the behavior observed in the early adolescent girl, including her sexual activity, represents defensive maneuvers against the regressive pull of the mother. This entails a thrust of activity and turn to reality (away from fantasy) that helps the girl overcome her dependent longings. The girl's offensive bulwark against these longings are buttressed by a defensive flight into heterosexual activity. This early heterosexual activity can be seen as a defense against the regressive pull toward the pre-oedipal mother, a pull that triggers anxiety because it means remaining attached to a same-sex object (Deutsch, 1944). It must be emphasized that the girl's heterosexual activity in preadolescence does not represent feminine sexuality, but is rather a defensive effort to deny the homosexual, dependent longings for mother.

With the development of visible, secondary sex characteristics, culminating in the menarche, the girl moves into puberty. During this phase, she must become accustomed to her new physical self and begin to relinquish her infantile love objects in favor of new and eventually nonincestuous relationships. This phase is often compared to growth in early childhood when, at 3 to 4 years of age, the child must cope with "high drive combined with a fluid mental organization" (Gesell, Ilg, & Ames, 1956). Her struggle is manifested, in part, in her intense and often fickle relationships with girlfriends and older women; these friendships take on the quality of a "crush" at this point, as the girl struggles both to let go of and retain her attachment to her mother.

Within the psychoanalytic theory of puberty, there is some disagreement about the specific effects of the emergence of the secondary sex characteristics, especially the menarche. The traditional view is that menarche represents an unsettling and stressful event for the girl, confirming infantile fears and fantasies of castration. This view fails to account, however, for the girl's positive identification with her feminine mother as a reproductive prototype, as essential to the girl's development as is her renunciation of maternal dependence (Blos, 1962). More recent writers, therefore, emphasize the role of the menarche as a constructive, organizing event for girls. Indeed, Diamond (1983) found that menarche triggers a renewed closeness with the mother, likely representing both an identification with her as a menstruating woman and a means of gaining additional support as she embarks on the exciting, but frightening path toward independence. The girl thus enters adolescence proper identified with her mother and seeking her father's acceptance to consolidate her role as a near woman.

Middle adolescence

Middle adolescence has perhaps received the most publicity in both the scholarly and the popular literature, undoubtedly due to the flamboyant and dramatic flair that so many children at this stage bring to events and relationships. While the early adolescent struggles to break the early tie with the mother, the middle adolescent has the task of relinquishing oedipal fantasies and establishing appropriate heterosexual relationships outside the family and the oedipal triangle. Her self-esteem is still affected, however, by her need to see herself as a worthy rival to her mother. Her experience is thus marked by two broad affective states, that of "mourning" and "being in love" (Blos, 1962). The girl must mourn the loss of her childhood attachment to her father as she works to find appropriate substitutes for this tie. Thus, we see the intensity of emotions ranging from depression to euphoria as the girl "falls in love" to replace the old ties to her parents, filling the sense of void left by her separation from them. The adolescent's frequent complaints and criticisms of her parents and her intense attachments to peers aid the girl in her effort to distance herself from her family.

Late adolescence

As the girl matures and begins to integrate her new sense of herself as an independent person, she moves into late adolescence. Hatcher (1973) points out that this phase has received the least attention in the psychoanalytic literature, probably because the emotional tasks of the late adolescent are more psychosocial than psychosexual. This is the time during which the girl solidifies her sense of self, with an aim toward consolidating her identity and achieving mature heterosexuality (Blos, 1962). Vocational and family goals become clearer and the adolescent's character becomes more fixed (Hatcher, 1973). Though earlier conflicts may not be completely resolved, they become part of the personality and the individual is freer to pursue her goals and aspirations in the external world of reality rather than the internal world of fantasy.

In sum, the stages of adolescence involve a process of relinquishing childhood attachments to the parents, opening the way for mature, reality-based, heterosexual relationships. As the girl lets go of the mother, she fills the void in early adolescence with intense relationships with girlfriends and idealized older women and defends against her dependent longings by a flight into heterosexuality. As she matures and becomes independent of her mother, she is increasingly able to move into and rework oedipal-level issues with her parents and begin to experience boys, and her sexuality, in a less need-oriented way. In late adolescence, she consolidates this sense of herself as an independent person, able to pursue goals and aspirations unencumbered by the fantasies and conflicts of earlier years. When we see, then, how much the adolescent changes psychologically over time, it becomes obvious that a pregnancy will have vastly different motivations and meanings depending on when it occurs. Not only can this awareness help us understand discrepant research findings, but it can guide us in the design and implementation of programs aimed at helping the pregnant adolescent and teen parents.

The psychological development of boys at adolescence

A brief word on the psychological development of adolescent boys is appropriate here, although teenage fathers have just begun to be studied by researchers on adolescent pregnancy (e.g., Elster & Lamb, 1986). Like the girl, the boy traverses stages of adolescence and must cope with the upsurge of drives at puberty and the accompanying regressive pull to the pre-oedipal mother. The differences between boys and girls lie primarily in their response to the regressive pull, their handling of aggression, and their use of people in their struggle against their instincts.

In psychological terms, if the early adolescent girl's central conflictual fear is that of merging with the pre-oedipal mother, the boy's fear is of castration by the pre-oedipal mother. Van der Leeuw (1958) notes that in early childhood "childbearing is experienced as achievement, power and competition with the mother." For the boy, this is the "archaic" mother, the active, phallic childbearer and caregiver. The boy's fears revolve around his identification with and surrender to this archaic figure and the castration that would accompany such surrender. At early puberty, the boy must finally renounce his passive, feminine longings, represented in part by wishes for a baby, so that he can proceed into the final resolution of the Oedipus complex. (It is important to note that, at this phase, the boy's castration anxiety is pre-oedipal, related to the mother, and is not to be confused with the positive oedipal castration fear of the father, which does not emerge until midadolescence.)

The boy in part defends against the regressive identification with the pre-oedipal mother, with its castration threats, by aggressively turning against her. As A. Freud (1936) points out, his defense is enhanced by his sexual maturation, in which the boy's growing musculature reinforces his aggressive display and reassures him of his masculinity. Indeed, Blos (1965) points out that boys in early puberty lack any passive means of drive discharge that does *not* interfere with their sex-adequate masculinity. The boy thus actualizes his pregenital conflicts through a *genital* model. The phallus becomes the primary organ for discharge of tension and becomes the instrument through which to release his intense, defensive aggression.

With the boy's continued maturation he eventually separates from the pre-oedipal mother, shifting his identification from mother to father as he progresses through the negative and positive stages of the Oedipus complex en route to appropriate heterosexual relationships. Like the girl at an earlier stage, he may defend against the homosexual connotation of the negative oedipal complex by turning forcefully to the opposite sex, to be followed by the eventual establishment of true, nondefensive heterosexual relationships.

Although little research has been done on the psychological underpinnings of adolescent fatherhood, our clinical and theoretical knowledge provides some context in which to begin to understand the phenomenon. It is important to remember that the developmental stages outlined above are psychological, not chronological. A boy's chronological age and physical maturity do not necessarily coincide with his psychological maturity. For example, if a 16-year-old boy is psychologically still in early adolescence, he may become sexually active and unconsciously wish to make a baby as an expression of his identification with the powerful, pre-oedipal mother; furthermore, his sexuality at this time may reflect the aggression he directs toward females, in defense against his passive longings. In turn, if a boy is in the negative oedipal phase of development, he too may become sexually active and wish to procreate to reassure himself of his masculinity in the face of his homosexual longing for his father. Finally, as he enters the competitive stage of the positive oedipal relationship to his father, the boy may impregnate a girl to prove that he is "as much of a man" and a worthy rival of his father. Empirical research with normal subjects is badly needed to validate such hypotheses, derived as they are from clinical theory, but the topic clearly offers a rich array of thought-provoking issues.

Cognitive development during adolescence

Before turning to a discussion of the psychological adjustment of adult women to pregnancy, it will be useful to review the cognitive changes that occur during adolescence in order to broaden the context in which to analyze the meaning of teenage pregnancy. The discussion will focus on Piaget's model of intellectual development, which, despite recent criticism beyond the scope of this chapter (see Keating, 1980, for an excellent review), remains the most comprehensive and influential theory of cognitive growth.

The intellectual changes distinguishing adolescence from childhood begin at 11 to 12 years old, although they are not fully established until age 14 or 15. "From a strictly cognitive view . . . the major task of early adolescence can be regarded as having to do with the conquest of thought" (Elkind, 1974, p. 90). In the Piagetian framework, this is accomplished through the establishment of formal operational thought, viewed by Piaget (1969) as "the crowning of an entire process of evolution that originates at birth and whose stages can be observed throughout the development of the child" (p. 104).

In Piaget's model, the primary characteristic of adolescent cognition is the capacity to think hypothetically. This ability develops through a process of detaching the concrete logic of childhood (concrete operation) from the objects themselves, so that the logic functions solely on verbal or symbolic statements (Piaget, 1969). The liberation of logic from the concrete allows the adolescent child to think not just in terms of observable facts, but in terms of possibilities, that is, to think hypothetically. Thus, the main difference between the intelligence of children and adolescents in Piaget's view is that the adolescent can reason on the basis of propositions that are not fact but that are experimentally formulated to derive all possible consequences, which are then *compared* with facts; formal operations is thus a logic of propositions rather than a logic of classes and relationships (Piaget, 1969).

The importance to the adolescent of the ability to think hypothetically is far reaching. No longer tied to the concrete, he or she can now compensate mentally for changes in reality. Representational logic also allows the assumption of contradictory opinions, which may facilitate the necessary adolescent task of opposing parents in the quest for independence. It also allows children to construct ideals and fantasies that further help them to separate from their family.

The new flexibility of thought resulting from formal operations also allows "the adolescent to take his own thought as an object" (Elkind, 1974, p. 102); that is, he can now introspect on himself. This adds to teenagers' self-conscious preoccupation with their developing body, for they are now also able to consider what others think of them and recognize discrepancies between their real self and their ideal.

In light of the impact of formal operational thought on the adolescent's functional maturity, the role of cognition in the case of teenage pregnancy gains importance. For example, the adolescent who chooses to be sexually active must deal with the *possibility* of pregnancy and must be able to consider the consequences of his or her actions; a sexually active teenager who has not attained formal operational thought is clearly at a high risk for pregnancy because he or she may not be able to recognize, emotionally or cognitively, the possibility of pregnancy and take appropriate precautions. It must be recognized, too, that the attainment of formal operations is by no means universal, either cross-culturally or across classes (Piaget, 1969). It would be interesting indeed to compare the level of cognitive functioning in adolescents who do or do not become pregnant to see how the attainment of formal operations affects impulse control, decision making, and planning for the future.

Let us now turn to a discussion of the psychological adjustment of normal adult women to pregnancy, with which to compare the experiences of pregnant adolescents.

Psychological adjustment of the mother

Many investigators have viewed pregnancy as a biologically determined period of psychological stress. Benedek (1970) suggested that pregnancy represents a developmental phase, one that is profoundly influenced by concurrent metabolic and hormonal shifts. She further suggested that pregnancy results in a continuation of previous developmental processes and that it brings up earlier conflictual feelings that must be worked through and resolved within the individual and between the couple in order to research a new level of maturation. According to Benedek, the maturational potential is influenced both by the level of evolved psychic structural development and by psychobiological factors in interaction with the woman's new experiences of reality.

Bibring, Dyer, Huntington, and Valenstein (1961) described pregnancy for women, like puberty or menopause, as a period of crisis involving profound psychological as well as somatic changes. On the basis of their work, primarily with women whom they followed longitudinally with psychoanalytically oriented interviews, social work interviews, and psychological testing, they postulated that the disturbance in equilibrium that occurs at this time resembles a more severe disintegration; however, the outcome of the crisis most often leads to healthy solutions. They stated that the more severe the psychological disturbances before pregnancy, the more likely it is that dramatic problems will emerge during this period. At other times, depending on the inner conflicts, the pregnancy may relieve the difficulties and promote solutions of the neurotic tensions.

Caplan (1960) also described pregnancy as a "crisis." He suggested that the woman's emotional state varies at different stages during pregnancy depending on her adjustment to the physiological and psychological changes. He suggested that a woman's emotional status during pregnancy is influenced by her reactions to the sexual aspects of the reproductive process; these are associated with the details of her personality structure and the vicissitudes of her sexual development. In other words, a woman's reaction to her pregnancy may reflect unresolved sexual conflicts. Her emotional status also reflects her psychological growth during the course of pregnancy into the role of mother; this process is influenced by her relationships with her own mother and women who serve as important models.

Caplan also noted that in pregnancy, as in all human crises, the outcome is dependent not only on the long-standing personality patterns of the participants, but also on their current life circumstances. Thus, the outcome may be influenced by helping figures in the family and environment and services in the community. Caplan stated that preventive intervention actually has a potentially greater effect during this period than it would during a period of stability. He also stressed that even minimal intervention during pregnancy is often remarkably effective in promoting and safeguarding not only the relationship of the mother to her future child, but other relationships among family members as well.

Studies of normative psychological adjustment as well as emotional disturbance and pregnancy are reviewed in other chapters in this volume. In general, studies on normative adjustment indicate that, although reactions may differ for an individual woman or couple during pregnancy, other factors, including age of the parents, available support systems, previous adjustment, and parenting experience, play significant roles in the process. Emotional disturbances during pregnancy seem to be related to maturational and psychological readiness for the process, emotional stability and instability at the time of pregnancy, early life experiences, the overall social situation, and probably the very significant hormonal shifts that occur.

In our combined clinical and research efforts on adaptation to pregnancy and new parenthood and risk factors for parents and infants, we also have found that women experience profound psychological changes during the course of pregnancy and after the birth of their baby. These struggles, in general, are most profound with a first pregnancy and are influenced by maternal and infant medical complications, life circumstances, and economic conditions. We (Osofsky & Osofsky) are currently carrying out a longitudinal study at the University of Kansas Health Sciences Center in which we are evaluating factors for parents and infants related to the transition to parenthood. Married primiparous women ages 18 to 35 and their husbands are being followed prospectively during the pregnancy before the occurrence of difficulties, and assessments are then being carried out on the impact of psychosocial, maternal medical, infant medical, and multiple risk factors on the individual parents, their relationship, their interaction with their infants, and their infant's development.

Let us now turn to the literature on pregnancy during adolescence.

Adjustment of adolescent mothers: preventive intervention program for pregnant adolescents

When one considers the stresses and disequilibrium that individuals experience in the process of becoming parents and the impact on the family, the age and maturity of the parents seem to be extremely important. One of us (Joy D. Osofsky) is the principal investigator of an ongoing research grant funded by the Center for Prevention Research of the National Institute of Mental Health, entitled "Mental Health Program for High Risk Infants and Their Families." The program is designed to evaluate patterns of adolescent parent–infant interaction and infant development, as well as to develop and evaluate the effectiveness of several intervention strategies for adolescent mothers and their infants. Evaluations of the developmental status of the infants and adaptation of the young parents, together with factors that influence strengths and risks, are being carried out. Physically and psychologically based interventions for mothers and infants are important components of the program. A main objective of the ongoing study has been to evaluate patterns of socioemotional development in the infants of adolescent mothers. Another important objective has been to determine which interventions may facilitate growth in the infants of the young mothers and which factors are the most important contributors to problematic patterns of development.

Incidence of adolescent pregnancies

Klein (1984) has summarized data indicating that more than half of the teenagers in the United States are sexually active; more than 1.1 million become pregnant each year. It has been estimated that in 1981 approximately 22% of sexually active teens 15 to 19 experienced a pregnancy (Hofferth, 1984). Seventy to 80% of teen pregnancies are unintended and unwanted (Nadelson, Notman, & Gillon, 1980; Planned Parenthood Federation of America [PPFA], 1984). Approximately 50% of all teen pregnancies result in live births; the majority of the remaining pregnancies are terminated by abortion (Klein, 1978; Tietze, 1978). Adolescents account for one-third of all abortions performed in the United States (PPFA, 1984). Although the birthrate for black adolescents remains higher than that for whites and hispanics, the birthrate for black adolescents has declined since 1971 whereas that of whites and hispanics has risen (PPFA, 1984). Adolescents are less likely than in the past to resolve a premarital pregnancy by marrying. The proportion who married during the pregnancy dropped by 50% between 1971 and 1979 (Hofferth, 1984). Relatively few young women give up a child for adoption. By 1976, the figure had dropped to 7% of white women and almost no black women (Zelnik & Kanter, 1977).

In spite of the wide availability of and recourse to abortion, a high proportion of pregnant adolescents become mothers in the United States. With the scope and complexity of these figures in mind, we shall look at the various issues and tasks that confront adolescents during the transition to parenthood.

Medical risk

Adolescent mothers and their infants appear to be at higher risk than older mothers and their infants for a variety of medical complications. Maternal medical complications may have short- or long-range implications for the mother and may affect her interaction with her infant. In addition, maternal medical complications may directly affect fetal well-being and subsequent infant health in ways that may have an impact on the parent–infant interaction and infant development.

Among the complications with increased incidence in adolescent mothers are anemia, toxemia, cephalopelvic disproportion, pregnancy-induced hypertension, abruptio placentae, urinary tract infections, prolonged labor, and difficult delivery (Baldwin, 1981; Carey, McCann-Sanford, & Davidson, Jr., 1981, 1983; Fielding & Russo, 1978; H. Osofsky, 1968, 1985; H. Osofsky & J. Osofsky, 1970; Phipps-Yonas, 1980; Schinke, Gilchrist, & Blythe, 1980). Labor and delivery complications caused by cephalopelvic disproportion are more frequent among adolescents than among older mothers, and as a result the incidence of cesarean section is higher. Hutchins, Kendall, & Rubino, Jr., (1979) have reported that the risk of premature delivery is twice as high for adolescent mothers as for mothers in their twenties. The risk of maternal death is considerably higher for adolescent mothers; for teenagers under age 15 it is 60% higher than for women in their twenties (Carey et al., 1983; Block, Saltzman, & Block, 1981; PPFA, 1984). Other teenage patterns that increase pregnancy risk include poor nutrition and nutritional fads and the abuse of alcohol and drugs, particularly drugs that can induce fetal abnormality. Gonorrhea and syphilis are also risks in this group and can produce complications for both mother and infant. The increasing incidences of chlamydial and genital herpes infections in adolescents are also of concern.

A number of major complications are increased for infants of adolescent mothers (Lawrence & Merritt, 1981, 1983). These include prematurity, small size for gestational age, neurological difficulties, respiratory difficulties, and infant death rate. The death rate for infants born to mothers under age 19 is nearly twice that for infants born to women in their early twenties (PPFA, 1984). Six percent of firstborn infants and 10% of secondborn infants of mothers under 15 years of age die during the first year of life (Baldwin & Cain, 1980). These rates are three to five times greater, respectively, than among the population at large. There are suggestions that the infants may be at greater risk of death during the first year from sudden infant death syndrome (SIDS) (Bergman et al., 1972; Kraus, Franti, & Borhani, 1972a,b). Fielding and Russo (1978) have reported a small for gestational age rate 30% higher than in the population at large. Schinke et al. (1980) has described a higher incidence of a number of major neurological complications in infants of adolescent mothers.

Some studies have indicated that the biomedical risk for teenage mothers, especially those ages 15 and older, can be decreased considerably – and perhaps normalized – with adequate nutrition and proper prenatal care (Carey et al., 1981, 1983; H. Osofsky, 1968; H. Osofsky & J. Osofsky, 1970). However, because of a combination of factors, most pregnant adolescents do not receive the type of prenatal care that would give the greatest likelihood of minimizing risk and optimizing outcome. Whatever the contribution of gynecological age, socioeconomic difficulties, poor dietary patterns, late diagnosis of pregnancy, and fragmentary services available to pregnant teenagers all operate against good prenatal care and optimal pregnancy outcome (J. Osofsky, 1985).

The obvious question is why adolescents do not obtain appropriate care if they become pregnant, assuming health care is available. The answer, in part, lies in the defensive style of adolescents, so aptly illustrated by Hatcher (1973). She found, for example, that early adolescent girls respond to news of their pregnancy with massive denial and by isolating and distancing themselves from their feelings. The middle adolescent, who may be using her pregnancy as a means of asserting herself as her mother's rival and gaining independence, experiences her pregnancy with pride, but also with guilt, which may interfere with her ability to treat herself well by obtaining appropriate help. The late adolescent, who is developmentally closest to wanting and being ready for motherhood, may express her ambivalence passively, by not actively seeking care.

Adolescent pregnancy and the mother's prognosis

As we noted earlier, pregnancy and new parenthood provide an opportunity for major developmental growth. However, even under optimal circumstances, significant adaptations are required for the parents as individuals and as a couple and in their relationship with their child, adaptations that are considerably greater for adolescent parents than for older parents. In this section we review data concerning educational and vocational outcome, marriage and marital success, subsequent fertility, and psychological antecedents and consequences of adolescent pregnancy.

Questions have been raised about possible differences between pregnant teenagers and their peers on measures of educational achievement before the initiation of the pregnancy (Baldwin, 1983; Wilson, 1980). Although to date there are no data that clearly link adolescent pregnancy to differences in educational ability, there are suggestions that a relative lack of success in school may be one factor that presages adolescent pregnancy (PPFA, 1984). In our experience, a recent history of worsening school performance, erratic school attendance, or the development of minor problems with delinquency may be apparent in the year before the onset of an adolescent pregnancy. Again, the meaning of such acting out varies according to the girl's psychological stage of development, an important consideration if one is to develop appropriate interventions.

The impact of the pregnancy on future educational attainment is well documented. A number of investigators have found that pregnant teenagers are less likely to complete as many years of schooling as their classmates. Card and Wise (1978) found marked differences in the attainment of a high school diploma between pregnant adolescents and their peers even when educational aspirations were comparable before the pregnancy. The younger the age at the onset of pregnancy, the fewer were the years of education attained. This makes sense given the limited ability, especially of the young adolescent, to care for herself, to say nothing of caring for an infant and continuing her education as well. Moore and Waite (1977) showed a strong association between teenage pregnancy and less education even when other factors linked to school achievement were controlled. Furstenberg (1976) described pregnancy as the main reason that adolescent females drop out of school, a finding noted in other studies as well (Osofsky & Osofsky, 1984). In follow-up evaluations, the poor educational prognosis has persisted, with marked educational discrepancies up to 11 years after the completion of the pregnancy (Card & Wise, 1978; Fielding & Russo, 1978; Furstenberg, 1976; McAnarney et al., 1978). There are indications that pregnant teenagers fare better educationally in special programs, especially programs that focus on educational needs and that provide education beyond the period following delivery (Burt, Kimmich, Goldmuntz, & Sonenstein, 1984; Hofferth, 1984; Klerman & Jekel, 1973; Polit, Tannen, & Kahn, 1983). Although the discrepancies are somewhat less apparent for adolescent fathers, in part because they are, on the average, 2 to 3 years older than adolescent mothers and in part because they less consistently have a continuing commitment to the relationship and responsibility for the infant, they also tend to complete less education than their peers (Card & Wise, 1978).

Related to these educational discrepancies and the links between educational achievement and quality of job attained, pregnant adolescents are more likely subsequently to have less satisfying and lower-paying jobs than their peers. Again, although the discrepancies are somewhat less apparent for adolescent fathers, they, too, are less likely to have financially rewarding jobs than their peers (Card & Wise, 1978). As with education, special programs that encourage continuation in the program and childcare services after delivery appear to improve the vocational prognosis for adolescent mothers (Burt et al., 1984; Hofferth, 1984; H. Osofsky, 1968, 1973; Polit et al., 1983). Moore and Waite (1977) summarized data indicating that teenage mothers are more likely than older mothers to receive welfare assistance following the birth of their infant and in subsequent years. Data concerning older mothers who are receiving Aid for Dependent Children indicate that they were likely to have had their first child while in their teen years.

As noted earlier, pregnant teenagers at present are less likely to marry following the confirmation of pregnancy than they were in the past. However, when they marry either before or during the course of the pregnancy, special tasks and problems emerge. Because it is frequently preceded by conception, the couple may have to struggle with consolidating their marriage with a limited courtship and the burdens accompanying the care of a child. In our experience, struggles over divided loyalties to their new family and their family of origin are somewhat greater than they are for individuals who marry in their twenties. Frequently because of economic necessity, the young couple are financially dependent upon or live with parents who may provide support but perceive the marriage as an intrusion upon prior family relationships. As noted previously, when pregnancy precedes marriage, couples tend not to fare as well financially as their peers. A combination of factors, including age, economic instability, family pressures, individual problems, and inadequate social supports, contributes to a much higher incidence of marital disruption or divorce among these couples than the population at large (Baldwin, 1983; Card & Wise, 1978; Fielding & Russo, 1978; McCarthy & Menken, 1979; Moore, Hofferth, & Wertheimer, 1979; H. Osofsky & J. Osofsky, 1983; Phipps-Yonas, 1980; Stack, 1974). Related to these instabilities and pressures is the tendency for pregnant adolescents to marry a greater number of times than their peers (Card & Wise, 1978). Presser (1980) found that 34% of pregnant adolescents, age 15 to 19, who were married before childbirth were separated or divorced by the time the infants were 6 months of age. In the Menninger Infant Project (J. Osofsky, 1985), among a group of adolescent mothers age 17 and younger who married before or during the course of the pregnancy, approximately three-quarters experienced marital difficulty or breakup by the time their infants were 1 year of age.

These findings on marital disruption are not really surprising if one considers the motivations for pregnancy at the different stages of adolescence. Specifically, if we realize that the early or middle adolescent becomes pregnant for unconscious as well as conscious reasons based on unresolved infantile conflicts, we see that there is little reason to expect that marriage would be an appropriate course of action or solution to the problem. Specifically, the young adolescent may unconsciously become pregnant both as a way of fighting her regressive longings for her mother (flight into heterosexuality) and as a way of extending her dependent bond with mother through her identification with her own infant. Indeed, in such cases, the young father or husband may be experienced as an intruder in the mother–child dyad rather than as a support, rendering a successful marriage highly unlikely. Though the middle adolescent has an increased capacity to sustain relationships with the opposite sex, she, too, brings many of her own needs to her heterosexual relationships, notably her need to prove herself a worthy rival to her mother and the narcissistic vulnerability that entails. In Hatcher's (1973) study, only the late adolescent subjects expressed (consciously or unconsciously) hope that their boyfriends would propose marriage, offering them a commitment that was not forthcoming before conception. In all of these situations, however, the motivation for marriage is based on need rather than maturity, hardly an auspicious way for a couple to begin a life together.

A further compounding of the educational, social, and at times relationship difficulties results because adolescent mothers are prone to having more offspring before they complete their teens and a larger number of offspring over their reproductive careers than are their peers (Card & Wise, 1978; Trussell & Menken, 1978). They are also likely to be pleased about becoming pregnant and experience satisfaction in the parenting role (Baldwin, 1983; Brooks-Gunn & Furstenberg, 1986; Card, 1977; Furstenberg, 1976; Phipps-Yonas, 1980). Given the numerous external problems experienced by the pregnant adolescent, this sense of pleasure seems surprising. When we consider the psychological tasks and motives of the adolescent in becoming pregnant, however, it makes more sense. To the extent that the adolescent is playing out infantile conflicts and fantasies, a pregnancy may be very gratifying (although Hatcher, 1973, found otherwise). The tendency of adolescents who become pregnant to repeat the experience suggests, however, that the sense of gratification is superficial at best and that these girls are, in fact, making repeated efforts to resolve their internal conflicts through their sexual and reproductive acting out.

In our own earlier experience, a comprehensive program for pregnant teenagers that provided extensive postdelivery continuity of services including education, childcare, health care, and family planning resulted in considerable decreases in unwanted, repeat pregnancies (H. Osofsky & J. Osofsky, 1970, 1973). Most studies have indicated relatively short-term effects of special programs in reducing the incidence of unwanted, repeat pregnancies (Burt et al., 1984; Hofferth, 1984; Klerman & Jekel, 1973; Polit et al., 1983). Some factors that appear to contribute to program success in this area include maintaining continuity of services beyond delivery, the adolescent mother remaining in school, the provision of family planning education and services, and the provision of childcare services. Economic factors, opportunities for the young mother, social supports, and issues related to self-esteem also appear to be important factors.

As must be obvious by now, the pregnancy and new infant can be expected to bring up and represent important developmental considerations and struggles for young parents. However, other than Hatcher's (1973) study, none of the research on the specific psychology of adolescent pregnancy takes into account the developmental age of the subjects, rendering generalizations confusing and possibly inaccurate. Early studies that focused on psychological antecedents and consequences of teenage pregnancy frequently employed clinical case study approaches. They addressed such issues as dependency and object losses, need to be cared for, and hysterical and other emotional reactions. A number of studies then focused on traits of adolescent mothers, usually employing a cross-sectional approach; they revealed higher incidences of such traits as external locus of control (Connolly, 1975; Meyerowitz & Malev, 1973), social isolation and anomie (Goode, 1961; Roberts, 1966), increased risk taking (Miller, 1973), a tendency toward denial (Rader, Bekker, Brown, & Richardt, 1978), low self-worth and self-devaluation (Faigel, 1967; Kaplan, Smith, & Pokorny, 1979), and problems with ego strength (Babikan & Goldman, 1971; Miller, 1973) in pregnant adolescents. In a cross-sectional study, Barth, Schinke, and Maxwell (1985) found lower than normal self-esteem and a tendency toward greater depression in pregnant adolescents and adolescent parents than in a nonpregnant group. Adolescent mothers in the Menninger Infant Project have more frequently evidenced signs of clinical depression on a self-report scale than nonpregnant peers (J. Osofsky & A. Culp, 1985), a finding consistent with other recent data. These findings may seem to contradict those of Baldwin (1983) and others who found that adolescents were pleased and satisfied with their pregnancies. The depression is not surprising, however, when we realize that the adolescent who becomes pregnant does so for a reason, specifically in an effort to resolve through action the intrapsychic conflicts and struggles associated with her past and with her current stage of development, including the depression itself. Her disappointment at discovering that having a baby did not make her feelings go away is likely to be profound and may be manifested as depression. Developmental constructs such as ego strength and maturity would appear to be related to outcomes for the parents and to effective parenting. Brunnquell, Crichton, and Egeland (1981) found a relationship between maternal responsivity and reciprocity toward their infant and ego strength. As pointed out by Brooks-Gunn and Furstenberg (1986) and Hamburg (1980), adolescent mothers likely have lower ego strength and are less mature socially and emotionally than older mothers. Again, these girls may become pregnant in order to deal with or avoid their feelings, rather than develop more adaptive ways of coping with their developmental crises.

Adolescent parenthood and the infant's development

As indicated previously, and related to a variety of circumstances, the infants of adolescent mothers have a higher mortality and morbidity than those born to more mature women. These include a variety of important medical problems that can contribute to developmental problems. There are some suggestions that the physical growth of children born to adolescent mothers may lag behind that of children of older mothers.

Lester and Zeskind (1978) found that infants of teenage mothers were more likely than infants of older mothers to be underaroused or overaroused on Brazelton Neonatal Assessment Scale scores. These scores are related to obstetrical history and perinatal risk factors. In our early work, we found that young mothers demonstrated some warmth and physical interaction with their infants, but relatively less verbal interaction. Their infants scored high on measures of activity but appeared to be less responsive and lower on affective expressions (H. Osofsky & J. Osofsky, 1970). This finding is consistent with subsequent work of Field (1981) and Sandler, Vietze, and O'Connor (1981) and our more recent study (H. Osofsky, 1985) indicating that adolescent mothers spend less time talking to and possibly looking at their infants than do older mothers. We have found that prenatal interview clusters indicating greater acceptance of pregnancy, emotional support, and more positive family dynamics and relationships within the nuclear family are positively related to maternal behaviors among adolescent mothers during newborn and 6-month feeding and 6-month play observations (J. Osofsky & A. Culp, 1985).

McAnarney et al. (1978) found that the younger the adolescent mother, the less she used typical maternal behavior such as touching, synchronous movement, high-pitched voice, and closeness to the infant. Young adolescent mothers were prone to using teasing and pinching behaviors. We confirmed this frequent testing and teasing behavior of young mothers toward their infants in videotaped observations in the Menninger Infant Project (J. Osofsky & L. Ware, 1984). Such behavior likely stems both from the young adolescent's lack of maturity and from her unconscious hostility toward the baby, who inevitably has been unable to satisfy her needs. Adolescent mothers in our study also appear to have considerable difficulty relating to their infant when the infant begins to evidence more autonomous behaviors. These mothers, most likely entrenched in their own separation conflicts, have difficulty being sensitive to their child's autonomy. In preliminary observations of attachment behaviors at 13 months, the infants more frequently appear insecurely attached than do infants in a low-risk population. In other studies (Main, Kaplan, & Cassidy, 1985; Matas, Arend, & Sroufe, 1978; Waters, Wippman, & Sroufe, 1979) there is evidence that these attachment patterns may be predictive of subsequent socioemotional, developmental difficulties.

A number of studies have indicated that pregnant teenagers have less realistic expectations about children's developmental milestones than do older mothers (de Lissovey, 1973; Field, 1981; J. Osofsky & A. Culp,

1985). Discrepancies appear prominent in areas related to cognition, language, and social functioning. Furstenberg (1976) found that, in children of adolescent mothers, marital stability and economic security were related to greater efficacy and trust at 42 to 60 months of age. Marecek (1979) reported little relationship between maternal age and the child's behavior at age 4, but a higher likelihood of overactivity, hostility, restlessness, and lack of impulse control at age 7 in children born to mothers younger than 18. It should be noted that relationships between maternal age and the child's social and emotional development at school-age years remain relatively unclear at present. Baldwin and Cain (1980) point to some of the contradictory findings in this area and the need for further studies to elucidate the socioemotional consequences to the infants of being born to adolescent parents.

As Brooks-Gunn and Furstenberg (1985), Baldwin and Cain (1980), and Kinard and Klerman (1983) have described, most studies of cognitive development have found a worse prognosis for children of adolescent mothers than for those of controls. Multiple factors, including poverty, diminished maternal educational attainment, family instability, life stresses and circumstances, and a relative lack of support play contributing roles. There is some evidence that the cognitive functioning of children of adolescent mothers begins to diverge from that of children of older mothers in the preschool years and remains divergent in subsequent years. Socioeconomic and maternal educational factors appear to be important contributors to the outcomes for the children of these adolescent mothers.

Conclusion

As documented in this chapter, adolescent pregnancy appears to result in greater risk for both the young mothers and their infants on a number of important dimensions. Most typically, adolescents become parents in an effort to resolve important age-related developmental issues, only to find that their action has not made their conflicts disappear. Instead, they are often faced with educational and economic instability, family pressures, and, if they marry, considerable marital disruption. The family, religious, and community support systems may be fragmentary and provide inadequate support, leaving the adolescent alone with her baby, potentially quite depressed.

It is important to understand the increased difficulties that often occur during both adolescence and pregnancy. Erikson (1950) described major steps in human growth and stressed the reactions and upheavals of the growth process. Considerable disequilibrium and crisis can herald the beginning of a new growth process. However, in adolescence, the primary developmental task to be accomplished is that of relinquishing infantile ties to the parents and establishing one's own identity. Adolescents must deal with issues of "Who am I? and "Who do I want to be?" separate from their actual and fantasized relationships with their parents. Having to go through the struggle of finding a direction in one's life at the same time as accepting the responsibilities of parenting can create major problems and conflicts. Such a situation can be disruptive to both parent and adolescent. The adjustments and conflicts that result may depend on the individual's personality and life circumstances at the beginning of and during the process. The outcome for adolescent parents and their offspring will depend both on inner resources and on support from family, community, and environment. Under optimal circumstances and with appropriate support and intervention, pregnancy and parenthood may offer the opportunity for an enhancement of the maturational process and a positive outcome for the adolescent parents and their offspring. Under less optimal circumstances, greater support, understanding, and comprehensive interventions are necessary to face, and perhaps resolve, the complex problems and optimize the outcome for the adolescent parents, their offspring, and society at large.

References

Babikian, H. M., & Goldman, A. (1971). A study of teenage pregnancy. *American Journal of Psychiatry, 128,* 755–60.

Baldwin, W. (1981). Adolescent pregnancy and childbearing. *Seminars in Perinatology, 5,* 1.

Baldwin, W. (1983). *Trends and consequences of adolescent childbearing in the United States.* Paper presented before the Select Committee on Children, Youth and Families, Washington, DC.

Baldwin, W., & Cain, V. (1980). The children of teenage parents. *Family Planning Perspectives, 12,* 34–43.

Barth, R. P., Schinke, S. P., and Maxwell, J. S. (1985). Coping skills training for school-aged mothers. *Journal of Social Service Research, 8,* 75–94.

Belsky, J. (1984). The determinants of parenting: A process model. *Child Development, 55,* 83–96.

Benedek, T. (1970). The psychobiology of pregnancy. In E. J. Anthony & T. Benedek (Eds.), *Parenthood: Its psychology and psychopathology* (pp. 137–52) Boston: Little, Brown.

Bergman, A. B., Ray, C. G., Pomeroy, M. A., Wahl, P. W., and Beckwith, J. B. (1972). Studies of the sudden infant death syndrome in King County, Washington. 3: Epidemiology. *Pediatrics* 49, 860–70.

Bibring, G. L., Dwyer, T. F., Huntington, D. S., & Valenstein, A. F. (1961). A study of the psychological processes in pregnancy and of the earliest mother–child relationship. 1: Some propositions and comments. *Psychoanalytic Study of the Child, 16,* 9–24.

Block, R. W., Saltzman, S., & Block, S. A. (1981). Teenage pregnancy. *Advances in Pediatrics, 28,* 75–98.

Blos, P., (1962). *On adolescence: A psychoanalytic interpretation.* New York: Free Press.

Blos, P. (1965). The initial stage of male adolescence. *Psychoanalytic Study of the Child,* 22, 145–64.

Blos, P. (1970). *The young adolescent: Clinical studies.* New York: Free Press.

Brooks-Gunn, J., & Furstenberg, F. F., Jr. (1986). Antecedents and consequences of parenting: The case of adolescent motherhood. In A. Fogel & G. Melson (Eds.), *The origins of nurturance* (pp. 233–58). Hillsdale, NJ: Erlbaum.

Brunnquell, D., Crichton, L., & Egeland, B. (1981). Maternal personality and attitude in disturbances of child rearing. *American Journal of Orthopsychiatry,* 51, 680–91.

Burt, M., Kimmich, M., Goldmuntz, J., & Sonenstein, F. (1984). *Helping pregnant adolescents: Outcomes and costs of service delivery* (final report to OAPP). Washington, DC: Urban Institute.

Caplan, G. (1960). Emotional implications of pregnancy and influences on family relationships. In H. C. Stuart & D. G. Prugh (Eds.), *The healthy child: His physical, psychological, and social development* (pp. 72–81). Cambridge, MA: Harvard University Press.

Card, J. J. (1977). *Long-term consequences for children born to adolescent parents* (final report to NICHD). Palo Alto, CA: American Institutes for Research.

Card, J. J., & Wise, L. L. (1978). Teenage mothers and teenage fathers: The impact of early childbearing on the parents' personal and professional lives. *Family Planning Perspectives,* 10, 199–205.

Carey, W., McCann-Sanford, T., & Davidson, E., Jr. (1981). Adolescent age and obstetric risk. *Seminars in Perinatology,* 5, 9.

Carey, W., McCann-Sanford, T., Davidson, E., Jr. (1983). Adolescent age and obstetric risk. In E. McAnarney (Ed.), *Premature adolescent pregnancy and parenthood* (pp. 109–18). New York: Grune & Stratton.

Connolly, L. (1975). Little mothers. *Human Behavior,* 11, 17–23.

de Lissovey, V. (1973, July–August). Child care by adolescent parents. *Children Today,* 22–5.

Deutsch, H. (1944). *The psychology of women* (Vol. 1). New York: Grune & Stratton.

Diamond, M. (1983). *The transition to adolescence in girls: Conscious and unconscious experiences of puberty.* Unpublished doctoral dissertation, University of Michigan.

Elkind, D. (1974). *Children and adolescents: Interpretive essays on Jean Piaget.* New York: Oxford University Press.

Elster, A., & Lamb, M. E. (Eds.). (1986). *Adolescent fatherhood.* Hillsdale, NJ: Erlbaum.

Erikson, E. (1950). *Childhood and society.* New York: Norton.

Faigel, H. C. (1967). Unwed pregnant adolescents: A synthesis of current viewpoints. *Clinical Pediatrics,* 6, 281–5.

Field, T. (1981). Early development of the preterm offspring of teenage mothers. In K. Scott, T. Field, & E. Robertson (Eds.), *Teenage parents and their offspring* (pp. 145–75). New York: Grune & Stratton.

Fielding, J. E., & Russo, P. K. (1978). Adolescent pregnancy revisited. *New England Journal of Medicine,* 299, 893–6.

Freud, A. (1966). Instinctual anxiety during puberty. In *The writings of Anna Freud: Vol. 2. The ego and the mechanisms of defense* (2nd ed.). New York: International University Press. (Original work published 1936.)

Furstenberg, F., Jr. (1976). The social consequences of teenage parenthood. *Family Planning Perspectives,* 8, 148–64.

Gesell, A., Ilg, F., and Ames, L. (1956). *Youth: The years from 10 to 16.* New York: Harper & Row.

Goode, W. J. (1961). Illegitimacy, anomie, and cultural penetration. *American Sociological Review,* 26, 910–25.

Greenacre, D. (1950). The pre-pubertal trauma in girls. *Psychoanalytic Quarterly, 19,* 298–317.

Hamburg, B. A. (1980). Developmental issues in school-age pregnancy. In E. Purcell (Ed.), *Aspects of psychiatric problems of childhood and adolescence* (pp. 299–325). New York: Josiah Macy, Jr., Foundation.

Harley, M. (1961). Some observations on the relationships between genitality and structural development at adolescence. *Journal of the American Psychoanalytic Association, 9,* 434–60.

Harley, M. (1970). On some problems of technique in the analysis of early adolescents. *Psychoanalytic Study of the Child, 25,* 99–121.

Hatcher, S. (1973). The adolescent experience of pregnancy and abortion: A developmental analysis. *Journal of Youth and Adolescence, 2,* 53–102.

Hofferth, S. L. (1984). *Review of adolescent pregnancy.* Unpublished manuscript, Center for Population Research/National Institute for Child Health and Human Development, Washington, DC.

Hutchins, F. L., Kendall, N., & Rubino, J. (1979). Experience with teenage pregnancy. *Obstetrics & Gynecology, 54,* 1–5.

Kaplan, H. B., Smith, P. B., & Pokorny, A. D. (1979). Psychosocial antecedents of unwed motherhood among indigent adolescents. *Journal of Youth and Adolescence, 8,* 181–207.

Keating, P. (1980). Thinking processes in adolescence. In J. Adelson (Ed.), *Handbook of adolescent psychology* (pp. 211–46). New York: Wiley, 1980.

Kinard, E., & Klerman, L. (1983). Effects of early parenthood on the cognitive development of children. In E. McAnarney (Ed.), *Premature adolescent pregnancy and parenthood* (pp. 253–65). New York: Grune & Stratton.

Klein, L. (1978). Antecedents of teenage pregnancy. *Clinical Obstetrics and Gynecology, 21,* 1151–9.

Klein, L. (1984, May). Presidential address to the American College of Obstetricians and Gynecologists, San Francisco.

Klerman, L., & Jekel, J. (1973). School-age mothers: Problems, programs and policy. Hamden, CT: Linnet.

Kraus, J. F., Franti, C. E., & Borhani, N. O. (1972a). Discriminatory risk factors in post-neonatal sudden unexplained death. *American Journal of Epidemiology, 96,* 328–33.

Kraus, J. F., Franti, C. E., & Borhani, N. O. (1972b). Post-neonatal sudden unexpected death in California: A cohort study. *American Journal of Epidemiology, 95,* 497–510.

Lawrence, R., & Merritt, T. (1981). Infants of adolescent mothers. *Seminars in Perinatology, 5,* 19.

Lawrence, R., & Merritt, T. (1983). Infants of adolescent mothers, perinatal, neonatal and infancy outcome. In E. McAnarney (Ed.), *Premature adolescent pregnancy and parenthood* (pp. 149–68). New York: Grune & Stratton.

Lester, B., & Zeskind, P. (1978). Brazelton scale and physical size correlates of neonatal cry features. *Infant Behavior and Development, 4,* 393–402.

Main, M., Kaplan, N., & Cassidy, J. (1985). Security in infancy, childhood, and adulthood: A move to the level of representation. *Monographs of the Society for Research in Child Development, 50* (1–2, Serial No. 209), 66–104.

Marecek, J. (1979). *Economic, social, and psychological consequences of adolescent childbearing: An analysis of data from the Philadelphia Collaborative Perinatal Project* (final report to NICHD). Palo Alto, CA: American Institutes for Research.

Matas, L., Arend, R. A., & Sroufe, L. A. (1978). Continuity and adaptation in the second year: The relationship between quality of attachment and later competence. *Child Development, 49,* 547–56.

McAnarney, E. R., Roghmann, K. J., Adams, B. N., Tatelbaum, R. C., Kash, C., Coulter, M., Plume, M., & Charney, E. (1978). Obstetric, neonatal, and psychosocial outcome of pregnant adolescents. *Pediatrics, 61,* 199–205.

McCarthy, J., & Menken, J. (1979). Marriage, remarriage, marital disruption and age at first birth. *Family Planning Perspectives, 11*(1), 21–30.

Meyerowitz, J. H., & Malev, J. S. (1973). Pubescent attitudinal correlates antecedent to adolescent illegitimate pregnancy. *Journal of Youth and Adolescence, 2,* 251–8.

Miller, W. B. (1973). Conception mastery: Ego control of the psychological and behavioral antecedents to conception. *Comments on Contemporary Psychiatry, 1,* 157–177.

Moore, K., Hofferth, S., & Wertheimer, R. (1979). Teenage motherhood: Its social and economic costs. *Children Today, 8*(5), 12–16.

Moore, K. A., & Waite, L. J. (1977). Early childbearing educational attainment. *Family Planning Perspectives, 9,* 220–5.

Nadelson, C. C., Notman, M. T., & Gillon, J. W. (1980). Sexual knowledge and attitudes of adolescents: Relationship to contraceptive use. *Obstetrics and Gynecology, 55,* 340–5.

Osofsky, H. (1968). *The pregnant teenager: A medical, educational, and social analysis.* Springfield, IL: Thomas.

Osofsky, H. J. (1985). Mitigating the adverse effects of early parenthood. *Contemporary OB/GYN, 25*(1), 57–68.

Osofsky, H., & Osofsky, J. (1970). Adolescent mothers: Results of a program for low income pregnant teenagers with some emphasis upon infant development. *American Journal of Orthopsychiatry, 40,* 825.

Osofsky, H., & Osofsky, J. (1980). *Answers for new parents.* New York: Walker.

Osofsky, H., & Osofsky, J. (1983). Adolescent adaptation to pregnancy and new parenthood. In E. McAnarney (Ed.), *Premature adolescent pregnancy and parenthood* (pp. 195–206). New York: Grune & Stratton.

Osofsky, H. J., Osofsky, J. D., Kendall, N., & Rajan, R. (1973). Adolescents as mothers: An interdisciplinary approach to a complex problem. *Journal of Youth and Adolescence, 2,* 233.

Osofsky, J. (1985). *Progress report on Menninger Infant Project.* Unpublished manuscript, Menninger Foundation, Topeka, Kansas.

Osofsky, J., & Culp, A. (1985, April). *Patterns of attachment in adolescent mothers and their infants.* Paper presented at biennial meeting of Society for Research in Child Development, Toronto.

Osofsky, J. D., & Osofsky, H. J. (1984). Developmental and psychological perspectives on expectant and new parenthood. In R. D. Parke, R. N. Emde, H. McAdoo, & G. Sackett (Eds.), *Review of child development research* (Vol. 7, pp. 372–97). University of Chicago Press.

Osofsky, J., & Ware, L. (1984, October). *Developmental and clinical perspectives on adolescent mothers and their infants.* Paper presented at the American Academy of Child Psychiatry, Toronto.

Phipps-Yonas, S. (1980). Teenage pregnancy and motherhood: A review of the literature. *American Journal of Orthopsychiatry, 50,* 403–31.

Piaget, J. (1969). The intellectual development of the adolescent. In G. Caplan & S. Lebovici (Eds.), *Adolescence: Psychosocial perspective.* New York: Basic Books.

Planned Parenthood Federation of America. (1984). *Task force on adolescent pregnancy.* New York: Author.

Polit, D. F., Tannen, M. B., & Kahn, J. R. (1983). *School, work and family planning: Interim impacts in project redirection.* New York: Manpower Demonstration Research Corporation.

Presser, H. (1980). *The social and demographic consequences of teenage childbearing for urban women* (final report to NICHD). Washington, DC: National Technical Information Service.

Rader, G. E., Bekker, L. D., Brown, L., & Richardt, C. (1978). Psychological correlates of unwanted pregnancy. *Journal of Abnormal Psychology, 87,* 373–6.

Roberts, R. W. (1966). *The unwed mother.* New York: Harper & Row.

Sandler, H., Vietze, P., & O'Connor, S. (1981). Obstetric and neonatal outcomes following intervention with pregnant teenagers. In K. Scott, T. Field, & E. Robertson (Eds.), *Teenage parents and their offspring.* New York: Grune & Stratton.

Schinke, S. P., Gilchrist, L. D., & Blythe, B. J. (1980). Role of communication in the prevention of teenage pregnancy. *Health and Social Work, 5,* 54–9.

Stack, C. (1974). *All our kin.* Chicago: Aldine.

Tietze, C. (1978). Teenage pregnancies: Looking ahead to 1984. *Family Planning Perspectives, 10,* 205–7.

Trussell, J., & Menken, J. (1978). Early childbearing and subsequent fertility. *Family Planning Perspectives, 10,* 209–18.

van der Leeuw, P. (1958). On the preoedipal phase of the male. *International Journal of Psychoanalysis, 39,* 112–15.

Waters, E., Wippman, J., & Sroufe, L. A. (1979). Attachment, positive affect, and competence in the peer group: Two studies in construct validation. *Child Development, 50,* 821–9.

Wilson, F. (1980). The antecedents of adolescent pregnancy. *Journal of Biosocial Science, 12*(2), 141–52.

Zelnik, M., & Kanter, J. F. (1977). Sexual and contraceptive experience of young unmarried women in the United States 1976 and 1971. *Family Planning Perspectives, 9,* 55–71.

Part III

Intervention strategies for individuals, couples, and families

8   Social networks and the transition to parenthood

Benjamin H. Gottlieb and S. Mark Pancer

Except in unusual circumstances, the birth of a first child is an occasion for celebration and congratulation. For the parents, it brings relief from worries about the health of the baby and dispels anxieties about potential complications in labor and delivery. For the close social network of family members and friends, it constitutes a new opportunity to show solidarity, affection, and pride in their relationship with the new parents. Moreover, the attending physician is not the only person who gains satisfaction from the knowledge that the counsel and support he or she offered during the prior nine months culminated in a thriving neonate and a joyful father and mother. The couple's parents and parents-in-law, as well as their close friends, are also congratulating themselves on the wisdom and foresight they imparted to the new parents.

Throughout the course of the pregnancy, the new parents' social network was actively engaged in providing feedback about the significance for the mother's and baby's health of certain somatic and emotional symptoms she experienced and in recommending certain health practices to avert or accommodate these symptoms. It also shaped the couple's expectations about the effects the newborn's arrival would have on their lives and, generally, smoothed the transition from a childless domestic context to parenthood. Moreover, the new parents' social network remains active in the immediate postpartum period and during the subsequent weeks and months when other adjustments must be made to meet the new psychological, practical, and emotional demands of parenting and marriage in the context of parenthood. Even the network itself undergoes certain changes in size, composition, and function as a result of the changing needs and identities of the new parents. Certain actors in the couple's preparenthood network may withdraw because they sense that their relationship with the new mother no longer hinges on shared career interests. Others, formerly on the margins of the couple's network, may gradually occupy more central positions because, as parents themselves, they can

235

provide support and guidance for the parenting role and its attendant daily demands. In short, the course and outcome of the transition to parenthood are influenced by the social ecology in which the couple is enveloped. In turn, the transition alters the forms and functions of the network, including the salience of certain actors and the support they can provide.

This chapter reviews the social network's cognitive, emotional, and behavioral impact on the transition to parenthood, emphasizing how the social field responds to the psychosocial needs of the couple and how its structure and significance to the couple are affected by the transition. In addressing the interplay between the couple's network and the adjustments this transition calls for, it spotlights the findings of empirical studies conducted among general community samples of expectant and new parents, the results of selected interventions intended to protect the health of new mothers and promote adaptation to the new parent role by altering the social ecology, and it considers topics for future research. For the most part, the chapter deals with mental health issues surrounding the transition, highlighting the social network's capacity to render the quality and quantity of social support needed to cushion the impact of stressors encountered during the transition and shore up the couple's mastery of the new parent role. Since other chapters in this volume address the special supportive needs of new parents who are at risk due to biological disorders or social adversity, we do not deal with these exceptional populations. Nor do we pay special attention to very early (e.g., teenage) or late (over thirty-five) childbearers or to parents who adopt a first child or conceive with the help of medical intervention. Our primary focus is on the experience and circumstances of couples who have no exceptional medical, emotional, or social handicaps, who want to become parents, and whose marriage is a first marriage, formal or common law.

The social network: composition, density, and dimensionality of relationships

To date, no one has systematically and critically reviewed the different ways in which social support has been measured in the context of the transition to new parenthood. Therefore, we do not know how much agreement there is about the kinds and sources of support that are most germane at different stages of the transition. However, there have been several general reviews of measurement techniques in the social support field (Bruhn & Philips, 1984; House & Kahn, 1985; Tardy, 1985), and they have been very useful in alerting researchers to such important issues as the distinction between perceived versus received support, the delivery versus the receipt of support, the description versus the evaluation of support, the variety of supportive provisions that can be assessed, and the structural features of social networks that may constrain or foster the expression of support among their members. Tardy's (1985) review is particularly informative because it reveals how these measurement issues are addressed and sometimes overlooked in seven social support instruments for which there are some reliability and validity data.

Researchers who wish to discern the social network's influence on norms, decisions, and health behaviors during the transition to parenthood must first establish the boundaries of this social aggregate, identify its structural properties, and gauge the types of supportive provisions it can render. Although the social network consists of a group of individuals and the connections among them, we advise researchers to focus on a subsystem of the couple's entire social network, composed of people who are of paramount significance in the couple's affective life, their feelings of esteem for themselves, and their sense of competence in the major life roles they occupy or wish to assume. This primary or first-order social network is typically composed of achieved and ascribed relationships, the former consisting of close friends who are recruited into the network via the couple's separate and joint patterns of affiliation before and during their marital relationship, and the latter consisting of the couple's closest blood ties, including siblings, parents, aunts, and grandparents. Although the couple's second-order or weak ties to acquaintances, more distant relatives, and associates at work may be important because of the novel information they provide about resources that may be unknown to the couple's close ties (e.g., services for new parents), they exert less influence on the couple's affective life and on their psychosocial adjustment to the transition. More generally, in research on social support and on help-seeking behavior, it is the primary network of kin and kith that is tapped to meet the bulk of the respondent's needs for instrumental and emotional aid.

Practically, one can determine the membership of the couple's primary social network either by asking about the people to whom the husband and wife feel closest and who have the greatest impact on their feelings about themselves and their lives, or by asking about the people to whom they typically turn for various types of support. Whether the primary social network's size and composition are gauged by inquiry into the couple's perceptions of relational intimacy or by assessment of the supportive functions that certain actors fulfill, a common additional criterion that should be imposed is some minimum level of contact with the nominees both in face-to-face interaction and in telephone and written communications. Studies mapping the primary social network in these ways reveal that it averages between 6 and 10 intimates for general community samples (see Gottlieb, 1983, pp. 115–20) as well as for single, low-income parents (Gottlieb & Carveth, 1981).

Husbands' and wives' social networks differ, of course, in accordance with a host of situational and personality variables. On the former score, their employment status and type of occupation if employed, their participation in voluntary organizations such as religious institutions and civic clubs, and their neighborhood and housing characteristics affect their opportunities for social interaction and relationship formation (Unger & Wandersman, 1985; Warren, 1981). Personality characteristics that may indirectly influence the size of their networks by affecting their ability to initiate and maintain close relationships include their locus of control, self-esteem, level of self-disclosure, and n-affiliation (Cohen & Syme, 1985). Moreover, there is bound to be considerable interaction between the situational and personality determinants of social networks, a topic that has been largely ignored by network analysts. Researchers are therefore advised to assess the partners' networks separately in order to identify shared and separate social intimates. For example, they can expect to find that working-class couples are involved in intimate friendship relations on a sex-segregated basis, whereas middle-class couples associate with friends on a husband–wife basis (Adams, 1967; Babchuck, 1965; Bott, 1957; Gans, 1962; Laumann, 1973).

Consideration of the extent of overlap in the composition of the husband's and wife's personal community draws attention to another important structural property of networks, namely, their density or degree of internal connectedness. Before and during their marriage the partners may decide which of their close associates they wish to share with each other and which they prefer to enjoy independently. They may keep certain relationships to themselves if they have largely revolved around mutual interests that are not shared by their spouse or if this exclusive relationship supports a valued identity that their spouse cannot or does not wish to support. In addition, some relationships that are segregated from the spouse may stem from childhood and adolescence and are valued for the nostalgia they arouse rather than for their pertinence to the present roles that the friends occupy. These durable chumships are not likely to become joint friendships unless they can be made relevant to the couple's present identities, lifestyles, values, or other psychosocial needs. Moreover, "outside relationships" are sometimes a subject of contention between spouses. They can be threatening if the outsider is perceived as a supplemental or substitute source of emotional support, supplanting the spouse's prominent role as confidant and thereby detracting from the intimacy of the couple bond.

It follows that couples who have brought their outside relationships into the marital relationship will have a denser or more closely knit social orbit that affords both greater communication between the parties and greater solidarity. Moreover, if the friends shared by the couple are introduced to one another, the density of the friendship sector of the network increases and if these friends, in turn, are introduced to the family members who inhabit the couple's primary network, the whole network's density increases. Density can therefore be assessed separately for the family sector of the network, for the friendship sector, between these two sectors (the family–friendship boundary density), and for the entire network. It is calculated as a proportion, the number of actual ties among network members being divided by the number of possible ties.

Denser networks have been found to furnish more consistent feedback than loose-knit networks because more channels of communication are open, allowing network members to confer with one another and achieve consensus about how to respond (Birkel & Reppucci, 1983). Denser networks can also engender feelings of reactance, signifying a perceived loss of freedom in decision making, when the combined and unified pressure of the social environment constrains behavior. For example, if one member of a close-knit network learns that the expectant mother is spotting during her fourth month of pregnancy, she may communicate this to the entire group of actors in the mother's network since she has ongoing friendship ties with them. They may then confer about the possible meanings of this symptom and about the most appropriate course of action, ultimately achieving consensus about the health behaviors and/or help-seeking directions the mother ought to pursue. However, from the mother's perspective, this conspiracy of network counsel may be too constraining and may leave her feeling she has lost control. Thus, despite its best intentions, the network's unified response may undermine the mother's sense of free movement and decision making, incurring resentment and even spiteful behavior.

Thus far, we have advised researchers to determine the size, composition, and density of the new parents' network in order to analyze how the structure of the social ecology affects the couple's social and emotional integration during the course of the transition and how the transition itself affects the morphology of the network. In addition, researchers should attend to the character of the couple's ties to others and to the types of supportive provisions rendered by these ties. The dimensionality of the couple's ties to each actor refers to the extent to which each tie is based on only one or more than one role partnership (Hirsch, 1980). Multidimensional ties encompass two or more role partnerships such as colleagues at work, cocongregationalists, *and* coparticipants in a cooperative daycare arrangement. Unidimensional ties are dyadic relationships based on only one important activity or role partnership. According to Hirsch (1980), multidimensional relationships "have a greater social exchange value to the parties involved, leading them to be stronger and more reliable sources of support" (p. 161). In a study of the social networks of college students, he found that satisfaction with multidimensional relationships was the strongest predictor of overall satisfaction with their networks (Hirsch 1979).

More relevant to our present focus on transitional issues, Hirsch (1980) found that recent, young widows and women returning to college after a period of absence adjusted more smoothly to these new life circumstances if their friendships were multidimensional. Apparently, multidimensional relationships provided opportunities to emphasize and expand involvement in spheres of the womens' relationships that supported the new identities they were trying to forge outside the domestic context. By selectively emphasizing dimensions of the relationships that had become more salient in their lives, they did not have to find new relationships to support their extradomestic interests.

By inference, new parents may not need to recruit new members into their networks if they can simply place a greater emphasis on parental roles and interests they share with existing network members. Hence, couples who launch their families at about the same time as do their close friends are actually adding another common dimension to these relationships and thereby minimizing the efforts they would otherwise have to make to find new relationships that shore up their parenting role. We are not aware of any research examining the possibility that adaptation to new parenthood is accelerated or fostered when parenting becomes a new focus for interaction with existing social ties. From another perspective, unidimensional relationships that are based exclusively on shared parental roles with network members may be the least satisfying for new parents because their very concentration on parenting issues threatens to submerge other valued identities of the partners. Indeed, one of the most salient threats of imminent parenthood is that the child will become the centerpiece of the couples' lives and the raison d'être of the marriage, the partners becoming so consumed by the demands and challenges of parenting that prior commitments and goals are sacrificed. New parents are often cautioned not to follow the example of other couples who became so preoccupied with childrearing that other aspects of life recede in meaningfulness. In sum, we hypothesize that multidimensional ties to network members foster a smoother integration of the parenting role within the role set the couple already occupies because they are more readily activated to meet the supportive needs of the new parents and yet do not exclusively emphasize this role identity.

Types of social support

Although recently several researchers have developed typologies of the supportive provisions rendered by lay associates (see, e.g., Barrera, Sandler, & Ramsay, 1981; Cohen, Mermelstein, Kamarck, & Hoberman, 1985; Gottlieb, 1978; Procidano & Heller, 1983; Sarason, Levine, Basham, & Sarason, 1983), we propose that four types of support are called for to meet the parents' psychosocial and practical needs during the course of this transition. The first, *emotional support,* consists of expressions of attachment to and esteem for the individual that are typically communicated in confiding interactions that foster the ventilation of feelings and insecurities in particular. Hence, emotional support buttresses feelings of self-esteem, security, and reliable alliance while also providing feedback about the appropriateness of the individual's feelings about himself or herself and the situation. *Cognitive guidance,* the second type of support, consists of advice, counsel, and normative information about the individual's handling of his or her situation or about his or her plans for handling situations. It is typically called for when major decisions must be made about ways of coping with present or anticipated demands and can be provided by network members either overtly through discussions or covertly through the process of social comparison. The third type of support is *tangible aid,* consisting of services and material resources that are extended by network members free of charge. They include outright gifts, loans, and favors that help the couple to arrange conditions for the child's birth in the most auspicious ways. Examples include helping to repaint a bedroom that will be the child's nursery, accompanying the expectant mother to the obstetrician's office or to the hospital, lending an infant carseat, and providing free babysitting.

Network members can extend a fourth type of support that conditions the couple's appraisals of the significance of the transition for the stability, continuity, and meaning of each partner's life and of the couple's relationship. We call this provision *coherence support,* crediting Antonovsky (1979), who has written so eloquently about the impact of people's "sense of coherence'' on their ability to withstand or come to terms with environmental turbulence and adversity. He defines the sense of coherence as ''a global orientation that expresses the extent to which one has a pervasive, enduring though dynamic feeling of confidence that one's internal and external environments are predictable and that there is a high probability that things will work out as well as can reasonably be expected'' (p. 123). Although he suggests that it is a personality construct, Antonovsky notes that discrete experiences can disturb the sense of coherence and that major changes in people's structural situations, such as the shift from couplehood to parenthood, can induce significant modifications in the sense of coherence. For new parents, the issues of control, stability, predictability, and meaning that underlie the construct of coherence are salient throughout the transition. They arise both within the context of discrete stressors, such as threats to the health of the mother and newborn, and within the context of broader life issues that have profound psychological significance, such as the trajectory of the marital relationship and the continuity of past and present life commitments.

Like cognitive guidance, coherence support can be provided overtly by the network or, indirectly, through unintended social influences. Overt coherence support can occur in discussions of the significance of the transition and events unfolding during the transition for personal and marital well-being. Indirect coherence support can occur through observation of similar peers and social comparisons. For example, couples may take particular notice of the ways their peers prepare for parenthood and of the impact of the baby's arrival on their marital relationship, household routines, working life, and even the maintenance and atrophy of their extra-domestic relationships. These observations may prompt the couple to discuss how they will try to integrate the changes wrought by the transition or minimize the pressure to make changes in the first place. Ultimately, coherence support maintains or boosts the couple's confidence that they will not be overwhelmed by the changes wrought by the transition and that these changes will be accommodated both within their personal life courses and in their marital relationship.

Our discussion of the interplay between network structure, its four supportive provisions, and the psychosocial issues arising during the course of the transition focuses on a set of demands and needs the partners face over time. Although there are numerous ways of dividing the transition into stages or phases, we have organized our discussion into three transitional periods: the period before conception, the period of pregnancy, and the postnatal period stretching from the baby's birth to the first birth-

The social network

Structural properties   *Characteristics of ties*

    1. Size   1. Intensity
    2. Composition   2. Multiplexity
    3. Density   3. Durability
                         4. Reciprocity

Supportive provisions

Emotional support	Cognitive guidance	Tangible aid	Coherence support

Psychosocial needs, by transitional stage

Pre-conception

- Decision to have a child
- Timing of first child

Pregnancy

- Physical fatigue, discomfort, symptoms
- Attitudes toward the pregnancy
- Perceptions of self and body
- Utilization of prenatal services

Postnatal period

- Financial needs
- Need for respite
- Postpartum depression
- Attitudes toward infant

- Feeling overburdened
- Feeling confined
- Division of labor
- Family disruption

Figure 8.1. Overview of the social network's structural properties and supportive functions bearing on the psychosocial needs experienced during three stages of the transition to parenthood.

day. The transition commences when the couple first consider having a child in the near future and experience attendant changes in their psychological and interpersonal functioning. It concludes when their pattern of functioning stabilizes. Moreover, as Connell and Furman (1984) point out in their conceptualization of normative, developmental transitions, the changes occuring during these three transitional periods, "are enduring in the sense that the organism does not return to the pretransitional pattern of adaptation after the transition but instead adopts a new pattern of adaptation" (p. 161). Figure 8.1 summarizes the critical psychosocial issues (needs and demands) arising during these three periods and presents a capsule overview of the supportive provisions and structural properties that are most germane to our analysis of the ways that the social network affects and is affected by the transition to parenthood.

The pre-conception transitional period

A couple's decision to have a first child is influenced by their appraisal of the status of their marital relationship, their personal development, their anticipation of the impact of parenthood on both of these domains, and their present and past exposure to the primary social network's norms and behaviors. We shall focus on the network's contribution to the decision process, emphasizing how its norms, structure, and supportive provisions come into play. The couple's decision about the timing of the first child illustrates the interaction among these forces. Both historical and current factors must be taken into account in determining the social network's influence. First, each partner brings to the decision relevant aspects of his or her own family biography and retrospective sentiments about that biography. For example, if one of the partners was raised in a large family and attaches positive sentiments to that experience, he or she may wish to launch a family quite early so that the desired family size can be achieved within the most propitious childbearing years. Similarly, if one of the partner's parents postponed childbearing until their late thirties, the partner may reject this pattern of delayed family formation, having experienced the drawbacks of older parents with few friends whose children were age-mates.

Presser's (1978) study of social factors affecting the timing of the first child provides empirical evidence that certain aspects of the prospective new mother's family background influence her decision about when to have her first child. She found that the prospective mother's age at first birth was strongly predicted by the timing of her own mother's first birth. Specifically, respondents whose mothers were teenagers when they bore their first child were, on average, approximately 4 years younger when they had their first child than were respondents whose mothers were 24 years old or older when they started their families. Regrettably, Presser (1978) did not gather similar biographical information from prospective fathers, and to our knowledge, no studies have examined how certain aspects of both partners' prior family experiences shape their negotiations about the timing of the first child.

Second, we speculate that the couple's awareness of family norms and customs regarding ideal family size influences the timing of the first child. If past generations of the husband's or wife's family have always had four or five children, the couple may feel pressured to repeat this pattern in part because they anticipate the approval of their parents and grandparents. In fact, in some families, rearing several children is a measure of the mother's competence and power; hence, the challenge of forming a large family indirectly testifies to the maternal competence of all the women who are family descendants or who marry into the family. It follows that those who take up the challenge must begin their families early.

Third, Brown and his colleagues (Brown, Harris, & Bifulco, 1986) have gathered some preliminary evidence suggesting that the early loss of a parent in childhood is a historical influence among women who were later diagnosed as depressed. Specifically, women who had children at a relatively immature age, either within or out of wedlock, and who suffered a lack of care in relation to an early parental loss were overrepresented among those showing marked depression later in life. The authors speculate that this childhood experience may have aroused strong needs to form secure attachments, which were expressed both in premature heterosexual ties and in early pregnancy. Later depression resulted, in part, from an absence of support from the husband or boyfriend. Brown and his colleagues are presently investigating these etiological links to depression (Harris, Brown, & Bifulco, 1986), which tentatively suggest that, in certain instances, early family formation is a product of an intense psychosocial need to give and get nurturance provoked by a childhood history of insufficient care and support.

In addition to the network's historical influence on the couple's decision about when to have a first child, the messages the network communicates to the couple, by example and precept, must be taken into account. For example, the partners' parents may express their feelings about the most auspicious timing of the first child, based on their own experience in launching a family and on their knowledge of other young couples of the same age who have commenced or postponed childbearing. On the latter score, it is not unusual for a mother or mother-in-law to hold up examples of the couple's friends, particularly childhood friends, who are far ahead in raising a family and to make comparisons with the couple's older siblings. Parents and parents-in-law may also force the couple to recognize that, if they do not launch their family soon, there will not be enough time for the children to get to know their grandparents and the couple will be denied the practical support of childcare that older relatives can offer. Moreover, the couple's contacts with relatives of the preceding generations may even force the awareness that they will have less time with their own grandchildren if they delay their family too long. Each partner's older, married siblings may also offer examples of the costs and benefits of different timing decisions and may extend abundant advice to the couple.

The timing decisions made by a couple's own friends, as well as the implications of these decisions for continued enjoyment of these friendships, also weigh heavily in the couple's decision making. This point is

vividly illustrated in the following comments made by a respondent in
Flapan's (1969) study of married women's childbearing motivations before
the birth of their first child:

If you don't have children you seem like on the outside of everything. As much
as you socialize with them, the conversation always comes back to children, and
did the kids do this or did they do that, and you always seem left out of that
conversation. (p. 409)

These words signal her appreciation of the need to have a child in order
to maintain her network of associates and to be fully involved with it. If,
however, a couple is exposed to peers who launched their families early
in their marriage, before they established a solid footing with one another
and before they gained secure employment, they will likely be determined
to avoid the same course and its attendant adversities. Similarly, if they
observe workmates whose careers were derailed or set back due to maternity leaves or because of lost productivity arising from new parenting
demands, they may also have greater trepidations about starting a family.
Indeed, women who are pursuing professional or managerial careers run
the risk of their peers judging them less committed to their careers if they
opt to have children before they have achieved their full potential in the
work place. Their network may begin to send them messages suggesting
that their career identity will be submerged or even lost in the face of
their emergent identity as new mothers. The fact that these women agonize
about the very decision of informing their supervisors about their pregnancy testifies to the cross-pressures arising from their work and domestic
lives. In sum, the couple's sense of security and stability will be threatened
or reinforced by what they see in their primary network, by what it communicates to them, and by their anticipation of its reactions to their childbearing plans.

Given that issues of security and stability weigh heavily in a couple's
decision about whether and when to have a first child, their perceptions
of the support available to them are bound to play a central part in their
appraisal of their ability to maintain equilibrium during the transition's
course. That is, the work of preparing for the transitional periods of pregnancy and parenthood involves anticipations of both the strains the couple
may experience and the social resources available to avert or offset them.
For example, the couple's confidence in their ability to master the transition would be bolstered by expectations of support from workmates who
could temporarily fill in for them at crucial times and by the promise of
an experienced older sibling's practical help during the first 2 weeks after
the baby's birth. In addition, the couple's knowledge that they could draw

on other couples who have recently gone through the transition themselves for advice about the care of the newborn or even for companionship during the first few weeks when they are housebound can mitigate tensions about the future. Moreover, their confidence in one another's continuing support and the effective care of a physician also diminishes the threat of the transition.

It is important to recognize that a couple's expectations of support from their network and from one another stem largely from their past experience in obtaining support from close associates for other stressors. Since they are now facing a novel transition, it is very difficult for them to predict accurately whether certain sources and types of support will materialize. Moreover, to the extent that they expect more support of certain kinds and from certain sources than is actually delivered, they may suffer particularly intense disappointment and may cope less effectively with certain transitional events. For example, although the husband's emotional support may be evident at the time of conception, work pressures may make it impossible for him to attend prenatal classes, and he may be unwilling to assume certain household chores during the first trimester of the pregnancy when his wife is feeling particularly tired. In contrast, a neighborhood friend of the expectant mother may provide far more tangible support than was expected, and a new friend met at prenatal classes may render more emotional support than long-term friends. Similarly, although an older sister may lend her practical experience with infant care during the first 2 weeks after the newborn comes home, she may do so in a way that undermines the parents' confidence in their handling of the baby while also demanding to be treated as an honored guest in the household.

Peters-Golden (1982) and Wortman and Conway (1985) have outlined many of the problems that seriously ill medical patients may face in obtaining support from network members. They found that patients were misunderstood, avoided, or feared by the people from whom they expected to receive support. In the context of the transition to parenthood, there may be other reasons that the expected sources, quality, or quantity of support may not materialize. They include the possibility that network members will be preoccupied with life events of their own, that they will lack understanding of the special strains the expectant or new parents are experiencing, and that they will withhold support to express their disapproval of the couple's decision to have a child in the first place. Support from expected sources may also fail to materialize if the couple develop new friendships with peers who are also going through the transition and whose support is a more effective substitute for the support offered by long-term ties. Researchers are therefore advised to measure anticipated and actual support separately in order to gauge the impact of each, as well as any discrepancies between them on the couple's adjustment. In addition, by measuring the sources and types of support that are expected and actually delivered, researchers will gain insight into both anticipated and unexpected demands for support that arise during the transition and, in addition, will discern changes in the salience of certain network members as potential and actual sources of support.

The preceding discussion has emphasized how the social network can undermine or shore up the couple's feelings of security and stability about starting a family and how it can boost or shake their confidence in their own resources for mastering the transition. Accordingly, we propose that the coherence support they receive from one another and from their kith and kin figures most prominently during the pre-conception transitional period. The expression of this type of support, either overt or covert, reassures the couple that childbearing will not disrupt the marital relationship, that it will not submerge other valued identities and life commitments, and that both their personal resources and the supportive provisions of their network will enable them to achieve control and maintain emotional stability over the course of the transition. Rather than minimizing the demands and adjustments the couple will face, the network's coherence support promotes greater awareness of the nature of these demands and conditions the couple's confidence in their ability to master them.

The transitional period of pregnancy

The literature that examines the psychosocial issues arising during the period of pregnancy, and the mental health of the expectant mother in particular, reveals a rich and consistent set of findings. Studies comparing the mental health status of pregnant women with that of nonpregnant control subjects reveal that, although the former experience some degree of realistic anxiety about pregnancy, labor, and the health of the fetus, they have a lower incidence of psychopathology than normative samples (Elliott, Rugg, Watson, & Brough, 1983; Gorsuch & Key, 1974; Heymans & Winter, 1975; Hooke & Marks, 1962; Lubin, Gardener, & Roth, 1975; Murai & Murai, 1975; Pleshette, Asch, & Chase, 1956). Although pregnant women report higher levels of tiredness, greater bodily discomfort, especially in the third trimester, and less interest in and satisfaction with sexual activity, their ratings of psychological distress and negative moods neither are higher than those of controls nor show any particular pattern over the course of the pregnancy (Elliott, 1984). Only one of the preceding studies examined the relationship between one aspect of social support and psychiatric symptom scores, both during and after pregnancy, documenting a significant association between symptoms and a less than satisfactory marital relationship (Elliott et al., 1983). We have not found any parallel studies of the mental health status of men during their wives' pregnancies, nor studies examining the interplay between the partners' psychological functioning during this transitional period.

Only two controlled, prospective studies of primaparas have examined the relationship between social support during pregnancy and physical health outcomes (Norbeck & Tilden, 1983; Nuckolls et al., 1972). However, because they differed so markedly in their operationalization of the support construct, in the samples they studied, and in the dependent measures they adopted, their finding are not comparable. For example, Nuckolls, Cassel, and Kaplan (1972) tapped social support among the wives of enlisted men by aggregating their ratings of the state of their marriage, their friendship patterns and perceived social resources, their attitudes toward their pregnancy, and their ego strength. This broad measure of "psychosocial assets" bears little correspondence to Norbeck and Tilden's (1983) purer measure of social support, consisting of ratings of perceived and actual informational, emotional, and tangible support from key network members. The women in their sample of army wives were also younger and less educated than the new mothers in Norbeck and Tilden's study, and they measured social support an average of 24 weeks after conception, compared with 16 weeks after in the Norbeck and Tilden investigation. The latters' findings reveal that tangible support moderated the impact of life stress during pregnancy on complications in labor, gestation, and delivery of the neonate. Emotional support proved to be significantly related to the women's emotional equilibrium during pregnancy but did not have the stress-buffering impact that tangible aid produced. The authors speculate that the importance of tangible support may derive from its impact on self-care behaviors that affect gestational and delivery complications. If the expectant mother's close associates cover for her at work, provide transportation to prenatal classes and medical appointments, and provide other concrete goods and services that make it easier for her to handle concurrent stressors, then she will experience less drain on her energy, engage in sound health behaviors, and gain greater emotional and physiological resilience. Future research should be directed toward specifying exactly how the network's resources are mobilized to promote positive health practices during the pregnancy so that a better understanding is gained of the processes or mechanisms whereby social support accomplishes its health-protective effects.

McKinlay's (1973) study of the social network's influence on the utilization of prenatal services aptly illustrates how the expectant mother's close ties influence health behaviors during pregnancy. It also illuminates how the social network's structure affects its provision of cognitive guidance during this transitional period. In this study, 87 low-income expectant mothers were divided into two groups, utilizers and underutilizers, on the basis of their pattern of attending a hospital-based maternity clinic in Aberdeen, Scotland. They included both primaparous and multiparous women who resided within the city, the underutilizers consisting of more multiparous women. Strict criteria were used to designate the members of each group (e.g., the underutilizers missed clinic appointments three times consecutively without offering an excuse and the utilizers attended regularly), and formal techniques of network analysis were used to determine whether and how the groups' networks differed structurally. Data were collected about the women's proximity to friends and relatives, the frequency and place of interaction with these two categories of associates, and the extent to which kin and kith were connected and consulted about issues surrounding pregnancy, childbirth, and the use of prenatal services.

McKinlay's (1973) findings reveal that the utilizers participated in social networks marked by a segregation of relatives from friends, visited relatives less frequently than did the underutilizers, and made much greater use of friends and husbands for advice about pregnancy, childbirth, and clinic attendance than the underutilizers. In contrast, the latter women had much denser social networks consisting of interlocking social ties between family members and friends, lived closer to their associates, and relied more on "a variety of readily available relatives and friends as lay consultants (McKinlay, 1973, p. 287). McKinlay (1973) argues that the very density of the underutilizers' social networks gives them greater social control because the members' interactions with one another create greater uniformity of opinion and stronger social pressure. Morever, the underutilizers' heavy reliance on their mothers, who typically downplayed the importance of attending clinic services, and their easier access to nearby lay consultants further discouraged them from clinic attendance.

Considered together, the studies by Norbeck and Tilden (1983) and McKinlay (1973) show that the social network's tangible aid and its cognitive guidance can improve the physical health of the mother by moderating the impact of life stressors she experiences during her pregnancy and by encouraging her to use medical services. McKinlay's (1973) study also reveals how the organization of the primary network and the influence of certain key actors in the network affect the focal individuals' health behaviors.

Evidence from a third study of new mothers sheds light on yet another avenue whereby social support can ameliorate adjustment in this phase of the transition. Cutrona (1984) found that women who received cognitive guidance from their close ties during the third trimester experienced fewer infant-related stressful events 2 weeks after delivery. This finding suggests that the earlier advice and normative information imparted by associates helped the new mothers to avert later child-related tensions (e.g., conflicts with other adults, problems with infant feeding and sleep schedules, and maternal and infant health problems). In short, the network's anticipatory guidance accomplished a primary preventive function for the new mothers. None of the other types of support that Cutrona (1984) inquired about predicted early postpartum stressful events.

Although there is a need for more research on the types and sources of support that cushion the impact of events occurring during pregnancy and foster improved coping during the onset of parenting, the preceding studies suggest that tangible aid and cognitive guidance in particular are the network's most influential resources. Functioning as an informal referral system (Gottlieb, 1984), the network provides advice about the choice of an obstetrician and a pediatrician, attendance at prenatal classes, utilization of childcare resources in the community, and participation in other support programs for expectant mothers such as the La Leche League. It also makes referrals to lay consultants, sponsoring introductions to other women and couples who are also expecting a first child and familiarizing the expectant parents with self-help groups and other voluntary associations serving new parents. In its capacity as a lay diagnostic system, the network also provides cognitive guidance, helping to interpret the significance of various somatic changes and symptoms, recommending certain self-care practices involving diet, exercise, and the use of medications, and even offering judgments of the physician's diagnoses and prognoses during the course of the pregnancy.

The social network's counsel can be fallible as well as supportive. It can aggravate the tensions the expectant parents experience by making them too vigilant about the health of mother and baby or by exhorting them to make changes in their lifestyle or household routines that conflict with the couple's needs and plans. For example, a mother may irritate her expectant daughter by her frequent reminders to monitor her blood pressure, or a workmate may strongly recommend an earlier or longer maternity leave than desired. Virtually no attention has been paid to the ways that the network interferes with or disrupts the couple's adjustment and how it may contradict or undermine the mother's compliance with self-care practices recommended by her physician. The study of the social network's influence on adaptation to new parenthood must take into account both its supportive and its conflictual functions if a balanced, realistic picture of its role during the transition is to be gained. Moreover, by giving closer attention to supportive deficiencies in the network and the tensions they create, researchers might better understand why certain actors become more salient sources of support and why new actors are recruited into the network. For example, Cronenwett (1980) found that the main reason women joined a Lamaze-sponsored postpartum support group was simply because their own networks did not afford sufficient opportunities to meet other highly educated, employed new mothers. Here, a deficiency of similar peers in the network spurred new affiliations.

Childbirth and the postnatal transitional period

Postpartum depression

The arrival of the baby places a host of new demands on the first-time parents. They must learn how to hold, feed, and bathe the child, cope with crying and illnesses, and deal with major changes in their family system. These events often produce considerable stress (Alpert, Richardson, & Fodaski, 1983; Walker & Silver, 1986). In the extreme, the stressors accompanying the onset of parenthood can combine and trigger serious emotional distress. This is supported by evidence of higher psychiatric admissions for women in the early postnatal months than during pregnancy (Kendell, Wainwright, Hailey, & Shannon, 1976; Kendell, Rennie, Clarke, & Dean, 1981), a higher incidence of depressive illness at 3 months postpartum than during pregnancy (Cox, Connor, & Kendell, 1982), and higher levels of psychiatric disorder in the first three postnatal months (Watson, Elliott, Rugg, & Brough, 1983). In a review of the literature on postpartum depression, Hopkins, Marcus, and Campbell (1984) conclude that postpartum depression affects approximately 20% of mothers and may last for up to a year after childbirth. It should be noted, however, that the majority of new mothers do not experience serious postpartum disorders. In a carefully controlled longitudinal study of 128 women who were followed through pregnancy and the first postnatal year, *higher* mood levels were recorded after the birth than before it (Elliott et al., 1983).

In their discussion of potential etiological links to postpartum depression, Hopkins et al. (1984) note that the support provided by the mother's social network, and by the spouse in particular, plays a crucial role in forestalling the development of postpartum emotional disorders. They review several studies linking postpartum depression to marital discord (Grossman, Eichler, & Winickoff, 1980; Kumar & Robson, 1978) and to low or absent support from relatives (Gordon & Gordon, 1959), findings that echo Colletta's (1983) report that network support, particularly emotional support and material aid, was related to lower levels of depression among teenaged mothers.

Additional evidence that the support provided by social intimates in particular can have a salutary influence on the emotional adjustment of new mothers has been offered by Paykel, Emms, Fletcher, and Rassaby (1980). Six weeks after childbirth, they assessed the instrumental help and perceived adequacy of support from husbands and a confidant other than the spouse in order to determine whether the support of an intimate cushioned the impact of life events on depressive symptoms. They found that women who showed evidence of postpartum depression reported experiencing a greater number of stressful events than did nondepressed women. More important, depressed women had significantly lower social support scores than did nondepressed controls, poor marital quality accounting for the greatest proportion of variance in depression scores following life events. These correlational data invite alternative interpretations, including the possibility that preexisting depression either caused marital discord or negatively colored the subjects' perceptions of their spouses' support.

Failure to control for preexisting depression also detracts from a study of network support and postpartum depression conducted by O'Hara, Rehm, and Campbell (1983). They, too, found differences in the support provided to depressed and nondepressed mothers 10 weeks postpartum; the depressed reported receiving less emotional support from their spouses, parents, and confidants than did the nondepressed. In addition, the depressed women reported that their confidants were less available and that they felt less free to discuss personal matters with them. Here, too, a competing interpretation is that earlier depression either caused the network to withdraw or negatively colored the subjects' perceptions of support. These methodological drawbacks underscore the need for prospective studies of the role of social support in postpartum adjustment that control for initial psychiatric status.

Most of the studies of social support and postpartum depression have inquired into the sources of support or parental satisfaction with the support received from different network members but have not distinguished among types of support. Therefore, Cutrona's (1984) research merits more detailed attention because she focused on the kinds of supportive provisions supplied by the social network in relation to postpartum depression. In her study, 71 primaparous women completed measures of social support, child-related stressful events, and depression at 2 and 8 weeks postpartum. A multidimensional social support measure called the Social Provisions Scale (Russell, Cutrona, Rose, & Yurko, 1984) was also administered 1 year postpartum, gauging six types of perceived social support from network members: attachment (a sense of security and safety), social integration (shared interests and concerns), opportunity for nurturance (a feeling of responsibility for the well-being of another), reassurance of worth (an acknowledgment of one's skills and abilities), reliable alliance (counting on others for support and assistance), and guidance. None of the supportive provisions assessed during pregnancy was significantly related to depression at 2 weeks postpartum, possibly because these early symptoms were brought about by hormonal changes. However, several provisions were significantly correlated with depression at 8 weeks postpartum, *even when initial levels of depression were controlled.* Specifically, social integration predicted 9% of the variance in depression scores at 8 weeks after delivery; reliable alliance, guidance, and reassurance of worth also proved to be significant, but weaker predictors of depression.

To summarize, the preceding studies reveal a consistent empirical trend supporting the proposition that social support reduces vulnerability to postpartum depression. However, because of the methodological problems noted above and because the studies differ sharply in the measures used to tap social support, conclusive statements about the impact of social support on postpartum emotional disturbance are not yet warranted. Moreover, with the exception of spousal support, there is little agreement about critical sources of support, the kinds of support that soften the emotional impact of the transition, and the processes underlying the salutary impact of social support. More generally, qualitative, process-oriented research is needed to enrich our appreciation of the interplay between the couple's social ecology, their separate and joint coping efforts, and their emotional and behavioral adjustment to new parenthood.

Coping with the first demands of parenting

Early investigations suggested that the birth of a first child represents a crisis in the lives of the parents, necessitating a major reorganization of the family system (Dyer, 1963; LeMasters, 1957). The current consensus (Elliott, 1984; Zajicek, 1981) is that the birth of a first child represents a transition rather than a crisis in the lives of the parents, albeit a transition that often entails some difficulty in adjustment. Regardless of whether the transition to parenthood represents a crisis for the new parents, it certainly presents them with a set of novel challenges, disrupting previously established behaviors and relationships (Walker & Silver, 1986). Alpert et al. (1983) developed a list of stressful events associated with the onset of parenting by interviewing 35 parents of children under the age of 5. By adopting only events mentioned by at least 10 respondents, they generated a list of 21 stressful events, 19 of them occurring after childbirth. Many of these stressors concern the physical care of the infant, such as holding, feeding, and bathing the child, dealing with illness and colic, and controlling the baby's crying. Others concern the effects of the infant on the family system, such as the need to reallocate the partners' household responsibilities and to manage the tensions stemming from conflicting demands on the parents' time.

The sheer number and intensity of child-related demands that new parents face draw attention to their needs for social support. Practically, they may need help to pay for medical expenses, baby furnishings, and childcare at a time when their income may be reduced because of one parent's leave from work. Loans of equipment and clothing from friends and outright financial gifts from relatives can help defray the costs they would otherwise incur, and the social network can also provide free services such as babysitting and daycare.

Two of the most common complaints voiced by new mothers are constant feelings of fatigue and of being tied down. Seventy-eight percent of the mothers in Russell's (1974) study of the problems and gratifications of new parents reported that physical fatigue bothered them somewhat or very much. Similarly, in Leifer's (1977) study of new mothers, more than two-thirds reported feeling that parenthood was more stressful than they had expected, largely because they felt "burdened and tied down by the unrelieved responsibility" (p. 81) of being at home alone for long periods of time with the baby. Hence, when family members or friends who have experience with infant care offer them respite, new parents can rest or spend time with one another without the cost (material and psychological) of hiring a babysitter. Moreover, as Crockenberg (1981) notes, the provision of such practical support allows mothers to feel "less harried, less overwhelmed, [that they] have fewer competing demands on their time, and as a consequence [that they] are more available to their babies" (p. 863). Specifically, in her study of the relationship between infant–mother attachment and social support, Crockenberg (1981) found that the adequacy of the support provided both by household members and by the mother's community contacts at 3 months postpartum was the best predictor of secure mother–infant attachment, especially for mothers with irritable babies.

Although new parents have intense needs for support, Hopkins et al.

(1984) point out that they also face a dilemma in obtaining support: "Because they are relatively housebound and drained by the demands of childcare, [they] may have difficulty obtaining adequate support from other network members" (p. 510). Sheer fatigue may prevent them from mobilizing support from their networks at a time when it is most needed. This dilemma may be most pronounced for women who experience postpartum depression, since their dysphoria may adversely affect their parenting behavior *and* alienate potential sources of support (Coyne, 1976). The mobilization of support may also be constrained by real or perceived demands for reciprocation of the aid provided by the network. As Cochran and Brassard (1979) observe: "Repayment to a network member for assistance previously provided may require the parent to give up valuable resources or be away from home for long periods of time, and in so doing limit the capacity of the adult to perform in the parental role" (p. 603). Yet another factor in the new parents' reluctance to seek assistance is their fear that network members will regard them as less than adequate parents who are unprepared to care for their own child.

New parents must also perform a variety of caretaking tasks for which they have had little if any training or experience. Prenatal training, if any, has dealt primarily with managing the events surrounding labor and delivery, not with the care of a new baby (Cronenwett, 1980). They must now learn how to bathe the infant, diaper and clothe the infant properly, and establish a feeding schedule that meets the needs of both infant and parents. Even holding a newborn is a skill the parents must acquire. Moreover, they must learn how to deal with a range of normative problems, from crying or colic to fever, rashes, and cradle cap. Having little conception of normal infant development, they must acquire information with which to judge the progress of their child's gains in physical, motor, and cognitive development (Fargo, Tokuno, & Migan, 1981). Some of this information can be gleaned from popular parenting magazines and from baby manuals such as Dr. Spock's (1976) classic *Baby and Child Care*, and some can be provided by the family physician or pediatrician (Cook & Ballenski, 1981). In addition, new parents actively seek guidance from their social network, calling upon its information and advice and using it as a point of reference for judging their own competence in the parenting role and their infant's development.

A recent empirical study provides details about influential sources of childrearing information and guidance (Cook & Ballenski, 1981). Mothers scheduling appointments for their children at a private pediatric clinic rated important sources of influence on their behavior as parents, including professionals, television and film, books, the mother's parents, parent education classes, and personal experience. The investigators found that the mother's own parents were the strongest source of influence on her parenting practices and attitudes. Besides being a major source of information, advice, and guidance, parents serve as important models (Cochran & Brassard, 1979; Leifer, 1977). Leifer found, for example, that the decision to nurse among new mothers could be predicted by whether or not their own mothers had nursed. Abernethy (1973), in a study of social networks and maternal roles, found that the single best predictor of maternal confidence was the frequency of contact between the new mother and her own mother.

Parents' and in-laws' counsel is not always welcome, even if it is highly influential. Alpert et al. (1983) list "interferences from in-laws related to child" as one of the stressful events associated with the onset of parenting, and in Russell's (1974) survey of 568 new mothers and fathers, 54% of husbands rated suggestions from in-laws as bothering them either somewhat or very much. In addition, parents may serve as negative as well as positive models. Couples participating in a pre- and postnatal discussion group often cited practices of their parents that they would not follow with their own children (Cowan, Cowan, Coie, & Coie, 1978). In part, this may be due to the fact that expectations regarding the roles of mothers and fathers are dramatically different now than they were a generation ago. Fathers regularly take part in the delivery of the baby and are expected to participate to a greater extent in the care and rearing of their children. Mothers not only are expected to assume their maternal roles competently, but often must juggle the maternal role with their careers. Thus, since social changes have redefined parental roles, the modern couple's own parents may be less relevant models while contemporaries may gain in importance. Older siblings and friends with children, as well as extended family members of the same generation as the new parents take on greater significance as role models.

Adjusting to the new parent role

The realities of caring for a newborn may contrast sharply with the parents' romanticized notions before the birth (Entwisle & Doering, 1981; Le-Masters, 1957; Walker & Silver, 1986). Consequently, they may experience unanticipated feelings of ambivalence toward the new baby, and a considerable amount of guilt and distress. Crnic, Greenberg, Ragozin, Robinson, and Basham (1983) studied attitudes toward parenting and mother–infant interactions in relation to maternal stress and social support. They examined maternal attitudes by means of the Satisfaction with Parenting

Scale, which assessed the mother's degree of pleasure in her baby and her parenting role. In addition, they examined the extent of support provided by intimate relationships (the spouse or partner), friends, and neighborhood or community members. All measures were administered in a structured home interview 1 month after the mothers and their infants had returned home from the hospital. They found that all three kinds of support predicted satisfaction with parenting 1 month postpartum. There was also evidence that the support received from intimates and community members predicted general life satisfaction, and even the quality of interaction between the infant and mother. Thus, social support may condition more positive attitudes toward parenting, dispelling feelings of ambivalence and consequent distress.

Another means of dealing with the guilt that may be aroused by ambivalence toward the new baby is participation in peer support groups. Coates and Winston (1983) maintain that support groups can help depressed individuals see themselves as responding in a normal way to a stressful situation, rather than defining themselves as deviant or abnormal. By talking to other people who have experienced, or are experiencing, the same kinds of feelings, the new mother may learn to accept them, viewing them as normal and transitory. For example, when Cronenwett (1980) asked the participants in a postpartum support group what they had found most meaningful, 73% mentioned that their realization that other women were experiencing the same feelings reassured them about the normalcy of their own experiences.

Confronted with a novel set of child-related stressors, new parents engage in a process of cognitive appraisal, which determines whether the event entails a threat to their identities, relationships, or physical and emotional well-being (Walker & Silver, 1986). If it is seen as a threat, they experience distress and attempt to cope with it in some manner; if not, no action is necessary. For example, if the baby does not appear to be nursing often enough, the appraisal process would involve determining whether something is wrong with the infant (Is the baby sick? not developing properly? Is this normal?) or with the parents' handling of the infant. If the feeding problem is appraised as benign – a sign of normal infant behavior – no action is taken. If, however, it is appraised as a symptom of illness or of parental mismanagement, the parents may invoke their physician's expertise or marshal the experiential knowledge of neighbors, friends, or family members. The social network can influence this process of appraisal through the provision of coherence support and cognitive guidance. It can do so directly by offering feedback about the meaning or significance of potentially threatening events and, indirectly, by modeling and providing a basis for social comparisons.

The effects of childbirth on the social network

Most of the research relating social networks and social support to the transition to parenthood has treated the network as an independent variable, examining its effects on the adjustment of new parents. However, strong reciprocal effects occur, the transition also shifting the structure and composition of the social network and altering the perceived adequacy of its supportive provisions. The few studies that examine the network and its help as a dependent variable support this assertion. For example, Cutrona (1984) discerned a number of changes in new mothers' perceptions of their access to social support between pregnancy and 1 year postpartum. Their networks were perceived to offer significantly less reassurance of their worth, less attachment, and less social integration in the period between pregnancy and the baby's first birthday. Either these decrements simply reflect a reduction in the size of the network, or they signal that changes in its membership or diminished involvement in it leave the new mother with impoverished supportive provisions. It is also possible that the network actually provided a steady level of support during this 12-month interval but that the mother's greater needs for these three supportive provisions caused her to view the network as deficient in meeting them.

Other relationships may be strengthened during the transition to parenthood, new members added to the network, and some dropped. Two longitudinal studies offer converging evidence about changes in the new parents' patterns of contact with network members. Both Belsky and Rovine (1984) and McCannell (1987) measured new parents' social contacts during the third trimester of pregnancy and twice thereafter, shortly following the baby's birth and several months later. They found an increase in contact with other parents of young children during the postpartum period and with family members. McCannell (1987) also found a significant decrease in the new mothers' average network size, from a mean of 16.6 members during pregnancy to 13.5 members 1 year after the birth. Consistent with Belsky and Rovine (1984), she found that the proportion of other parents within the network increased over time, from 24% during pregnancy to 36% 1 year postpartum.

The picture that emerges from this research reveals a transition to a smaller, denser, and more homogeneous network, friends who have or are about to have children and family members comprising a large portion of the network. One reason for the increased interaction with family members may be that family members do not expect reciprocation for their help during this period. Lerner and Meindl (1981) have suggested that family members are in an "identity" relationship with one another; help for family members is tantamount to help for oneself and therefore does not require reciprocal benefits. Because friends have a "unit" relationship with the couple, they would be more likely to expect reciprocity for the help they provide. These distinctions may also explain why other parents of new babies become a larger part of the couple's network; the common needs that stem from their shared identity as parents create many opportunities to balance exchanges of emotional support, cognitive guidance, and tangible aid.

A great deal more research is needed to understand the ways in which networks and their supportive provisions change throughout the transition to parenthood. Why do certain members drop out of the network? How are new members added? Are changes in the network related to the kinds of support needed at different points in time? Ecological variables such as maternal employment may also influence changes in the network. Moreover, McCannell (1987) underscores the importance of examining how network changes differ for the mother and father. If networks play as important a role in this transition as the research indicates, it is necessary to develop a deeper understanding of how they influence, and are influenced by, the onset of parenthood.

Support programs for new parents

Until recently, most programs available to couples undergoing the transition to parenthood were designed primarily to ease childbirth, not to help the partners assume the parent role. Within the past few years, however, a number of programs have been designed by professionals and ordinary citizens who recognized the need for additional support during the immediate postnatal transitional period. Many of these programs have been described in a volume prepared by the Family Resource Coalition with the assistance of the Yale University Bush Center in Child Development and Social Policy (1984; see also Kagan & Seitz, Chapter 10, this volume). In addition, Wandersman (1982) has critically reviewed eight support programs for new parents, concentrating on ways of matching program goals to the needs of new parents, increasing the intervention's impact on parental behaviors, and enriching the support process that unfolds in the group sessions. She shows that these programs generally have not had much impact on objective measures of parental functioning despite their consumers' relatively high levels of participation in and satisfaction with group sessions. Moreover, she attributes much of the difficulty of achieving desired objectives to a mismatch between the ambitious and specific goals of these interventions and their diffuse focus in the actual programming of the group sessions: "While programs can still combine support and education on a variety of important issues in the transition of parenthood, programs which specify their emphasis may be more effective than those which disperse their efforts equally to all areas entailed in the transition of parenthood" (Wandersman, 1982, p. 107).

Although most postnatal support programs combine cognitive guidance from veteran parents or experts with the emotional support of peers, they differ sharply in the ways members are recruited, the composition of the groups, the location of meetings, the number and duration of group sessions, and the extent to which the group sessions are structured and focused on skill acquisition. Their goals also differ markedly, some aimed purely at the reduction of social isolation, some attempting to effect major changes in parenting attitudes and behaviors, and some striving to avert child maltreatment and neglect among high-risk parents. Powell's (1987) Child and Family Neighborhood Program and the Pride in Parenthood Program described by Gray (1982) epitomize peer support initiatives that are aimed to reduce social isolation among low-income and navy families, respectively. Badger's (1981) intervention aimed to shore up the parenting skills of high-risk adolescent mothers. Two studies that used experimental designs to evaluate the impact of postnatal support groups failed to detect any changes in the health and adjustment of program participants, although both received glowing reports from the new parents about the value of their attendance (McGuire & Gottlieb, 1979; Wandersman, Wandersman, & Kahn, 1980). The former study deserves more detailed attention because it provides preliminary evidence that support group participation can encourage greater reliance on the informal resources available in the parents' own social networks.

McGuire and Gottlieb (1979) collaborated with two family physicians who were interested in teaching new parents more about infant development and care so that they would make less use of the physicians' services for problems that were self-limiting. However, instead of providing them with educational materials or instructing them about parenting, the physicians agreed to assign new parent couples randomly to a support group convened by the physician and his wife in their own home and to a control group, which received educational material in the mail. Accordingly, 24 couples participated in the study, 6 attending one physician's support group and 6 attending the other's; 12 couples constituted the comparison group. Following a pretest of the respondents' levels of stress and well-being, their parenting behaviors and attitudes, and their use of their own social networks for help in dealing with child-related matters and concerns, the support group members met with their respective physicians weekly for 7 weeks, completing an identical posttest 5 weeks after the final group session. Couples in both the intervention and the comparison groups were told that the posttest would provide the physicians with information about whether and how couples' attitudes and behaviors change as their children mature.

The results of this intervention showed that it had no effects on the health or the attitudes of the group members but did prompt them to make greater use of their own social networks to support the parenting role. Specifically, 5 weeks after the last group session, couples in both support groups discussed childrearing matters with members of their own social networks more frequently than did control couples, and participants in one of the groups also enlarged the range of associates with whom they discussed such matters. Moreover, this finding does not reflect the integration of support group members in the intervention groups' networks since they were told not to include these new contacts. Thus, it appears that "their group experience in the use of informal social support generalized to the natural networks in which they participated" (McGuire & Gottlieb, 1979, p. 115). More generally, these results suggest that peer support groups for new parents may reduce inhibitions about seeking help from informal sources. The intervention itself demonstrates that physicians and other community caregivers can sponsor such groups and that peer support can reduce the demand for and cost associated with the use of professional health and welfare services for new parents.

Whereas the preceding study provides evidence that peer support groups can foster greater reliance on the support of ongoing networks, other reports show that members attend precisely because their networks fail to offer support for the parenting role or because they have few ties from which to draw relevant support in the first place. As noted earlier, Cronenwett (1980) found that women joined a Lamaze postnatal support group mainly because they wished to meet persons in the same situation as themselves (having their first child and returning to work soon after the baby's birth) and desired to meet mothers with children who were the same age as their own child. These new mothers did not lack a network of peer ties, but attended because their networks were deficient in types and sources of support germane to the participants' special circumstances and identities as career-oriented new mothers. In short, for these women, the new ties afforded by the support group assisted them in integrating the transition with other ongoing life commitments. Additional evidence that the social ecology in which new mothers are embedded exerts an influence on their use of parent education and support programs comes from a study conducted by Birkel and Reppucci (1983). Echoing Mc-Kinlay's (1973) findings in relation to social network differences among high and low utilizers of prenatal medical services, they found that low utilizers of a professionally organized parent education program participated in denser, more kin-dominated networks that were located closer to the mothers' homes than did the high utilizers. They speculate that the process underlying these contrasting network configurations may have to do with the possibility that denser networks "fail in providing connections to other social systems, exert pressure to pursue help-seeking in normatively approved fashion (for example, only from network members), or are so efficient in providing aid and advice as to obviate the need for professional assistance" (Birkel & Reppucci, 1983, p. 198). Unlike McKinlay (1973), the authors did not examine whether the two groups differed in their reliance on certain actors in their networks for advice about attending the parent education program.

Finally, two additional interventions deserve mention here because they involve the delivery of social support from a single source rather than from a group of similar peers and because they are focused specifically on mitigating pain, discomfort, and complications in labor and delivery. The first is the father's involvement as a coach in the Lamaze method of childbirth preparation, and the second is the introduction of a supportive lay companion at the time of labor and delivery.

In their cogent analysis of the psychological mechanisms underlying the Lamaze method of childbirth preparation, Wideman and Singer (1984) observe that the father's coaching activities "provide reassurance and confidence as well as feelings of caring and support to the mother" (p. 1360). His attendance at classes, supervision of home practice, and actual participation during labor and delivery, consisting of physical stroking, timing of contractions, and reminders to relax, are tangible expressions of his support. However, since this support is only one of five mechanisms that may contribute to the efficacy of Lamaze training, Wideman and Singer (1984) conclude that its specific impact is as yet unknown. They call for experimental studies with appropriate controls to discern the effects of the separate components underlying this kind of training.

The second intervention does, indeed, provide evidence that support delivered by an empathic companion during childbirth produces health-protective effects. Sosa, Kennell, Klaus, Robertson, and Urrutia (1980) conducted a study in a Guatemalan hospital in which they randomly assigned a *doula*, or supportive companion, to accompany half of the women admitted for their first delivery. This untrained layperson, who was a stranger to the expectant mothers, was constantly present from the time of admission until delivery, providing physical contact, friendly dialogue, and simple companionship. In comparison with the control group of women, who received routine care from the hospital's medical staff, the group receiving companionate care had far fewer complications in labor and delivery; only 13 of the 33 women assigned a *doula* experienced any complications, whereas 83 of the 103 women assigned to the routine-care condition experienced serious complications. Furthermore, the presence of the *doula* speeded delivery time; an average of 8.7 hours elapsed from the point of admission to delivery in comparison with 19.3 hours for the routine-care group. The groups also differed dramatically in maternal behaviors deemed to foster bonding between mother and infant; during the first hour after birth, mothers who received informal support were observed to stay awake longer than those in the routine-care group, stroked their infants more, talked to them more, and smiled at them more.

Hence, the presence of a calm, supportive ally had impressive effects on the health of mother and neonate, although, once again, it is not clear why. The psychoprophylactic impact of the *doula* may have spurred the production of a larger amount of natural analgesics (Wideman & Singer, 1984); it may have created greater physiological relaxation, which inhibited the sympathetic arousal system (Connor, 1974); or it may have directly conditioned less threatening appraisals of the dual stressors of labor and childbirth. Moreover, the powerful results of the Guatemalan study require replication in other cultures before conclusive statements can be made about the protective effect of social support during parturition. For example, it is possible that the *doula*'s support was particularly salutary because these women were unaccustomed to receiving such support from their ongoing network ties or because they received much more support in the hospital than they had expected. The *doula*'s presence may also have diverted their attention from the intimidating medical equipment with which they were surrounded in the labor and delivery rooms, further attenuating their anxiety.

Conclusion

In this chapter we have tried to bring into sharper focus the direct and indirect ways in which the social network helps new parents anticipate and adjust to the multiple demands they face over the course of the transition, as well as the ways in which the needs aroused by the transition affect the network's structure and the perceived adequacy of its supportive provisions. We have also identified four types of support that ought to be taken into consideration in future research among prospective or new parents, highlighting the importance of distinguishing between the support the partners expect to receive from one another and their associates and the support they actually receive. In addition, we have faulted prior research for its disproportionate emphasis on the positive side of network interactions, and we have lamented the fact that few studies have offered insights about the processes whereby social support accomplishes its health-protective effects. Even the interventions we have reviewed fail to illuminate why a supportive companion or a peer support group exerts a beneficial impact on the health and adjustment of new mothers. In the absence of a theory of social support, there is simply no basis for testing hypotheses relating specific support functions to specific stressful demands or for determining the mechanisms, cognitive, physiological, and/or behavioral, underlying the positive health effects of social support. Moreover, methodological shortcomings within studies and sharp differences among the measures of support they have adopted make it impossible to accept and integrate their findings.

There is a need for more qualitative, descriptive research documenting the supportive and stressful transactions that prospective or new parents engage in with members of their social networks. Also needed are interventions designed to reveal how the support process arises and how different ways of matching peer allies and programming their activities affect new parents' adjustment over time. Researchers can collaborate with public health departments that offer prenatal classes, experimenting with alternative methods of establishing supportive interactions among the participants. Although the Lamaze method casts the father into the role of a supportive ally vis-à-vis his wife, it does not make any provisions for *him* to receive support either from other fathers or from the whole class. The literature on the transition to parenthood tends to ignore the ways that the father's social network socializes him into the parent role and aids or constrains his strivings to integrate this identity within his marital and work life. Finally, we believe that much more attention should be paid to the interplay between the social network and the professional services that are available to new parents. We need to gain a better understanding of how the network can undermine the physician's recommendations for self-care and infant care, how it can deter new parents from using formal health and human services or encourage their use, and how its experiential knowledge can be marshaled to promote healthy marital and family functioning.

References

Abernethy, V. D. (1973). Social network and response to the maternal role. *International Journal of Sociology of the Family, 3*, 86–92.

Adams, B. A. (1967). *Kinship in an urban setting*. Chicago: Markham.

Alpert, J. L., Richardson, M. S., & Fodaski, L. (1983). Onset of parenting and stressful events. *Journal of Primary Prevention, 3*, 149–59.

Antonovsky, A. (1979). *Health, stress, and coping*. San Francisco: Jossey-Bass.

Babchuk, N. (1965). Primary friends and kin: A study of the associations of middle class couples. *Social Forces, 43*, 483–93.

Badger, E. (1981). Effects of parent education program on teenage mothers and their offspring. In K. G. Scott, T. Fields, & E. Robertson (Eds.), *Teenage parents and their offspring* (pp. 93–121). New York: Grune & Stratton.

Barrera, M., Sandler, I., & Ramsay, T. B. (1981). Preliminary development of a scale of social support: Studies on college students. *American Journal of Community Psychology, 9*, 435–47.

Belsky, J., & Rovine, M. (1984). Social network contact, family support, and the transition to parenthood. *Journal of Marriage and the Family, 45*, 567–79.

Birkel, R. C., & Reppucci, N. D. (1983). Social networks, information seeking, and the utilization of services. *American Journal of Community Psychology, 11*, 185–205.

Bott, E. (1957). *Family and social networks*. London: Tavistock.

Brown, G. W., Harris, T. O., & Bifulco, A. (1986). Long-term effect of early loss of parent. In M. Rutter, C. Izard, & P. Read (Eds.), *Depression in young people: Developmental and clinical perspectives*. New York: Guilford Press.

Bruhn, J. G., & Philips, B. U. (1984). Measuring social support: A synthesis of current approaches. *Journal of Behavioral Medicine, 7*, 151–69.

Coates, D., & Winston, T. (1983). Counteracting the deviance of depression: Peer support groups for victims. *Journal of Social Issues, 39*, 169–94.

Cochran, M. M., & Brassard, J. A. (1979). Child development and personal social networks. *Child Development, 50*, 601–6.

Cohen, S., Mermelstein, R., Kamarck, T., & Hoberman, H. (1985). Measuring the functional components of social support. In I. G. Sarason & B. R. Sarason (Eds.), *Social support: Theory, research, and applications* (pp. 73–94). The Hague: Nijhoff.

Cohen, S., & Syme, S. L. (1985). Issues in the study and application of social support. In S. Cohen & S. L. Syme (Eds.), *Social support and health* (pp. 3–22). New York: Academic Press.

Colletta, N. D. (1983). At risk for depression: A study of young mothers. *Journal of Genetic Psychology, 142*, 301–10.

Connell, J., & Furman, W. (1984). The study of transitions: Conceptual and methodological issues. In R. Emde & R. Harmon (Eds.), *Continuities and discontinuities in development* (pp. 153–73). New York: Plenum.

Connor, W. H. (1974). Effects of brief relaxation training on autonomic response to anxiety-evoking stimuli. *Psychophysiology, 11*, 591–9.

Cook, A. S., & Ballenski, C. B. (1981). Perceived influences on parenting. *Family Perspectives, 15*, 11–14.

Cowan, C., Cowan, P., Coie, L., & Coie, J. (1978). Becoming a family: The impact of a first child's birth on the couple's relationship. In W. Miller & L. Newman (Eds.), *The first child and family formation* (pp. 296–324). Chapel Hill: University of North Carolina, Carolina Population Center.

Cox, J. L., Connor, Y. M., & Kendell, R. E. (1982). Prospective study of the psychiatric disorders of childbirth. *British Journal of Psychiatry, 140*, 111–17.

Coyne, J. C. (1976). Depression and the response of others. *Journal of Abnormal Psychology,* *85,* 186–93.

Crnic, K. A., Greenberg, M. T., Ragozin, A. S., Robinson, N. M., & Basham, R. B. (1983). Effects of stress and social support on mothers and premature and full term infants. *Child Development, 54,* 209–17.

Crockenberg, S. B. (1981). Infant irritability, mother responsiveness and social support influences on the security of infant–mother attachment. *Child Development, 52,* 857–65.

Cronenwett, L. R. (1980). Elements and outcomes of a postpartum support group program. *Research in Nursing and Health, 3,* 33–41.

Cutrona, C. E. (1984). Social support and stress in the transition to parenthood. *Journal of Abnormal Psychology, 93,* 378–90.

Dyer, E. D. (1963). Parenthood as crisis: A restudy. *Marriage and Family Living, 25,* 296–301.

Elliott, S. A. (1984). Pregnancy and after. In S. Rachman (Ed.), *Contributions to medical psychology* (Vol. 3, pp. 93–116). New York: Pergamon Press.

Elliott, S. A., Rugg, A. J., Watson, J. P., & Brough, D. I. (1983). Mood changes during pregnancy and after the birth of a child. *British Journal of Clinical Psychology, 22,* 295–308.

Entwisle, D. R., & Doering, S. G. (1981). *The first birth: A family turning point.* Baltimore, MD: Johns Hopkins University Press.

Fargo, J., Tokuno, K., & Migan, M. A. (1981). Comfort/discomfort in the parenting role: Implications for the provision of child rearing information. *Family Perspectives, 15,* 63–71.

Flapan, M. (1969). A paradigm for the analysis of childbearing motivations of married women prior to the birth of the first child. *American Journal of Orthopsychiatry, 39,* 402–17.

Gans, H. J. (1962). *The urban villagers.* New York: Free Press.

Gordon, R. E., & Gordon, K. K. (1959). Social factors in the prediction and treatment of emotional disorders of pregnancy. *American Journal of Obstetrics and Gynecology, 77,* 1074–83.

Gorsuch, R. L., & Key, M. K. (1974). Abnormalities of pregnancy as a function of anxiety and life stress. *Psychosomatic Medicine, 36,* 352–62.

Gottlieb, B. H. (1978). The development and application of a classification scheme of informal helping behaviors. *Canadian Journal of Behavioural Science, 10,* 105–15.

Gottlieb, B. H. (1983). *Social support strategies: Guidelines for mental health practice.* Beverly Hills, CA: Sage.

Gottlieb, B. H. (1984). The informal system of employee assistance on campus. In R. W. Thoreson & E. P. Hosokawa (Eds.), *Employee assistance programs in higher education* (pp. 65–84). Springfield, IL: Thomas.

Gottlieb, B. H., & Carveth, W. B. (1981). *An investigation into the use of formal and informal helping resources by low income families.* Unpublished manuscript, University of Guelph, Department of Psychology, Guelph, Ontario.

Gray, E. B. (1982). Perinatal support programs: A strategy for the primary prevention of child abuse. *Journal of Primary Prevention, 3,* 138–52.

Grossman, F. K., Eichler, L. S., & Winickoff, S. A. (1980). *Pregnancy, birth, and parenthood.* San Francisco: Jossey-Bass.

Harris, T. O., Brown, G. W., & Bifulco, A. (1986). Loss of parent in childhood and adult psychiatric disorder: The Walthamstow study 1. The role of lack of adequate parental care. *Psychological Medicine, 16,* 641–59.

Heymans, H., & Winter, S. T. (1975). Fears during pregnancy: An interview study of 200 postpartum women. *Israel Journal of Medical Science, 11,* 1102–5.

Hirsch, B. J. (1979). Psychological dimensions of social networks: A multimethod analysis. *American Journal of Community Psychology, 7,* 263–77.

Hirsch, B. J. (1980). Natural support systems and coping with major life changes. *American Journal of Community Psychology, 8,* 159–72.

Hooke, J. F., & Marks, P. A. (1962). MMPI characteristics of pregnancy. *Journal of Clinical Psychology, 18,* 316–17.

Hopkins, J., Marcus, M., & Campbell, S. B. (1984). Postpartum depression: A critical review. *Psychological Bulletin, 95,* 498–515.

House, J. S., & Kahn, K. L. (1985). Measures and concepts of social support. In S. Cohen & S. L. Syme (Eds.), *Social support and health* (pp. 83–108). New York: Academic Press.

Kendell, R. E., Wainright, S., Hailey, A., & Shannon, B. (1976). The influence of childbirth on psychiatric morbidity. *Psychological Medicine, 6,* 297–302.

Kendell, R. E., Rennie, D., Clarke, J. A., & Dean, C. (1981). The social and obstetric correlates of psychiatric admission in the puerperium. *Psychological Medicine, 11,* 341–50.

Kumar, R., & Robson, K. (1978). Neurotic disturbance during pregnancy and the puerperium: Preliminary report of a prospective survey of 119 primaparae. In M. Sandler (Ed.), *Mental illness in pregnancy and the puerperium* (pp. 40–51). Oxford: Oxford Medical Publications.

Laumann, E. O. (1973). *Bonds of pluralism.* New York: Wiley.

Leifer, M. (1977). Psychological changes accompanying pregnancy and motherhood. *Genetic Psychology Monographs, 95,* 55–96.

LeMasters, E. E. (1957). Parenthood as crisis. *Journal of Marriage and Family Living, 19,* 352–5.

Lerner, M. J., & Meindl, J. R. (1981). Justice and altruism. In J. P. Rushton & R. M. Sorrentino (Eds.), *Altruism and helping behavior: Social, personality and developmental perspectives* (pp. 213–32). Hillsdale, NJ: Erlbaum.

Lubin, B., Gardener, S. H., & Roth, A. (1975). Mood and somatic symptoms during pregnancy. *Psychosomatic Medicine, 37,* 136–46.

McCannell, K. (1987). Social networks and the transition to motherhood. In R. Milardo (Ed.), *Families and social networks.* Beverly Hills, CA: Sage.

McGuire, J. C., & Gottlieb, B. H. (1979). Social support groups among new parents: An experimental study in primary prevention. *Journal of Clinical Child Psychology, 8,* 111–16.

McKinlay, J. B. (1973). Social networks, lay consultation, and help-seeking behavior. *Social Forces, 51,* 275–92.

Murai, N., & Murai, N. (1975). The study of moods in pregnant women. *Tohoku Psychologia Folia, 34,* 10–16.

Norbeck, J. S., & Tilden, V. P. (1983). Life stress, social support, and emotional disequilibrium in complications of pregnancy: A prospective, multivariate study. *Journal of Health and Social Behavior, 24,* 30–46.

Nuckolls, K. B., Cassel, J., & Kaplan, B. H. (1972). Psychosocial assets, life crisis, and the prognosis of pregnancy. *American Journal of Epidemiology, 95,* 431–41.

O'Hara, M. W., Rehm, L. P., & Campbell, S. B. (1983). Postpartum depression: A role for social network and life stress variables. *Journal of Nervous and Mental Disease, 171,* 336–41.

Paykel, E. S., Emms, E. M., Fletcher, J., & Rassaby, E. S. (1980). Life events and social support in puerperal depression. *British Journal of Psychiatry, 136,* 339–46.

Peters-Golden, H. (1982). Breast cancer: Varied perceptions of social support in the illness experience. *Social Science and Medicine, 16,* 483–91.

Pleshette, N., Asch, S. A., & Chase, M. A. (1956). A study of anxieties during pregnancy, labour, and the early and late puerperium. *Bulletin of New York Academy of Medicine, 32,* 436–55.

Powell, D. (1987). A neighborhood approach to parent support groups. *Journal of Community Psychology, 15,* 51–62.

Presser, H. (1978). Social factors affecting the timing of the first child. In W. B. Miller & L. F. Newman (Eds.), *The first child and family formation* (pp. 159–79). Chapel Hill: University of North Carolina, Carolina Population Center.

Procidano, M. E., & Heller, K. (1983). Measures of perceived social support from friends and from family: Three validation studies. *American Journal of Community Psychology, 11,* 1–24.

Russell, C. (1974). Transition to parenthood: Problems and gratifications. *Journal of Marriage and the Family, 36,* 294–301.

Russell, D., Cutrona, C. E., Rose, J., & Yurko, K. (1984). Social and emotional loneliness: An examination of Weiss' typology of loneliness. *Journal of Personality and Social Psychology, 46,* 1313–21.

Sarason, I. G., Levine, H. M., Basham, R. B., & Sarason, B. R. (1983). Assessing social support: The Social Support Questionnaire. *Journal of Personality and Social Psychology, 44,* 127–39.

Sosa, R., Kennell, J., Klaus, M., Robertson, S., & Urrutia, J. (1980). The effect of a supportive companion on perinatal problems, length of labor, mother–infant interaction. *New England Journal of Medicine, 303,* 597–600.

Spock, B. (1976). *Baby and child care.* New York: Pocket Books.

Tardy, C. H. (1985). Social support measurement. *American Journal of Community Psychology, 13*(2), 187–202.

Unger, D. G., & Wandersman, A. (1985). The importance of neighbors: The social cognitive and affective components of neighboring. *American Journal of Community Psychology, 13*(2), 139–70.

Walker, M. P., & Silver, R. L. (1986). *The transition to motherhood: The role of appraisals of threat and expectations in depressive symptomatology during pregnancy and the postpartum.* Manuscript submitted for publication.

Wandersman, L. P. (1982). An analysis of the effectiveness of parent–infant support groups. *Journal of Primary Prevention, 3,* 99–115.

Wandersman, L. P., Wandersman, A., & Kahn, S. (1980). Social support in the transition to parenthood. *Journal of Community Psychology, 8,* 332–42.

Warren, D. I. (1981). *Helping networks.* Notre Dame, IN: University of Notre Dame Press.

Watson, J. P., Elliot, S. A., Rugg, A. J., & Brough, D. F. (1983). Psychiatric status during pregnancy and the first postnatal year. *British Journal of Psychiatry, 144,* 453–62.

Wideman, M. V., & Singer, J. E. (1984). The role of psychological mechanisms in preparation for childbirth. *American Psychologist, 39,* 1357–71.

Wortman, C. B., & Conway, T. L. (1985). The role of social support in adaptation and recovery from illness. In S. Cohen & S. L. Syme (Eds.), *Social support and health* (pp. 281–302). New York: Academic Press.

Yale University Bush Center in Child Development and Social Policy. (1984). *Programs to strengthen families.* Available from the Family Resource Coalition, 230 N. Michigan Ave., Chicago, IL 60601.

Zajicek, E. (1981). The experience of being pregnant. In S. Wolkin & E. Zajicek (Eds.), *Pregnancy: A psychological and social study* (pp. 98–119). New York: Academic Press.

9 Intervention programs for the transition to parenthood: current status from a prevention perspective

S. Wayne Duncan and Howard J. Markman

What might we not achieve if we could persuade women to prepare for pregnancy and labor with the care that we train our young men for war, or even with the care that a prize fighter gives to preparing for a fight.

C. Tupper, "Conditioning for Childbirth" (1956)

Preparation for childbirth has been a topic of scientific interest for more than three decades and represents the most extensively studied and widespread intervention strategy with couples in the transition to parenthood. In recent years, however, attention has expanded from preparation for labor and delivery to decision making concerning the desirability and timing of parenthood and to the period of transition adults experience during pregnancy and the early years of childrearing. A result has been an increased interest in preparation for parenthood and in the impact of parenting on the marital relationship, and vice versa. This chapter provides an overview of these intervention areas.

Such a review is necessarily far reaching, given the many disciplines that have focused on some aspect of the transition to parenthood. Programs and approaches we will review emanate from a variety of disciplinary homes – obstetrics and gynecology, psychology, psychiatry, nursing, public health, home economics, prevention, and sociology. The time frame we have adopted starts with pre-conception planning and proceeds through the first year of the infant's life. The first section of the chapter reviews key concepts in the area of prevention programs and their evaluation. Prevention concepts are then used to explore this large literature. We start our review with programs aimed at helping individuals decide whether and when to become parents. Then we examine the variety of childbirth preparation programs, giving special attention to studies examining the effects of Lamaze programs. We also consider the effects of childbirth preparation programs on fathers and highlight issues of subject selection and motivation in this research area. Our third major section focuses on programs designed to enhance parents' adaptation to the demands of parenting and to the changes in their relationship with one another. We conclude with a discussion of some conceptual, research design, measurement, and clinical issues that cut across these different, though clearly related, domains. This section includes our recommendations for future work in this area.

The programs we review in this chapter come from such a variety of areas that it has been difficult to survey fully the many journals and books that might contain relevant articles. It is inevitable that we missed some programs and articles. Nevertheless, we believe that our review is representative of these areas, though we do not claim that it is exhaustive. Our hope is that these sections will provide a helpful picture of the types of programs available in the different areas, their relative levels of research and theoretical sophistication, and the areas of work needed in future years.

Prevention programs and their evaluation

Although the goals and objectives of the programs we will review vary and in some cases are not clearly stated, an implicit overarching goal of many programs is to increase couples' competencies and reduce rates of marital and family problems and, if possible, to prevent problems before they develop. It is clear that the goals of many childbirth preparation programs are more short term (e.g., the reduction of pain and medication usage during childbirth), though there is the implicit longer-term goal of fostering happier, more supportive marital and family relationships. These are important goals because, although divorce rates are currently decreasing, there are still more than 1 million new divorces every year in the United States, directly affecting more than 1 million children (National Center for Health Statistics, 1986). These rates are alarming given the research documenting the negative effects of marital conflict, separation, and divorce on children and their parents (Emery, 1982; Hetherington, 1979). Until recently, the response of mental health professionals to the problems of couples and families was to offer treatment programs designed to alleviate distress (Markman & Floyd, 1980). However, increasing attention has been given to developing interventions that can benefit couples before problems develop and thereby prevent marital distress and dissolution (see Markman, Floyd, & Dickson-Markman, 1982, for a review). The purpose of this section is to review current conceptions of prevention in order to provide both a rationale for working with couples in the transition to parenthood and a framework for the review of programs that follows.

The concept of prevention has its origin in the public health domain, and prevention programs have classically been divided into three types: primary, secondary, and tertiary. Primary prevention programs are designed to prevent problems before they develop by modifying the external conditions that cause problems or by helping people cope with these conditions. In contrast, secondary prevention programs are designed to intervene with people who have developed "early signs" of a problem, and tertiary prevention programs are meant to help people cope with existing problems and to decrease the chances of the problem developing again. Contemporary conceptions of prevention in the mental health field have focused on primary and secondary prevention since tertiary programs resemble traditional treatment programs. Drawing on crisis theory (e.g., Caplan, 1964), recent discussions of primary and early secondary prevention have stressed the importance of intervening during milestone or transition periods, such as the transition to parenthood (Bloom, 1984). These are times when stress is potentially high, new skills are often required, and people are generally considered to be unusually receptive to interventions. Thus, they are highly motivated. Motivation to participate in prevention programs is a key factor because, unlike targets for treatment programs, candidates for prevention programs, by definition, are not experiencing current distress.

The theoretical rationale for working with people in the transition to parenthood derives partially from family development theory with its emphasis on the tasks and transitions couples and families encounter as they negotiate the family life cycle (Carter & McGoldrick, 1980; Mattessich & Hill, in press; Napier, 1980). This emphasis reflects our belief that, as noted elsewhere, "the manner in which this early phase of the family life cycle is handled may have far-reaching consequences for the psychological adjustment of both children and parents" (Markman, Floyd, Stanley, & Lewis, 1986, pp. 174–5). Thus, the establishment of effective patterns of family communication and problem solving is likely to lead to more harmonious functioning over time.

In addition to the focus on transition periods, contemporary conceptions of prevention programs view goals in terms of promoting health rather than preventing disease. The goal of disease prevention stems from the public health origins of prevention concepts and is appropriate when the cause of a specific disorder is known. However, in the mental health field in general and in the marital and family field in particular, there is a paucity of knowledge about causal processes and there is the recognition that most disorders have multiple determinants. Therefore, programs attempt to modify multiple aspects of functioning (i.e., behavior, cognitions, and feelings) that are thought to increase the well-being of the participants (Bloom, 1984). Hence, many preventive interventions are conceptualized as health promotion programs (McPheeters, 1976). One characteristic of such programs is that they involve a set of nonspecific interventions that are intended to increase the general well-being of the participants or "targets." In this chapter it will be clear that some of the programs we review can be considered health promotion programs, whereas others are characterized by specific interventions and goals.

Evaluation of prevention programs

Evaluating prevention programs is difficult because the goals of prevention (e.g., preventing divorce, enhancing child functioning) are *long term* by definition. Thus, *longitudinal* studies are necessary to evaluate adequately the long-term preventive goals of programs. Evaluation of the short-term (e.g., pre-/post-) effects of prevention programs is also important to establish the immediate effects of the program (psychotherapy researchers sometimes call this "outcome research") and to assess the therapeutic processes that lead to change (psychotherapy researchers sometimes call this "process research"; Gottman & Markman, 1978). An example may help clarify the difference between short- and long-term goals and process and outcome research. We have developed a prevention program for couples planning marriage (Markman, Floyd, Stanley, & Jamieson, 1984). The short-term process goals are to enhance couples' communication and problem-solving skills. The short-term outcome goal, although not a primary focus, is to improve relationship satisfaction. The long-term outcome goals include maintaining a high level of relationship satisfaction, decreasing conflict, improving parent–child communication, and enhancing child functioning. The long-term process goals are to maintain high levels of communication and problem-solving skills.

To summarize, we have reviewed current conceptions of prevention theory and research in order to suggest that the programs reviewed in this chapter can be considered prevention programs. Consistent with most prevention effects, the programs we will review are aimed at healthy "targets" during a life transition, and their goals are to promote well-being rather than to prevent disorder. Once the reader considers the programs we review to be prevention programs, they can be evaluated in terms of their prevention potential and the degree to which short- and long-term process and outcome goals have been articulated and evaluated. We will use this framework to evaluate the conceptualization and evaluation of programs. Although we will occasionally comment on programs as we describe them, we will save our critique of the three types of programs for the last section of the chapter.

The use of a prevention perspective should not necessarily be taken to represent the program developers' own orientation, but our own orientation and one that we believe will be useful in this review. Using a prevention framework may at times raise issues or criticisms that arise naturally out of a prevention orientation but not necessarily out of the one held by the program developers. Thus, we are not attempting to be unfairly critical but simply to demonstrate the usefulness of a prevention perspective in thinking about program design, development, and evaluation in the transition to parenthood period.

Planning for pregnancy: group intervention programs for nonparent couples

The decision to become a parent is one that individuals and couples are paying increasing attention to in the United States. The availability of effective birth control methods, the impact of children on parents' educational and career opportunities, the increased financial cost of children, and the possibility of marital difficulties involving children have no doubt contributed to an increased introspection on the part of couples concerning their plans for parenthood (Kantrowitz, 1986). Perhaps as a result of these factors, along with others, some couples are waiting longer to have children and are having fewer children (Leridon, 1981; Westoff, 1978).

The issue of parenthood elicits considerable attention from many U.S. couples. One study of the problems couples report in the early stage of marriage indicated that "potential children" was rated as one of the top three problem areas by 24% of couples (Markman, Jamieson, & Floyd, 1983). Thus, the issues of whether to become parents and when to do so are ones that intervention programs could address and thereby, potentially, help prevent unplanned pregnancies and accompanying problems. A number of books provide couples with information about parenthood that is presumed to be helpful in the decision-making process (e.g., Cohen, 1985; Feldman, 1984; Whelan, 1975), and many hospitals and medical centers now offer prepregnancy classes on the changes that accompany parenthood. For example, one flyer announced, "A three-week class to help you learn everything you should know *before* pregnancy." Yet only a handful of programs have been described in the professional literature, and even fewer have been systematically evaluated.

Although there is a sizable literature on family planning and psychological factors related to fertility (e.g., Fawcett, 1973; Fox, 1982; Pohlman, 1969), little attention has been given to intervention programs designed to aid couples and individuals in deciding whether and/or when to parent. Such programs have been a fairly recent development in the prevention field, and our search of the literature suggests that these programs are found only in the United States. Family-planning programs in many developing countries are geared toward altering attitudes about family size, not whether to have a child at all or the spacing of births (e.g., Toohey & Valenzuela, 1983). However, for many adults in the United States the central question is whether one will be a parent.

In this section we briefly review four group intervention programs for couples and then examine a single study, based on three of the earlier studies. The group intervention programs have as an underlying assumption the prevention orientation discussed above (Caplan, 1964). Such an approach emphasizes the prevention of a disorder by the provision of information about the potential disorder. For the decision to become a parent, the implicit disorder is a constellation of possible problems, including postpartum depression (e.g., Hopkins, Marcus, & Campbell, 1984), disturbances of parenting (e.g., Cohler, Weiss, & Grunebaum, 1970), and decreased relationship satisfaction (e.g., Rollins & Galligan, 1978). By providing potential parents with information about the demands and satisfactions of parenting, the assumption is that couples will be able to make a more realistic evaluation of their own needs and desires as a couple and as individuals and that the decision to become parents will be grounded in facts, discussion, and introspection, and not on cultural myths and ignorance.

In his dissertation research Ginsberg (1981) examined the value of an educational program in helping couples decide about becoming parents or remaining childless. He used groups with two different levels of structure (high, low) as well as a waiting-list control group. Each group consisted of three to five couples and was led by nonprofessional volunteers. Thirty-two couples (mean age, 28 years) were involved in the four-session program. The sessions emphasized factors and motivations that might affect one's decision to parent or to remain childless (e.g., financial, social, personal), encouraged participants to explore the possible impact of having and not having children on their marital relationship, and presented a decision-making model and encouraged couples to use it in this area. Group, dyadic, and individual activities were used, as were homework assign-ments. Ginsberg described the fundamental goal as teaching participants skills (e.g., decision making) that "will facilitate for participants both a greater awareness of important factors concerning the questions of par-enthood and decision-making competency regarding this important de-cision" (1981, p. 152). Postintervention assessments revealed increases in knowledge about factors related to parenting (e.g., potential impact on the couple's relationship) as well as high satisfaction of participants in the intervention groups with the program. Few differences emerged between the low- and high-structure groups. Ginsberg concluded that the inter-vention program was successful and warrants further attention in helping couples decide about parenthood.

Another program with a couple focus is that reported by Prochaska and Coyle (1979). Entitled "Choosing Parenthood: The Pros and Cons of Hav-ing Children," their six-session program was aimed at helping couples identify and deal with issues, fears, and pressures involved with parent-hood. The groups, led by clinical social workers, had about 10 members each and followed a family life education approach. Such an approach emphasizes some group structure, feedback from both peers and profes-sionals, and structured learning exercises. The women in the groups were about 30 years old; no data are provided regarding the men. Topics dis-cussed in the sessions were generated by the participants and varied from group to group, though in each of the groups dual-career families and childless marriages were covered.

The evaluation of the program was based on the responses of the par-ticipants to a questionnaire given out at the last session. The questionnaire was designed to assess the overall program, individual sessions, and the effects of the program on participants. The results are reported only in a general, descriptive manner, and given the lack of a control group, it is impossible to obtain much more than an impressionistic grasp of the pro-gram's effects. In general, group members reported greater satisfaction with the group discussions and exercises that centered around personal feelings and experiences. The purely information-centered sessions were, apparently, less well received. Participants did report increased com-munication with spouses, though the absence of information about who participated in the groups makes this information difficult to interpret: Were the groups helpful in fostering communication if only one member of a couple participated? Was there a minimum number of sessions in which the couple needed to participate before this effect was evident? Such questions were apparently not addressed in the evaluation of the groups' effectiveness. With one group of seven couples the authors conducted a 1-year reunion. At this time three couples had decided to have a child, two couples were still discussing the matter, one couple had decided against becoming parents, and one couple had begun divorce proceedings. Such results are impossible to interpret, given the absence of an appropriate control group. The authors indicated that the former group members reported "less conflictual feelings about the subject of child-bearing" (p. 295) and felt less defensive about their decision regarding parenting. It is clear that this research answers few questions, but it does pose some interesting issues regarding intervention strategies and the psychological value of group support in decision making about whether to become a parent.

"Considering Parenthood" was the name of a program run by a psychotherapist, Potts (1980), to aid couples in "a shared exploration of an apparently normal developmental issue" (p. 630). The experiences of five different groups of couples, totaling 20 couples, were reported. Most participants were in their late twenties and early thirties. The couples met in weekly sessions over a period of 6 to 8 weeks. The 2-hour sessions were focused on decision making and were based on the exploration of "critical issues" that might influence couples' parenting decisions (e.g., personal goals and values, own childhood experiences, partner or marital relationships). Again, sessions involved individual activities, group activities, discussions, and guest speakers. However, the author reports that, at later sessions, much time was spent on issues of individuals and couples and that group members began serving in cotherapist roles.

The evaluation provided by Potts consists primarily of case examples of participants in the program. Although the goal of the groups had been to foster decision making by the couples, Potts reports, "Most frequently, couples did not make final decisions by the conclusion of the group" (p. 636). Most couples, however, reported feeling "clearer" about their eventual decision. At a 6-month reunion Potts reported perfect attendance by the group participants, leading her to suggest that these groups may provide an important source of social support for "older" couples who are considering parenthood. At the time of the reunion 50% of the 20 couples had decided in favor of parenthood, and most of the others were leaning toward parenthood. Ten percent of the couples, however, had decided against becoming parents, and one couple had separated over differences about the decision. The great homogeneity of the couples in these groups (i.e., older, highly educated with dual careers) led the author to suggest that these volunteer couples may actually have been "seeking support and help for making a decision to *have* children" (p. 637).

A study by Kimball and McCabe (1981) also involved a decision-making group composed of four couples facing the decision of whether to become parents. Again, the participants were older (26–37 years), were highly educated, and had been married from 4 to 11 years. There were seven group sessions and, in addition, pre- and postgroup sessions with the group leaders for the exchange of individual information and feedback. There was no emphasis on therapy in this group; most attention was focused on decision making. The group's goals were twofold: to clarify and understand one's own and one's spouse's views concerning the timing and desirability of parenthood and to gain an accurate view of parenthood and of childless adulthood.

Values clarification, outside reading, decision-making exercises, and other activities were used to foster couples' movement toward a decision. However, none of the four couples had reached a clear decision by the close of the program. Couples' reactions to the program were generally quite positive. As in the study by Prochaska and Coyle (1979), the couples reported great satisfaction with having guest couples speak who had made different decisions about whether to become parents. Kimball and McCabe (1981) also report that "a majority of members stated they would have preferred combining a small-group or workshop format with couples counseling" (p. 155). Thus, again a decision-making group appears not to have achieved its objective of helping couples make a decision about becoming parents during the course of the group meetings, but the group appears to have provided a useful structured forum for examining ideas, opinions, and information with similar couples.

Daniluk and Herman (1984), in a study modeled after earlier work by Kimball and McCabe (1981), Prochaska and Coyle (1979), and Potts (1980), examined the decision-making process concerning parenthood among 20 career women. This self-selected sample of women, whose ages averaged a little less than 30 years, participated in a 20-hour workshop whose purpose was to help the participants make "better informed and more personally satisfying choices regarding the decision to accept or reject motherhood, and to increase participants' level of comfort in dealing with the parenthood decision" (p. 608). The workshop was open only to women under the assumption that it might be helpful for women to clarify their own views on becoming parents before dealing with the issue in a relationship context. The women met for eight weekly sessions, each lasting 2½ hours. A female facilitator and two female small-group leaders led the sessions. The approach emphasized the provision of information to the participants concerning a variety of issues: reasons for having or not having children, careers and motherhood, effects of children on adults' relationships, financial aspects of parenthood, and division of childcare and child-rearing responsibilities.

This approach was based on decision-making research in the transition to parenthood (Beach, Townes, & Campbell, 1978) that emphasizes the role of adequate information in making satisfying decisions. Before the workshop and again before its completion, the women filled out the Optional Parenthood Questionnaire (OPQ; Beach et al., 1978). This instrument assesses individuals' attitudes about parenthood and helps them identify the pros and cons (Beach et al., 1978). In addition, participants filled out the Personality Research Form (Jackson, 1974) and an evaluation form focusing on participants' subjective responses to the workshop. The results indicated no differences in the pre- and postworkshop scores of participants on the OPQ, and post hoc analyses with the Personality Research Form showed only that women who had decided to have a child scored lower on the autonomy variable than those who had decided to remain childless or who were undecided. The subjective evaluations of the participants provided more encouraging results: Participants reported increased communication with spouses, friends, and family as well as stimulation to seek more information on becoming parents. In addition, they reported a greater awareness about fertility issues. The workshop leaders observed that the OPQ had served to focus participants' thoughts about parenthood, directing their attention from general issues to specific attitudes and feelings. One change the authors recommended for future work in this area was switching the emphasis to a dyadic focus in order to consider both couple and individual decision making.

Summary

The programs described here to aid couples in their decision making about parenthood clearly represent differing levels of theoretical and empirical development. The small samples involved in some of the programs, the absence of spouses in one, and the absence of long-term follow-up in all of the programs suggest areas where future work will have to show improvement. The importance of long-term follow-up is especially clear in this area since many couples have not reached a "final" decision about whether to parent at the end of the intervention program. This fact is not necessarily a criticism of the programs themselves given the complexity and importance of the decision being undertaken, yet it points to the need for long-term follow-up so that longer-term effects of the program on such variables as marital communication and satisfaction can be assessed.

Preparation for childbirth

Several decades ago, Dean McIntosh of the Yale Medical School stated, "If physicians and educators work together, they will recognize that preparation for maternity is the most important task of our society" (cited in Thoms & Wyatt, 1951, p. 209). Indeed, preparation for childbirth has become the intervention area receiving the greatest attention in the United States. In this section we first briefly review the types of childbirth preparation programs available and their histories. We then examine a variety of empirical studies conducted during the past two decades that examine the effectiveness of various programs and highlight a group of studies examining Lamaze childbirth preparation programs. We conclude this section by focusing on the impact of prepared childbirth on fathers and also by considering the characteristics and motivation of participants in childbirth preparation classes.

Historical overview

Preparation for childbirth has been a topic of discussion since the time of Hippocrates (Dick-Read, 1959), but it was only in the late 1800s that physicians began studying the effects of prepared childbirth. Beck, Geden, and Brouder (1979) present a useful summary of the three major childbirth preparation movements: the "hypnosis" school, the Velvovsky–Lamaze movement (Lamaze, 1965; Velvovsky, 1972; Velvovsky, Platonov, Ploticher, & Shugom, 1960), and the movement following the views of Dick-Read (1959). It is clear from these reviews that preparation for childbirth has had a controversial history. At various times the techniques have been heavily criticized. For instance, after the presentation of a paper (Davis & Morrone, 1962) at the American Gynecological Society that reported no difference in trained and untrained mothers on such variables as the length of labor and the amount of medication used, one physician commented that the absence of effects of preparation "support the skepticism that many of us have shared about any physical benefits derived from this program," and another reported having "enjoyed this objective evaluation of mothers' classes . . . [that] disproved certain ephemeral effects which had been claimed for them" (Davis & Morrone, 1962, pp. 1201, 1204). Such resistance to and skepticism about prepared childbirth was not always the case, however. For example, in 1951 the Soviet Ministry of Health made an official policy strongly recommending the use of the childbirth preparation techniques of Velvovsky, and in 1956 Pope Pious XII gave official papal sanction to the use of natural childbirth principles (Chertok, 1967).

Such widely divergent views on the value of preparation for labor and childbirth are often forgotten today, as both the medical establishment and groups supporting alternative approaches to health care endorse the value of prepared childbirth. The gradual acceptance of psychoprophylaxis in the United States has been chronicled by various authors (e.g., Beck et al., 1979; Bing, 1972; Chertok, 1959, 1967). Whatever resistance to prepared childbirth that remains today in the U.S. medical community is considered to be related to physicians' training that generally emphasizes the use of analgesics and anesthetics (e.g., Chertok, 1959) or to the extra time and expense prepared childbirth is thought to require (Barnes, 1976). Since the demonstration of the negative effects of maternal medication on newborns (e.g., Brackbill, 1979), acceptance of "natural childbirth" has increased. This scientific impetus for change in obstetric practices has been accompanied by social and political movements that have emphasized women's knowledge and control over decisions regarding childbirth (e.g., Boston Women's Health Book Collective, 1976), by increased consideration of childbirth as a developmental achievement as opposed to a medical problem (e.g., Brazelton, 1981), and by enhanced focus on the father's role in childrearing and socialization (e.g., Pedersen, 1980).

These movements have had an impact as more and more U.S. couples have chosen to participate in either independent (e.g., Lamaze) or hospital-affiliated programs (Wideman & Singer, 1983). Some hospitals, in fact, require participation in a childbirth preparation course for fathers who wish to accompany the mother during labor and delivery. One unpublished survey of hospitals revealed that "almost 80% of the women who delivered at these hospitals had undergone some form of childbirth preparation" (Wideman & Singer, 1983), though childbirth educators' estimates tend to hover around 50 to 60% (A. Berman, personal communication, June 24, 1986; L. Kondrat, personal communication, June 24, 1986). Given the rate of 3.6 million births per year in the United States, from 1.8 to 2.9 million mothers are involved yearly in some sort of childbirth preparation program. Since about 40% of the births each year are first births, a large percentage of these mothers are seeking training for the first time (Brown, Spragins, Engardio, Ringe, & Klinkerman, 1985). Dated estimates (Ball, 1960, in Beck et al., 1979; Chertok, 1967; Lundh, 1975) of rates of prepared childbirth in other countries suggest a lower rate in Sweden (38%), a similar rate of participation in France (50%) and a higher rate in the Soviet Union (87%).

As Chertok (1959), Beck et al. (1979), and others have indicated, three main "schools" of childbirth preparation have emerged through the decades, though as many as "21 ways to have a baby" have been identified in the United States (Lesko, 1986). The earliest, the hypnosuggestive method, dates back to the late nineteenth century (Chertok, 1959, 1967) and has been criticized because of its individual focus, making group training impossible. The requirement of specialized training in hypnosis by medical personnel has contributed to the infrequent use and lack of popularity of this approach (Morishima, 1982). The other two methods, that of British obstetrician Grantly Dick-Read (1959) and that of Velvovsky (1972), have received the greatest attention. They share an emphasis on education about the anatomy and physiology of pregnancy, labor, and delivery, on proper breathing techniques and physical conditioning, and on the creation of a general mental outlook that deemphasizes thoughts of pain during childbirth. The work of Velvovsky (Velvovsky et al., 1960) in the Soviet Union was popularized first in France by Fernand Lamaze in 1952 after his visit to the Soviet Union and observation of a "painless delivery." In France the Lamaze approach took hold, consistent with the liberal political movements of the 1950s and the support of the Catholic church.

The Lamaze technique became a U.S. import in 1959 when Marjorie Karmel published a description of her own experience with natural childbirth in Paris under Dr. Lamaze's care. Her book, *Thank You, Dr. Lamaze: A Mother's Experience in Painless Childbirth* (1959), stimulated great interest in the United States among expectant mothers and even some skeptical physicians (Tanzer & Block, 1972). The impact of the work was gradual but considerable. Lamaze is now considered a fundamental approach to childbirth preparation in the United States, and we shall focus on it in a later section. Next, however, we shall examine some of the early studies of prepared childbirth. These studies will help provide the historical context for the more recent studies.

The evaluation of prepared childbirth

Early studies. The sentiment expressed by Dean McIntosh concerning childbirth preparation was both atypical for a medical professional during this time and prescient of future developments in the area of obstetrics. A faculty member at Yale, Herbert Thoms, had been one of the early U.S. leaders to explore seriously the writings of Dick-Read as well as relaxation exercises of Jacobson (1938) and Heardman (1951). These ideas were incorporated into an educational program that had "a twofold purpose, that of allaying fear and that of preparing the patient to perform her part in the labor process" (Thoms & Goodrich, 1949, p. 1256). The program originally consisted of lectures by a physician on the physiology of pregnancy, aspects of labor and delivery, as well as breathing and relaxation exercises, supplemented with exercise classes led by nurses who also answered prospective mothers' questions about pregnancy, labor, and delivery. Although women were not required to participate in the classes, they were encouraged to do so. Thoms and Goodrich did not have a control group of women with which to compare the classes' participants but, nevertheless, asserted that the prepared mothers differed from non-class participants in several important ways: They expressed less anxiety during labor, greater physical stamina during labor and childbirth, and greater satisfaction with the delivery. The authors deemphasized the fear reduction aspect of the program that Dick-Read had stressed, instead focusing on an educational program for "childbirth with understanding and support" (p. 1258).

Numerous studies appeared in the obstetric and gynecology journals in the 1950s describing the results of various childbirth preparation programs (e.g., Tupper, 1956). Most reported consecutive birth series but without any control group. One exception was the study by van Auken and Tomlinson (1953). These obstetricians compared 200 primiparous patients who had attended four antepartum classes based on Dick-Read's and Heardman's approaches with 200 patients who had not done so. Though statistical analyses were not performed on the data, van Auken and Tomlinson (1953) reported the following:

From the study it is evident that labors are shortened by at least 2 hours and that the incidence of delivery by artificial means [use of forceps] lessened by 17 percent among those trained. It appears that the training decreases perineal trauma by 5 percent and there is marked diminution in the use of drugs and anesthesia that tend to asphyxiate the baby as well as produce postpartum hemorrhage. The psychological benefit to the patient is beyond description. (p. 104)

Such work led to continued interest in prepared childbirth as well as frequent controversy over philosophy, techniques, and outcomes. One result was the carrying out of studies to assess the effects of prepared childbirth. Typically, these studies reflected improvements in design and analysis, especially in the inclusion of control groups. We review these studies in the following section.

Controlled evaluation studies. In 1962, following the presentation of the Davis and Morrone (1962) paper mentioned above, one obstetrician observed, "Having been around Western Europe where I visited 35 or 40 different clinics and many others, I have about come to the conclusion that it is almost impossible to arrive at any objective evaluation of any of these programs" (C. L. Buxton, cited in Davis & Morrone, 1962, p. 1205). Gradually, however, this view has been modified as efforts have been made to examine the effectiveness of various childbirth preparation approaches. In this section we briefly consider studies that have examined the efficacy of preparation programs. This review is not exhaustive. Studies have been included that meet the criterion of having a comparison group in addition to the experimental group. In all the studies mothers attended a series of, usually, six to eight classes that emphasized information about the physiology of pregnancy and childbirth, breathing and relaxation exercises, as well as practical knowledge concerning hospital and labor room procedures and policies.

Table 9.1 summarizes the effects of childbirth preparation on a number of outcome measures that reflect the short-term outcome goals of prepared childbirth: (1) the emotional reaction of the mother to labor and delivery, (2) the pain of the birth reported by the mother, (3) the length of labor, (4) the amount of medication used, and (5) the number of spontaneous deliveries. We will review the effects on each of these outcome measures. Although "box score approaches" have shortcomings (Block, 1976; Gardner, 1966), we believe that they are helpful in pointing out general trends in results.

1. *Reaction to childbirth.* Examination of the "Cognitive and affective variables and outcomes" column of Table 9.1 indicates that women who went through childbirth preparation programs tended to report less negative affect (anxiety and depression) during labor and delivery as well as, in one study, a greater number of positive emotions.

2. *Painfulness of childbirth.* Although only two studies examined this outcome, both found that prepared mothers experienced less pain than comparison mothers.

3. *Length of labor.* The results suggest that preparation for childbirth has no effect on the length of labor. Three studies found no difference between the experimental and comparison groups, though one study reported significantly shorter labors for prepared mothers.

4. *Amount of medication.* The results from four studies indicate that prepared mothers utilized less medication. In contrast, Davis and Morrone (1962) found no effect of preparation on the amount of maternal medication used during delivery. (The reasons for this decreased usage of medication are likely to be quite complex; see Wideman & Singer, 1984, for a discussion.)

5. *Spontaneous deliveries*. The results are inconclusive on this outcome variable examining the prevalence of spontaneous (e.g., nonforceps, unassisted) deliveries. Two studies found no difference in the trained and nontrained groups, and one found a difference favoring trained mothers.

In summary, the evidence is somewhat consistent for only three of the outcome categories: affective reactions, reported pain, and amount of medication. Mothers who have prepared for childbirth tend to report more positive emotional reactions to the experience as well as less pain. They also use less medication during the labor and delivery.

Studies of Lamaze participants. Probably the most widely known method of childbirth preparation in the United States is the Lamaze approach (Wideman & Singer, 1984). Estimates suggest that as many as 80% of the women who take a childbirth preparation class enroll in a Lamaze course (A. Berman, personal communication, June 24, 1986; Yarrow, 1982). Taught by certified instructors, this series of, usually, six classes focuses on five different areas of preparation: knowledge of the anatomy and physiology of pregnancy and childbirth, breathing exercises, relaxation exercises, cognitive restructuring, and assistance from a coach (Ewy & Ewy, 1982; Wideman & Singer, 1984). Because of the widespread existence of these classes, we devote this section to the results of the six studies that have examined the effects of Lamaze training on mothers and couples. Table 9.1 contains descriptions of these six studies. Three studies (those of Huttel, Mitchell, Fischer, & Meyer, 1972; Hughey, McElin, & Young, 1978; and Scott & Rose, 1976) resemble the studies reported in the previous section, whereas the other three move the focus from physiological outcome variables to psychological ones.

Inspection of the table reveals that most of these studies did not examine the effect of Lamaze preparation on mothers' reported pain during labor and delivery. The one that did so found that trained mothers reported less pain. Consistent with studies of other childbirth preparation approaches, length of labor was not significantly different for the groups in any study that examined this variable. As with the previous group of studies, trained mothers generally received less medication. Also, trained mothers generally had greater success in giving birth without the use of forceps. These findings are quite consistent with those from the previous section.

Furthermore, the Markman and Kadushin (1986) study and the Entwisle and Doering (1981) and Doering and Entwisle (1975) studies suggest some potentially important nonphysiological effects of Lamaze participation by couples. In the Markman and Kadushin study those couples who had par-

Table 9.1. *Prepared childbirth evaluation studies*

Reference	Popu-lation	Sample size NT	T	Mean age	Assessment times
Non-Lamaze studies					
Davis and Morrone (1962)	M	108[a]	355	NR	P(3), LD, PP
Bergstrom-Walan (1963)	M	150[b]	100[b]	NR[c]	LD
Tanzer (1967)	M[e]	22	14	NR	P(2), PP
Enkin et al. (1972)	M[e]	56	28	NR	PP
Zax et al. (1975)	M[e]	41	118	NR	P(2), LD
Lamaze studies					
Huttel et al.[g] (1972)	M	41	31	NT: 26.3 T: 26.3	P, LD, PP
Doering and Entwisle (1975)	M[e]	137	132	26.7	PP
Scott and Rose (1976)	M	129	129	NT: 24 T: 25	LD
Hughey et al. (1978)	M[e]	500	500	NT: 27.8 T: 28.5	LD
Entwisle and Doering (1981)	M, F	35M 14F	80M ≺8F	M: 24.7[h] F: 26.9[h]	M: P(2), PP(2) F: P, PP
Markman and Kadushin (1986)	M, F	37	39	NTF: 27.8 NTM: 26.4 TF: 29.5 TM: 27.3	P, PP(2)

Abbreviations: M, mothers; F, fathers; P, pregnancy; LD, labor and delivery; PP, postpartum; (if more than one assessment was conducted during the time period, the number is indicated in parentheses); NR, not reported; NS, not significant; NT, not trained (i.e., no Lamaze course and very little other preparation); T, trained (i.e., had Lamaze or other childbirth preparation course); some samples contained both multiparous and primiparous mothers.

[a]Patients who attended five or more classes were compared with those who had attended one or none.

Cognitive and affective variables and outcomes	Reported pain	Length of labor	Amount of medication	Spontaneous deliveries
Fears: NS Anxiety: NT	NR	NS	NS	NS
—	NT > T	NT > T	NT > T[d]	NS
Ratio of positive to negative emotions: NT < T	NT > T	NR	NT > T	NR
Depression: NT > T	NR	NS	NT > T	NT < T
Anxiety: NS	NR	NS[f]	NT > T[f]	NR
Complaints: NT > T Depression: NS Perceived difficulty: NT > T Wish for more children: NT < T	NR	NS	NT > T	NS
Level of awareness during LD: NT < T Positive attitudes toward infant and birth: NT < T	NR	NS	NR	NR
NR	NR	NS	NT > T	NT < T
NR	NR	NS	NS	NT < T
Level of awareness during LD: more trained > less trained Positive feelings about childbirth: more trained > less trained Positive feelings about baby: more trained > less trained	NT > T	NS	NR	NR
Marital satisfaction: NT < T State anxiety: NT > T Parenting problems: NT > T	NR	NR	NT > T	NR

[b] Total patients in trained and not trained groups.
[c] All subjects were between 18 and 30 years of age.
[d] For sedatives, NT > T; for analgesia, NS.
[e] Sample contains both primiparous and multiparous women.
[f] Historical hospital controls used for these comparisons.
[g] Other data reported in Fischer et al. (1972).
[h] Two trained groups combined; compared with a less trained group.

ticipated in Lamaze classes reported no change in their marital satisfaction and level of anxiety from prebirth measures to postpartum measures obtained 2 months postpartum. In contrast, non-Lamaze parents reported greater anxiety, lower marital satisfaction, as well as increased parenting problems postpartum than did Lamaze parents. The Entwisle and Doering studies indicate that prepared childbirth is associated with more positive feelings about the birth process and the infant. In addition, Lamaze mothers have greater awareness during the childbirth than do less prepared mothers. The authors assert that positive effects of Lamaze are mediated by the mother's awareness, which is partially influenced by medication level (lower levels of medication are related to greater awareness). Greater awareness may be associated with increased feelings of mastery over the stressful experiences associated with childbirth. Both Markman and Kadushin and Entwisle and Doering suggest that the husband's presence during Lamaze lends support to the mother and may foster improvements in the marital relationship. These two factors may operate in tandem with the physiological effects of Lamaze to facilitate adjustment to parenthood.

Prepared childbirth: effects on fathers

We have not found it well to have the husband in the room at the time of delivery. We tried that many years ago in home deliveries, and my experience was that the husband was useless. Grandmothers and aunts and mothers were all right, but the husband was in the way and frequently so frightened that he had bolstered himself with several drinks and was very much in the way. It may be a good idea to have him in the delivery room but I have not been converted to that yet. (Dr. Edward L. King, in Davis & Morrone, 1962, p. 1205)

Although the father's role in labor and delivery varies considerably with the cultural context (Newton & Newton, 1972), his role in the United States has changed drastically during the past two decades. Father involvement was spurred on by the lack of partners (e.g., qualified teachers) for women who desired Lamaze training. Thus, having husbands coach their wives during the birth of their child was a pragmatic alternative (Bing, 1972). However, increased father involvement was not immediately accepted by all involved parties:

There was a slow awareness of this revolutionary idea. But once couples heard of the possibility of sharing their labor and delivery, they started to demand it. Pressure was exerted on hospital administrators, on physicians, on nurses. First one, then two hospitals tentatively opened their doors and allowed husbands to accompany their wife into labor and delivery. But generally, this new concept in obstetric care was not easily accepted, in fact, in many cases all hell broke lose [*sic*]. (Bing, 1972, p. 72)

Though involving the husband in labor and delivery was revolutionary in the United States, Dick-Read in England had been involving fathers for decades and implored husbands to take advantage of the pregnancy and birth as "a heaven-sent opportunity for an association in marriage of the highest level" (Dick-Read, 1959, p. 276).

Since many hospitals were reluctant to allow fathers in the labor and delivery room without prior preparation, many established regulations requiring husbands to have attended some form of childbirth preparation class before the birth. According to one recent poll, four of five fathers (79%) are now present in the delivery room when their child is born, a sharp contrast to the 27% rate reported a decade earlier (Gallup Organization, 1983). Researchers have been studying these fathers for some time now, examining questions such as the effect of their presence on their wives' reported pain and likelihood of receiving medication. To date, four studies have examined the effect of childbirth preparation classes on fathers' adjustment to parenthood. Table 9.2 summarizes the design and results of these studies. An examination of the "Results" column indicates that participation in the preparation classes had no demonstrable effect on the fathers' concepts of themselves and their spouse, their adjustment difficulties, or their interaction with their newborn infant, but participation was related to their evaluation of the childbirth experience and their marital relationship.

The weak effects on fathers are not surprising when one examines the process and outcome goals of childbirth preparation. In general the outcome goals have centered around the reduction of pain for the mother and decreased need for medication. Little has been specified about the presumed effect on the father, though it has been suggested that the experience helps solidify the marital relationship (e.g., Tanzer, 1967). Certainly, theory has not suggested that participation in such classes should have an impact on self-concept or on problems of parenting, as examined in the research by Hott (1972). Helping a partner learn certain breathing techniques and supporting the partner in their use during labor and delivery are likely to have an impact on the mother's childbirth experience, but they are not likely to have a direct impact on the father's self-esteem or feelings about his spouse.

Another important aspect to consider when evaluating these results is that preparation for childbirth is not preparation for parenting. Thus, to expect childbirth preparation to have an effect on parenting skill and adjustment would be inconsistent with our knowledge of parents' feelings of uncertainty and anxiety over the care of an infant (e.g., Entwisle & Doering, 1981) and the potential value of parent–infant education programs

Table 9.2. *Effects of childbirth preparation classes on fathers*

Reference	Comparison group	Type of class[a]	Age	N	Outcome measure	Results
Hott (1972)	Yes	Psychoprophylactic	NR	44	Questionnaire on concepts of self and wife	No significant differences in groups on pre- or postbirth scores
Cronenwett and Newmark (1974)	Yes	Lamaze	NR	PA: 64 UA: 58 NA: 30	Questionnaire on father–child, couple relationships	No effect on father–child relationship, but Lamaze fathers viewed childbirth and marital relationship more positively
Wente and Crockenberg (1976)	Yes[b]	Lamaze	21–37	46	Questionnaire on difficulty of adjustment to parenting	No difference in Lamaze and non-Lamaze fathers
Miller and Bowen[c] (1982)	Yes	Preparenthood	18–39[d]	48	Observed attachment behaviors of father to infant	No difference on basis of class attendance

Abbreviations: NR, not reported; PA, prepared attenders; UA, unprepared attenders; NA, nonattenders.
[a] Authors' own descriptions are listed here.
[b] Non-Lamaze fathers had not taken classes but were present during labor and delivery.
[c] Additional information reported in Bowen and Miller (1980).
[d] Mean age, 27 years.

(Joy, Davidson, Williams, & Painter, 1980). The findings of Wente and Crockenberg (1976) are predictable when considered in this light.

Another consideration relevant to these findings concerns the early research and writing on fathers and their infants that suggested the importance of early postpartum contact, such as in the labor and delivery room, for facilitating fathers' "bonding" with their children (e.g., Greenberg & Morris, 1974). Subsequent research, however, has demonstrated the inappropriateness of applying models of development or theoretical concepts (e.g., sensitive period) based on rodents' and ungulates' parenting behavior to that of humans (e.g., Lamb, 1983). More important is the parent–child interaction over the infant's first year of life in determining the quality of the parent–child relationship, irrespective of parent–infant contact in the first minutes or hours following the baby's birth (Rode, Chang, Fisch, & Sroufe, 1981). Thus, to expect childbirth preparation to have an effect on attachment behaviors is also inconsistent with our knowledge of the development of the parent–child relationship.

Still, fathers can benefit from participation in childbirth, and these benefits are evident even without formal preparation. For example, Cronenwett and Newmark (1974) found "unprepared attenders" reflecting more positively on the birth of their child and on their marital relationship than "nonattenders," though "prepared attenders" reported the greatest positive effects. One likely reason for such additional benefits of prepared assistance is suggested in an article by Block, Norr, Meyering, Norr, and Charles (1981). These researchers found that husbands' helpfulness during labor and delivery (e.g., by coaching breathing and timing contractions) was strongly related to their preparation level; that is, those husbands who had participated in Lamaze courses provided the greatest assistance, according to the wives' reports. Further support for the importance of fathers' presence at the birth of their child is Wente and Crockenberg's (1976) finding of no differences between Lamaze and non-Lamaze fathers in parenting adjustment. This is especially interesting in light of the fact that almost all non-Lamaze fathers were present at birth. Thus, there seem to be some important benefits to be gained by simple presence at the birth, though this is heightened by preparation for the event.

Prepared childbirth: issues of subject selection and motivation

A major problem in interpreting the results of the studies comparing trained versus nontrained parents is that most studies do not control for the influence of subject self-selection and motivation, because, in general, trained and nontrained groups were self-selected. Thus, the group differences that emerge may be attributable to factors other than the training. The major alternative explanation of the positive effects shown by training couples is that some who select training may be different from the other couples in ways that are related to the positive outcomes. However, two studies had control groups that did not suffer from the possible bias inherent in self-selected groups. Enkin, Smith, Dermer, and Emmett (1972) included a group that wanted training but could not receive it because demand for the program was higher than the resources available. The training group showed lower usage of medication, and felt labor and delivery to be a more positive experience, than did this control group.

Entwisle and Doering (1981) compared mothers with various levels of preparation, assuming that the influence of motivation for preparation was equal across groups. Their results indicated that the highly trained group generally showed more positive results than the group that received less training. While it is true that the research participants were not originally assigned to groups on a random basis, the researchers' assumption of equivalent motivation across groups seems plausible, though it is certainly possible that those individuals who choose to attend a more time-consuming, fee-required course (e.g., Lamaze) may be more motivated than those opting for a shorter, free course. Nevertheless, these two studies are important because they suggest that the effects of training are above and beyond any positive effects engendered by motivation or placebo effects.

In general, an important issue in this area is the characteristics of participants in these programs and research studies. Few studies have been conducted specifically to ascertain the characteristics of participants and nonparticipants in these programs. The few studies that have been conducted have looked at individuals and couples going through the transition to parenthood and choosing to take a childbirth preparation course (e.g., Lamaze), a hospital-based prenatal course, or no course at all. Leonard (1973) compared 26 women who had attended childbirth preparation classes with 16 who had not and found that the "attenders" were significantly older, better educated, more interested in breastfeeding, and more likely to use some form of birth control.

Such findings are consistent with Watson's (1977) and are supportive of data indicating sharp differences in participation rates in Lamaze classes by social class (e.g., 63 vs. 12% for upper-middle vs. lower class, in Dharamraj et al., 1981). Such sharp differences in participation take on new importance when viewed in light of research delineating differential effects of preparation for childbirth on women and couples with differing social class backgrounds. For example, Nelson (1982) found much stronger effects of childbirth preparation among working-class women: They were less likely to use medication during labor and delivery and more likely to breastfeed, for example, than their unprepared working-class counterparts. The origin of these differing effects is an important topic for future research and is especially noteworthy given the apparent equal availability of and support for prepared childbirth in U.S. hospitals, regardless of locale (rural, urban) or characteristics of the patients served (ethnicity, socioeconomic status; Wideman & Singer, 1983; J. E. Singer, personal communication, August 12, 1986).

Preparation for parenthood

According to a Gallup poll, "Americans tend to be woefully unprepared for the future. One-third say they don't feel equipped to deal with being a parent" (Jones, 1985). A wide variety of programs have been developed to help couples prepare for the demands, experiences, and feelings following the birth of their first child. The need for such programs is clear given the number of adults who state they feel ill-prepared for parenting and especially caring for infants (Entwisle & Doering, 1981; Jones, 1985). One area that many couples say changes drastically with the birth of a child is that of their marital relationship. Studies conducted as far back as the 1950s (e.g., LeMasters, 1957) reported couples experiencing the changes in their life as a result of parenthood as stressful; the decrease in time, energy, and money that can be devoted to the marital relationship is a major complaint. Programs are now focusing specifically on this aspect of the transition. In this section we examine six such programs (Table 9.3). Although more programs no doubt exist, reports on the six we review have appeared in the literature and there has been some evaluation of their effectiveness. These programs not only share a focus on the couple's relationship but also emphasize the adaptive value of a strong marital relationship for dealing with the stresses that accompany the transition to parenthood (Duncan, 1984).

Previous reviews have examined intervention programs for infants (e.g., Beller, 1979) as well as support programs for new parents (see Kagan & Seitz, Chapter 10, this volume), but little attention has been given to this time of transition for couples as they move from the marital dyad to a family triad. As noted before, the birth of the first child has been considered a milestone by scholars of the family (e.g., Hill, 1978) and as an opportune time for preventive intervention. For example, Caplan (1964) discusses the transition to parenthood as a time of greater flexibility and openness to new information by individuals and couples. Such a perspective has led researchers and therapists to develop programs that would ideally tap this developmental readiness for learning and adaptive change.

Table 9.3. *Programs for prospective or new parents*

Reference	Comparison group	Goals	Participants' ages[a]	N[b]	Recruitment method	Program Approach	Program Deliverers	Program Length	Program Content	Evaluation out-come measures
Shereshefsky and Yarrow (1973)	Yes	To be ego supportive in a program of psychotherapy	M: 24 F: 27	29	Obstetrical clinic	Counseling (3 types)	Women counselors	M: 12–15 sessions; F: 7 sessions, pregnancy through 6 months postpartum	1. Personal insight 2. Clarification of feelings; object relations 3. Anticipatory guidance	1. Labor/delivery 2. Maternal/infant adaptation 3. Marital adjustment
Aranoff and Lewis (1979)	No	To make couples aware of communication and social support needs during TP	NR	48	NR	Lecture/discussion	Mental health professionals	8 weekly sessions, 2 hr each, during pregnancy	1. Couple's expectations 2. Change in couple relationship 3. Emotional needs of infant	1. Questionnaires 2. Postpartum meeting with couples
Wandersman et al. (1980)	Yes	To provide social support to new parents	Mid-20s	23M, 18F[c]	Childbirth preparation classes	Discussion	NR	Began 6–10 wk postpartum; met weekly for 6 wk then monthly for 4 wk	Topics of early parenting	Questionnaires: 1. Well-being 2. Marital adaptation 3. Parental sense of competence

Study		Goal	Age	N	Recruitment	Format	Leader	Meetings	Changes in couple's relationship	Questionnaire
Clulow (1982)	No	To strengthen the couples' relationship	20–38	42	Letters to expectant couples	Discussion	Health visitor	6 meetings, beginning in late pregnancy and continuing through early parenting; 1 meeting/month		
Sudsberry et al. (personal communication, 1980)	No	To facilitate adults' adjustment to parenting role	21–32	43[d]	Mass media, brochures, word of mouth	Lectures, group activities, discussion	Family educators	9 weekly sessions postpartum	1. Balancing multiple roles, values 2. Parenting self-confidence 3. Family communication and satisfaction 4. Family development	Questionnaires: 1. Parenting confidence 2. Parenting knowledge 3. Family worries
Cowan and Cowan (1987)	Yes	To focus on changes in couple relationship	M: 29 F: 30	24	Ob/Gyn practices, newsletters	Discussion	Trained couples	25 meetings over 6 months pregnancy through postpartum	1. Sense of self/self-esteem 2. Role arrangements 3. Couple communication	Questionnaires: 1. Marital satisfaction 2. Conflict/disagreement

Abbreviations: M, mothers; F, fathers; NR, not reported; TP, transition to parenthood.

[a] May not reflect full age range of intended target groups.

[b] Couples in experimental group only.

[c] Eighteen couples plus five mothers.

[d] Authors report attendance only in terms of individual parents' participation, though program is designed for couples.

The work of Shereshefsky and Yarrow (1973) is based on the idea that the birth of the first child provides an opportune period for intervention with couples, utilizing their greater openness to learning and change to effect changes in their relationship and to establish patterns that will, one hopes, persist beyond the pregnancy period. Expectant couples were recruited from a Washington, D.C., prepaid health care organization and offered individual psychotherapy. A randomly selected control group was also formed. Although there were some differences related to the type of psychotherapy (three different approaches were utilized), the overall effect of counseling was significant. Specifically, women who received counseling were found to be more successful in visualizing themselves as mothers, to be more closely identified with their new family, to have functioned better during labor and delivery, and to be doing better in their marital relationship postnatally. Husbands also received counseling, though less frequently, and it centered around providing emotional support for the wife during pregnancy. Marital adjustment was greatest for the couples when the wife had received "anticipatory guidance." This focused on helping women anticipate the stresses of pregnancy, childbirth, and early parenting, as well as encouraging them to generate strategies for dealing with problems that would likely emerge.

Other studies focused either on the pregnancy period (Aranoff & Lewis, 1979) or on the postpartum period (Myers-Walls & Sudsberry, 1982) and shared the goal of fostering positive adjustment to parenthood by the provision of information on early parenting. In addition, they sought to provide a comfortable context in which couples could discuss problems, express satisfactions and fears, as well as solicit help and advice. The Family Enrichment for New Parents program of Sudsberry, Myers-Walls, and Coward (1980) has now been offered by the program's developers five times to a total of 43 parents. Usually led by female and male coleaders experienced in group work, this nine-session program focuses on the acquisition both of knowledge about the transition to parenthood and parenting and of skills in the areas of time management and communication. Most participants have been first-time parents, but others have been involved in the program following the birth of a second or third child. Participants have indicated increased self-confidence about themselves and their ability to care for an infant and have suggested that the program eased their adjustment to parenting a new child. The program's developers have reported low attendance, however, and hope that further evaluation efforts will provide insight into this problem (Myers-Walls & Sudsberry, 1982; J. A. Myers-Walls, personal communication, June 25, 1986).

Another program is that described by Aranoff and Lewis (1979). Their experience with 48 couples has been positive and corroborated by participants' responses to postpartum and postgroup questionnaires. The emphasis on couple communication and sources of social support in the pregnancy period appeared to direct participants' attention to previously unidentified issues, reduce fears and anxieties, and increase awareness of communication and problem-solving skills. Of course, the absence of any comparison group makes it difficult to place these comments in perspective. Similarly, the work of Clulow (1982) in London with neighborhood-based couples discussion groups during pregnancy and early parenthood contains a wealth of interesting and well-presented information on forming intervention groups, and yet the absence of a comparison group and prebirth data on couples' functioning makes interpretation of much of his postpartum questionnaire data impossible. Nevertheless, this volume should prove invaluable to others planning work in this area because of the author's thoughtful treatment of theoretical and practical issues related to the development of a prevention program and its implementation.

The work by Cowan and Cowan (1983, 1987) should prove, however, to be paradigmatic for future researchers in this area. Their Becoming a Family Project at the University of California, Berkeley, is a model of careful design and is described in detail in this volume (Chapter 4). Their work has involved the random assignment of couples to one of three groups for expectant couples that permit the delineation of the effects of group participation and of repeated assessments. In addition, there is a fourth group of couples who are not going through the transition to parenthood. All of the families are continuing to be followed, so the long-term preventive effects of an intervention program during pregnancy and early parenting can be assessed.

The results at 6 months postpartum indicated that both experimental and control couples were sharing household tasks less than they had before becoming parents and were experiencing more marital conflict and disagreement. At 6 months, experimental parents "showed a tendency toward *lower* self-esteem than control parents" (C. Cowan, 1983, p. 2). Other results indicated that the couples who had participated in the treatment groups were experiencing at least as much, if not more, dissatisfaction than couples who had not participated in them. However, marital satisfaction remained generally stable for the group couples and declined for the nongroup couples. At 1-year postgroup follow-up (when the babies were 18 months old), a clearer picture emerged: Group couples regained the level of self-esteem and life satisfaction they had lost in the early postpartum period, and they maintained their level of marital adjustment; in contrast, the nongroup women showed decreases in self-esteem, and both they and their husbands reported decreased marital satisfaction. Most striking, however, were differences in rates of marital distress and dissolution: None of the couples who had participated in the intervention had separated or divorced, whereas 12.5% of the control couples had. Cowan and Cowan are continuing to analyze the massive amount of data they have gathered on these couples and young families, and their current and future reports should continue to provide important insights into the value and processes involved in preventive intervention programs for expectant parents.

Recommendations and conclusion

We have reviewed three areas in which intervention programs have been developed and evaluated for couples considering or going through the transition to parenthood. We have seen that these programs cover a wide range of emphases, approaches, and outcomes. The program developers and evaluators represent a diverse group of disciplines, and it is not surprising that the quality of the research and conceptualization varies and that the quality and quantity of the material presented describing the programs and their evaluation varies as well. In general, these three intervention areas are in different stages of development, with childbirth preparation programs having the longest history and greatest development, followed by preparation for parenting programs, and recently joined by the programs helping couples to decide whether and when they wish to become parents. In order to help provide a group of standards and expectations for future work in these three areas, we conclude with a set of recommendations, grouped into four major areas: conceptual, design, measurement, and clinical issues.

Conceptual recommendations and issues

The major conceptual issue is the need for program developers to articulate clearly the short- and long-term process and outcome goals in their conceptualization of their intervention programs, as discussed earlier. As an example of the process–outcome distinction, consider the decision making for parenthood studies. The process evaluation of these studies involves assessing the extent to which couples learn the information presented in the study. Then the outcome goal is the making of a better decision. But did that happen? Of course, "better decision" must be operationally defined. This could simply be the couple's satisfaction with the decision or the decision-making process as evaluated by objective observers or experts. These processes and outcomes are short term; longer-term goals remain unstated. However, these may include greater satisfaction among program couples than among control couples with having a child if they decide to have one, or greater satisfaction with remaining childless if that was their decision.

As another example of the short-term/long-term distinction, consider the majority of the programs we have reviewed. Some programs are aimed at rather immediate or short-term outcomes (e.g., reduction of pain and use of medication during childbirth), and others have longer-term goals (e.g., parenting programs' goal of enhancing adults' competencies as parents, ideally leading to improved parent–child relations and better child adjustment). Programs vary in the degree to which they delineate outcome goals, long-term goals generally receiving less attention than short-term goals. Such articulation of both short- and long-term outcome goals should lead to the generation of hypotheses concerning the expected progress over time as a function of the intervention. This hypothesis generation should lead to the testing of specific theories and models of individual and couple functioning during the transition to parenthood.

The second major conceptual issue is the need to consider what Hartup (1979) refers to as the "levels of analysis" issue. Program developers can choose to intervene at the individual, couple, group, or community level. Similarly, program evaluators can choose to assess the impact of the intervention delivered on any of these four levels. For example, many of the childbirth preparation studies focus on mothers (at the individual level of analysis) for both intervention and evaluation. Little attention has been paid to the influence of the marital relationship, families and friends, previous childbirth experiences (primiparous vs. multiparous births), and other aspects of the mother's world on the efficacy of intervention programs. Conspicuous in its omission is the role of the father, considering the emerging research on his role in childrearing (Parke, 1981; Pedersen, 1980). Clearly, focusing on one level versus another will present constraints for the researcher or program developer; all variables cannot be examined in the same study. Consequently, investigators will need to consider the goals of their programs and their research carefully if the program is to represent the theory accurately and if the evaluation is to assess the work of the program developers fairly.

Finally, many intervention programs in the community appear to be based solely on common sense or clinical intuition rather than on empirical data concerning parents' success in coping with the transition to parenthood. For example, one brochure advertising prepregnancy classes in Denver suggested that, in 3 weeks, prospective parents could learn "everything you should know before pregnancy." But do we really know what couples should know before pregnancy? Future researchers must not only study what information is most useful to expectant couples but also examine affective and personality factors that may limit individuals' motivation for fully assimilating such information during the pregnancy period (Clulow, 1982). Similarly, the decision making for parenthood programs have in common the provision of information to couples about the demands of parenting. There are a number of assumptions that should be made explicit. First is the assumption that people need information to make better decisions. Is there empirical evidence that supports this? If so, what is the information that is required? Are there any empirical studies that suggest that providing certain information helps couples feel they made a better decision?

Many of the programs are developed by well-meaning clinicians who base the content on their clinical experience but who may be professionally removed from the "basic research" on decision making, childbirth preparation, human development, and other areas that could clearly assist program developers. Myers-Walls and Sudsberry (1982) have emphasized the need for program developers to collaborate with university researchers so that the work of each group can be enriched and refined by the efforts of the other. Such collaboration is especially important in a multidisciplinary field such as this one, where relevant work can emanate from any number of disciplines. Thus, we recommend that programs be based as much as possible on empirical evidence (see Markman et al., 1982, for a description of a preventive intervention framework).

Design issues

The major design issue is that studies and programs often do not include appropriate comparison groups, and ideally randomly assigned control groups should be used. When random assignment is not possible, researchers should attempt to control for several factors that might influence the participants' selection of groups, such as motivation and commitment to the relationship. These are essential if the effects of the programs are to be fully appreciated and if some understanding of the mechanisms whereby the programs have their effects is to be obtained. As the research progresses, strategies other than the use of no-intervention control groups will be important to consider. These will include placebo control groups as well as others that help delineate mechanisms whereby the effects may be achieved (e.g., Kondas & Scetnicka, 1972). Innovative research designs such as those used by Entwisle and Doering (1981) and by Cowan and Cowan (1987) should be encouraged and supported.

A second issue is the need for more heterogeneous samples. As noted in the section entitled "Prepared childbirth: issues of subject selection and motivation," this is particularly true with regard to socioeconomic status and ethnicity. The potentially differing impacts of these programs on different groups behooves the researcher or program developer to include different target groups. Of course, the inclusion of these groups will have an impact on the outcomes such programs are predicted to have, requiring the development of more specific theoretical models and increased attention to process issues.

A third design issue is the need for long-term follow-up. This point is consistent with the fact that the objectives of prevention programs are by definition long term. In many instances evaluations of programs should also include a minimum of two follow-up assessments. Given that most of the programs have long-term goals, we would recommend that studies include at least one assessment during the pregnancy, one assessment immediately following the birth of the child, and one at a later point when theory would dictate.

Measurement issues

The major measurement issue is that researchers have used different measures to assess similar dimensions of functioning, thereby hindering the comparison of findings across studies. For example, the measurement of anxiety in various studies has involved at least four different instruments. The problem is compounded when investigators develop their own instruments without adequate attention to the psychometric properties of the measure (e.g., reliability and validity). Then it is almost impossible to ascertain the importance of the findings for future research and theory in the area. We recommend that a common set of validated measures be used by researchers in the transition-to-parenthood area. We do not intend to diminish researchers' and program developers' creativity in developing new measures but to encourage the development and validation of measures *before* their inclusion in studies and evaluation programs as well as to encourage the increased use of common measures.

A second issue is the appropriateness of instruments for transition-to-parenthood groups (e.g., Barnett, Hanna, & Parker, 1983), as well as the sensitivity and validity of indicators of developmental status. For example, Ainsworth's Strange Situation (Ainsworth, Blehar, Waters, & Wall, 1978) procedure for assessing the quality of the parent–infant relationship is an excellent example of a measure that has demonstrated both concurrent and predictive validity (Cronbach & Meehl, 1955) and that provides "outcome" data that reflect important knowledge about developmental processes as well.

Clinical issues

Each of the three areas reviewed focused on different aspects of the transition to parenthood. Common to all three areas is the potential for marital issues to interact with the tasks facing the parents-to-be or new parents. Only a few of the programs reviewed in this chapter focused directly on the marital relationship. And yet the transition to parenthood, similar to other transition periods, is potentially an optimal time for people to make changes in important areas of their lives, including their marital relationship. The need for intervention in the marital relationship is apparent when one examines the high rates of divorce and marital distress and considers the link between stress on families and decreases in marital satisfaction (Miller & Sollie, 1980). Thus, couples in the transition to parenthood, particularly those with dysfunctional relationships going in, are "at risk" for experiencing increased marital problems, often centering around childcare and childrearing. Dissatisfaction with the marital relationship has been found to be related to greater reported feelings of anxiety and sadness by new parents, as well as to reports of greater problems with parenting (Duncan, 1984). Research and clinical experience, then, suggest that couples anticipating the birth of a child may want to take some time before the child is born to examine issues in their marriage and to make their relationship stronger, in the process helping to provide a better environment for their child. Yet high levels of stress and demands for changes on the couple during the time of transition to parenthood may make it unlikely that couples will want to deal directly with issues that produce anxiety (G. Y. Michaels, personal communication, July 19, 1985; Shereshefsky & Yarrow, 1973).Thus, an important issue for clinicians is the degree to which issues that are opened up during the transition to parenthood in some type of intervention program have the potential to affect the marital relationship in a positive way.

Another alternative that bypasses to a degree the above issue is to adapt programs aimed at improving couples' ability to communicate (e.g., Gottman, Notarius, Gonso, & Markman, 1976) so that they "target" each of the domains described in this chapter. The rationale for communication enhancement would be that the quality of a couple's communication is one of the best predictors of future marital satisfaction (Markman, Duncan, Storaasli, & Howes, 1987), so that couples have the communication skills to talk about problems as they move through the transition to parenthood. Belsky, Spanier, and Rovine (1983) note that one of the major changes in couples' relationships during the transition to parenthood is an enhanced feeling that they are working as a team. Improvement in communication skills is one way of increasing couples' working together as a team.

Another observation derived from considering the couple as the unit of analysis and based in part on the research reviewed above is that, when couples participate in interventions together, even if the focus is not specifically on communication or the couple's relationship per se, the intervention often has a positive impact on the couples' feelings of closeness and affection. There are several possible reasons for this outcome. First, couples share an experience and develop a common language system to talk about their experience. Second, couples engage in the activity together, fostering a sense of couple identity and shared mastery or efficacy over the aspect of the transition they are experiencing and with which they are coping. When one individual experiences an intervention that has to do with the couple's relationship, directly or indirectly, and the other does not, research indicates that relationship functioning is at risk (Gurman & Kniskern, 1978).

Thus, mutual participation in an intervention program may serve as a joining, positive experience for couples, whereas the participation of only one member of the couple often seems to serve as a separating, distancing experience. When couples participate in an intervention with other couples sharing the same experience, this provides them with a feeling of social support that has been linked to better functioning during the transition and subsequently (Heller & Monahan, 1977; Markman & Kadushin, 1986). Thus, we would recommend that intervention programs be focused on couples, not on individuals. Cronenwett (1980), however, reported that women who had participated in a postpartum support group without their partners said overwhelmingly (59 of 66) that they preferred not having their partners present. Thus, single and couple group participation may have different effects depending on the goals of the group and when the measures of outcome functioning and satisfaction are obtained.

Conclusion

Our review has indicated that great strides have been made in preparing parents for childbirth. We have seen that the majority of programs are still aimed at mothers, but there are signs that fathers are becoming increasingly included. Although most programs focus on childbirth, the need also to prepare couples for parenthood is becoming more widely recognized, and efforts to prepare couples for this are now well underway. Consistent with other clinical enterprises, evaluation efforts lag behind the program development efforts in both quality and quantity. The results of evaluations to date, despite their limitations, clearly indicate that these programs have had a positive impact on couples going through the transition to parenthood.

Nevertheless, this field is still in its infancy, and its interdisciplinary nature sometimes impairs its growth because of poor communication among disciplines. In this chapter we have attempted to provide a shared context using a prevention framework for the diverse programs that comprise the transition-to-parenthood intervention domain. We have attempted to identify common issues and solutions. We hope that we have demonstrated the importance of improved methodological and conceptual program development and evaluation efforts along the dimensions specified, as well as the benefits of increased linkage between program development and evaluation.

Acknowledgments

The authors thank Carla Bigelow and Nancy Pleiman for their assistance in preparing the manuscript. Correspondence should be directed to the authors at the Center for Marital and Family Studies, Department of Psychology, 2450 So. Vine St., University of Denver, Denver, Colorado 80208.

References

Ainsworth, M. D. S., Blehar, M. C., Waters, E., & Wall, S. (1978). *Patterns of attachment: A psychological study of the strange situation.* Hillsdale, NJ: Erlbaum.

Aranoff, J. L., & Lewis, S. (1979). An innovative group experience for couples expecting their first child. *American Journal of Family Therapy, 7,* 51–5.

Ball, T. L. (1960). The psychoprophylactic preparation of pregnant women for childbirth in the U.S.S.R. *Transactions of the New York Academy of Sciences, 22,* 578–80.

Barnes, A. B. (1976, May 27). Prophylaxis in labor and delivery [letter to the editor]. *New England Journal of Medicine,* pp. 1235–6.

Barnett, B. E. W., Hanna, B., & Parker, G. (1983). Life event scales for obstetric groups. *Journal of Psychosomatic Research, 27,* 313–20.

Beach, L. R., Townes, B. D., & Campbell, F. L. (1978). *The Optional Parenthood Questionnaire: A guide to decision making about parenthood* (available from National Alliance for Optional Parenthood, 2010 Massachusetts Ave., N.W., Washington, DC 20036).

Beck, N. C., Geden, E. A., & Brouder, G. T. (1979). Preparation for labor: A historical perspective. *Psychosomatic Medicine, 41,* 243–58.

Beller, E. K. (1979). Early intervention programs. In J. D. Osofsky (Ed.), *Handbook of infant development* (pp. 852–94). New York: Wiley.

Belsky, J., Spanier, G. B., & Rovine, M. (1983). Stability and change in marriage across the transition to parenthood. *Journal of Marriage and the Family, 45,* 567–77.

Bergstrom-Walan, M.-B. (1963). Efficacy of education for childbirth. *Journal of Psychosomatic Research, 7,* 131–46.

Bing, E. D. (1972). Psychoprophylaxis and family-centered maternity: A historical development in the U.S.A. In N. Morris (Ed.), *Psychosomatic medicine in obstetrics and gynaecology* (pp. 71–3). London: Karger.

Block, C. R., Norr, K. L., Meyering, S., Norr, J. L., & Charles, A. G. (1981). Husband gatekeeping in childbirth. *Family Relations, 30,* 197–204.

Block, J. H. (1976). Issues, problems, and pitfalls in assessing sex differences: A critical review of *The psychology of sex differences. Merrill–Palmer Quarterly, 22,* 283–308.

Bloom, B. L. (1984). *Community mental health: A general introduction* (2d ed.). Monterey, CA: Brooks/Cole.

Boston Women's Health Book Collective. (1976). *Our bodies, ourselves: A book by and for women* (2d ed.). New York: Simon & Schuster.

Bowen, S. M., & Miller, B. C. (1980). Paternal attachment behavior as related to presence at delivery and preparenthood classes: A pilot study. *Nursing Research, 29,* 307–11.

Brackbill, Y. (1979). Obstetrical medication and infant behavior. In J. D. Osofsky (Ed.), *Handbook of infant development* (pp. 76–125). New York: Wiley.

Brazelton, T. B. (1981). *On becoming a family: The growth of attachment.* New York: Delacorte Press/Seymour Lawrence.

Brown, P. B., Spragins, E. E., Engardio, P., Ringe, K., & Klinkerman, S. (1985, April 22). Bringing up baby: A new kind of marketing boom. *Business Week,* pp. 58–9, 62, 65.

Caplan, G. (1964). *Principles of preventive psychiatry.* New York: Basic Books.

Carter, E. A., & McGoldrick, M. (1980). *The family life cycle: A framework for family therapy.* New York: Gardner Press.

Chertok, L. (1959). *Psychosomatic methods in painless childbirth: History, theory and practice* (D. Leigh, Trans.). New York: Pergamon Press.

Chertok, L. (1967). Psychosomatic methods of preparation for childbirth: Spread of the methods, theory, and research. *American Journal of Obstetrics and Gynecology, 98,* 698–707.

Clulow, C. F. (1982). *To have and to hold: Marriage, the first baby and preparing couples for parenthood.* Aberdeen, Scotland: Aberdeen University Press.

Cohen, J. B. (1985). *Parenthood after 30? A guide to personal choice.* Lexington, MA: Lexington Books.

Cohler, B. J., Weiss, J. L., & Grunebaum, H. U. (1970). Child-care attitudes and emotional disturbance among mothers of young children. *Genetic Psychology Monographs, 82,* 3–47.

Cowan, C. P. (1983, August). *A preventive clinical intervention aimed at the marriages of new parents.* Paper presented at the meeting of the American Psychological Association, Anaheim, CA.

Cowan, C. P., & Cowan, P. A. (1987). A preventive intervention for couples becoming parents. In C. F. Z. Boukydis (Ed.), *Research on support for parents and infants in the postnatal period.* Norwood, NJ: Ablex.

Cowan, P. A., & Cowan, C. P. (1983, April). *Quality of couple relationships and parenting stress in beginning families.* Paper presented at the biennial meeting of the Society for Research in Child Development, Detroit, MI.

Cronbach, L. J., & Meehl, P. E. (1955). Construct validity in psychological tests. *Psychological Bulletin, 52,* 281–302.

Cronenwett, L. R. (1980). Elements and outcomes of a postpartum support group program. *Research in Nursing and Health, 3,* 33–41.

Cronenwett, L. R., & Newmark, L. L. (1974). Fathers' responses to childbirth. *Nursing Research, 23,* 210–17.

Daniluk, J. C., & Herman, A. (1984). Parenthood decision-making. *Family Relations, 33,* 607–12.

Davis, C. D., & Morrone, F. A. (1962). An objective evaluation of a prepared childbirth program. *American Journal of Obstetrics and Gynecology, 84,* 1196–1206.

Dharamraj, C., Sia, C. G., Kierney, C. M. P., Parekh, A., Harper, R. G., & Weissman, B. (1981). Observations on maternal preference for rooming-in facilities. *Pediatrics, 67,* 638–40.

Dick-Read, G. (1959). *Childbirth without fear: The principles and practice of natural childbirth* (2d ed.). New York: Harper & Row.

Doering, S. G., & Entwisle, D. R. (1975). Preparation during pregnancy and ability to cope with labor and delivery. *American Journal of Orthopsychiatry, 45,* 825–37.

Duncan, S. W. (1984). The transition to parenthood: Coping and adaptation of couples to pregnancy and the birth of their first child (doctoral dissertation, University of Minnesota, 1984). *Dissertation Abstracts International, 45,* 1600-B.

Emery, R. E. (1982). Interparental conflict and the children of discord and divorce. *Psychological Bulletin, 92,* 310–30.

Enkin, M. W., Smith, S. L., Dermer, S. W., & Emmett, J. O. (1972). An adequately controlled study of the effectiveness of PPM training. In N. Morris (Ed.), *Psychosomatic medicine in obstetrics and gynaecology* (pp. 62–7). London: Karger.

Entwisle, D. R., & Doering, S. G. (1981). *The first birth: A family turning point.* Baltimore, MD: Johns Hopkins University Press.

Ewy, D., & Ewy, R. (1982). *Preparation for childbirth: A Lamaze guide* (3rd ed.). New York: New American Library.

Fawcett, J. T. (Ed.). (1973). *Psychological perspectives on population.* New York: Basic Books.

Feldman, S. (1984). *Making up your mind about motherhood.* New York: Bantam.

Fischer, W. M., Huttel, F. A., Mitchell, I., & Meyer, A.-E. (1972). The efficacy of psychoprophylactic method of prepared childbirth. In N. Morris (Ed.), *Psychosomatic medicine in obstetrics and gynaecology* (pp. 38–44). London: Karger.

Fox, G. L. (Ed.). (1982). *The childbearing decision: Fertility attitudes and behavior.* Beverly Hills, CA: Sage.

Gallup Organization. (1983, Sept. 7). *Opinions about motherhood: A Gallup/Levi's maternity wear national poll of pregnant women and new mothers* (available from Levi Strauss & Co., Levi's Plaza, 1155 Battery St., San Francisco, CA 94111).

Gardner, R. A. (1966). On box score methodology as illustrated by three reviews of overtraining reversal effects. *Psychological Bulletin, 66,* 416–18.

Ginsberg, M. R. (1981). An evaluation of an educational program to promote couples' decision-making skills concerning parenthood (doctoral dissertation, Pennsylvania State University, 1981). *Dissertation Abstracts International, 42,* 140-A.

Gottman, J. M., & Markman, H. J. (1978). Experimental designs in psychotherapy research. In S. Garfield & A. Bergin (Eds.), *Handbook of psychotherapy and behavior change* (2d ed., pp. 23–62). New York: Wiley.

Gottman, J., Notarius, C., Gonso, J., & Markman, H. (1976). *A couple's guide to communication.* Champaign, IL: Research Press.

Greenberg, M., & Morris, N. (1974). Engrossment: The newborn's impact upon the father. *American Journal of Orthopsychiatry, 44,* 520–31.

Gurman, A. S., & Kniskern, D. P. (1978). Deterioration in marital and family therapy: Empirical, clinical, and conceptual issues. *Family Process, 17,* 3–20.

Hartup, W. W. (1979). Levels of analysis in the study of social interaction: An historical perspective. In M. E. Lamb, S. J. Suomi, & G. R. Stephenson (Eds.), *Social interaction analysis: Methodological issues* (pp. 11–32). Madison: University of Wisconsin Press.

Heardman, H. (1951). *Relaxation and exercise for natural childbirth.* Baltimore, MD: Williams & Wilkins.

Heller, K., & Monahan, J. (1977). *Psychology and community change.* Homewood, IL: Dorsey Press.

Hetherington, E. M. (1979). Divorce: A child's perspective. *American Psychologist, 34,* 851–8.

Hill, R. (1978). Psychosocial consequences of the first birth: A discussion. In W. B. Miller & L. F. Newman (Eds.), *The first child and family formation* (pp. 392–401). Chapel Hill: University of North Carolina, Carolina Population Center.

Hopkins, J., Marcus, M., & Campbell, S. B. (1984). Postpartum depression: A critical review. *Psychological Bulletin, 95,* 498–515.

Hott, J. R. (1972). An investigation of the relationship between psychoprophylaxis in childbirth and changes in self-concept of the participant husband and his concept of his wife (doctoral dissertation, New York University, 1972). *Dissertation Abstracts International, 33,* 296B–297B.

Hughey, M. J., McElin, T. W., & Young, T. (1978). Maternal and fetal outcome of Lamaze-prepared patients. *Journal of Obstetrics and Gynecology, 51,* 643–7.

Huttel, F. A., Mitchell, I., Fischer, W. M., & Meyer, A.-E. (1972). A quantitative evaluation of psychoprophylaxis in childbirth. *Journal of Psychosomatic Research, 16,* 81–92.

Jackson, D. N. (1974). *Personality research form manual.* Goshen, New York: Research Psychologists Press.

Jacobson, E. (1938). *Progressive relaxation.* University of Chicago Press.

Jones, R. (1985, June 26). U.S. optimism tops, Gallup says. *Rocky Mountain News,* p. 8.

Joy, L. A., Davidson, S., Williams, T. MacB., & Painter, S. L. (1980). Parent education in the perinatal period: A critical review of the literature. In P. M. Taylor (Ed.), *Parent–infant relationships* (pp. 211–37). New York: Grune & Stratton.

Kantrowitz, B. (1986, Sept. 1). Three's a crowd. *Newsweek,* pp. 68–74, 76.

Karmel, M. J. (1959). *Thank you, Dr. Lamaze: A mother's experience in painless childbirth.* Philadelphia: Lippincott.

Kimball, K. K., & McCabe, M. E. (1981). Should we have children? A decision-making group for couples. *Personnel and Guidance Journal, 60,* 153–6.

Kondas, O., & Scetnicka, B. (1972). Systematic desensitization as a method of preparation for childbirth. *Journal of Behavior Therapy and Experimental Psychiatry, 3,* 51–4.

Lamaze, F. (1965). *Painless childbirth: Psychoprophylactic method* (L. R. Celestin, Trans.). New York: Pocket Books. (Original work published 1956.)

Lamb, M. E. (1983). Early mother–neonate contact and the mother–child relationship. *Journal of Child Psychology and Psychiatry, 24,* 487–94.

LeMasters, E. E. (1957). Parenthood as crisis. *Marriage and Family Living, 19,* 352–5.

Leonard, R. F. (1973). Evaluation of selection tendencies of patients preferring prepared childbirth. *Obstetrics and Gynecology, 42,* 371–7.

Leridon, H. (1981). Fertility and contraception in 12 developed countries. *Family Planning Perspectives, 13,* 93–6, 98–102.

Lesko, W. (1986, June). The birth chart. *Good Housekeeping,* pp. 123–6.

Lundh, W. (1975). Preparation for childbirth or planning for parenthood: A change in emphasis? In H. Hirsch (Ed.), *The family* (pp. 180–4). London: Karger.

Markman, H. J., Duncan, S. W., Storaasli, R. D., & Howes, P. W. (1987). The prediction and prevention of marital distress: A longitudinal investigation. In K. Hahlweg & M. J. Goldstein (Eds.), *Understanding major mental disorder: The contribution of family interaction research* (pp. 266–89). New York: Family Process Press.

Markman, H. J., & Floyd, F. J. (1980). Possibilities for the prevention of marital discord: A behavioral perspective. *American Journal of Family Therapy, 8*, 29–48.

Markman, H. J., Floyd, F., & Dickson-Markman, F. (1982). Towards a model for the prediction and primary prevention of marital and family distress and dissolution. In S. Duck (Ed.), *Personal relationships. 4: Dissolving personal relationships* (pp. 233–61). New York: Academic Press.

Markman, H. J., Floyd, F. J., Stanley, S. M., & Jamieson, K. (1984). A cognitive-behavioral program for the prevention of marital and family distress: Issues in program development and delivery. In K. Hahlweg & N. S. Jacobson (Eds.), *Marital interaction: Analysis and modification* (pp. 396–428). New York: Guilford Press.

Markman, H. J., Floyd, F. J., Stanley, S. M., & Lewis, H. C. (1986). Prevention. In N. S. Jacobson & A. S. Gurman (Eds.), *Clinical handbook of marital therapy* (pp. 173–95). New York: Guilford Press.

Markman, H. J., Jamieson, K. J., & Floyd, F. J. (1983). The assessment and modification of premarital relationships: Preliminary findings on the etiology and prevention of marital and family distress. In J. Vincent (Ed.), *Advances in family intervention, assessment and theory* (Vol. 3; pp. 41–90). Greenwich, CT: JAI Press.

Markman, H. J., & Kadushin, F. S. (1986). Preventive effects of Lamaze training for first-time parents: A short-term longitudinal study. *Journal of Consulting and Clinical Psychology, 54*, 872–4.

Mattessich, P., & Hill, R. (in press). Family development and life cycle research and theory revisited. In M. Sussman & S. Steinmetz (Eds.), *Handbook of marriage and the family*. New York: Plenum.

McPheeters, H. L. (1976). Primary prevention and health promotion in mental health. *Preventive Medicine, 5*, 187–98.

Miller, B. C., & Bowen, S. L. (1982). Father-to-newborn attachment behavior in relation to prenatal classes and presence at delivery. *Family Relations, 31*, 71–8.

Miller, B. C., & Sollie, D. L. (1980). Normal stresses during the transition to parenthood. *Family Relations, 29*, 459–65.

Morishima, H. O. (1982). Obstetric analgesia and anesthesia. In D. N. Danforth (Ed.), *Obstetrics and gynecology* (4th ed.; pp. 663–79). New York: Harper & Row.

Myers-Walls, J. A., & Sudsberry, R. L. (1982). Parent education during the transition into parenthood. In N. Stinnet, J. DeFrain, K. King, H. Lingren, G. Rowe, S. van Zandt, & R. Williams (Eds.), *Family strengths. 4: Positive support systems* (pp. 55–70). Lincoln: University of Nebraska Press.

Napier, A. (1980). Primary prevention: A family therapist's perspective. In N. Stinnet, B. Chesser, J. DeFrain, & P. Knaub (Eds.), *Family strengths: Positive models for family life* (pp. 49–65). Lincoln: University of Nebraska Press.

National Center for Health Statistics. (1986, July 17). Births, marriages, divorces, and deaths for April 1986. *Monthly Vital Statistics Report, 35*, 1–11.

Nelson, M. K. (1982). The effect of childbirth preparation on women of different social classes. *Journal of Health and Social Behavior, 23*, 339–52.

Newton, N., & Newton, M. (1972). Childbirth in crosscultural perspective. In J. G. Howells (Ed.), *Modern perspectives in psycho-obstetrics* (Vol. 5; pp. 150–72). New York: Brunner/Mazel.

Parke, R. D. (1981). *Fathers*. Cambridge, MA: Harvard University Press.

Pedersen, F. A. (Ed.). (1980). *The father–infant relationship: Observational studies in the family setting.* New York: Praeger.

Pohlman, E. (1969). *The psychology of birth planning.* Cambridge, MA: Schenkman.

Potts, L. (1980). Considering parenthood: Group support for a critical life decision. *American Journal of Orthopsychiatry, 50,* 629–38.

Prochaska, J., & Coyle, J. R. (1979). Choosing parenthood: A needed family life education group. *Social Casework, 60,* 289–95.

Rode, S. S., Chang, P.-N., Fisch, R. O., & Sroufe, L. A. (1981). Attachment patterns of infants separated at birth. *Developmental Psychology, 17,* 188–91.

Rollins, B. C., & Galligan, R. (1978). The developing child and marital satisfaction of parents. In R. M. Lerner & G. B. Spanier (Eds.), *Child influences on marital and family interaction: A life-span perspective* (pp. 71–105). New York: Academic Press.

Scott, J. R., & Rose, N. B. (1976). Effect of psychoprophylaxis (Lamaze preparation) on labor and delivery in primiparas. *New England Journal of Medicine, 294,* 1205–7.

Shereshefsky, P. M., & Yarrow, L. J. (Eds.). (1973). *Psychological aspects of a first pregnancy and early postnatal adaptation.* New York: Raven Press.

Sudsberry, R. L., Myers-Walls, J. A., & Coward, R. T. (1980). *Family enrichment for new parents* (available from J. A. Myers-Walls, Human Development, Child Development and Family Studies, Purdue University, West Lafayette, IN 47907.)

Tanzer, D. R. W. (1967). The psychology of pregnancy and childbirth: An investigation of natural childbirth (doctoral dissertation, Brandeis University, 1967). *Dissertation Abstracts International, 28,* 2615B.

Tanzer, D., & Block, J. L. (1972). *Why natural childbirth? A psychologist's report on the benefits to mothers, fathers, and babies.* New York: Doubleday.

Thoms, H., & Goodrich, F. W., Jr. (1949). Training for childbirth. *Journal of the American Medical Association, 140,* 1256–8.

Thoms, H., & Wyatt, R. H. (1951). One thousand consecutive deliveries under a training for childbirth program. *American Journal of Obstetrics and Gynecology, 61,* 205–9.

Toohey, J. V., & Valenzuela, G. L. (1983). Values clarification as a technique for family planning education. *Journal of School Health, 53,* 121–5.

Tupper, C. (1956). Conditioning for childbirth. *American Journal of Obstetrics and Gynecology, 71,* 733–40.

van Auken, W. B. D., & Tomlinson, D. R. (1953). An appraisal of patient training for childbirth. *American Journal of Obstetrics and Gynecology, 66,* 100–5.

Velvovsky, I. Z. (1972). Psychoprophylaxis in obstetrics: A Soviet method. In J. G. Howells (Ed.), *Modern perspectives in psycho-obstetrics* (Vol. 5; pp. 314–27). New York: Brunner/ Mazel.

Velvovsky, I. Z., Platonov, K., Ploticher, V., & Shugom, E. (1960). *Painless childbirth through psychoprophylaxis.* Moscow: Foreign Languages Publishing House.

Wandersman, L., Wandersman, A., & Kahn, S. (1980). Social support in the transition to parenthood. *Journal of Community Psychology, 8,* 332–42.

Watson, J. (1977). Who attends prepared childbirth classes? A demographic study of CEA classes in Rhode Island. *JOGN Nursing, 6,* 36–9.

Wente, A. S., & Crockenberg, S. B. (1976). Transition to fatherhood: Lamaze preparation, adjustment difficulty and the husband–wife relationship. *Family Coordinator, 25,* 351–7.

Westoff, C. F. (1978). Marriage and fertility in the developed countries. *Scientific American, 239,* 51–7.

Whelan, E. M. (1975). *A baby? . . . maybe: A guide to making the most fateful decision of your life.* New York: Bobbs-Merrill.

Wideman, M. V., & Singer, J. E. (1983). *Psychosocial trends in obstetrical practices in American hospitals.* Unpublished manuscript, Uniformed Services University of the Health Sciences, Bethesda, MD.

Wideman, M. V., & Singer, J. E. (1984). The role of psychological mechanisms in preparation for childbirth. *American Psychologist, 39,* 1357–71.

Yarrow, L. (1982, August). When my baby was born. *Parents Magazine,* pp. 43–7.

Zax, M., Sameroff, A. J., & Farnum, J. E. (1975). Childbirth attitudes, maternal attitudes, and delivery. *American Journal of Obstetrics & Gynecology, 123,* 185–90.

10   Family support programs for new parents

Sharon L. Kagan and Victoria Seitz

In Santa Barbara, California,[1] a terrified teenmother calls a 24-hour warm line to find out what to do when her infant will not nurse or where to turn when she needs some respite from the demands of parenting. One of many supports offered to the postpartum family, the warm line is augmented by parent support groups and referral services.

In Fort Wayne, Indiana,[2] adoptive couples particpate in weekly classes where they discuss psychological tasks unique to those who elect to build their families through adoption. Led by an adoptive parent, the classes deal with routine parenting information and provide the special supports needed by couples as they may deal with their own infertility and with the special challenges and joys of parenting an adopted child.

In Denver, Colorado,[3] a pregnant woman who is uncertain about her readiness and ability to care for the child she will soon give birth to welcomes a home visitor, a parent from the community. During weekly visits from midpregnancy through the first year of life, the home visitor listens, shares, reassures, and provides practical information about babying, child development, and community resources available to new parents. The home visitor helps the woman deal with a range of functions and emotions by acting as "friend," "guide," and "inspiration."

These three examples convey the nature and intent of hundreds of support programs and services that have emerged throughout America in recent years. The array of supports available to families multiplies when one considers efforts in numerous sectors: the myriad written materials available in popular magazines, journals, and government publications and the bevy of broadcast media programs devoted to parents and parenting education; the many programs and services offered by the traditional bureaucratic human service sector; and the increasing efforts of business,

---

[1] Postpartum Education for Parents, P. O. Box 6154, Santa Barbara, CA 93160.

[2] Indiana Resolve, Inc., 5629 Chester Blvd., Fort Wayne, IN 46819.

[3] The Home Visitor Program of Family Support Services, Inc., 820 Clermont Street, Suite 210, Denver, CO 80220.

311

industry, and countless other groups to support individuals as they become parents.

Services to assist adults as they make the transition to parenthood fall along a continuum, ranging from those that are totally informal and private to those that are bureaucratized and public. At the informal end, support is rendered by friends, families, and neighbors, as has been the case throughout history. At the opposite end, highly bureaucratized social services are available for those who are otherwise unable to meet their needs. The vast arena between contains a host of support efforts – some remaining very informal, some codified into ongoing programs. This chapter will concentrate not on supports too informal to chronicle or those so bureaucratized that they have been described ad infinitum, but rather on the range of services in the center of the continuum: family support programs. Historical antecedents of programs to assist teens and adults as they become parents will be presented; emphasis will be placed on supports for families after a child's birth. Problems and challenges in the implementation and evaluation of family support designs will be considered and policy recommendations put forth. We should underscore that in focusing on family support programs, as opposed to informal supports, on the one hand, or highly bureaucratized services, on the other, we highlight an emerging aspect of the widespread effort to assist new parents.

Antecedents of family support programs

Historical and demographic antecedents

Traditionally, supporting adults as they became parents, as in other periods of transition (marriage, illness, death), had been the responsibility of the family. When the immediate family could not meet the needs of members under stress, extended family or friends from the church or neighborhood were called upon to lend necessary support and solace. Essentially, then, as Moroney (1980) has pointed out, the family itself functions as a social service.

The need for care beyond the family network was precipitated in the 1800s in America by urbanization and industrialization. The move from rural to urban centers separated the family from traditional sources of support at the same time as it faced the new exigencies of an industrialized society. At this time, formal social service agencies were created to fill the void by providing needed support.

The social philosophy that guided the development of America's early service network was characterized by opposing values – values that continue to shape the social service milieu in America. Garbarino (1982) points out that social Darwinism represents one value orientation: the survival of the fittest. This orientation supports a hands-off attitude toward social problems. In contrast, a second value – that of equality as an American ideal – led social reformers to try to provide opportunities that would help reduce the disparity between the "fit" and the "not-so-fit." Thus, in the more conservative periods in our history, social problems are attributed to an individual's failure. In contrast, in reforming eras, social problems are viewed as a societal failure to provide equality. In these periods, change focuses on restructuring societal agents, institutions, and social structures.

Against this philosophic pendulum, a pattern of social services emerged in America. Rooted in the work of voluntary charitable organizations, such as settlement houses and churches, social services in the late nineteenth century were neighborhood-based and emphasized the provision of opportunities in the form of employment rather than dole. As the early efforts became more bureaucratized, and as a helping profession emerged in the 1920s and 1930s, the social distance between those needing and those giving support widened. With the acceptance of psychotherapy, expert advice became the norm, further widening the gap between the professional and the client. With few exceptions, the predominant norm of service has been remediative, predicated on the theory of social Darwinism: Those who can, survive; those who cannot, fail and become dependent. Correcting the behaviors, attitudes, and deficits of the latter group was a predominant goal of social services through the late 1960s.

Although attempts at social reform abounded (Kagan, 1984; Pizzo, 1983), systematic alterations to the basic social service mode were implemented very sporadically. Families typically sought to avoid involvement with the social service network for fear of being swept in and subsumed by it. Then, as in the past, families turned to informal networks, so that a system of "personal social services" (Kahn, 1976) developed alongside the more structured social service bureaucracy.

The 1960s witnessed an ideological shift. First, recipients and providers acknowledged their dissatisfaction with traditional social service delivery modes. Second, a renewed emphasis on equality called for vigorous efforts to redress imbalances between the professional and the client. Parents were portrayed as partners in schools, and their participation was required for federal funding. Antipoverty agencies predicated programs on a model of collaboration between professionals and community residents, and grass-roots organizations flourished. Pizzo (1983) points out how the very special experiences of the 1960s activists affected their visions of parenthood in the 1970s:

Would a young man who had been willing to deny the American selective service system accept the obstetric ward's policy of "fathers aren't allowed?" Would the young woman who had been willing to confront the Birmingham or Chicago police . . . be cowed by her daughter's school principal? Many of the parents of the seventies and eighties were prepared for making decisions of conscience and acting on those decisions. (p. 47)

The emphasis on equality forecasted a new direction, broadly, for social services and, specifically, for parent support.

Today's informal support programs are rooted in more than the activism of the 1960s. Recent demographic changes have also accelerated a movement toward this new mode of social service delivery. Given enormous changes in families, adults are now experiencing unprecedented stress. A 65% increase in the number of divorces leaves one in every five children in a single-parent family (Bane, 1976). In fact, it is predicted that, by 1990, nearly one in four children will live in single-parent households – an increase of 3 million youngsters, or a 48% increase since 1980 (U.S. Congressional Budget Office, 1983). The full impact of these figures is masked until we acknowledge the close correlation between family structure (in this case, single parenthood) and income (or lack thereof). By 1990, of 23 million children *under 6 years of age,* 17% will be from single-parent households, one-half of which will have household incomes below the poverty level (U.S. Congressional Budget Office, 1983). With increasing economic needs, women are returning to the work force in unprecedented numbers. Among working mothers, a striking fact is the number of mothers of young children who are employed out of the home: 44.9% of mothers with children under 6 are in the labor force, and this rate is expected to continue to rise (U.S. Bureau of the Census, 1981). With this social revolution comes need for increased support.

Another important demographic trend that has given rise to family support programs is an increase in the number of teenage parents, particularly among young (15- to 16-year-old) and unmarried adolescents. The number of women under 15 who gave birth rose from 7,500 in 1960 to 13,000 in 1973. During the 1970s, the number of babies born to unmarried women also rose significantly, from less than 10,000 in 1960 to almost 200,000 in 1970 to 270,000 in 1980. Nearly half (48%) of births to teens were out of wedlock in 1980, as contrasted with 15% in 1960 (Baldwin, 1984). The concern regarding the marital status of the mother is critical, because it often affects access to economic and social supports. In addition to age and marital status, race, in concert with age, is important to consider. According to data from the National Center for Health Statistics (1981), the younger the adolescent, the greater are the racial differences in birthrates. Nearly five times as many black 14-year-olds have babies as do whites, but by age 19, this number is reduced to less than twice as many. Whatever the marital status, age, or race of the mother, the problems concomitant with teenage motherhood are now well documented – reduced educational and occupational attainment, higher mental instability, and higher subsequent fertility (see Osofsky, Osofsky, & Diamond, Chapter 7, this volume).

In addition to these demographic factors, the growth in family support programs can also be traced to federal budget cuts. Constrained by reduced funding, traditional social service agencies are simply unable to meet existing, much less increasing, demands for services. In addition to new fiscal limitations, the political philosophy of the 1980s espouses a limited government role in family life. Increased needs among families coupled with reduced federal commitment have forced individuals to fashion a new system of supports, independent of the traditional bureaucracy and reflective of a novel set of orientations.

Theoretical antecedents

In an assessment of the rationale for the ascendency of family support programs, theoretical antecedents must be considered along with the historical and demographic antecedents discussed. Three theories hold particular relevance to the early parenting support efforts: a nonpathological competency-based orientation, an ecological perspective, and an orientation toward preventive rather than ameliorative services.

A nonpathological competency-based orientation. Whittaker, Garbarino, and Associates (1983) trace the increasingly perceived need for a competency orientation in the delivery of social services. They suggest that there has been a steady move away from a pathological model of practice toward a competence model. This model refocuses on the strengths people have within themselves and on resources they can use in their environments. It stresses the existence of competence, skills, and motivation within the individual. Such an orientation, like others that characterize family support, stress teaching and learning by the individual as cofunctions. In teaching and modeling coping and mastery skills, individuals learn to maximize their own talents and resources.

An ecological perspective. The ecological perspective in human service practice posits environmentally oriented intervention to strengthen social supports. The ecological perspective is akin to the competency point of view in advocating individually oriented interventions that promote personal strengths. Whittaker, Garbarino, and Associates (1983) indicate that the ecological perspective consists of a broadly inclusive view of effective human service that

1. recognizes the complementarity of person-in-environment and seeks to strengthen each component;
2. accepts the fact that an exclusive focus on *either* the individual *or* his or her immediate environment will generally not produce effective helping;
3. acknowledges that interpersonal help may take many forms, as long as its goal is to teach skills for effectively coping with the environment;
4. views social support not simply as a desirable concomitant to professional help but as an inextricable component of an overall helping strategy; and
5. recognizes the distinct and salutary features of both professional and lay helping efforts in an overall framework for services.

This orientation, then, shifts us from the individual as the sole unit of intervention by extending the focus of support to the interaction of the individual, the family, and the social context. Operationally, this perspective promotes collaboration between and among clients and service providers, and between and among informal programs and traditional bureaucracies.

A preventive orientation. Prevention is an important approach to social problem solving. Garbarino (1982) notes that, traditionally, human services have existed to minimize negative outcomes. This orientation presumes that "the client must step over an invisible line of failure or inadequacy before service begins" (Garbarino, 1982, pp. 177–8). The inherent goal is to restore the individual or family to an *acceptable* level of functioning. In contrast, a focus on optimizing positive outcomes yields a substantively different approach. This position (like the competency orientation discussed earlier) organizes resources so that *optimal* functioning can be facilitated and problems averted. It implies a nondeficit orientation and includes all individuals, not simply families with specific problems. This perspective acknowledges that the need for support is universal and that the timing of support – before a problem occurs – is critical.

Empirical antecedents

As theoretical assumptions have helped to reshape attitudes about human service delivery, empirical evidence has reshaped tenets of infant development, which in turn determine the design of programs to facilitate the transition to parenthood. Empirical data have refined our attitudes toward infants so that we no longer view them as passive organisms, shaped by their environment. Rather, as Yarrow (1979) and Huntington (1979) point out, studies reveal the infant to be a skilled and active partner in relationships, seeking stimulation from birth and needing the opportunity to learn. Empirical studies also identify the adult as a figure for identification, as a model for learning how to cope and interact, and as a figure who sets expectations.

With this widening body of information, parents' expectations for themselves are heightened. The job of parenting an infant is being taken more seriously by more young adults than ever before. For some, the desire to be a more effective parent motivates their involvement in family support programs. For others, this process is exacerbated by demographic realities that produce stress and the related need for support.

As we have seen, family support programs are rooted in the history of social services in this country, are legacies of the activism and empowerment of the 1960s, and are shaped by theoretical and empirical developments. We shall see that these programs, dramatically increasing in number, are as varied and rich as this groundwork suggests.

Contemporary family support programs

In an attempt to clarify the nature, organization, and range of participants in programs that support individuals as they become parents, various theoretical constructs have been used. Wandersman (1987) postulates that five categories of service characterize many programs: (1) unstructured mutual help groups, (2) parent skills training, (3) couple discussion groups, (4) home visits by professionals, and (5) home visits by paraprofessionals. Harmon and Brim (1980), in discussing methods of parenting education, present a useful typology: They focus not on the activity involved, but on the *scope* of the audience, which in turn influences the nature of involvement by the participant. For example, in the mass mode – a category that includes books, pamphlets, magazines, newspapers, radio, and television – the individual must take the initiative, but his or her involvement remains private, as does the presenting problem. In contrast, the group mode, including group discussion, is oriented toward an organized clientele, individuals who are willing and able to share in some systematic manner. In the final category, the individual mode – consisting of counseling, guidance, and referral – the orientation is geared toward the individual in need of support or intervention from a more traditional service mode.

Our framework for discussion of contemporary efforts focuses not on the scope of the audience or the activities generated, but on the interaction of the two. We believe that family support programs are shaped by differing family needs and, consequently, the programs and supports that emerge may be understood most easily when seen within the context of family structure. For the purposes of this chapter, we will categorize families into three broad groups: (1) mainstream families, (2) nontraditional families, and (3) high-risk families. By mainstream families we mean those families who are intact, with a husband and wife who are not at risk, either physically or emotionally, and those who hold promise for establishing a positive nurturing environment for the child. Mainstream families are not free from stress, nor are they of any single economic, religious, or racial group. Rather, they are subject to societal pressures, but because of the absence of any draining conditions their energies can be vested in parenting.

Nontraditional families are those that do not fit the "average family" stereotype and who may need additional supports, on either an episodic or a long-term basis, because of their unique family structure. Nontraditional families include (1) blended or remarriage families, (2) adoptive families, (3) families with foster children, and (4) families with twins. The inclusion of families with twins in this category is based on considerations of family structure, not biological state.

High-risk families are those who, by virtue of biological, economic, or structural factors, are most likely to need intensive support. Their circumstance is likely to be of long duration and frequently would be served by the traditional social service bureaucracy in addition to family support programs or services. The high-risk category includes (1) families with premature infants, (2) families below the poverty level, (3) families headed by a single teenager, (4) families with an adult or infant who is retarded or has other biological handicaps, and (5) families with mentally ill or severely depressed parents.

Activities offered by family support programs are multiple and varied, but they do fall along a continuum from unstructured to structured. In our construct a "drop-in" center would be an unstructured service available "on demand" to parents, whereas regularly scheduled home visits, because they entail definite time commitments, are a more structured activity type. An initial hypothesis that we explored was that a correlation existed between family type (e.g., mainstream, nontraditional, and high-risk) and activity type (structured or unstructured). Although we found that no such correlation existed universally, we did discover that many programs for high-risk families offered a range of activity types, and they also stressed more formal activities. Conversely, within the range of efforts for mainstream families, more informal activities existed.

We also noted that the specific kinds of activities were somewhat cumulative; that is, programs for mainstream families typically focused on resource and referral, parenting education, and parent support groups. Efforts for nontraditional and high-risk families included these activities, but also became more targeted and had home-visitor and/or counseling components. Our work suggests that, although there is considerable overlap of specific activities among support efforts for mainstream, nontraditional and high-risk families, some differentiation of activities between groups is also discernible.

Mainstream families

Mainstream families, although intact, may feel uncertain about their readiness or ability to parent effectively. To meet these concerns, programs typically offer two basic services: information and referral (I/R) and parenting education. I/R may provide information to parents on available services in the community, including babysitting, child care, and health care. Hot lines, warm lines, and newsletters are additional vehicles through which parents are kept abreast of the activities of programs and parents can gain child development, health, nutrition, and community service news.

Recently, many I/Rs have changed their names to *resource* and referral (R/R), reflecting a change in orientation. Beyond simply providing information, R/Rs actually involve the sharing or exchanging of resources including toys, books, or children's clothing. At Parents Place[4] in San Francisco, for example, information and resources are shared by parents who come to a restored Victorian home to learn about child development.

Another very popular component of prenatal and infant support programs is parenting education. Typically done with a group of parents, parenting education may take the form of sharing child development information or may focus on assisting the parent in coping with new responsibilities. One example is the Family Enrichment for New Parents, a packaged program guide that is used by experienced leaders of parent groups (Myers-Walls & Sudsberry, 1982). This curriculum helps parents understand their responsibilities and provides them with the basic skills

---

[4] Parents Place, Jewish Family and Children's Services, 3272 California Street, San Francisco, CA 94118.

needed to carry them out. In addition, it assists parents in developing self-confidence, balancing responsibilities, and improving communication.

Parent support groups are also an important element in serving mainstream families. Some have a long history. For example, La Leche League was founded in 1958 as a self-help mutual support group for breastfeeding mothers. It was established so that nursing mothers could offer to one another the encouragement, support, and skills needed to breastfeed successfully.

More recently, new forms of support groups are gaining popularity. As interest in the father's role in family and child development grows and as more families truly coparent, support groups for fathers where they can share with and learn from one another are growing. Pasley, Ernst, and Gingles (1981) describe a father–infant program that is designed to enable fathers to gain skills in promoting their infants' development, to assist fathers in developing an awareness of materials, activities, and experiences suitable to their infant's current stage of development, and to provide resources and support for fathers through sharing experiences with others in similar situations. This program incorporates, as many do, elements of basic support, parent education, information and referral, and networking.

Less frequently noted, but nonetheless present in programs for mainstream families, are advocacy efforts and childcare. Advocacy has ranged from acting on parents' behalf to procure services, to helping an institution alter basic policies. In this context, the support unit functions as a mediating structure, navigating between the individual and the institution. Specific examples include the Family Support Service, Inc., in Denver,[5] which helps mothers get food stamps, find appropriate housing, or return to school. On another level, Coping with the Overall Pregnancy/Parenting Experience (COPE)[6] in Boston works with corporations, encouraging them to alter their policies to be more flexible and supportive of new parents, in addition to offering education programs.

In other programs, childcare is offered for infants while their parents participate in program activities. One example is a Mothers' Center Development Project,[7] of which there are 55 throughout the United States. In many of these, childcare is provided while discussion groups address childcare and developmental theory, among other topics. In establishing on-site child care, programs help parents understand and cope with tem-

[5] Family Support Services, Inc., 601 South Irving, Denver, CO 80219.
[6] Coping with the Overall Pregnancy/Parenting Experience (COPE), 37 Clarendon Street, Boston, MA 02116.
[7] The Mothers' Center Development Project, 129 Jackson Street, Hempstead, NY 11550.

porary separation from their infants. In other programs, parents observe their infants' responses to other caregivers through one-way mirrors.

An interesting variation includes programs that involve the parent and the infant together. For example, in the Infant Care Program at Evanston Hospital in Evanston,[8] Illinois, parents participate in checking their newborns' reflexes, along with their responses to cuddling, comforting, visual, and auditory stimulation. At the Franklin Maternity and Family Center in Philadelphia,[9] developmentally appropriate parent–child playgroups are held frequently and are quite popular.

Nontraditional Families

Nontraditional families differ from mainstream families in that they have a unique family structure. These families may be nontraditional from the perspective of the adult or the infant. In the first category – nontraditional from the adult perspective – are blended families and single-parent families. The latter include both families headed by custodial fathers and by single mothers. Families headed by single-parent *adolescents* are not included in this category. The second category focuses on the infant and includes families with foster children, adopted children, or multiple-birth children.

Family support programs for nontraditional families offer many of the same activities found in programs for mainstream families. Support groups, a common activity with mainstream parents, are also popular with nontraditional families. However, typically, the efforts are tailored to the specific group involved. For example, Mothers of Twins discussion groups focus on the unique challenge of fostering independent identities of twins. Discussion groups of single parents focus on the particular stresses they encounter in a world of "couples" and in a world where the conventional perception of family includes two parents.

Programs for nontraditional and high-risk families are more likely than programs for mainstream families to offer home visits and crisis intervention. In the home-visit component, a home visitor, typically another parent or person from the community, provides highly personalized information and guides the parent through the emotional stages that accompany pregnancy and early parenting. Discussion of health and nutrition is often incorporated into regularly scheduled home visits. In some cases,

---

[8] Infant Care Program, Department of Pediatrics, Evanston Hospital, 2650 Ridge Avenue, Evanston, IL 60201.

[9] Parenting Program, Franklin Maternity and Family Center, 6051 Overbrook Avenue, Philadelphia, PA 19131.

home visits follow prescribed curricula with information developed by the program itself. Occasionally, prepared packaged materials are used (Hamner & Turner, 1985). Prenatal and infant development programs for nontraditional families also tend to offer crisis intervention services to parents as they confront particularly difficult life events. Counseling is also offered in many programs, on either an individual or a group basis.

Services available to nontraditional families may be linked to a national organization that augments the local group's efforts. For example, the North American Council on Adoption is a national organization that individuals or local groups may join. In addition to providing networking services for its members, this group plays an important advocacy role in promoting the adoption of children with special needs.

The National Organization of Mothers of Twins Clubs, Inc.,[10] not only links hundreds of local twin parent groups, but promotes and facilitates the growing body of research on twins. Beyond supporting research on twins, other aims of the organization are disseminating public information and maintaining the involvement of twins themselves, as they mature. Nationally, there are hot lines for mothers of twins, magazines for parents of twins, as well as an elaborate array of local programs. One such program is Twin Topics, Inc.,[11] in Minnesota, where regular meetings include parenting education, equipment and clothing exchanges, and guest speakers. Many of the twins groups, though having "twins" in their title, actually offer support to any parent of "multiples."

High-risk families

It is increasingly recognized that certain situations pose a special long-term threat to stable family formation. Having an infant who is premature, has medical complications, or has a developmental disability places a family in a high-risk category. Living in poverty and becoming a parent before becoming an adult are risk factors, as is having a history of mental illness or depression. Similarly, delivering a baby that is not full term and healthy, or one that is unusually irritable, can pose special problems for the transition to parenthood. Many programs have been instituted in response to the needs of new parents in such high-risk circumstances.

---

[10] The National Organization of Mothers of Twins Clubs, Inc., 12404 Princess Jeanne, N.E., Albuquerque, NM 87112.

[11] Twin Topics, Inc., Minneapolis, MN, c/o Janice Paulson, 2045 Unity Avenue, Golden Valley, MN 55422.

Premature infants. Premature infants present a family with stress that may be great enough to call for special supportive efforts (see Easterbrooks, Chapter 6, this volume). Premature infants do not meet parental expectations of normal infant appearance or behavior. They are less alert, active, and responsive to stimulation for the first few months of life than are full-term babies, and mothers of preterm infants are likely to be less involved with them or to engage in inappropriate stimulation in trying to elicit responses from them (Bakeman & Brown, 1980; Field, 1977). Because preterm infants typically remain in the hospital after delivery, often attached to life support instruments, ordinary parent–child social interaction is also likely to be curtailed.

Both Field, Widmayer, Stringer, & Ignatoff (1980) and Scarr-Salaptek and Williams (1973) have shown that special programs for low-income, black, teenage mothers of premature infants promote better parent–child interactions and subsequent child development. Both programs studied employed home visitors who helped the young mother establish realistic expectations for her child's capabilities and who provided toys and information on how to interact with the child.

Minde and his associates (1980) have described a hospital-based support program for more typical parents of premature infants (e.g., parents who were not also undergoing the stresses of poverty or adolescence). Groups of 16 couples met weekly in sessions that were attended by a nurse, who was the group coordinator, and by a "veteran mother," who acted as the "official animator" of the group. In these sessions, which continued for 7 to 12 weeks, parents were encouraged to share their feelings. They were also given information about the special neonatal care procedures used with premature babies and, through staff referrals, were offered concrete assistance with such problems as finding babysitters or housing.

Parents in this program were compared with others who received the routine care offered by the premature nursery. Minde found that the mothers in the support groups visited their babies more often, interacted with them more extensively, felt more comfortable about their roles as caregivers, and were more knowledgeable about their babies' conditions. Minde suggests that programs such as these have considerable promise both in reducing the immediate severe stresses experienced by the parents and in promoting behavioral changes presumed to be beneficial to the parent–child relationship.

Poverty. One of the most intensive family support intervention programs for poverty-level families undergoing transition to parenthood was implemented by a Yale pediatrician, Dr. Sally Provence, and her colleagues (Provence & Naylor, 1983; Provence, Naylor, & Patterson, 1977). Working with poor, inner-city mothers who were expecting a healthy first child, Provence and her colleagues provided a network of four free services that began with the child's delivery and continued for 30 months. These services were regular pediatric care, regular home visits by a social worker or other trained clinician, regular psychological developmental examinations for the child, and daycare, if desired.

In receiving services, each family actually interacted with only four service providers, who constituted the "family team." The service providers and families thus came to know one another well over the 30-month period. This approach can be contrasted with a "clinic" model, in which services are provided by the person on call rather than consistently by the same individual.

The aim of the intervention was not specifically to teach parenting skills, nor to provide any predefined program, but rather to tailor services to each family's needs. For the family whose immediate need was safer housing, for example, the social worker facilitated contacts with appropriate community agencies. For the family whose child developed a life-threatening illness, readily available emergency medical care from the pediatrician was a more critical need. And for the family at self-acknowledged risk of abusing their infant, the daycare provided a therapeutic nursery setting while the parents received counseling from the rest of the team. According to Provence and her colleagues (1977), the philosophy of their program was "that helping young parents with child rearing and with the stresses that impinged upon them would increase their capacity to rear healthy children" (p. 11).

The results of this family support program have indicated lasting benefits for these families. At the 30-month mark, there were few differences between families in the experimental group and those in a matched control group (Provence et al., 1977). In follow-up studies 5 and 10 years later, however, the experimental families showed substantial improvement in their overall life circumstances (Rescorla, Provence, & Naylor, 1982; Trickett, Apfel, Rosenbaum, & Zigler, et al., 1982; Seitz, Rosenbaum, & Apfel, 1985). Ten years later, for example, the experimental mothers had obtained significantly more education than had controls, and they had limited their subsequent childbearing to an average of fewer than two total children. Not surprisingly, then, almost all experimental families were self-supporting, whereas only about half the control families were. Experimental families also evidenced enhanced warmth in the parent–child relationship, and their sons showed strikingly better school adjustment than boys in control families.

This project has been described in detail not because it necessarily represents the only model family support might profitably follow with impoverished families, but because it indicates the potential of support programs to offer benefits that last well after the programs terminate. The positive findings of the Provence project clearly signal that further research on providing support to impoverished parents during the transition to parenthood is well worth pursuing.

Adolescent parents. As noted in earlier chapters, the negative consequences of school-aged parenthood are now well documented. Hundreds of programs have been established in response to the special needs of very young parents. In a review of such programs, Jekel and Klerman (1982) stressed the importance of their being *comprehensive*. That is, such programs must address three kinds of problems associated with adolescent family formation: medical, educational, and social.

The need for medical intervention was recognized very early, because young mothers are at elevated risk of delivering babies who are not full term and healthy (Sarrel & Klerman, 1969; Zachler, Andelman, & Bauer, 1969). The risk differential between younger mothers and those in their twenties was once thought to be a reflection of some biological problem associated with very young motherhood. More recently, researchers have documented that the obstetrical and perinatal risks are largely a function of such adolescent behaviors as failing to obtain early and regular prenatal care and of failing to maintain good nutritional habits. It is now well established that intervention programs that lead teenagers to receive adequate prenatal health care and nutrition during pregnancy are highly effective in reducing the health risks associated with early parenthood (Sarrel & Klerman, 1969; Zachler et al., 1969). It is clear that family support for the adolescent undergoing the transition to parenthood must involve such a health care focus at the very least.

An additional concern for the school-aged mother is the likelihood of educational curtailment. Without special programs, the teenager who becomes pregnant before graduating from high school is likely to drop out (Hardy, Welcher, Stanley, & Dallas, 1978). In the past, such a situation was often forced upon the young mother by school attendance policies forbidding her to remain in school during pregnancy. Even though such regulations have now largely been abandoned, the stresses of balancing caring for a baby with meeting school requirements often make dropping out of school the teenage mother's eventual choice. Leaving school often results in a failure to develop employable skills, which can eventuate in the mother's becoming a welfare-supported head of a single-parent family. Thus, a second component of any comprehensive program for young mothers should address their educational needs.

A third necessity of comprehensive family support is social services. The serious social or psychological problems common to many young parents should not be ignored by those designing support services for them. Among an unbiased sample of inner-city school-aged mothers, at least one-third had serious problems predating the pregnancy, including having been an abused child, having an alcoholic, drug-abusing, or deceased parent, having a history of severe depression, or being mentally retarded (Seitz, Apfel, & Rosenbaum, 1983). The new young parent may thus have significant needs for social services that can address long-standing problems in addition to new problems created by the pregnancy.

A number of impressive comprehensive programs for school-aged parents have been in existence for a considerable time. The Young Mothers Educational Development (YMED) Program in Syracuse, New York, for example, provides an alternative high school for pregnant and parenting students (Osofsky & Osofsky, 1970). Classes are taught so that students can continue to earn academic credit, help is provided with daycare for the babies, and medical services are arranged. Compared with other student mothers, those in the YMED Program have been reported to have much higher rates of educational success, as well as healthier newborns (Osofsky & Osofsky, 1970). Although there are other well-known school-based interventions (Howard, 1968; New Futures School, 1984), such programs are difficult to evaluate in a formal way because of the absence of clear comparison groups. Given what is known of typical adolescent parents, however, the outcomes for teens attending these alternative schools appear to be highly favorable.

Hardy and her associates (Hardy, King, Shipp, & Welcher, 1981) have described a comprehensive program provided through a hospital rather than a school. All teenage mothers in the study received high-quality prenatal care; approximately half then received a postnatal program as well. Postnatal services were provided from 2 weeks postpartum until the baby was 3 years old. The services included health supervision and counseling as well as family planning and small-group parent training sessions for the teenager. Infant health screening and supervision were provided, as was active outreach with regular home visits, educational counseling, referrals to appropriate agencies as needed, and group activities with other young mothers. The results of this special approach to family support for new teenage parents were very positive. Eighty-five percent of the teenagers who received support were still in school or had graduated by the 2-year follow-up, compared with only about 20% of teens who received no services. The program also reduced the likelihood that teenagers would be pregnant again within 1 year (7.5% of experimental vs. 21% of controls) or within 2 years (21% of experimental versus 39% of controls). As Hardy and her associates (1981) note, "A supporting network of integrated community services to meet the educational, day care, and social support needs to help the young family become self-sustaining is essential" (p. 281).

Families with a mentally retarded or biologically handicapped child. There has been much more research on the effects of intervention programs for handicapped children than on programs providing support services for their parents. There is, however, widespread agreement that parents who have a handicapped child are greatly in need of such support efforts and that the transition to parenthood in such cases is extremely difficult. Ample research documents their risk of both short- and long-term stress, depression, and marital instability (Cummings, 1976; Cummings, Bayley, & Rie, 1966). Recently, some researchers have also noted risks to normal siblings in such families, especially the oldest daughter, who may come to assume caregiving responsibilities well beyond those customary for a child her age (Gath, 1974).

Handicapped or retarded children include those with specific diagnoses, such as Down syndrome or cerebral palsy, and those with less clearly defined diagnoses of mildly, moderately, severely, or multiply handicapped. Bromwich (1981) has characterized programs for the parents of such children as representing three models: parent therapy, parent training or infant curriculum, and parent–infant interaction. Each model provides family support, but the emphases differ. The parent therapy model is primarily parent-oriented. Counseling is provided to help the parent resolve negative feelings and stress associated with the birth of a handicapped child, with the expectation that this will also benefit the child by promoting more competent parenting. Recently, parent groups are replacing professional counseling in this model; often such groups are organized by the parents themselves.

The parent training model usually involves a program in which parents are taught strategies for teaching specific skills to their children. The aim of this model is the child's optimal development in motor and cognitive growth, language and social skills, and self-sufficiency. Although historically this model was separate from the parent therapy approach, more recently the two are often combined (Bricker & Dow, 1980; Connolly, Morgan, Russell, & Richardson, 1980).

One noteworthy research project representing a combination of both approaches is the Family, Infant, and Preschool Program (FIPP) in North Carolina reported by Dunst, Vance, & Gallagher (1983). This program offers a variety of services including both parent and sibling support groups, a parent preschool cooperative nursery, a lending library and informational newsletters, a home training program, and one-to-one contact between an experienced family with a handicapped child and the family of a child whose similar condition has been newly diagnosed.

Dunst (1982) has reported the effects of such supports for families. He divided participants into those receiving a high, moderate, or low amount of support, based on their responses to a questionnaire in which they were asked to rank 18 possible sources of support on a 5-point scale (*not helpful at all* to *extremely helpful*). A positive relationship was found between the amount of support, assessed in this manner, and the parents' health, mood, and reports that their child's time demands were not excessive. According to Dunst (1982), "Families with high degrees of social support available to them had less personal problems, were more integrated families, and perceived their children's handicaps as being less severe than those of parents having lesser degrees of social support" (p. 30).

Bromwich and her colleagues (1981) have developed a program exemplifying the third model, that of attempting to stimulate mutually satisfying parent–child relationships. This approach has a substantial theoretical foundation in developmental research on interactions between normally developing infants and caregivers. Bromwich and her associates have created a specific curriculum for stimulating better interactions, and an instrument, the Parent Behavior Progression (PBP), to assess the need for and the success of their intervention efforts. As Bromwich and her colleagues comment, "The Parent Behavior Progression is founded on the principle that when parents achieve mutually satisfying interactions with their infants and acquire sensitivity and responsiveness to their infants' needs in different areas of development, they create an environment in which infants are able to develop to their fullest potential" (p. 95).

Although this kind of approach does not lend itself easily to formal assessment, ample clinical evidence suggests that parents who are helped to learn what to expect from their child at each level of development, and how to obtain more satisfying interchanges with the child, are likely to feel increasingly competent. This systematic, personalized approach appears to have considerable potential for reducing the likelihood of parental withdrawal and frustration with the child and of setting off, instead, a positive spiral of increasingly satisfying interchanges and better development for the child.

Mentally ill or depressed parents. There is strong evidence that parental mental illness or depression constitutes a major risk factor for children's development (Beardslee, Bemporad, Keller, & Klerman 1983; Cohler, Grunebaum, Weiss, Garner, & Gallant, 1977; Sameroff, Seifer, & Zax, 1982; Weissman, Paykel, & Klerman, 1972). Because they perceive a great need for intervention with such parents, researchers are especially reluctant to deny services to some in order to create control groups. It is therefore difficult to make formal assessments of the effects of programs for this group of parents, and we will limit ourselves to a description of interventions that have been employed.

One extensive effort to offer services to such disturbed parents is a project implemented by Greenspan and his colleagues (1985). In this project, long-term therapeutic efforts are made with the parent (usually the mother) and child by a highly trained team of clinicians. In many cases, clinical reports document significant improvement in the parents' capacity to nurture following intensive therapeutic work over many months.

In another project, Musick, Klehr, Cohler, and Clark (1983) offered two types of support programs to mentally ill parents. One model, the Thresholds Program, is a 40 hour per week comprehensive social rehabilitation program for mentally ill mothers. It includes efforts to enhance the mother's skills and competence as a parent and as a person in her own right through vocational, educational, and social skills building. The Thresholds Program is also designed to facilitate the cognitive and psychosocial development of the children of these mothers. The second model Musick and her colleagues have evaluated is the Home Care Program, in which psychotic mothers and their children receive a home visit for 1 to 2 hours per week by a psychiatric nurse or social worker. In this program, emphasis is placed on making appropriate linkages with resources in the community.

Comparisons of the children in the two treatment approaches have not shown differences between them. However, in both groups, the children's performance on standardized cognitive tests improved markedly from initially low functioning to the normal range. As Musick and her colleagues (1983) noted, "These treatment findings in general speak to the efficacy of even minimal intervention with this apparently understimulated group of children, since in all aspects of functioning measured, approximately *half* of the children in *both* treatment conditions improved in their developmental abilities" (p. 11).

The design of family support programs targeted at a specific high-risk population reflects the specialized needs of participants. Although parents of premature infants might benefit most from parenting education that helps them respond to the unusual attributes of such newborns, families in which a parent is emotionally disturbed are best served by more global intervention geared partly toward weaving the family into lasting support networks. Programs for impoverished families and those with adolescent parents have been designed with the recognition that both tangible needs and educational and social problems have to be addressed, and this is best accomplished with comprehensive programs and an interdisciplinary staff. At the same time, however, family support programs for high-risk parents seek to maintain flexibility with respect to the idiosyncracies of each individual family. They face the further challenge of being committed to an informal, nonthreatening atmosphere, independent of the traditional social service bureaucracy, yet being frequently called upon to provide intensive, professional services. It is these and other structural tensions to which we turn in the next section.

Implementation and evaluation issues

Because informal programs designed to support new parents are so multifaceted and variegated, whether or not there are common implementation and evaluation issues may seem questionable. Yet in spite of their differences in goals or orientations, programs seem to experience a range of problems that overrides their specificity. The purpose of this section is to address broad challenges in the implementation and evaluation of programs that support new parents.

Implementation issues

In conceptualizing a family support effort, initiators, like initiators of any new program, must make key decisions that shape the long-term nature and success of the effort. Yet the challenge to initiators of family support programs is particularly acute because there are inherent contradictions in designing a program that will have longevity without a heavy bureaucratic overlay. Repeatedly, program initiators must decide where on the continuum from institutional dependence to institutional independence their program will reside. For example, becoming a part of a hospital program might provide easy access to delivering mothers, but the formidable environment of the hospital might militate against the flexibility and informality desired by program initiators. Program originators feel that structural decisions regarding organizational autonomy are critical and must be addressed at the outset if the effort is to succeed.

Beyond organizational structure, program initiators must decide on the focus of the services to be provided: Should the program stress direct services, education, advocacy, or all three? The natural tension between direct services and advocacy must be acknowledged, and planners must determine the appropriate balance among foci. Finally, given the unique role of staff in family support programs, decisions must be made about the roles staff will play and the criteria that will be established for their selection and evaluation. Special considerations must be given when paraprofessionals are involved (Mitchel & Hurley, 1981). Dealing with differences in the perception of problems, in training, and in standards of responsibility are issues to be addressed. If the program is composed fully of volunteers, consideration must be given to motivations and rewards for participation as well as to mechanisms for training.

Like decisions made at the outset, challenges that surface during operational phases are colored by the unique nature of family support efforts. For example, in most bureaucratic organizations, a table of organization exists, with a titular leader specified. Though organizational leadership does not always reside in the titular head, the chain of command is clear. But in programs that minimize role differentiation, the question of leadership is far more complex. Further, when low salaries and job stress result in heavy staff turnover, as is the case in many family support programs, sustaining quality leadership becomes even more difficult.

Other and equally important operational issues involve the integration of the family support program with other community services and agencies. Because family support efforts have an ecological orientation, a commitment to a systems or holistic approach prevails. Yet in many cases, linking programs with truly informal networks, on the one hand, and with traditional human services programs, on the other, remains a difficult challenge. Froland, Pancoast, Chapman, and Kimboko (1981), in addressing the relationship between informal (what we consider family support) and formal (what we consider traditional human service programs), indicate that there are very divergent assumptions and expectations about what constitutes support. In a survey that draws from the experiences of 30 agencies, Froland et al. note that there is considerable rationale for linking formal and informal approaches. The benefits cited include improving cost-effectiveness, overcoming the traditional inaccessibility of some professionals to grass-roots problems, and improving organizational effectiveness among the approaches. Yet the authors acknowledge that such a collaborative arrangement forces a renegotiation of the balance between the public and the private responsibility for support. Nonetheless, Froland et al., and others (Litwak, 1978; Whittaker, Garbarino, & Associates, 1983) indicate the necessity of instituting these links.

As a matter of practicality, many family support programs have sought linkages with community agencies and organizations to stay alive. It is not at all uncommon for infant and parent development programs to begin modestly. But as demands for services escalate, program leaders, pressed for funding, turn to local United Ways, Rotary Clubs, and other organizations for financial support. Furthermore, although they strive to maintain autonomy and informality, programs quickly become engaged in an array of agreements with local, state, and even federal agencies. In so doing, they move a step closer to the bureaucratic end of the human service continuum.

How family support efforts remain malleable enough to meet changing individual needs raises other implementation issues. These programs repeatedly face the dilemma of reconstituting themselves, in some cases programmatically and financially. Designed to support people (staff, volunteers, and participants), the programs often find that they in turn need support in dealing with operational challenges. Filling this void, providing resources and information for family support efforts, has been the responsibility of the Family Resource Coalition (FRC) of Chicago.[12] The FRC serves as a switching station where programmatic information can be exchanged through conferences, workshops, and a program newsletter. The FRC also has volunteers in nearly every state in the union who serve as resources for family support programs.

A final challenge to family support as a whole is to determine whether these are idiosyncratic, loosely affiliated efforts, or whether there is sufficient momentum to engender a national policy favoring the sustenance of family support programs. Hidden in this policy orientation is the assumption that national policy could, should, and would be beneficial to the total effort. Skeptics remain convinced that the nation is not ready for such an orientation. Advocates say, "Why not?" At bay are considerations of whether a national policy is advantageous and whether the research base is strong enough to justify such a policy. Have we learned enough from evaluations about the efficacy of these programs to shape a national policy? In the next section, we explore the issues and challenges inherent in the evaluation of family support programs.

[12] The Family Resource Coalition, 230 North Michigan Avenue, Suite 1625, Chicago, IL 60601.

Evaluation issues

In considering what research can tell us about programs, it is helpful to distinguish between the two major kinds of evaluation: those focused on describing the process by which a program is presumed to have its effects and those focused on determining how well a program works. A process evaluation assesses how *efficiently* a program works, in comparison to an outcome evaluation, which assesses its *effectiveness*. For practical and ethical reasons, outcome evaluations are not always possible; every program, however, can and should undergo process evaluation.

Process evaluation. As Meisel (1977) has noted:

[Process evaluation] answers such questions as "Does the program run smoothly?" "Is it administered well?" "Does it do what it says it is going to do when it says it is going to do it?" "Are resources used efficiently?" "Are the procedures of the program reasonable and clear?" "How many clients are served every day, week, month, year?" (p. 13)

As these questions suggest, many aspects of process evaluation can be adequately addressed by careful record keeping. If resources permit, it is also desirable to perform some kind of routine self-monitoring or to have the program visited by an observer on a regular basis. Ideally, the results of such monitoring can produce information useful in permitting others to replicate the program. Without a clear description of what actually occurs, it is unlikely that a program can be adopted successfully by others no matter how effective it may be.

Certain facets of programs are easier to describe than others. The staff-to-client ratio, the group or class size, the number of sessions, and similar objective information are relatively simple to tabulate. A number of programs have also developed clear-cut curricula describing their procedures in painstaking detail (Bromwich et al., 1981; Ramey & Haskins, 1981). The more intangible aspects of programs – the warmth of the staff, for example – are difficult to measure, yet they may often be a necessity for program effectiveness. One personalized, caring session with a sympathetic person might be much more important than 10 equally long sessions with a person perceived as cold and distant. The difficulty of pinpointing what ingredients make a program work well probably explains why a successful model is not always transferable to other settings. For this reason, there is a strong need for future process evaluations to include measures of such intangibles even though they pose significant measurement challenges.

There are often useful objective proxy variables for such qualities as warmth and caring. In a school for pregnant teenagers, for example, one might interview the staff about a random sample of students who had attended in earlier years, determining how much they knew about the girls' family situation and special problems. Such information is not routinely obtained by teachers unless they take a deep personal interest in their students. Yet in a study we have conducted in New Haven (Seitz, et al., 1983), we have been astonished at the richness of such information that is readily provided by teachers in a successful school for pregnant teenagers. In some programs, staff persons respond frequently to emergencies in the participants' lives, making home visits on their own time, making phone calls on the attenders' behalf, or taking them to appropriate agencies for help. A surprising degree of dedication is often found in the staff of support programs, and since this may well be a major ingredient in program success, greater efforts should be made to document it.

Outcome evaluation

The purpose of an outcome evaluation is to determine whether a program has a measurable impact on the people participating in it. This goal is easy to state, but often very difficult to accomplish. The strongest research design for evaluating a treatment involves randomly choosing from the persons who are eligible for it an experimental group, which will receive the treatment, and a control group, which will not. Without random assignment, selection bias often makes it impossible to ascertain a program's effects. People who choose to attend a program are usually very different from those who do not, and it is difficult to distinguish these preexisting differences from the effects of the program when it comes time to compare the groups.

For both ethical and practical reasons, random assignment is rarely used in studying family support programs. The ethical concerns are obvious, but the practical ones include the fact that persons may simply be unwilling to cooperate in an experiment. Persons who are assigned to the control group, for example, may refuse to allow the follow-up measures necessary to evaluate the program they were denied.

For these reasons, some experts in research design recommend more widespread use of slightly modified procedures called "quasi-experiments" (Cook & Campbell, 1979). Such research designs include using persons on a waiting list for a program as control subjects, or assigning persons randomly to different kinds of programs in order to compare them (Cook & Campbell, 1979; Seitz, 1982). Quasi-experiments are not always feasible (a program may not have a waiting list, for example), but they are likely to be possible more often than are true experiments, and they can play an important role in program evaluation.

It is unfortunate but understandable that the greater the need for a support program, the less likely it is that a convincing outcome evaluation can be conducted. True experiments have been employed to evaluate programs for families at risk because of poverty (Garber & Heber, 1981; Ramey & Haskins, 1981; Schweinhart & Weikart, 1983), but such designs would be unlikely for evaluating programs for such high-risk groups as parents of severely retarded infants. In general, the more obviously the parents are in distress, the greater are the ethical problems encountered in attempting to form control groups. We would thus recommend other approaches to evaluating such programs, even at the cost of failing to satisfy all possible critics of the evaluation design.

Meisel (1977) describes a number of other alternative research models in useful detail. The "educational model," for example, is based on achieving a preestablished percentage of objectives before a program is considered to have done an adequate job. The "consumer evaluation model" is based on systematic evaluations by the persons receiving the support service; the recipients indicate what they liked most and least, how the program could be changed, and how they feel about the staff. Other models described by Meisel include the "case study model," the "objective standards model," and the "outside evaluation model." For many support programs, these alternative approaches to a standard experiment may provide very useful outcome information.

In addition to design problems, there are other barriers to performing outcome studies of family support interventions. Evaluations are expensive, sometimes costing as much or more than the services themselves (Zigler & Seitz, 1982). This is especially true if outside evaluators are hired. The best information about program effects can often be obtained only by identifying people who are eligible for, but not served by, the program. Determining who such people are, locating them, and obtaining their cooperation is often much more expensive than limiting a study to the program attenders. Community records necessary to determine such obvious and basic information as the percentage of an eligible group that the program serves are often poorly kept or inaccessible. With all these problems, it is not surprising that few outcome evaluations are performed.

Nevertheless, where strong designs have been possible, the results have been very encouraging. The Provence project described above has indicated that results of intensive, early family support efforts can be profound and long lasting and that the effects of a program can be much greater than is apparent in the short run. A study recently published by Weikart and his colleagues (Berrueta-Clement, Schweinhart, Barnett, Epstein, & Weikart, 1984) similarly shows extremely persistent effects, in adulthood, for children who received intervention when they were very young. And Hardy and her colleagues' (1981) project indicates the potential of support for teenage mothers during the transition to parenthood in increasing their educational success and decreasing the likelihood of early repeated pregnancy. Despite the obstacles to gathering outcome evaluations of family support programs, those evaluations with strong research designs give considerable reason for optimism concerning the potential of such programs to benefit significantly the lives of those receiving them.

Recommendations

As this chapter has indicated, there is an extensive range of family support programs for new parents. Despite this diversity, several general recommendations can be offered:

1. We would suggest that there appears to be little need for formal governmental efforts to fund programs for normal, mainstream families. What is particularly striking about family support efforts for ordinary families is how ubiquitous they are. Such efforts have a lively, grass-roots quality that could easily be lost if they became enmeshed in bureaucratic requirements. Where outside stimulation could be beneficial, however, is in promoting the *development* of programs. "Seed money," rather than continuing funds, could provide an effective incentive for the establishment of programs. Procedures requiring matching funds could have a similar effect.

2. In contrast to the minimal governmental role we advocate for programs for mainstream families, such initiatives should be much greater for families that are at unusually high risk. The needs of psychotic or severely depressed parents, or of families with biologically handicapped children, for example, are likely to be so great that they cannot be left to grass-roots initiatives alone. There is increased need for incorporating persons with specialized training in support programs for high-risk families, as well as a need for longer-term commitments than are likely to be provided by purely volunteer efforts. In addition to seed money, therefore, federal or state funding for such programs might well include relatively permanent, ongoing commitments.

3. There is clearly a need for much more research on the effects of family support programs. Better process evaluations would permit better

dissemination of successfully functioning programs and might ultimately increase financial support for individual programs, as well as for family support in general. Despite the difficulties of performing outcome evaluations, when they have been undertaken their results have suggested that family support during the transition to parenthood has significant potential to benefit family members. Much more information is needed on timing, targeting, and the best specific form for programs to take.

4. There is a strong need for better networking efforts across programs. Often, new programs are established without awareness of similar programs elsewhere; as a result, there is a considerable degree of reinventing the wheel in support programs. Also, long-established programs could benefit greatly from information about how other, similar programs operate so that innovative procedures can be exchanged. A more concerted approach to providing a network of information would therefore be very valuable.

5. Finally, we suggest that there would be much benefit in more systematically linking traditional social support services to many of the less formalized family support programs we have been describing. Currently, the two approaches are viewed as being quite separate domains. Instead, however, interrelations could flow smoothly in both directions. Providers of bureaucratized services, such as formal social work, could make referrals to the less formal support or self-help groups as clients appeared ready to make such a transition. Staff in the latter programs might often need to refer persons to appropriate community agencies for greater services than informal groups can provide. Ideally, we would argue, there should be a broad continuum of social services with no sharp breaks among them.

In considering recommendations for the future, we endorse the coexistence and collaboration of formal and informal support efforts and suggest that the plentiful range of options currently available be sustained. We adhere to the principle that programs be designed with respect for the experience of practitioners and the knowledge gained from well-framed and well-executed evaluations. From the results of creative collaborations between practitioners and evaluators, solid programs and policies that support new parents will emerge.

Acknowledgments

The authors acknowledge the helpfulness of Linda Lipton and Lynn Pooley in assisting with program identification and of Alexandra Shelley for her editorial assistance.

References

Bakeman, R., & Brown, J. V. (1980). Early interaction: Consequences for social and mental development at three years. *Child Development, 51*, 437–47.

Baldwin, W. (1984). *Teen parents and their children: Issues and programs* (prepared testimony for U.S. House of Representatives Select Committee on Children, Youth and Families, July 20, 1983). Washington, DC: U.S. Government Printing Office.

Bane, M. J. (1976). *Here to stay: American families in the twentieth century.* New York: Basic Books, Inc.

Beardslee, W. R., Bemporad, J., Keller, M. B., & Klerman, G. L. (1983). Children of parents with major affective disorder: A review. *American Journal of Psychiatry, 140*, 825–32.

Berrueta-Clement, J. R., Schweinhart, L. J., Barnett, W. S., Epstein, A. S., & Weikart, D. P. (1984). *Changed lives: The effects of the Perry Preschool Program on youths through age 19.* Ypsilante, MI: High/Scope Press.

Bricker, D. D., & Dow, M. G. (1980). Early intervention with the young severely handicapped child. *Journal of the Association for the Severely Handicapped, 5*, 130–42.

Bromwich, R. (1981). *Working with parents and infants: An interactional approach.* Baltimore, MD: University Park Press.

Bromwich, R., Burge, D., Kass, W., Khokha, E., Baxter, E., & Fust, S. (1981). A parent behavior progression. In B. Weissbourd & J. Musick (Eds.), *Infants: Their social environments* (pp. 95–110). Washington, DC: National Association for the Education of Young Children.

Cohler, B. J., Grunebaum, H. U., Weiss, J. L., Gamer, E., & Gallant, D. H. (1977). Disturbance of attention among schizophrenic, depressed and well mothers and their young children. *Journal of Child Psychology and Psychiatry, 18*, 115–35.

Connolly, B., Morgan, W., Russell, F., & Richardson, B. (1980). Early intervention with Down syndrome children. *Physical Therapy, 60*, 1405–8.

Cook, T. D., & Campbell, D. T. (1979). *Quasi-experimentation: Design and analysis issues for field settings.* Chicago: Rand McNally.

Cummings, S. T. (1976). The impact of the child's deficiency on the father: A study of fathers of mentally retarded and of chronically ill children. *American Journal of Orthopsychiatry, 46*, 246–55.

Cummings, S. T., Bayley, H. C., & Rie, H. E. (1966). Effects of the child's deficiency on the mother: A study of mothers of mentally retarded, chronically ill, and neurotic children. *American Journal of Orthopsychiatry, 36*, 595–608.

Dunst, C. J. (1982, November). *Social support, early intervention, and institutional avoidance.* Paper presented at the annual meeting of Southeastern American Association on Mental Deficiency, Louisville, KY.

Dunst, C. J., Vance, S. D., & Gallagher, J. L. (1983, April). *Differential efficacy of early intervention with handicapped infants.* Paper presented at the biennial conference for the Society for Research in Child Development, Detroit, MI.

Field, T. M. (1977). Effects of early separation, interactive deficits, and experimental manipulation on mother–infant face-to-face interaction. *Child Development, 48*, 763–71.

Field, T. M., Widmayer, S. M., Stringer, S., & Ignatoff, E. (1980). Teenage, lower-class, black mothers and their preterm infants: An intervention and developmental follow-up. *Child Development, 51*, 426–36.

Froland, C., Pancoast, D., Chapman, N. J., & Kimboko, P. J. (1981). Linking formal and informal support systems. In B. H. Gottlieb (Ed.), *Social networks and social support* (pp. 259–75). Beverly Hills, CA: Sage.

Garbarino, J. (1982). *Children and families in the social environment.* New York: Aldine.

Garber, H. L., & Heber, R. (1981). The efficacy of early intervention with family rehabilitation. In M. J. Begab, H. C. Haywood, & H. Garber (Eds.), *Psychosocial influences in retarded performance: Vol. 2. Strategies for improving competence* (pp. 71–88). Baltimore, MD: University Park Press.

Gath, A. (1974). Sibling reactions to mental handicap: A comparison with brothers and sisters of normal children. *Journal of Child Psychology and Psychiatry, 15,* 187–98.

Greenspan, S. I., Wieder, S., Lieberman, A., Nover, R., Lourie, R., & Robinson, M. (1985). *Infants in multi-risk families: Case studies of preventive intervention.* New York: International Universities Press.

Hamner, T. J., & Turner, P. H. (1985). *Parenting in contemporary society.* Englewood Cliffs, NJ: Prentice-Hall.

Hardy, J. B., King, T. M., Shipp, D. A., & Welcher, D. W. (1981). A comprehensive approach to adolescent pregnancy. In K. G. Scott, T. Field, & E. Robertson (Eds.), *Teenage parents and their offspring* (pp. 265–82). New York: Grune & Stratton.

Hardy, J. B., Welcher, D. W., Stanley, J., & Dallas, J. R. (1978). Long-range outcome of adolescent pregnancy. *Clinical Obstetrics and Gynecology, 21,* 4.

Harmon, D., & Brim, O. G., Jr. (1980). *Learning to be parents: Principles, programs, and methods.* Beverly Hills, CA: Sage.

Howard, M. (1968). *The Webster School, a District of Columbia program for pregnant girls.* Washington, DC: Children's Bureau.

Huntington, D. S. (1979). Supportive programs for infants and parents. In J. D. Osofsky (Ed.), *Handbook of infant development* (pp. 837–51). New York: Wiley.

Jekel, J. F., & Klerman, L. V. (1982). Comprehensive service programs for pregnant and parenting adolescents. In E. R. McAnarney (Ed.), *Premature adolescent pregnancy and parenthood* (pp. 295–310). New York: Grune & Stratton.

Kagan, S. L. (1984). *Parent involvement research: A field in search of itself.* Boston: Institute for Responsive Education.

Kahn, A. (1976). Service delivery at the neighborhood level: Experience, theory and fads. *Social Service Review, 50,* 23–56.

Litwak, E. (1978). Agency and family linkages in providing neighborhood services. In D. Thurz & J. Vigilante (Eds.), *Reaching people: The structure of neighborhood services* (pp. 59–94). Beverly Hills, CA: Sage.

Meisel, J. (1977). *Programming for atypical infants and their families.* New York: United Cerebral Palsy Associates, Inc.

Minde, K., Shosenberg, N., Marton, P., Thompson, J., Ripley, J., & Burns, S. (1980). Self-help groups in a premature nursery: A controlled evaluation. *Journal of Pediatrics, 96,* 933–40.

Mitchel, R. E., & Hurley, D. J., Jr. (1981). Collaboration with natural helping networks: Lessons from studying paraprofessionals. In B. H. Gottlieb (Ed.), *Social networks and social support* (pp. 277–98). Beverly Hills, CA: Sage.

Moroney, R. (1980). *Families, social services, and social policy: The issue of shared responsibility* (DHHS Publication No. ADM 80-846). Washington, DC: U.S. Government Printing Office.

Musick, J. S., Klehr, K., Cohler, B., & Clark, R. (1983, April). *Results of a five year intervention program for young children at risk for psychopathology.* Paper presented at biennial conference for the Society for Research in Child Development, Detroit, MI.

Myers-Walls, J. A., & Sudsberry, R. L. (1982). Parent education during the transition to parenthood. In N. Stennett, J. DeFrain, K. Kerg, H. Lingren, G. Rowe, S. van Zandt, & R. Williams (Eds.), *Family strengths. IV: Positive support systems* (pp. 55–70). Lincoln: University of Nebraska Press.

National Center for Health Statistics. (1981). *Advance report of natality statistics, 1979: Monthly vital statistics report* (DHHS Publication No. PHS 81-1120). Washington, DC: U.S. Government Printing Office.

New Futures School (1984). *A comprehensive program for school-age parents.* Albuquerque, NM: Albuquerque Public Schools.

Osofsky, H. J., & Osofsky, J. D. (1970). Adolescents as mothers: Results of a program for low-income pregnant teenagers with some emphasis upon infants' development. *American Journal of Orthopsychiatry, 40,* 825–34.

Pasley, K., Ernst, J., & Gingles, J. (1981). The Father–Infant Program: A model of paternal education. In N. Stennett, J. DeFrain, K. King, P. Knaub, & G. Rowe (Eds.), *Family strengths. III: Roots of well-being* (pp. 313–22). Lincoln: University of Nebraska Press.

Pizzo, P. (1983). *Parent to parent.* Boston: Beacon Press.

Provence, S., & Naylor, A. (1983). *Working with disadvantaged parents and children: Scientific issues and practice.* New Haven, CT: Yale University Press.

Provence, S., Naylor, A., & Patterson, J. (1977). *The challenge of daycare.* New Haven, CT: Yale University Press.

Ramey, C. T., & Haskins, R. (1981). The causes and treatment of school failure: Insights from the Carolina Abecedarian Project. In M. J. Begab, H. C. Haywood, & H. Garber (Eds.), *Psychosocial influences in retarded performance: Vol. 2. Strategies for improving competence* (pp. 89–112). Baltimore, MD: University Park Press.

Rescorla, L. A., Provence, S., & Naylor, A. (1982). The Yale Child Welfare Research Program: Description and results. In E. F. Zigler & E. W. Gordon (Eds.), *Day care: Scientific and social policy issues* (pp. 183–99). Boston: Auburn House.

Sameroff, A. J., Seifer, R., & Zax, M. (1982). Early development of children at risk for emotional disorder. *Monographs of the Society for Research in Child Development, 47*(7, Serial No. 199).

Sarrell, P., & Klerman, L. (1969). The young unwed mother. *American Journal of Obstetrics and Gynecology, 105,* 575–8.

Scarr-Salapatek, S., & Williams, M. L. (1973). The effects of early stimulation on low-birth-weight infants. *Child Development, 44,* 94–101.

Schweinhart, L. J., & Weikart, D. P. (1983). The effects of the Perry Preschool Program on youths through age 15 – A summary. In Consortium for Longitudinal Studies (Ed.), *As the twig is bent . . . Lasting effects of preschool programs* (pp. 71–101). Hillsdale, NJ: Erlbaum.

Seitz, V. (1982). A methodological comment on the problem of infant day care. In E. Zigler & E. Gordon (Eds.), *Day care: Scientific and social policy issues* (pp. 243–51). Boston: Auburn House.

Seitz, V., Apfel, N. H., & Rosenbaum, L. K. (1983, April). *Schoolaged mothers: Infant development and maternal educational outcome.* Paper presented at the biennial conference for the Society for Research in Child Development, Detroit, MI.

Seitz, V., Rosenbaum, L. K., & Apfel, N. H. (1985). Long-term effects of family support intervention: A ten-year followup. *Child Development, 56,* 376–91.

Trickett, P. K., Apfel, N. H., Rosenbaum, L. K., & Zigler, E. F. (1982). A five-year followup of participants in the Yale Child Welfare Research Program. In E. F. Zigler & E. W. Gordon (Eds.), *Day care: Scientific and social policy issues* (pp. 200–22). Boston: Auburn House.

U.S. Bureau of the Census. (1981). Population profile of the United States, 1980. *Current Population Reports* (Series P-20, No. 363). Washington, DC: U.S. Government Printing Office.

U.S. Congressional Budget Office. (1983). *Demographic and social trends: Implications for federal support of dependent-care services for children and the elderly.* Washington, DC: U.S. Government Printing Office.

Wandersman, L. P. (1987). Parent–infant support groups: Matching programs to needs and strengths of families. In C. F. Zachariah Boukydes (Ed.), *Research on support for parents in the postnatal period.* Norwood, NJ: Ablex.

Weissman, M. M., Paykel, E. S., & Klerman, G. L. (1972). The depressed woman as a mother. *Social Psychiatry, 7,* 98–108.

Whittaker, J. K., Garbarino, J., & Associates. (1983). *Social support networks: Informal helping in the human services.* New York: Aldine.

Yarrow, L. J. (1979). Historical perspectives and future directions in infant development. In J. D. Osofsky (Ed.), *Handbook of infant development* (pp. 897–917). New York: Wiley.

Zachler, J., Andelman, S., & Bauer, F. (1969). The young adolescent as an obstetric risk. *American Journal of Obstetrics and Gynecology, 103,* 305–12.

Zigler, E., & Seitz, V. (1982). Head Start as a national laboratory. *Annals of the American Academy of Political and Social Science, 461,* 81–9.

Conclusion
The transition to parenthood: synthesis and future directions

Wendy A. Goldberg and Gerald Y. Michaels

This chapter provides an analysis of the state of the art in transition to parenthood theory and research. In doing so, it attempts to synthesize and add to some of the conceptual analyses, critiques, research findings, and proposals for future study that have been presented by the contributors to this volume. Each of these contributors has written in the context of his or her own area of special interest. We will try to point to some directions for inquiry that apply to the field as a whole. Though our treatment of these issues is not exhaustive, our hope is to set the stage for the next phase of inquiry into the transition to parenthood.

The chapter begins with a discussion of conceptual issues that have emerged from the work done to date. These include recognition of the effect of previous life events on the transition to parenthood, the difference in the impact of a first versus a second or later transition, identification of the critical factors that shape adaptation to parenthood, and the growing awareness of the ways in which innovation in medical technology is influencing the psychological experience of this life-span event. Then, on the basis of these discussions, the section on conceptual issues closes with a presentation of a three-tiered synthesis of the transition to parenthood. Included are factors that promote competency in the adjustment to parenthood, factors that suggest risk and strategies for intervention.

The second section of the chapter focuses on methodological issues that have emerged from the chapters of this volume. A series of suggestions for designing future research are presented. Then, several of these issues are discussed in more detail and specific strategies for facilitating research in this challenging area of study are described.

342

Conceptual issues

The impact of past life experiences on the transition to parenthood

When examining the effects of a critical life event on the individual, it is all too common to restrict the window in time to the event and its sequelae. This tendency to focus exclusively on the transition experience per se (e.g., in literatures on the transition to parenthood and the transition to adolescence) has led to an emphasis on the short- and long-term consequences of the pivotal transition experience but has largely ignored prior and concurrent experiences. A life event, whether it be the loss of a job, a long-distance move, or the birth of a baby, occurs within the life span of the individual and a larger social context. Historical time, social time, social support, and the individual's prior experiences all interact to influence the individual's response and eventual adaptation to the event. Thus, there is a history and a context for the transition experience such that its sequelae – the quality and extent of adaptation and adjustment – cannot be pinned exclusively to the transition event itself.

In this volume, we have seen that the state of functioning of individuals and couples early in the transition to parenthood is an important predictor of postpartum functioning, both for marital relations and for individual development. Cowan and Cowan (Chapter 4, this volume) discuss whether we should be blaming the baby for strained marital relations in the postpartum months. They review several studies that indicate that the prebaby level of marital quality predicts the quality of the relationship following birth: By and large, couples who were satisfied with their marriage before the baby was born continue to fare well, whereas those who had problems initially continue to face difficulties after the baby's arrival. Thus, despite the regularly noted finding of a decline in marital satisfaction among groups of couples following the birth of a baby, given couples tend to maintain their relative ranking across the transition to parenthood.

Antecedent to the transition to parenthood, but affecting its outcome, is the adults' prior state of mental health. As they become parents, adults carry their "psychological baggage" with them. Among women, a history of psychological problems or the onset of high anxiety and depression during the months of pregnancy predicts the level of mental health during the first few months postpartum. For both men and women, unresolved issues concerning dependency can be exacerbated by the dependency needs of the newborn baby. The stimulation of their own needs to be cared for or the stimulation of a feeling of inadequacy in the parenting role can interfere with the nascent parent–child relationship. Fedele, Golding, Grossman, and Pollack (Chapter 3) report that the reactivation of dependency needs without adequate resolution is predictive of depression in the postpartum period. Even the potential effectiveness of social interventions is affected by prior patterns of functioning. Social support can boost the individual's mental health during the transition to parenthood, but the capacity for obtaining the needed support depends on the individual's past experiences in seeking and using support during stressful periods (Gottlieb & Pancer, Chapter 8).

The importance of expanding the window of the transition experience to include prior events is underscored by research on expectancies during the transition to parenthood. An important moderator of adaptation that was mentioned in several chapters in the context of individual, couple, and family adaptation is the contrast between what was desired or expected before the baby's birth and what actually transpired postpartum. Antonucci and Mikus (Chapter 2) discuss this dichotomy in the context of developing a positive self-identity as a parent. Actualization of this goal depends in part on how the individual resolves the discrepancy between ideal and real conceptualizations of self. Failure to reconcile these images hinders adult development; successful resolution promotes personality development.

Michaels (Chapter 1) also discusses this issue of expectancies versus outcomes in terms of prospective parents' expectations about the types of satisfactions that children will bring. Whether these expectations are met can affect not only adults' self-concept as parents, but their sense of fulfillment in the parenting role.

In their chapters, Cowan and Cowan and Gottlieb and Pancer describe the impact on marital relationships of fulfilled and unfulfilled expectations concerning role arrangements and couple interaction. Couples whose expectations were violated about household and childcare task assignments and the nature and extent of emotional support from the spouse (e.g., one spouse was doing or giving more or less than was expected) report greater disappointment and marital dissatisfaction postpartum than couples whose expectations were realized (see also Belsky, 1985). Such violation of expectancies could explain part of the drop in marital satisfaction that characterizes some relationships during the transition to parenthood.

Fulfilled and unfilled expectations also affect the family's adaptation. In terms of parent–infant relationships, Easterbrooks (Chapter 6) emphasizes the impact of the contrast at birth between the fantasized and romanticized baby and the real baby. All parents must contend with the discrepancy between the idealized vision of the way the baby will look (and sound and behave) and the actual appearance of the baby. However, this contrast acquires additional poignancy upon the birth of an ill or handicapped infant, when the discrepant, and negative, perceptions may lead to guilt, blame, and ambivalence toward the baby. Adolescent parents face potentially great discrepancies between their fantasies of needs that will be fulfilled by having a baby and the reality of problems and conflict that persist after the baby's birth (Osofsky, Osofsky, & Diamond, Chapter 7). A viable preventive intervention for risk and nonrisk families is to inform prospective or expectant parents about what to expect from pregnancy, childbirth, and childrearing. As Duncan and Markman (Chapter 9) describe, "anticipatory guidance" can help individuals to develop realistic expectations and strategies for meeting the forthcoming demands of childbearing and childrearing.

The significance of the "first" transition versus later transitions

Another commonplace in "transition" research is the tendency to emphasize the first occurrence of a transition event – for example, the impact of the first baby on the family, the first child's experience of adolescence, or the effects on a child's life of the birth of the first sibling. Certainly, the first occurrence of a life transitional event is uniquely important. From a methodological point of view, this is the "cleanest" occurrence to investigate and it provides the greatest contrast. However, it then remains to be determined to what extent additional transitional events of this type are experienced similarly. Specifically, in transition-to-parenthood research, attention has been given only recently to the experience of having a second or later child and to the important dyadic, triadic, and quadratic changes that occur (e.g., Kreppner, Paulsen, & Schuetze, 1982; Mebert & Kalinowski, 1986; Stewart, 1985). One of the major differences between first-time and second-time parenthood is that second-time parents are not taking on a whole new role, and to this extent the psychological impact may be less dramatic. Multiparous women and their husbands have already experienced the structural shift from being a couple to being a family. The similarities and differences in the impact of a first and that of a later pregnancy on self-image, couple dynamics, and social network relations call for further empirical research.

The parenting experience with the first child may differ widely from that with subsequent children. Research is needed to investigate the extent to which expectations about a later transition-to-parenthood experience that are based on a first pregnancy experience may be mistaken, either because of systematic differences in the two experiences or because of the unique personality or temperamental characteristics of the two babies. The violation of expectations regarding the subsequent child(ren) can be a source of considerable stress in the family. For example, with regard to systematic differences, parents who anticipate as influential a change in their lives or as intense an experience at the birth of a second or later child may feel that something is wrong with them if they do not feel this intensity. At the individual level, parents who have had a temperamentally "easy" first baby may find themselves frustrated and distressed with the need to cope with a colicky second child. Furthermore, the second-time parent may anticipate that the second child will be different and may worry about this in advance, which itself may influence the transition process. The clinical experience of one of the authors (Michaels) suggests that it is not unusual for second-time expectant parents to wonder whether they will feel the same intensity of bonding and attachment to their second child as they felt to their first.

At the same time, the violation of expectations can have positive results. Some parents express surprise and delight that their second child is much easier than expected, perhaps reflecting their own sense of efficacy as experienced parents (Daniels & Weingarten, 1982). They may be able to relax and enjoy their second baby in ways that they were not able to do with their first.

Another major difference between the first and later transitions to parenthood is that later transitions involve changes in the family system; that is, they involve a reorganization of the existing family structure and function. To put it succinctly, "First children are born to couples; second children are born to families" (Daniels & Weingarten, 1982, p. 222). With the arrival of a second child, changes occur in the network of family relationships, including redistribution of parental involvement with the first child and with one another (Kreppner, 1987). The birth of a second child involves a budding sibling relationship and adjustments for the first child, who is an important player in the transition process. Although the impact of a second child may be less "dramatic" than that of the first, it clearly is more complex in terms of the number of relationships that it affects and is affected by.

Given the added complexity in relationships, researchers examining the transition to second or later parenthood may want to include more detailed assessments of family functioning in their research, drawing on research on sibling interaction (e.g., Dunn, 1983, Nadelman & Begun, 1982), as well as on the theoretical writings, research literature, and measures that have emerged out of family process and family therapy research. In fact, research on the second transition to parenthood may provide a needed point of contact between family researchers and transition-to-parenthood researchers.

Continuity and change in the adaptation to parenthood

Evidence has amassed in this volume for consistency in couple and individual levels of functioning across time, that is, from the pre- to the postpartum period across the transition to parenthood. There is evidence as well for consistency in the quality of functioning across domains of family life at any given time. Support has been found for continuity in the quality of interactions in various family subsystems such as marriage and parenting. Both before and after the birth of a first baby, men and women who are satisfied with themselves also report satisfying relations with their spouse, child, and social network (see Cowan & Cowan, Chapter 4). These claims for consistency of functioning across domains and over time are not intended to rule out the possibility of change. Indeed, the transition to parenthood, along with other pivotal transition experiences, provides an opportunity for reevaluation and change, in both positive and negative directions. Challenges to adjustment can provoke problems but also provide opportunities for growth and change.

Even without a history of psychological problems, individuals during the transition to parenthood face potential adjustment difficulties. One way that the transition can act as a catalyst for change in adult functioning is through the encountering of "old issues" during this time (see also Antonucci & Mikus, Chapter 2). An opportunity arises to resolve issues concerning separation anxiety, needs for dependency and control, and the relationship with one's own parents, which are reactivated by the pregnancy experience and impending parenthood. New parents whom we interviewed in our research (Goldberg, Michaels, & Lamb, 1985; Michaels, 1981) reported a negotiation of several issues: the sharing of affection between spouse and baby, the disruption of old routines (household division of labor, work roles), restrictions on freedom and independence, and a reexamination of their commitment to the marriage. These changes are challenges for the individual, couple, and family system.

Satisfactory resolution of old issues and personal growth can involve change in one's self-concept, as through the addition of a "possible self of parent" (Antonucci & Mikus, Chapter 2), the acquisition of a sense of being an adult (Hoffman & Manis, 1978), or the expansion of one's identity and relationships within the family system (Fedele et al., Chapter 3). The development of new skills, or the maturation of abilities already possessed, through the experience of caring for a baby can also influence self-concept in a positive way. Becoming a parent may be a welcomed license for adults to expose emotions that have been dormant: For men, it could sanction the expression of nurturing feelings (Antonucci & Mikus, Chapter 2); for women, it may kindle protective feelings; for both men and women, it can unleash spontaneity and delight in everyday occurrences.

Even when new parents define their parenting roles along traditional sex-typed boundaries, the transition to parenthood may awaken new avenues of expression that may not be obvious because they are channeled into conventional modes of expression. The same activities may be approached with renewed interest or be motivated by different factors. For example, a new father may experience renewed commitment to his occupation, motivated by his love and affection for his baby and wish to provide well for the baby. In this example, the source of the motivation is new, although its behavioral manifestation in work involvement may obscure the impact of the baby on the father's self-concept.

At least in a temporal sense, the motivation to become a parent is a primary factor in the process of adaptation to pregnancy and parenthood. Motivations may vary depending on the point in the life span when the individual becomes a parent (Goldberg, this volume). The timing of first parenthood is a proxy for the rewards and costs of childrearing that individuals can expect to experience. In his chapter, Michaels presents several lines of theory and research on the value of parenthood. One aspect of adaptation is the individual's capacity to achieve a balance between seeing parenthood as an opportunity to expand arenas for personal achievement and fulfillment, on the one hand, and the desire to fulfill existing roles, on the other. The actual or anticipated benefits and costs of childrearing – both the reasons that adults want children and their concerns about having children – affect their fertility behavior and readiness for parenthood. Intervention programs launched before conception can help couples evaluate their motives for having a child and assist efforts to determine the optimal timing for childbearing (Duncan & Markman, Chapter 9).

It is important for parents to have strong personal resources as they adjust aspects of their personality to the developing child. Indeed, the diminished opportunity among adolescent parents for having achieved a level of maturity marked by flexibility and ego strength appears to be one of the factors that makes young age a risk for parenting problems. Osofsky et al. (Chapter 7) point out that pregnancy and parenthood during the teenage years impede the adolescent's negotiation of his or her own developmental needs. These authors, along with Kagan and Seitz (Chapter 10), discuss the types of interventions that may facilitate the transition to parenthood for adolescents.

What might be considered optimal in terms of individual and family functioning varies with the phase of the transition to parenthood under question. Factors that predict success in *becoming* a parent may not operate in the same way when the issue turns to *being* a parent. Fedele et al. (Chapter 3) report research evidence to support this distinction. A high affiliative orientation during pregnancy bodes well for maternal psychological health during the first few months postpartum, a time when nurturing behavior from the mother "fits" well with the dependent state of her infant. As the months pass and the infant develops a more separate sense of self, maternal autonomy becomes an important predictor of infant and maternal well-being. This distinction between becoming and being a parent also applies to the timing and content of intervention programs (see Gottlieb & Pancer, Chapter 8; Duncan & Markman, Chapter 9; and Kagan & Seitz, Chapter 10). Pre-conception, pregnancy, and postpartum periods carry unique demands and challenges for individuals and families. The type of program that prospective and active parents should choose (e.g., drop-in center, peer support group, counseling, home visitor) depends in part on their "risk" status; those with low social and medical risk status are better suited to informal, loosely structured support programs than those who are at risk for social and/or medical problems (Kagan & Seitz, Chapter 10).

In studying adaptation to parenthood and in developing phase-specific interventions, researchers have assumed an end point for the transition period set anywhere from a few months to 1 year or more. We do not have established criteria for determining when this life-span event is "over" and hence do not know when the adjustment process can be expected to be complete. Of course, there will be individual and group differences in this timing, but for all, the last phase of the transition period should entail an end to a sense of crisis, overwhelming change, or structural reorganization. Following the transition per se should be a more stable period of parenthood functioning. This stability is relative, however. The quickly developing child requires continual adjustments from the parent. Another period of greater instability may be triggered by a second pregnancy as the new transition experience is layered onto the continuing adjustments already being made to first parenthood. This makes it difficult to delineate objectively the end to the transition to parenthood.

The transition to parenthood at the end of the twentieth century

Becoming a parent in the latter years of this century has taken on new meaning in part because of changing expectations for marriage and fertility behavior (see Goldberg, this volume) and in part because of technological advances that have influenced how we conceive, gestate, and give birth to our children. In Chapter 5, Holt describes many of these advances and discusses some of the implications for physicians and parents. More adults are able to conceive and bring to term healthy infants thanks to these advances. Holt points out that what may appear to be a highly favorable advance, one that from the medical perspective promotes the well-being of the mother or her offspring, is occasionally, from a psychological perspective, a two-edged sword. Technological innovations may have a potentially negative psychological impact on the expectant parent or they may simply raise unanticipated psychological issues for which the parent has little preparation to resolve.

At times, expectant parents actively seek out the information provided by the new technology, for example, in situations of infertility, high-risk pregnancy, or fetal sex selection. At other times, expectant parents find themselves confronted with new technological procedures without choosing or expecting them because they have become part of established obstetrical practice, such as is becoming the case with ultrasound. Sometimes procedures like ultrasound or amniocentesis are undertaken for a specific reason, but end up providing a wide array of diagnostic material. In these instances, the expectant parents may find themselves in possession of information they did not seek; for example, they may learn the sex of the fetus from ultrasonic imaging or learn about a "secondary" genetic disorder (one that was not the primary reason for having the amniocentesis). The new technology may then be experienced as an intrusion, pose dilemmas for the expectant parents ("If the medical staff know my baby's sex, shouldn't I?" or "Should we continue the pregnancy knowing that the baby has a XYY genotype?"), and potentially threaten existing coping strategies.

Technological developments in the area of obstetrical practice such as in vitro fertilization (so-called test tube babies), embryo transfers, prenatal genetic screening for an ever widening array of defects and diseases, and selection of sex of offspring raise immediate and sometimes far-reaching ethical, cultural, and legal questions, and require adjustment and accommodation of the existing legal and ethical value system to the new technology. For example, advances in genetic typing of the fetus will allow for the identification of a far greater number of structural problems and susceptibility factors than has ever been possible, and parents, as well as society as a whole, will be faced with the ethical and legal question of when it is proper to terminate the pregnancy. Similarly, the progressive decrease in the age of survivability of the fetus may eventually present a situation in which the time of permissible abortion and that of fetal survivability overlap. How the new parent experiences the new technology and the legal and ethical issues emerging in the 1980s is an important area for study.

A synthesis of the major variables that influence the transition to parenthood

One of the major advances made by this volume is the identification and discussion of factors that explain why some individuals and relationships adapt smoothly to the transition to parenthood whereas others face numerous difficulties that may even reach crisis proportions. In their respective chapters, the authors elaborate particular antecedents and correlates of adaptation or maladaptation. In this final chapter, we provide a compendium of the key factors. We have organized these factors in a three-tiered synthesis of the transition to parenthood (see Table 1). The first phase delineates correlates and predictors of competency during the transition process. "Competency" refers to modes of functioning that have been deemed adaptive by theory and research. In the main, factors associated with competency reflect psychological, physical, and socioeconomic health, as well as well-functioning interpersonal relationships. In the second tier, we present factors that denote risk for individuals, couples, and/or families during the transition to parenthood. These factors are largely indicators of biomedical and socioeconomic risk conditions. In the third tier, we list intervention strategies that can assist prospective and active parents at each phase of the transition to parenthood. The interventions cover both formal and informal programs that are designed to enhance positive outcomes; that is, they have an orientation toward competency.

Our integrative summary also has a temporal dimension. Under "Preconception" we list characteristics of the individual's social ecology that precede, but nonetheless affect, the transition to parenthood. In the column headed "Pregnancy," we mention characteristics and events that assume special significance during the childbearing period, from conception through birth. The third column, labeled "Postnatal," covers the period following birth through the end of the infant's first year. For the competency and risk tiers, the third column contains possible consequences of the preceding periods. However, each phase of the transition to parenthood reflects prior events and experiences (i.e., is an outcome) and sets the stage for adaptation in the next period (i.e., is a causal factor of a future phase). In the intervention tier, the third column includes intervention programs suitable for the whole family.

Our synthesis is limited to a two-dimensional, abbreviated form of presentation; however, we wish to underscore our position that the transition to parenthood takes place within the context of the individual's life span

Table 1. *Phases of the transition period*

	Pre-conception	Pregnancy	Postnatal
Competency profile (predictors and correlates)	Well-functioning marriage Adequate social support network Good relationship with own parents Adequate socioeconomic status History of psychological health History of physical health Strong motivation to become a parent Social climate supportive of children and families	Supportive spousal relationship Adequate social support network (emotional, tangible, and cognitive support from family and friends) Adequate socioeconomic status Adequate prenatal care Good relationship with obstetrician Psychological health (low anxiety, low depression, high self-esteem, good self-concept, high autonomy, high affiliation) Medically and psychologically satisfactory birth experience	Well-functioning marriage; satisfaction with division of labor Psychological health Satisfaction with work and family roles Positive change and growth in self-concept Successful adaptation to parenthood (synchronous parent–infant interaction, development of secure attachment, sensitivity to child's developmental needs) Closer intergenerational ties Well-functioning social support network Adequate socioeconomic status Adequate well-baby care
Risk profile (predictors and correlates)	History of psychiatric problems Low motivation to become a parent Psychological conflicts over femininity, masculinity History of physical health problems Economic hardship	Maternal anxiety and depression Psychological problems Economic problems Teenager; teenage head of household Advanced maternal or parental age	Poor adjustment to parenthood Reactivation of unresolved psychological needs Role conflict, strain, overload Extended postpartum depression Negative change in self-concept

Marital distress
Stress and deficits in support from family, friends, and community

Maternal or fetal medical complications during pregnancy
Birth problems (maternal medical complications; birth of an ill, premature, or handicapped infant)
Marital distress; lack of spousal support
Stress and deficits in social support network

Guilt, ambivalence, grief, and mourning if infant ill, premature, or handicapped
Separation from infant due to maternal or infant health problems
Financial problems
Marital distress
Stress and deficits in social support network

Intervention
(types and objectives)

Learn decision-making skills to assist decisions about whether and when to have a baby
Learn to use social support network effectively
Couple (marital) therapy to resolve conflicts; work on communication skills

Childbirth preparation to impart educational information, promote spousal support, alleviate maternal experience of pain and need for medication during labor
Preparation for parenthood – anticipatory guidance (what to expect from baby, changes to expect in lifestyle, marital and employment roles)
Communication skills for couples
Prenatal care
Medical, educational, and social-psychological care for pregnant teenagers
Government subsidies for economically disadvantaged women (e.g., the WIC Program)

Informal support programs, e.g., drop-in center, peer support group, resource and referral
Formal support programs, e.g., parent education, home visitors, counseling, group therapy
Learn special caregiving for ill or handicapped infant
Pediatric well-baby care
Good-quality childcare
Emotional, tangible, and cognitive support from family and friends

and culture. In addition, the experience of the transition to parenthood is not the same for men and women (for an extended discussion, see Rossi, 1985). We hope that our integration is sufficiently general to allow for these subtle and not so subtle gender differences.

The depiction in Table 1 is linear, and although the reality may not be, we intend only to provide a heuristic for the investigation of interdependent and causal relations across the transition to parenthood. In reality, there are interactive relationships among the factors. Psychological well-being following the birth of a child is not merely the absence of a history of psychiatric illness, nor is it simply the consequence of a highly affiliative style during pregnancy. Similarly, high-risk parent–child relationships are not the invariable result of the presence of one risk factor during pregnancy, but likely are the consequence of multiple risk factors during the pre-conception and gestational periods. Even in the face of multiple risk factors, there are parents and children who will fare well despite these adverse circumstances. However, individuals most likely to adapt well to pregnancy and parenthood are those with "multiple competency factors": healthy, psychologically well-adjusted adults who look forward to parenthood and are buoyed by a supportive network of family and friends. Greater attention must be directed toward the identification of the timing, combination, and intensity of factors that may anticipate a negative or positive trajectory through the transition to parenthood. Findings from academic research, for example, from studies of parents' responses to premature or handicapped infants (Easterbrooks, Chapter 6), should be integrated into the design of appropriate interventions for new families.

Methodological issues

Recent years have born witness to advances in methodological sophistication in research and intervention designs for the study of the transition to parenthood. The work of many of the contributors to this volume is testament to this progress. Below, we summarize the major methodological suggestions put forth by the authors of this volume to guide future research. For the reader interested in the application of particular methodological strategies, we include selected examples of research. (These references are intended to be illustrative; they are not intended to be extensive or exhaustive.) Thus, we recommend the following:

1. longitudinal research designs that begin before conception (e.g., McHale & Huston, 1985) or early in the prenatal period (e.g., Goldberg et al., 1985; Grossman, Eichler, & Winickoff, 1980) to facilitate the study of stability and change and influences over time; also the inclusion of multiple points of assessment in follow-up studies, that is, more than one assessment following the baby's birth (e.g., Cowan & Cowan, 1987);

2. designs that adopt a process orientation, that is, that address mechanisms of influence and view response to the transition to parenthood as continuous interplay between the person and the social and physical environment; also the inclusion of both direct and indirect paths of influence;

3. the inclusion of socioeconomically and ethnically heterogeneous samples; also samples that reflect the plurality of contemporary family forms (e.g., female-headed households, blended families);

4. comparison groups of nonparents in studies of individual and couple functioning across the transition to parenthood (e.g., Cowan et al., 1985; McHale & Huston, 1985; White & Booth, 1985);

5. appropriate control groups in intervention studies for individuals, couples, and families (e.g., Cowan & Cowan, 1983; McGuire & Gottlieb, 1979) (when random assignment is not feasible, creative and workable alternatives should be pursued; see Kagan & Seitz, Chapter 10);

6. expansion of the unit of analysis to include men as well as women (men are too frequently omitted from studies of marital relations, parent–child relations, and social support networks), children (the new baby and siblings in studies of the arrival of second and subsequent children), and the family network as a whole (the family both as a context for individual development and as a systematic entity);

7. reliable, valid, and readily interpreted measures of individual, dyadic, and familial functioning;

8. greater consistency across studies in the selection of measures to assess similar aspects of individual, dyadic, family, or social network functioning in order to promote comparisons across studies;

9. use of multiple assessment techniques and multiple measures to evaluate complex aspects of individual and interpersonal relations (e.g., use of self-report, projective, interview, and observational techniques and measures); and

10. collection and integration of qualitative and quantitative data.

Several of these recommendations merit elaboration from the vantage point of the field as a whole. To this end, we focus next on concerns related to the composition of samples; the selection of measures for use in heterogeneous samples; and the selection, recruitment, and retention of subjects.

The transition to parenthood in diverse populations

One area needing enhancement is the examination of the transition to parenthood among adults from socioeconomically and ethnically diverse backgrounds. Most research studies that investigate such factors as marital satisfaction and role change have been conducted with white middle-class samples of married persons.

In some studies with adult subjects, other ethnic, racial (e.g., Hobbs & Wimbish, 1977), or socioeconomic groups (e.g., Cowan & Cowan, 1987) have been represented, but typically not in sufficient number to make comparative analyses. It is not known, for example, whether the shift toward more traditional household role relationships reported by many researchers holds true for black families, Hispanic families, or Asian families, or whether in these groups there may be other types of role changes not seen in the white families. Similarities and differences in individual and family development by culture and subculture should be further investigated.

In contrast to research with adults, the study of the transition to parenthood among adolescent parents has addressed possible racial and cultural differences. Studies of teenage parents often draw upon poverty samples and/or samples of black and Hispanic youth (e.g., Furstenberg, 1976). Yet with considerable theoretical justification, the transition to parenthood of very young parents has been treated as posing a separate set of research questions than the transition to parenthood among adults.

Once systematic study of non-Caucasian families is undertaken, the issue of the suitability of current measures will have to be addressed. We cannot assume that items on a measure developed with a normative white sample will be interpreted identically by expectant parents from another racial or cultural group, or that important dimensions salient to these groups will not be neglected entirely by a measure developed for white middle-class couples. For example, the current form of the widely used Locke–Wallace measure of marital adjustment (Locke & Wallace, 1959) does not take into account important aspects of relationships among unmarried couples and therefore might not be appropriate in samples of adults with children born out of wedlock. Even couple adjustment measures that were developed to include situations in which the couple lives together without being married, such as the Dyadic Adjustment Scale (Spanier, 1976), contain assumptions about what constitutes desirable communication patterns and modes of decision making that may not apply to different racial and ethnic groups.

As another example, it has commonly been acknowledged by researchers in the field that the quality of the couple or marital relationship is the most critical factor in the family's adjustment to new parenthood. Yet in cultural groups where extended family living arrangements are more common, the marital or couple relationship may be less important for parenthood adjustment than is support provided by other family members. Thus, if attention is now going to be given to ethnic differences in the transition to parenthood, much initial work will have to be done to determine the validity of the frequently used measures for other ethnic groups. New measures that address unique aspects of the pregnancy and early parenthood experience of these groups will have to be developed and validated.

Subject selection, recruitment, and retention

The important issue of subject selection has been addressed infrequently up to now by transition-to-parenthood researchers. The reliance on self-selected volunteers in this area of research raises the question of what factors may differentiate this self-selected group from those in the same population who have not chosen to participate. The transition to parenthood has some characteristics that may affect whether an expectant mother or father volunteers to participate in a research study. For example, couples under a great deal of psychological stress during the pregnancy period may not have the time or energy to participate in research. This means that a researcher studying adjustment to parenthood may not have access to the most poorly adjusted couples.

We have noted in our research that it is more difficult to recruit the voluntary participation of fathers than mothers. Fathers may be less inclined to share emotional experiences associated with the pregnancy with a relatively unknown investigator or interviewer than are mothers, who may be more used to sharing their experiences about the pregnancy with their doctor, nurse, friends, and associates. If researchers are intent on studying couples, and therefore need the agreement of both the husband and the wife, selection factors may bias the recruitment of a group of volunteer fathers toward those who are more open and more verbal than is typical for the population as a whole.

Some researchers are able to pay subjects for their participation, and this may enhance the participation rate as well as lower the attrition from longitudinal studies. However, because longitudinal studies of the transition to parenthood are labor-intensive operations, even when subject payments are available, these payments may function as tokens of appreciation rather than as adequate compensation for the hours contributed and may not induce subjects to continue over a period of years. Despite the difficulty with reliance on volunteer samples, we have found in our research that couples who do volunteer tend to be quite open and even enthusiastic about participating in studies, and they often appreciate the opportunity to communicate something about what they are experiencing at this important time of life. Prospective and new parents are generally tolerant of the time required, even when they are involved in longitudinal research with identical or similar measures being administered at multiple assessment points.

Aside from investigating the characteristics of volunteer subjects, researchers should attempt to keep track of the subject participation rate (i.e., response rate) to the extent that is possible in their studies. Researchers in the transition-to-parenthood area recruit expectant couples by a variety of strategies, including posting notices in obstetricians' offices and obstetrics clinics, placing advertisements in newspapers, and requesting referrals from study participants who know other couples who are expecting a child. In these cases the researchers are not able to determine how many adults passed up the opportunity to sign up for a research study. If possible, more formal solicitation of potential subjects should be done so that the participation rate can be better evaluated.

Finally, with regard to subject recruitment, we have found in our research that a good way to increase the participation rate in studies of the transition to parenthood is to solicit the involvement in subject recruitment and/or in the research itself of an obstetrician or another health care provider, such as a nurse, with whom prospective female subjects have close and continuous contact over the course of their pregnancy. When women and their husbands are aware that their physician or nurse is involved in the research and that they are helping him or her, they tend to be more trustful and interested in being involved themselves. In some instances, the physician or nurse becomes an active member of the research team with an investment in the study outcomes. Such an interdisciplinary approach to research on the transition to parenthood is highly advocated for its potential payoff in increased understanding of the impact of this life event at all levels of the mother's and father's social, psychological, and biopsychological experience.

Conclusion

Research on the transition to parenthood is reaching a new level of sophistication. Reliance on anecdotal evidence and case studies is being supplanted by rigorously designed empirical studies that attempt to meet the methodological specifications set out above. Furthermore, the unit of analysis has broadened to include fathers as well as mothers, and couples and families as well as individuals. The past several years have been witness to the development of a number of important theoretical models that can guide these research efforts into their next phase. We are beginning to see integration of concepts from the fields of life-span development, family development, and family systems theory into research on the transition to parenthood. There is much room for further research that compares the transition-to-parenthood experience in the life course of the parent with other major life-span events in both quality and intensity. This type of research could then help define the salient dimensions of the transition to parenthood, some of which are presumably shared with other life transitions. Ultimately, outcome studies in which either the child's or the parent's adjustment is the primary focus would also benefit from this kind of comparative analysis. However, we again caution that little is known about the generalizability of either the theoretical models or the empirical findings beyond the middle-class North American couples who have served as subjects in most of these investigations. As we move into the next decade, it is essential that the developing theoretical and empirical models, with their concepts of individual, couple, and family change, be broad enough to include the diversity of family forms and sociocultural influences that prevail.

References

Belsky, J. (1985). Exploring individual differences in marital change across the transition to parenthood: The role of violated expectations. *Journal of Marriage and the Family, 47*, 1037–44.

Cowan, P. A., & Cowan, C. P. (1983, April). *Preventive therapy for couples at the transition to parenthood.* Paper presented at the meetings of the Society for Research in Child Development, Detroit, MI.

Cowan, P. A., & Cowan, C. P. (1987, April). *Couple relationships, parenting styles, and the child's development at three.* Paper presented at the meetings of the Society for Research in Child Development, Baltimore, MD.

Cowan, C. P., Cowan, P. A., Heming, G., Garrett, F., Coysh, W., Curtis-Boles, H., & Boles, A. (1985). Transition to parenthood: His, hers, theirs. *Journal of Family Issues, 6*, 451–82.

Daniels, P., & Weingarten, K. (1982). *Sooner or later: The timing of parenthood in adult lives.* New York: Norton.

Dunn, J. (1983). Sibling relationships in early childhood. *Child Development, 54*, 787–811.

Furstenberg, F. F., Jr. (1976). *Unplanned parenthood: The social consequences of teenage childbearing.* New York: Free Press.

Goldberg, W. A., Michaels, G. Y., & Lamb, M. E. (1985). Husbands' and wives' adjustment to pregnancy and first parenthood. *Journal of Family Issues, 6*, 483–504.

Grossman, F., Eichler, L., & Winickoff, S. (1980). *Pregnancy, birth, and parenthood.* San Francisco: Jossey-Bass.

Hobbs, D., & Wimbish, J. M. (1977). Transition to parenthood by black couples. *Journal of Marriage and the Family, 39*, 677–89.

Hoffman, L. W., & Manis, J. (1978). Influences of children on marital interaction and parental satisfactions and dissatisfactions. In R. M. Lerner & G. W. Spanier (Eds.), *Child influences on marital and family interaction: A life-span perspective* (pp. 165–213). New York: Academic Press.

Kreppner, K. (1987, April). *Changes in family interaction patterns after the arrival of a second child.* Paper presented to the meetings of Society for Research in Child Development, Baltimore, MD.

Kreppner, K., Paulsen, S., & Schuetze, Y. (1982). Infant and family development: From triads to tetrads. *Human Development, 25*, 373–91.

Locke, H., & Wallace, K. (1959). Short marital adjustment and prediction tests: Their reliability and validity. *Marriage and Family Living, 21*, 251–5.

McGuire, J. C., & Gottlieb, B. H. (1979). Social support groups among new parents: An experimental study in primary prevention. *Journal of Clinical Child Psychology, 8*, 111–16.

McHale, S., & Huston, T. (1985). The effect of the transition to parenthood on the marriage relationship. *Journal of Family Issues, 6,* 409–34.

Mebert, C., & Kalinowski, M. (1986, April). *Parity differences in the transition to parenthood.* Paper presented to the meetings of the International Conference on Infant Studies, Los Angeles.

Michaels, G. Y. (1981). *Transition to parenthood: Impact on moral–personal values, attitudes and life goals.* Unpublished doctoral dissertation, University of Michigan, Ann Arbor.

Nadelman, L., & Begun, A. (1982). The effect of the newborn on the older sibling: Mothers' questionnaires. In M. E. Lamb & B. Sutton-Smith (Eds.), *Sibling relationships: Their nature and significance across the lifespan* (pp. 13–37). Hillsdale, NJ: Erlbaum.

Rossi, A. S. (1985). Gender and parenthood. In A. S. Rossi (Ed.), *Gender and the life course.* New York: Aldine.

Spanier, G. (1976). Measuring dyadic adjustment: New scales for assessing the quality of marriage and similar dyads. *Journal of Marriage and the Family, 38,* 15–28.

Stewart, R. J. (1985, April). *Transition to parenthood. Part II: Familial role adjustment following the birth of a second child.* Paper presented to the meetings of Society for Research in Child Development, Toronto.

White, L. K., & Booth, A. (1985). The transition to parenthood and marital quality. *Journal of Family Issues, 6,* 435–50.

Index of names

Abdulla, U., 167
Abernathy, S., 194
Abernethy, V. D., 257
Adams, B. A., 238
Adelson, E., 67
Adland, M. L., 118
Adler, N.E., 27
Ahammer, I., 67
Ainsworth, M. D., 200, 301
Allen, L. C., 168
Allen, V. L., 63
Alpert, J. L., 252, 255, 257
Als, H., 194
Ames, L., 211
Andelman, S., 325
Anderson, B. J., 92, 131, 177
Anthony, E. J., 68, 70
Antonovsky, A., 241, 242
Antonucci, T. C., 13, 126, 344, 347, 348
Apfel, N. H., 324, 326
Aranoff, J. L., 294, 296, 297
Arend, R. A., 226
Arms, S., 162, 164, 165, 170, 171
Aschenbrenner, B., 92, 137
Ashe, M., 194
Awalt, S. J., 120, 145

Babchuck, N., 238
Babikan, H. M., 225
Badger, E., 261
Bain, J., 118, 142
Bakan, D., 93
Bakeman, R., 195, 321
Baldwin, W., 219, 220, 221, 223, 225, 227
Ball, J., 139
Ball, T. L., 281
Ballard, R. A., 182
Ballenski, C. B., 256
Ballinger, C. G., 88, 89
Baltes, P. B., 63
Bane, M. J., 9, 10, 312

Barash, D., 24
Barnard, K. E., 190, 195
Barnes, A. B., 281
Barnes, M., 74
Barnett, B. E. W., 301
Barnett, C. R., 183, 186, 191, 193, 201
Barrera, M. E., 197
Barry, W. A., 130, 133
Barth, R. P., 255
Basham, R. B., 182, 241, 257
Bauer, F., 325
Bayley, H. C., 327
Beach, L. R., 27, 28, 279
Beardslee, W. R., 329
Beauchamp, D., 115
Beck, N. C., 162, 280, 281, 282
Becker, P. T., 194
Beckman, L. T., 9, 10, 27
Beckwith, L., 195, 196, 198
Begun, A., 346
Bekker, L. D., 225
Bell, R. Q., 66, 67
Beller, E. K., 293
Belsky, J., 62, 67, 68, 75, 132, 137, 138, 176, 177, 178, 180, 201, 210, 259, 303, 344
Bem, S. L., 38
Bemporad, J., 329
Benedek, T., 24, 38, 64, 67, 76, 126, 127, 216,
Benson, L., 187
Berezin, N., 189, 190
Bergman, A. B., 220
Berman, A., 285
Bergstrom-Walan, M. B., 286
Berrueta-Clement, J. R., 336
Bibring, G. L., 209, 217
Biller, H. B., 95
Billings, A. G., 135, 147
Bing, E. D., 288
Birkel, R. C., 263

361

Blake, R. R., 27
Blase, B., 201
Blehar, M., 200, 301
Block, C. R., 291
Block, J., 132
Block, J. H., 132
Block, J. L., 282
Block, R. W., 220
Block, S. A., 220
Blood, R. O., 118
Bloom, B. L., 272, 273
Blos, P., 209, 210, 211, 212, 213, 214
Blum, M. E., 120
Blythe, B. J., 219
Boehm, F., 26
Bombardieri, M., 57
Booth, A., 120, 355
Borg, S., 179, 180, 183, 185, 186, 187, 189
Borhanyi, N. O., 220
Boston Women's Health Book Collective,
    1976, 281
Bott, E., 238
Bowen, M., 138
Bowen S. L., 290
Boyer, R., 9
Brackbill, Y., 164, 281
Bradburn, N., 118, 127, 142
Bram, S., 38
Brassard, J. A., 256, 257
Brasted, W. S., 179
Brazelton, T. B., 194, 196
Breen, D., 70
Brenner, P., 165
Bricker, D. D., 328
Brim, O. G., Jr., 63, 317, 319
Brockington, F., 118
Brody, E. B., 158
Bromwich, R., 327, 328, 329, 330
Bronfenbrenner, U., 122
Bronte, B., 197
Brooks, V., 192
Brooks-Gunn, J., 225, 227
Brouder, G. T., 280
Brough, D. I., 248, 252
Brown, C., 192, 193
Brown, G. W., 78, 245
Brown, L., 225
Brown, J., 195, 323
Brown, P. G., 281
Brown, R., 39, 40
Bruhn, J. G., 236
Brunquell, D., 225
Buckley, D. E., 88
Bumpass, L., 8
Burr, W., 63
Burt, M., 222, 224
Buss, D. M., 73, 74, 75

Butts, H. F., 166
Buxton, C. L., 284

Cabenar, J. O., 90
Cain, R. L., 92, 131, 177
Cain, V., 227
Call, J., 184
Callahan, E. J., 179, 183, 189
Campbell, A., 64, 65, 78, 118
Campbell, D. T., 334
Campbell, F. L., 27, 28, 279
Campbell, S. B., 86, 252, 253, 275
Cannel, W. B., 78
Caplan, G., 63, 158, 178, 183, 188, 191,
    217, 293
Caplan, S., 147
Caplovitz, D., 118, 127, 142
Card, J. J., 221, 222, 223, 224
Carey, W., 219, 220
Carter, E. A., 272
Cassel, J., 135, 177, 249
Cath, S. H., 89
Cavenar, J. D., 90, 126
CBA Foundation, 180
Cetrulo, C., 170
Chaikin, A. L., 27
Chandler, M. J., 198, 200
Chang, P. N., 291
Chapman, N. J., 331, 333
Charles, A. G., 291
Chase, H. C., 178
Chase, M. A., 248
Cherlin, A., 7, 9, 10, 119
Chertok, L., 281, 282
Chesler, P., 62
Chess, S., 66, 182
Chialdini, R. B., 27
Chilman, C. S., 64, 65, 67
Chiriboga, D., 65
Chodorow, N., 94, 95
Chrichton, L., 225
Ciccetti, D., 193, 194
Clark, R., 329, 331
Clarke, J. E., 252
Clulow, C. F., 127, 294, 297, 300
Clyman, R. I., 182
Coates, D., 258
Cobb, S., 135
Cochran, M. M., 256
Cohen, J. B., 274
Cohen, R. S., 65, 68, 76
Cohen, S. E., 195, 196, 198
Cohler, B., 275, 329, 331
Coie, J. D., 67, 91, 125
Coie, L., 67, 91, 125
Cole, C. L., 119
Cole, S. P., 67, 78, 115, 116, 177

Coleman, M., 71
Coleman, R. W., 65
Coletta, N. D., 253
Collmer, C. W., 201
Colman, A., 65, 70, 90, 160, 161, 162
Colman, L., 65, 70, 90, 160, 161, 162
Comfort, R. L., 180, 191
Connell, J., 243
Connolly, B., 328
Connolly, L., 225
Connor, Y. M., 252
Converse, P. E., 64, 118
Conway, T. L., 247
Cook, A. S., 256
Cook, T. D., 334
Cowan, C. P., 5, 14, 65, 66, 67, 68, 70, 71,
    76, 91, 95, 110, 120, 122, 123, 125,
    127, 128, 129, 131, 133, 134, 136, 137,
    138, 139, 140, 142, 144, 176, 178, 180,
    257, 294, 297, 298, 301, 343, 344, 345,
    347, 354, 355
Cowan, P. A., 5, 14, 66, 67, 68, 91, 110,
    122, 123, 125, 126, 129, 131, 133, 134,
    176, 178, 180, 257, 294, 297, 298, 301,
    343, 344, 345, 347, 354, 355
Coward, R. T., 296
Coyle, J. R., 276, 278
Coyne, J. C., 256
Cox, J. L., 252
Cox, M. J., 1, 67
Craik, K. H., 73
Cramer, J. C., 9
Crawford, T. J., 9, 27
Crnic, K. A., 182, 195, 257
Crockenburg, S., 135, 177, 255, 290, 291
Cronbach, L. J., 302
Cronenwett, L. R., 252, 258, 262, 290, 291,
    303
Crosbie, P., 9
Crouter, A. C., 68
Culp, A. M., 186, 194, 195, 200
Cummings, S. T., 327
Curry, M. A., 165
Cutrona, C. E., 87, 88, 89, 251, 253, 259

Dabiri, C., 200
Dallas, J. R., 325
Daniels, P., 3, 346
Daniluk, J. C., 179
Darling, J., 179
Darling, R. B., 179, 183, 184, 188, 192
Datan, N., 3
Davenport, D. M., 170
Davenport, Y., 118
Davidson, A. R., 27
Davidson, E., 219
Davidson, S., 291

Davis, C. D., 283, 284
Davis, K., 9
Dean, C., 252
DeFrain, J. D., 188
deLissovey, V., 226
Dempsey, G., 200
Dempsey, J. R., 193
Dermer, S. W., 293
Detre, T., 87
Deutsch, H., 24, 25, 162, 210, 211
Diamond, M., 3, 15, 209, 210, 212, 312,
    343
Dickie, J. R., 92, 96
Dick-Read, G., 280, 282, 283, 289
Dicks, H. V., 127
Dickson-Markman, F., 271
DiVitto, B., 194, 195, 196, 197, 198
Doering, S., 120, 127, 128, 257, 285, 286,
    288, 289, 292, 293, 301
Doherty, R., 158
Dohrenwend, B. P., 63, 135
Dohrenwend, B. S., 63, 135
Donovan, W. L., 192
Douratsos, E., 168
Douvan, E., 64, 65
Drillien, C. M., 180
Dow, M. G., 326
Duncan, W., 3, 16, 17, 66, 120, 270, 293,
    302, 303, 345, 348, 349
Dunn, J., 346
Dunst, C. J., 328, 330
Duvall, E. C., 4, 5, 6
Dwyer, T. F., 209, 217
Dyer, E. D., 78, 79, 91
Dyer, T. F., 115, 116, 117, 217

Easterbrooks, M. A., 15, 132, 177, 191,
    200, 323, 344, 346, 354
Edwards, W., 27
Egeland, B., 225
Eggebeen, D., 11
Eichler, L., 120, 252, 354
Elkind, D., 215, 216
Elliot, S. A., 248, 249, 252, 254
Elson, M., 76, 79
Elster, A., 213
Emde, R. N., 185, 186, 192, 193, 194
Emery, R. E., 271
Emmett, J. O., 293
Emms, E. M., 253
Engardio, P., 281
Enkin, M. W., 293
Entwisle, S., 120, 127, 128, 257, 285, 286,
    288, 289, 292, 293, 301
Epstein, A. S., 336
Erikson, E., 2, 4, 5, 6, 26, 38, 54, 64, 94,
    95, 96, 115, 147, 188, 227

Ernst, J., 320
Ernst, L., 188
Ewy, D., 285
Ewy, R., 285

Faigel, H. C., 225
Farber, S. S., 147
Fargo, J., 256
Fasteau, M. F., 94
Faulstich, G., 194
Fawcett, J. T., 64, 76, 275
Fedele, N. M., 14, 78, 91, 93, 95, 96, 118, 126, 344, 347, 349, 351
Fein, R. A., 67, 76
Feinleid, M., 78
Feld, S., 65, 67, 68, 118
Feldman, H., 78, 115, 118, 119, 120, 130, 177
Feldman, S. S., 91, 92, 95, 97, 120, 121, 137, 274
Felner, R. D., 147
Fernandez, P., 182
Field, T. M., 193, 194, 196, 197, 199, 200, 226, 323, 325
Fielding, J. E., 219, 220, 222, 223
Figley, C., 176
Fisch, R. O., 291
Fischer, W. M., 285
Flapan, M., 246
Flavel, R., 158
Fletcher, J., 253
Fleugel, J. C., 26
Floyd, F., 271, 272, 273, 274
Fodaski, L., 252
Folkman, S., 135
Fournier, B. E., 57
Fournier, G., 57
Fox, G. L., 275
Fraiberg, S., 67, 194
Framo, J. L., 134, 138
Frank, L., 6
Franti, C. E., 220
Freedman, D., 158
Freeman, T., 90
Freese, M. P., 194
Freud, A., 209, 214
Freud S., 25, 26
Friedlander, B. Z., 180, 183
Friedman, S. L., 193
Frodi, A. M., 192, 193
Froland, C., 331, 332
Furman, W., 243
Furstenberg, F. F., 222, 225, 227, 356

Galinsky, E., 65, 70, 78
Gallagher, J. L., 330

Gallagher, R. J., 193
Gallant, D. H., 329
Galligan, R., 275
Gallup Organization, 289
Gans, H. J., 238
Gant, N. F., 163
Garbarino, J., 315, 316, 332
Garber, H. L., 335
Gardner, R. A., 284
Gardner, S. H., 248
Garner, E., 329
Garrett, E. T., 128
Gath, A., 191
Geden, E. A., 280
Gerber, S. C., 92, 96
Gerson, M. J., 37, 38, 39, 46, 49
Gesell, A., 211
Gil, D. F., 201
Gilchrist, L. D., 219
Gilligan, C., 94
Gillon, J. W., 219
Gingles, J., 320
Ginsberg, M. R., 275, 276
Gladieux, J., 133, 158
Glenn, N. D., 118, 119
Gleicher, N., 170
Gnedza, M. T., 9
Gold, P. W., 118
Goldberg, S., 185, 194, 195, 196, 197, 198, 199, 200
Goldberg, W. A., 2, 9, 17, 42, 67, 128, 129, 132, 177, 347, 354
Golding, E. R., 14, 93, 118, 344
Goldman, A., 225
Goldmuntz, J., 222
Gonso, J., 302
Goode, W. J., 225
Goodrich, F. W., 283
Goodwin, F. K., 118
Gorsuch, R. L., 99, 248
Goshen-Gottstein, E., 158
Gottlieb, B. H., 3, 16, 188, 238, 241, 251, 261, 262, 344, 346, 349, 355
Gottman, J., 130, 140, 273, 302
Graff, H., 8
Granados, J. L., 179
Granger, J., 9
Gray, E. B., 261
Green, V., 3
Greenacre, D., 210
Greenberg, M. T., 165, 177, 182, 257, 291
Greenberger, E., 9
Greene, B., 67, 76
Greenspan, S. I., 329, 331
Grobstein, R., 191, 201
Gronseth, E., 67

Grossman, F. K., 3, 14, 88, 91, 93, 95, 96, 97, 98, 100, 101, 103, 108, 118, 120, 121, 131, 134, 137, 252, 344, 354
Group for the Advancement of Psychiatry, 66, 76
Grunebaum, H. U., 275, 329
Guilleminault, C., 201
Gurin, G., 127
Gurman, A. S., 303
Gurusitt, A. R., 89
Gutmann, D., 79, 93
Gyurka, J., 192

Hailey, A., 252
Haire, D., 162, 165, 170, 171
Hall, D. E., 158
Hallock, N., 200
Hamburg, B. A., 118, 225
Hamilton, J. A., 118
Hamner, T. J., 322
Hanna, B., 301
Handwerker, W. P., 8
Hansen, D., 5, 147
Hardy, J. B., 325, 326, 327
Harley, M., 201, 211
Harmon, D., 317, 319
Harmon, R. J., 182, 185, 186, 190, 191, 194, 195, 200
Harper, L. V., 67
Harris, T. O., 78, 245
Harrison, M., 162, 165
Hartup, W. W., 299
Haskins, R., 333, 335
Hatcher, S., 210, 212, 213, 221, 223, 224
Havercamp, A. D., 170
Havighurst, R. J., 4, 6
Hay, R., 6
Haynes, S. G., 78
Heardman, H., 282, 283
Heath, D. H., 79
Heber, R., 335
Heinicke, C., 68, 121, 122, 132, 137
Heisler, V., 183, 184
Heller, K., 241, 303
Helmrath, T. A., 188
Heming, G., 119, 132, 134, 137, 141, 146
Herbst, A. L., 167
Herman, A., 278
Hernandez, D., 17
Hertel, R. K., 78, 130
Herzog, A., 87, 126, 190
Herzog, J. M., 190, 198
Hetherington, E. M., 271
Hewitt, D., 191
Heymans, H., 248
Hicks, M., 118

Hilderbrandt, K. A., 192
Hill, R., 5, 6, 115, 116, 147, 148, 272, 293
Hines, B., 188
Hiroto, D., 135
Hirsch, B. J., 240
Hoberman, H., 241
Hobbs, D. F., 67, 78, 91, 93, 115, 116, 117, 176, 177, 355
Hock, E., 9
Hockberg, J., 192
Hofferth, S. L., 219, 222, 223, 224
Hoffman, L. W., 2, 8, 9, 13, 24, 25, 29, 30, 31, 32, 33, 34, 35, 37, 39, 40, 41, 42, 44, 48, 49, 51, 52, 55, 64, 65, 76, 79, 80, 128, 142, 347
Hoffman, M., 13, 24, 29, 30, 31, 39, 40, 41, 48, 49, 142
Holt, L. H., 3, 15, 167, 350
Hooke, J. F., 248
Hopkins, J., 86, 87, 88, 89, 252, 275
Horowitz, M., 135
Hott, J. R., 289, 290
House, J. S., 236
Houseknecht, S. K., 119
Houser, B. B., 9, 27
Howard, J., 182, 183, 185, 186
Howard, M., 326
Howes, P. W., 303
Hubert, J., 158
Hudson, W. W., 119
Hughey, M., 170, 285, 286
Humphrey, M. E., 185
Hunter, R. S., 201
Huntington, D. S., 209, 217, 319
Hurley, D. J., 329
Huston, T. L., 120, 130, 354, 355
Hutchins, F. L., 220
Huttel, F. A., 285, 286
Hymel, S., 195

Ignatoff, E., 323, 325
Ilg, F., 211
Inazu, J., 27
Ingermarsson, E., 170
Ingermarsson, I., 170
Insko, C. A., 27

Jaccard, J. J., 27
Jackson, D. N., 279
Jacobson, E., 282
Jacobson, N., 140
Jacoby, A. P., 116
Jaffe, S., 201
Jamieson, K., 273, 274
Jeffcoate, J. A., 185, 186, 199
Jekel, J. F., 222, 224, 325, 327

Jens, K. G., 193
Jerath, B. K., 166
John, R., 160
Johnson, S. H., 192
Johnson, V., 147
Jones, E., 9, 26
Jones, F. A., 3
Jones, M. B., 178
Jones, R., 293
Jordan, J. V., 96
Joy, L. A., 291

Kadushin, F. S., 285, 286, 288
Kagan, S. L., 3, 17, 135, 313
Kagan, V., 293, 348, 349, 355
Kahn, A., 12, 313
Kahn, J. R., 222
Kahn, K. L., 236
Kaij, L., 87
Kalinowski, M., 345
Kamark, T., 241
Kamerman, S., 12
Kane, F., 166
Kanner, A. D., 135
Kanter, J. F., 219
Kantrowitz, B., 274
Kaplan, A. G., 96
Kaplan, B. H., 135, 249
Kaplan, D. M., 182, 183
Kaplan, H. B., 225
Kaplan, N., 226
Kaplan, S., 94, 102
Karagozlu, F., 168
Karmel, M., 282
Kattwinkel, J., 201
Katz, E. L., 194
Keating, G. W., 27
Keating, P., 215
Kegan, R., 93
Keller, M. B., 329
Kendall, N., 220
Kendell, R. E., 252
Kennell, J. H., 165, 176, 182, 185, 186, 195, 198, 201, 263
Kew, S., 66
Key, M. K., 248
Kililea, M., 188
Kimball, K. K., 277, 278
Kimboko, P. J., 331, 333
Kimmich, M., 222
Kinard, E., 227
King, E. L., 288
King, T. M., 326
Kingston, P., 12
Kirchner, E. P., 27, 37
Kitzinger, S., 162, 165

Klaus, M. H., 165, 176, 182, 185, 186, 195, 198, 201, 263
Klehr, K., 329, 331
Klein, L., 192, 219
Klerman, G. L., 329
Klerman, L., 222, 224, 227, 325, 329
Klinkerman, S., 281
Kniskern, D. P., 303
Kogan, K., 195
Kohut, H., 94
Kondas, O., 300
Kondrat, L., 281
Kopp, C. B., 179
Korn, S. J., 182, 188, 190, 191
Kothandpani, V., 27
Kraus, J. F., 220
Kraus, S., 3
Kraybill, E. N., 201
Kreppner, K., 345, 346
Kris, E., 65
Kulka, E., 64
Kumar, R., 253

Lachman, M. E., 67, 76, 77, 78
LaCoursiere, R., 90
Lamaze, F., 280, 282
Lamb, M. E., 11, 42, 67, 128, 129, 192, 213, 291, 347
Lang, M. E., 120
Langmayer, D., 27
LaPata, R. E., 170
LaRossa, M. M., 120
LaRossa, R., 120
Lasker, J., 179, 180, 183, 185, 186, 187, 189
Lesko, W., 282
Laumann, E. O., 238
Lawrence, R., 220
Lawton, J. T., 71
Lazarus, R., 135, 142
Leavitt, L., 192
Lee, K. S., 173
Leiderman, P. H., 183, 186, 191, 193, 201
Leifer, M., 71, 76
LeMasters, E. E., 1, 76, 115, 116, 117, 254, 257
Lenanne, K. J., 160
Leonard, R. F., 293
Leridon, H., 274
Lerner, M. J., 259, 260
Lester, B., 192, 193, 194, 197, 201, 226
Levenson, R. W., 140
Levin, B., 135
Levine, H. M., 241
Levine, J., 67, 76, 78
Levinson, D. J., 2, 94

Lewis, H. C., 272
Lewis, R., 118, 119
Lewis, S., 294, 296, 297
Lieberman, A. F., 177
Lieberman, M., 135
Lieberman, V., 145
Liefer, A. D., 183, 186
Liefer, M., 88, 126, 127, 178, 255, 257
Lindmann, H., 27
Lipsitt, L. P., 63, 194, 201
Litwak, E., 332
Lloyd, J. K., 185
Locke, H. J., 100, 120, 121, 143, 146, 356
Loda, F., 201
Lopata, H., 63, 66, 67
Lott, B. E., 38
Lowenthal, M. F., 65
Lubin, B., 248
Luckey, E., 118, 142
Lunde, D. T., 118, 281
Lundgren, D., 27
Lushene, R., 99
Lussky, R., 170

MacDonald, P. C., 163
Macre, J. N., 170
Mahler, M. S., 94
Maier, R., 192
Main, M., 226
Malev, J. S., 225
Manis, J. D., 31, 32, 33, 34, 51, 52, 64, 76, 80, 128, 347
Manning, D., 188
Marcus, M., 86, 252, 275
Marecek, J., 227
Margolin, G., 140
Markman, H. J., 3, 16, 17, 66, 120, 130, 270, 271, 272, 273, 274, 285, 286, 288, 300, 302, 303, 345, 348, 349
Marks, P. A., 248
Markus, H., 69, 70
Martin, P., 191
Marton, P., 188
Marut, J. S., 166, 171
Masi, W., 201
Masnick, G., 9, 10, 11
Mason, E. A., 182, 183
Matas, L., 226
Mattessich, P., 5, 6, 272
Maxwell, J. S., 225
Mayaux, M. J., 158
McAnarney, E. R., 222, 226
McBride, S. L., 9
McCabe, M. E., 118
McCann-Stanford, T., 219
McCannell, K., 259, 260

McCarthy, J., 223
McCubbin, H., 176
McElin, T. W., 285
McFee, J. G., 170
McGoldrick, M., 272
McGuire, J. C., 261, 262, 355
McHale, S. M., 120, 130, 354, 355
McIntosh, Dean, 280, 282
McIntyre, M. N., 191
McKinlay, J. B., 250, 263
McLanahan, S., 118, 119
McLaughlin, S. D., 77
Mead, M., 168
Mebert, C., 345
Meehl, P. E., 302
Meindl, J. R., 259, 260
Meisel, J., 333, 335, 337
Meisels, S. J., 200
Meisler, R., 158
Menken, J., 223, 224
Mercer, R., 2, 3, 166, 171
Mermelstein, R., 241
Merritt, T., 220
Meyer, A. E., 285
Meyering, S., 291
Meyerowitz, J. H., 115, 119, 130, 225
Michaels, G. Y., 2, 13, 17, 39, 40, 42, 67, 79, 128, 129, 344, 347, 348, 350
Micklin, M., 77
Middlestadt-Carter, S. E., 27
Migan, M. A., 256
Mikus, K., 13, 76, 77, 78, 126, 344, 347, 348
Miller, B., 118, 120, 212
Miller, B. C., 290, 302
Miller, J. B., 96
Miller, W. B., 5, 23, 225
Milofsky, E., 91
Milunsky, A., 168
Minde, K., 188, 197, 199, 323, 325
Minuchin, S., 138
Mitchel, R. E., 331
Mitchell, I., 285
Mitchell, R. E., 135, 147
Modell, B., 168
Mohr, G. J., 158
Mohr, J. C., 160, 168
Monahan, J., 303
Moore, K. A., 222, 223
Moos, R. H., 118, 133, 135, 147
Morgan, W., 328
Morishima, H. O., 282
Moroney, R., 314
Morris, N., 177, 291
Morrone, F. A., 280, 281, 283, 284, 286
Murai, N., 248

Murphy, G. J., 119
Musick, J. S., 329, 331
Myers-Walls, J. A., 296, 300, 319

Nadelman, L., 346
Nadelson, C. C., 87, 88, 219
Naeye, R. L., 161
Napier, A., 272
Nash, S. C., 92, 95, 120, 121, 137
National Center for Health Statistics, 158, 271, 312
Navran, L., 130
Naylor, A., 324
Naylor, G. J., 88
Nelson, M. K., 293
Neugarten, B., 3
Neunaber, D. J., 88
New Futures School, 326
Newmark, L. L., 291
Newman, L. F., 5
Newton, M., 288
Newton, N., 158, 168, 288
Nilsson, A., 87
Norbeck, J. S., 249, 250
Norr, J. L., 291
Norr, K. L., 291
Notarius, C., 130, 302
Notman, M. T., 87, 88, 219
Nuckolls, K. B., 135, 249
Nurius, P., 69, 70
Nye, F. I., 64, 65

Oates, D. S., 68
O'Connor, S., 226
O'Donnell, K. J., 193
Offer, D., 147
O'Hara, M. W., 88, 253
O'Leary, D., 46
Oppenheimer, V. K., 9
Ory, H. W., 157
Osgood, C. E., 39
Osofsky, J. D., 3, 15, 66, 120, 126, 127, 195, 209, 218, 219, 220, 222, 223, 224, 225, 226, 314, 326, 345, 348, 350
Osofsky, H., 3, 15, 118, 120, 126, 127, 195, 209, 218, 219, 220, 222, 223, 224, 226, 314, 326, 345

Paffenbarger, R. S., 118, 166
Painter, S. L., 291
Pancer, S. M., 3, 16, 188, 344, 349
Pancoast, D., 331, 333
Paneth, N., 173
Pannabecker, B. J., 185, 186
Parens, H., 126
Parke, R. D., 11, 66, 122, 134, 178, 188, 194, 195, 198, 201, 299

Parker, G., 301
Pasick, P. L., 200
Pasley, K., 320
Patterson, G., 147
Patterson, J., 324
Paulsen, S., 345
Pawl, J. H., 189
Paykel, E. S., 89, 253, 329
Pedersen, F. A., 92, 131, 177, 199, 281, 299
Pensky, E., 120
Penticuff, J. H., 180, 186
Peraita, R., 201
Perrotta, M., 199
Perry-Jenkins, M., 68
Petarsky, J. H., 189
Peters-Golden, H., 247
Peterson, G., 6
Peterson, L., 6
Petrou, M., 168
Philips, B. U., 236
Phillips, L. D., 27
Phipps-Yonas, S., 219, 223
Piaget, J., 215, 216
Picciotto, S., 145
Pious XII, 280, 281
Pizzo, P., 185, 313, 315
Placed, P. J., 171
Platonov, K., 280
Platt, M., 118
Pleck, J., 11
Pleshette, N., 248
Ploticher, V., 280
Plunkett, J. W., 200
Pohlman, E., 24, 25, 275
Pokorny, A. D., 225
Polit, D. F., 222, 224
Pollack, S., 342, 346
Pollack, W. S., 14, 92, 94, 101, 104
Potts, L., 277, 278
Powell, D., 261
Power, T. G., 178, 188, 195
Presser, H., 223, 244
Price, G. M., 100
Primavera, J., 147
Pritchard, J. A., 163, 168, 170, 171
Prochaska, J., 276, 278
Procidiano, M. E., 241
Protheroe, C., 87
Provence, S., 65, 334
Prugh, D. G., 183
Pugh, T. F., 166

Rader, G. E., 225
Ragozin, A. S., 182, 257
Rainwater, L., 25
Ramey, C. T., 333, 335

Ramsay, T. B., 241
Rapoport, R., 66, 95, 144
Rapoport, R. N., 66, 95, 144
Rassaby, E. S., 253
Raugh, V. A., 201
Raush, H., 78, 130, 141
Reed, D. M., 178
Reed, R. B., 166
Reese, H. W., 63
Rehm, L. P., 253
Reich, J. N., 192
Reilly, T. W., 127, 128
Reitterstol, N., 90
Rempel, J., 55
Renee, K., 118
Rennie, D., 252
Reppucci, N. D., 263, 239
Rescorla, L. A., 324
Rheingold, H. L., 66
Rich, A., 165
Richardson, B., 328
Richardson, M. S., 135, 252
Richardt, C., 225
Rie, H. E., 327
Rindfuss, R., 8
Ringe, K., 281
Roberts, G., 132
Roberts, R. W., 225
Robertson, S., 263
Robinson, N. M., 182, 257
Robson, K., 253
Rode, S. S., 291
Rodgers, W. L., 5, 6, 64, 118
Roghmann, K., 158
Rokeach, M., 53
Rollins, B. C., 119
Roloff, D. W., 200
Rose, J., 254
Rose, N. B., 285, 286
Rosenbaum, L. K., 46, 324, 326
Rosenberg, A. J., 166
Ross, J. M., 89
Roth, A., 248
Roth, R. S., 182
Routh, D., 120
Rovine, M., 120, 176, 259, 303
Rubino, J., 220
Rugg, A. J., 248, 252
Russell, C. S., 39, 67, 76, 78, 91, 93, 115,
    116, 142, 176, 256
Russell, D., 255, 257
Russell, F., 328
Russo, P. K., 219, 220, 222, 223
Ryder, R., 120, 177

Sabbagha, R., 167
Sabshin, M., 147

Salzman, S., 220
Sameroff, A. J., 66, 198, 200, 329
Sandler, H., 226
Sarason, B. R., 241
Sarason, I. G., 241
Sarbin, T. R., 63
Sarrel, P., 325
Satir, V., 138
Sawin, D. B., 66
Scarr-Salaptek, S., 201, 321, 325
Scetnicka, B., 300
Schaffer, C., 135
Schinke, S. P., 219, 220, 225
Schmidt, W. M., 166
Schott, T. L., 120
Schuetze, Y., 345
Schultz, S., 134
Schweinhart, L. J., 335, 336
Schwartz, B., 76, 77
Schwartz, D., 158
Scotch, N., 78
Scott, J. R., 285, 286
Seashore, M. J., 183, 191, 198
Seaver, W. B., 27
Seifer, R., 329
Seitz, V., 3, 17, 292, 324, 326, 334, 335,
    348, 349, 355
Shannon, B., 252
Shapiro, E. R., 92, 93
Shapiro, V., 67
Shereshefsky, P. M., 67, 70, 76, 78, 79, 88,
    100, 120, 131, 133, 178, 294, 296, 300
Shipp, D. A., 326
Shugon, E., 280
Shuman, H. H., 193, 200
Siegelman, M., 38
Silver, E., 166
Silver, R. E., 252, 255, 257, 258
Simon, R., 184, 189, 190
Singer, J. E., 263, 264, 281, 284, 285, 291,
    293
Sirignano, S. W., 67, 76, 77, 78
Smetlana, J. G., 27
Smith, P. B., 225
Smith, S. L., 293
Sniderman, S. H., 182
Snowden, L. R., 120
Soddy, J., 24
Solkoff, N., 201
Solnit, A., 182
Sonenstein, F., 222
Sosa, R., 263
Souquet, M., 201
Spanier, G., 100, 118, 119, 120, 176, 303,
    356
Spielberger, C., 99
Spock, B., 256

Spragins, E. E., 281
St. John, C., 8
Stack, C., 223
Stanley, F. J., 178
Stanley, J., 325
Stanley, S. M., 272, 273
Stansfield, D. A., 88
Starke, M., 182
Stechler, G., 94, 102
Steffensmeier, D. J., 67
Steffensmeier, R. H., 67
Steinberg, D., 67, 76
Stern, M., 192
Sternitz, E. M., 188
Stewart, R. J., 345
Storaasli, R. D., 303
Strelitz, Z., 66, 95, 144
Stringer, S., 314, 325
Suci, G. J., 39
Sudsberry, R. L., 294, 296, 300, 319
Sugarman, M., 166, 171
Surrey, J. L., 96
Svenningsen, N. W., 170
Swain, M. A., 78, 130, 194
Syme, S. L., 238

Tannen, M. B., 222
Tannenbaum, P. H., 39
Tanzer, D., 282, 286, 289
Tardy, C. H., 236, 237
Thoman, E. B., 194
Thomas, A., 66
Thompson, H. E., 170
Thoms, H., 280, 282, 283
Thornton, A., 31, 52, 158
Thorpe, J. K., 194
Tietze, C., 219
Tilden, V. P., 249, 250
Ting, E., 200
Tinsley, B. R., 122, 134, 178, 188, 195
Toffel, S. M., 171
Tokuno, K., 256
Tomlinson, D. R., 283
Toohey, J. V., 275
Townes, B. D., 27, 28, 29
Trickett, P. K., 324
Trussel, J., 224
Tupper, C., 270, 283
Turner, P. H., 322
Turner, R. H., 63, 64, 65
Tyler, N., 195

Uhlenberg, P., 11
Unger, D. G., 238
Urritia, J., 263
Usher, R. H., 178

U.S. Bureau of the Census, 314
U.S. Congressional Budget Office, 314

Vaillant, G., 91
Valenstein, A. F., 209, 217
Valenzuela, G. L., 275
Van Auken, W. B. D., 283
Vance, S. D., 236, 238
van der Leeuw, P., 213
Vaughn, V. C., 179
Vella, D., 197
Velovsky, I. Z., 280, 282
Veroff, J., 64, 65, 67, 68, 118
Vessey, M. P., 158
Vietze, P., 194, 226
Vinokur-Kaplan, D., 27, 35, 36, 37

Wainwright, S., 252
Wainright, W., 90
Waite, L. J., 222
Waldron, H., 120
Walker, M. P., 252, 255, 257, 258
Wall, S., 200, 301
Wallace, K. M., 100, 120, 121, 143, 146,
    356
Walsh, F., 135
Walters, J., 66, 67
Walters, L. H., 66, 67
Wandersman, A., 238, 261
Wandersman, L. P., 76, 260, 261, 294, 317,
    319
Ward, R. H. T., 168
Ware, L., 226
Warren, D. I., 238
Wasserman, G. A., 200
Waters, E., 200, 226, 301
Watson, J., 248, 252, 293
Watts, H., 17
Weaver, C. N., 119
Weddington, W. W., 90, 126
Weikart, D. P., 335, 336, 338
Weiner, A., 126
Weingarten, P., 2, 346
Weintraub, D., 201
Weiss, J. L., 275, 329
Weissman, M. M., 329
Weissman, S. H., 65, 68, 76
Welcher, D. W., 325, 326
Wengraf, F., 24
Wenner, N. K., 120, 126
Wente, A. S., 177, 291
Werner, P. D., 27
Wertheimer, R., 223
Westoff, C. F., 274
Wheeler, S., 63
Whelan, E. M., 274

White, L. K., 120, 355
Whittaker, J. K., 315, 316, 332
Wideman, M. V., 263, 264, 281, 284, 285, 293
Widmayer, S. M., 323, 325
Wile, D. B., 140
Wilke, J. R., 10
Williams, J., 186, 193
Williams, M. L., 201, 323, 325
Williams, T., 291
Wilner, F., 221
Wilner, N., 135
Wilson, F., 221
Wimbisch, J., 91, 93, 115, 117, 355
Winnicoff, S., 120, 252, 354
Winston, T., 258
Winter, S. T., 248
Wippman, J., 226
Wise, L. L., 3, 221, 222, 223, 224
Wolfe, D. M., 118
Wood, R. L., 27
Wortman, C. B., 247

Wyatt, F., 25, 38
Wyatt, R. H., 280
Wynne, L. C., 176

Yalom, I. D., 118
Yarrow, L. J., 67, 68, 70, 76, 78, 88, 89, 100, 120, 131, 133, 178, 285, 294, 296, 300, 317, 319
Yeates, D., 158
Yogman, M. W., 199
Young, T., 285
Yurko, K., 254

Zachler, J., 325
Zajicek, E., 254
Zaslow, M., 118
Zax, M., 286, 329
Zekoski, E. M., 219
Zelnik, M., 219
Zeskind, P., 192, 193, 197, 201, 226
Zigler, E. F., 324, 335
Zilboorg, G., 90

Index of subjects

abortion
  adolescents and, 219
  genetic screening and, 168
  incidence of (U.S.), 157
  second trimester and, 167
  ultrasound and, 167
adaptation to parenthood
  autonomy and affiliation and, 85–6,
    93–110
  behaviors, predictive of, 92
  conceptual models of, 90–3, 342
  correlates and predictors of, 347–9, 352–9
  crisis and, 63, 78, 115–18, 209, 216–18
  men's psychopathological responses
    and, 89–90
  role conflict in parental, 65, 342
  women's psychopathological responses
    and, 87–9; see also anxiety; crisis;
    depression (pregnancy and postpar-
    tum)
adolescent pregnancy and parenthood
  crisis conceptualization of, 209
  developmental tasks of, 210, 225–8,
  education and, 3, 221–2, 325–7
  expectations about, 343
  fathers and outcome of, 44, 213–15
  intervention programs for, 218, 323
  medical risks of, 219–21, 227, 327
  mothers and outcome of
    education and, 221–2
    infant development and, 225–7
    marriage and, 222–4
    psychological consequences for, 224–5
    subsequent fertility and, 224
  motivational factors and, 39–45
  phases of, 210–13
    cognitive development and, 215–16
    level of maturity and, 348
  programs for, 228, 313–20, 323–5, 330–2,
    334, 348–9
  rates of, 219, 314–15

adoption, 321
adult developmental stages, see life cycle
    (life-span perspective)
affective states
  parenthood and changes in, 78–9
  preterm infants and, 193
affiliation, 14, 95–8, 101–8; see also auton-
    omy
age, chronological
  adaptation to parenthood and, 91
  adolescent pregnancy and, 40, 43–4
  pregnancy and marriage at later, 158
  timing of parenthood and, 2–4
  U.S. fertility patterns and, 10, 11
alertness, preterm infants and, 194, 197
alphafetoprotein (AFP) blood test, 169–70
amniocentesis, 167, 168, 350
anxiety, 143
  adaptation to parenthood and, 88, 89
  infant temperament and, 78–9
  parenthood and, 302, 343
  pregnancy and, 161–2
  pubertal, 210–11
attachment, infant–parent, 186, 200, 226,
    264, 301, 346
autonomy, 14, 279, 349
  adaptation to parenthood model and, 93–6
  adult-to-parent transition, 93–5
  differences between men and women,
    94–5
  internal dimensions of, 102–3
  marital adaptation and, 103
  negotiation of, 96
  postpartum adjustment, 104–7
  psychological adjustment to parenthood
    and, 93
  research about
    clinical implications, 108–9
    family research in future and, 109–10
    methodology, 97–101
    study findings, 102–8

babies, *see* infants; infants, infancy (preterm and handicapped)
Baby and Child Care (Spock, 1976), 256
Baby Decision, The (Bombardieri, 1981),
  57
beliefs, parenthood and changes in, 79–80
birth of first child, *see* adaptation to parenthood
birthing rooms, 165
birth process, 164–6; *see also* cesarean
  section; childbirth preparation programs; Lamaze training; labor
  anesthesia during, 164–5
  preterm, 177, 179–80
  supportive companion during, 263–4
birthrates; *see also* fertility
  race and, 314–15
  in U.S., 10–11
blacks, *see* race
blues (postpartum), 88–9, 252–4; *see also*
  depression
body image, self-esteem during pregnancy
  and, 76, 126, 161
bonding
  father–child, 291
  high-risk infant and, 186
  mother–child, 108, 190, 200
  ultrasound and, 167
boys, psychological development of, 213–
  15; *see also* fathers; infants, infancy;
  men

careers; *see also* employment
  attitudes of co-workers toward pregnan-
    cy and, 161–2
  children and, 3, 23, 68
  family development perspective on, 6
  family size and, 9
  men and their, 4, 136
  pregnancy and, 161–2
  renewed sense of purpose in, 142
  women's work lives and, 136, 257
census, 17–18
cerebral palsy, 194, 195, 327
  programs for parents and, 325
cesarean section, 108, 171, 172, 220; *see
  also* birth process
child abuse, 201, 322, 324
  infant abuse, 201
childbirth, *see* birth process; labor
childbirth preparation programs; *see also*
  Lamaze training; pregnancy intervention programs
  communication between couple and,
    273, 276, 302–3
  couple participation and, 303

evaluation of
  in controlled studies, 283–5
  in early studies, 282–3
  in Lamaze participation studies, 285–8
  marriage as focus, 124–5, 143, 276–9,
    302
  measurement issues and, 301
  selection and motivation of subjects
    and, 291–3
  study design issues and, 300–1
fathers and, 288–91, 304
follow-up and, 279, 297, 301
goals of, 271, 298–9
historical overview of, 280–2
Lamaze, 252, 262–3, 280–2, 285–8, 291–2
preparation for, 293–8
prevention of problems (marital distress
  avoidance programs)
  conception of prevention and, 271–3
  research findings on, 273–7, 298–9
planning for pregnancy groups (for couples)
  "Choosing Parenthood" program,
    276–7
  "Considering Parenthood" program,
    277
  decision to become a parent and, 274–5
  evaluation of, 275–9
childrearing experts, 71
chorionic villus sampling (CVS), 168,
  169
cognitive development of adolescents,
  215–16
competency of new parents, 327, 328, 342,
  349
  behavior, predictive of, 351
continuity (stability) in parental behavior,
  197–8, 347
contraceptive technology, 23
control, sense of
  autonomy and affiliation and, 99, 102,
    103
  personal efficacy analysis and, 77
  pregnancy and loss of, 65, 347
counseling, 322, 327
couples, *see* marriage
couvade, 90, 126; *see also* fathers; men
crisis (psychological upheaval); *see also*
  adjustment to parenthood; anxiety;
  depression (pregnancy and postpartum)
  adolescent parents and, 209
  birth of first child and, 63, 78, 103
  couple and transition to parenthood as,
    5, 115–18, 131, 140, 146–8, 176, 254,
    351

crisis (*cont.*)
  three-generational perspective and, 133
  transition periods and, 272, 343
cross-cultural samples, 124, 355–6, 359
cry patterns (preterm infant), 192–3
Current Population Reports (U.S. Bureau
    of Census), 7
Current Population Survey, 18

decision-making process; *see also* problem
    solving
  clarification of motivations during, 57
  fertility behavior and, 27
  planning for pregnancy programs and,
    274–5, 277–9
depression (pregnancy and postpartum)
  affiliation and, 99–100, 103
  birth of a damaged infant and, 182
  family support programs and, 329–30
  nonpsychotic postpartum, 87–8
  postpartum blues, 87–9, 252–4
  pregnancy and, 86–8, 159
  psychological variables associated with,
    78, 89, 118, 245, 344
  rates of postpartum, 86–9, 252
  support and postpartum, 86–8, 252–4
developmental tasks of adolescence, 210,
    228
division of labor, *see* household chores
divorce, 158, 271
  fertility patterns and, 11
  infant risk status and, 191
  intervention programs and, 298, 302
  marital satisfaction and, 119
doula (supportive companion, Guatemala),
    263–4
Down syndrome, 170, 327
  affective responses and, 192–3
  appearance of infant and, 192
  programs for parents of, 327–9
  siblings and, 327
  social support and, 179, 188, 325
  stimulation and interactive behavior and,
    194
Dyadic Adjustment Scale, 100, 120, 146,
    356

education
  fertility rates and, 8
  family factors, influence on child's, 123
  interventions and, 275–6
  mothers and, 252
  motivation for having children and, 32
  teenage parents and, 3, 221–2, 325–6,
    334
electronic fetal monitoring (EFM), 170–1

employment; *see also* careers
  adolescent pregnancy and, 40, 43
  fertility and, 9, 12
  maternity leave and, 12
  mothers of handicapped children and,
    187, 195
  mothers of young children and, 314
  motivation for having children and, 32
  social support networks and, 238, 246,
    252
ethnicity
  adaptation to parenthood and, 124
  birthrates and, 10
  research design and, 124, 355–6, 359

Families under Stress (Hill, 1949), 115
family
  as focus of research, 2, 13, 148, 341
  one-child, 55–6
  of origin, 38, 244–5
  single-parent, 314, 321
  system changes and first and second ba-
    bies, 33–7, 128–9, 244–6, 342, 345–7
  three-generational perspective and, 133
  timing of parenthood and family size,
    245, 346
family development process (family life
    cycle); *see also* life cycle (life-span
    perspective)
  birth of first child and, 92–3
  life-span perspective on, 5–7, 358
family roles, parenthood and changes in,
    64–6, 128–9, 145
family size
  attitudes toward, 33, 275
  financial concerns and, 35
  influences on, 8, 55–6
  norms, 244–5
  patterns in U.S., 10–11
  race and, 33
  values of couples and, 36–7
family support programs; *see also* social
    support
  activities offered by, 317
  categorizing and defining, 318–19
  Child and Neighborhood Program, 261
  demographic background of, 312–15
  empirical studies and, 316–17
  evaluation issues and, 331–5
  Family Enrichment for New Parents,
    296, 319–20
  Family, Infant, and Preschool Program
    (FIPP), 328
  Family Resource Coalition (FRC), 260,
    332
  government and, 311, 313, 336

high-risk families, 318, 322–5, 330
historical background of, 312–14
Home Care Program, 329
implementation (operational) issues and, 330–3
Infant Care Program, 321
La Leche League, 320
mainstream families and, 319–21
Menninger Infant Project, 223
Mother's Center Development Project, 320
Mothers of Twins, 321, 322
networking efforts (community agency) and, 331–2, 335, 337
nontraditional families and, 321–2
range of programs available, 311–12
recommendations for, 336
theoretical antecedents, 315–16
Thresholds Program, 329
Twin Topics, Inc., 322
Young Mother's Education Development Program (YMED), 326
family systems theory, 85, 93, 96, 108–10, 346, 358; see also theory
fathers; see also men
    adaptation to parenthood and, 64, 90–2, 97, 105–8
    adolescent, 41, 213–15, 223
    adolescent girls and their own, 25, 44
    change in role of, 257
    childbirth preparation programs and, 288–91, 304
    couvade among, 90, 126
    Lamaze training and, 262, 263, 288
    motivation for parenthood and, 46–7, 49, 348
    parent support groups and, 321
    preterm infants and, 190, 195–96, 198–9, 200, 202
    personality changes in, 64, 68, 76,
    stress and, 64
    support for mothers by, 161, 191, 247, 249, 263
    temperament of child and, 78–9
    timing of parenthood and, 3–4
fatigue and new parenthood, 255
federally funded programs, 17, 311, 313, 336
    agency-community linkages and, 331–2, 335, 337
femininity and desire for parenthood, 38, 64
fertility; see also birthrates
    adolescent parents and, 224
    age of couple and decrease in, 158
    competency of parents and, 53

intervention programs and, 275, 279
survey of data sources and, 7
U.S. patterns of, 10–11
values of having children and, 26–9, 32–4, 53, 56
world patterns of, 7–9, 12
fetal defects, 166–70, 172
fetal monitoring, 170–1
financial concerns
    of adolescent couples, 223
    parenthood and, 255
    preterm infants and, 187–9
First Child and Family Formation, The (Miller and Newman, 1978), 1
friendships, 238–9, 245–6, 259–60

gender differences in transition to parent-hood, 137–8
gender identity, 94; see also sex roles
generativity, 4, 54
genetic disorders, 168, 350
genetic testing, 166–70, 350
grandparents, 122–3
    three-generational perspective and, 133–5
    timing of parenthood decision and, 245
grief and infant risk status, 182, 184–5, 188–9
guilt
    high-risk infant and, 183
    teenage pregnancies and, 221

health behaviors, pregnancy and social support and, 249–51
home visitor programs, 317, 321–2
homosexuality, 211, 214
household chores, 28–9, 104, 144–5
    infant risk status and, 199
    marital and family adaptation model and, 128–9, 144–5
    parenthood and, 297, 347
    social support and, 247, 344
human services, see family support pro-grams
husbands, see fathers; men
husband–wife relationship, see marriage

immortality, 32–3, 54
income
    effects on adjustment to parenthood, 350–1
    fertility and, 8
    transition to parenthood and loss of, 136
    values of having children and, 47
infant–parent separation, 184–7, 191
infant risk status, see infants, infancy

infant temperament, 66, 67, 346; *see also*
    infants, infancy
    parental anxiety and, 78–9
    personal efficacy and, 77
infants, infancy
    abused, 201
    adolescent parents and their, 255–7
    attachment, parents and, 200, 226,
        344
    disorders of, 170, 201, 220, 325
    interaction of parents and, 66
    marital distress and, 144–5
    preterm and handicapped
        characteristics of, 192–7
        continuity (stability) in parental be-
            havior, 197–8
        definitions of, 176, 179
        developmental outcome of infant and,
            199–200
        family support programs and, 323,
            327–9, 330
        fathers' interaction with, 190, 195–6,
            198–9, 200, 202
        financial costs of, 15, 187
        intervention programs and, 201–2,
            320–1
        leisure activity of parents and, 191
        marital relations and, 189–91
        mentally retarded infants' programs
            and, 325–6
        mothers' interaction with, 193–7, 202
        neonatal intensive-care units and, 194
        parental response to, 182–9, 191, 195,
            258
        parent-infant interaction and, 194–7
        transition to parenthood (general char-
            acteristics) and, 176–84
intervention; *see* childbirth preparation
    programs; family support programs

Journal of Family Issues, 1

labor, 164, 281, 284; *see also* birth process
labor force participation, *see* careers; em-
    ployment
Lamaze training
    childbirth preparation programs and,
        280–2, 285–8, 291–2
    peer support and, 262, 263
life cycle (life-span perspective); *see also*
        family development process (family
        life cycle)
    birth of first child and, 91, 343, 358
    marital satisfaction and, 118–22
    timing of parenthood and, 2–7, 68
    transitions in, 343–7
life satisfaction, 54–5

lifestyle change, infant risk status and,
        190–1
Locke-Wallace Marital Adjustment Scale,
        100, 121, 143, 146, 356

marital communication
    childbirth preparation programs and,
        273, 276, 302–3
    importance of, 140
    marital and family adaptation and, 130–1
marital conflict, 139–42
marital distress avoidance programs, *see*
        prevention programs for marital dys-
        function
marital relationship, *see* marriage
marital satisfaction; *see also* marriage;
        sexual relations
    decline in, 141–4
    household tasks and, 129
    intergenerational relationships and, 134
    life cycle and, 118–22
    measurement of, 146
marriage; *see also* divorce; household
        chores; sexual relations
    adolescent parents and, 222–4
    childbirth preparation programs and, 302
    communication, 130–1
    crisis and, 115–18, 144–8
    five-domain structural model of (Cowan
        and Cowan)
        consistency and, 136–7
        defining domains, 122–3
        gender differences, 137–8
        methodological issues and, 123–5
        three-generational perspective and,
            133
    high-risk and preterm infants and, 189–
        91
    individuality and mutuality, 138–9, 144
    intrapsychic relationships and, 91–2
    measures of
        Activity with the Child Questionnaire,
            42
        Dyadic Adjustment Scale, 100, 120,
            146, 354
        Hierarchy of Birth Planning Values,
            27–8
        How Are Your Feeling Questionnaire,
            42
        Locke-Wallace Marital Adjustment
            Inventory, 100, 121, 143, 146, 354
        Parenthood Relations Questionnaire,
            38
        The Pie Role Analysis Instrument,
            127, 145–6
        selection of, 145–6
        Semantic Differential Technique, 39

problem solving in, 139–41, 142, 273
process model of, 138–9, 141–5
satisfaction and, 91–2, 118–22, 141–4
maternal instinct, 24; see also motivation
    for parenthood
maternity leave, 12, 190
mate selection, 74
maturity
    adolescents and, 40–1
    adult status value and, 31, 33, 40–5
    having children and sense of, 29, 126–7
    measurement of, 42
    parenthood and personality changes and,
      79
medical risks of pregnancy, 166–70
    adolescence and, 219–21, 227, 325
    age of mother and, 3
    infants, preterm and handicapped, 38–9
medical technology, 15, 23, 342, 350
    predictors of postpartum functioning
      and, 349–50
    pregnancy and, 167–73
    prenatal care and, 178–9
men, 14, 67; see also fathers
    adaptation to parenthood and, 91–2
    autonomy and affiliation and, 94–5,
      103–8
    career and transition and, 136
    couples, groups and, 124
    crisis and, 117
    differences from women during transi-
      tion to parenthood, 137–8
    expression of feelings and, 189, 348
    family of origin, 134
    fertility pattern in U.S. and, 11–12
    household tasks and, 128–9, 144–5, 199,
      247
    marital conflict and, 91–2, 140
    motivation and values for having chil-
      dren and, 25–6, 28, 31, 35–7, 50–2
    parenthood and expansion of self and,
      77
    personality growth and change and, 13
    pregnancy reactions and, 126
    psychological development of boys and,
      213–15
    psychopathological responses to parent-
      hood and, 89–90
    self-image and, 64, 76
    social pressure during pregnancy and, 161
    timing of parenthood and, 3–4
mental health model, 16; see also adapta-
    tion to parenthood; psychopathologi-
    cal responses to first child
mentally ill parents and family support
    programs, 329–30
miscarriage, 160

mortality
    adolescent pregnancies and infant, 220
    infant and maternal, 169, 171
    infant perinatal, 179, 182, 185
mother–child bond, 108, 349; see also at-
    tachment; infant–parent; bonding
    infant risk status and, 190, 200
mothers; see also adolescent pregnancy
    and parenthood; women
    adaptation to parenthood and, 86–9, 92,
      102–5, 216–18, 354–9
    adolescent (outcomes for), 219–27
    femininity and, 89
    preterm infants and, 16, 193–7
motivation for parenthood
    adolescent parents and, 39–45
    college students and,, 37–9, 46
    conflicts in, 23
    evolutionary pespectives on, 24
    fathers and, 348
    fertility and, 26–9, 32–4, 53, 56, 348
    historical overview, 24–9
    Hoffman and Hoffman model, 29–39
    husband and wife differences and, 35–7,
      51–2
    innate factors, 24–5
    international (seven-nation) study and,
      30–2
    life-span perspective on, 3–4, 23–4
    longitudinal study of values of having
      children and, 45–50
    methodological shortcomings of model
      of, 2, 50–2
    postpartum depression and, 89
    psychological barriers, 51
    psychological processes underlying,
      13–14
    rationality models, 9
    research issues and, 53–8
    theoretical models of values of having
      children
      alternatives hypothesis, 30, 32, 43–4,
        50–1
      basic values in, 29–30
      costs (negative values) and, 28, 30,
        34–5, 37, 47–9, 55
      population research, 26–9
      psychoanalytic theories, 25–6
    unconscious, 57–8
    women's liberation movement and, 38
motor behavior (preterm infant), 193
multiple births, 15
mutuality, 138–9, 144

networking (agency-community), 331–2,
    335, 337
nightmares and pregnancy, 162

obstetrician–patient relationship, 162–4; *see also* pregnancy

oedipal attachment, 25–6

overpopulation, 35

parent advocacy groups, 320, 331

parental leave policy, 12

parental loss, depression and early, 245

parent–child interaction, 100–1; *see also* adolescent pregnancy and parenthood; attachment, infant–parent; bonding; fathers; infants, infancy; mothers

  high-risk infant and, 190, 194–7, 354

  marital and family adaptation model and, 131–3

parent–child separation, 184–7, 191

parenthood, *see* adaptation to parenthood; motivation for parenthood; parenthood intervention programs; personality changes and parenthood; timing of parenthood

parenthood intervention programs, 293–8

  childbirth programs

    Lamaze, 280–2

  family support programs

    Child and Neighborhood program, 261

    Family Enrichment for New Parents, 296, 319–20

    Family, Infant and Preschool Program (FIPP), 328

    Family Resource Coalition (FRC), 260, 332

    Home Care Program, 329

    Infant Care Program, (Evanston), 321

    Menninger Infant Project, 223, 225, 226

    Mother's Center Development Project, 320

    Thresholds Program, 329

    Twin Topics, Inc., 322

    Young Mother's Education Development Program (YMED), 326

  pregnancy decision programs

    Becoming a Family Project, 123, 297

    Choosing Parenthood Program, 276–7

    Coping with the Overall Pregnancy/ Parenting Experience (COPE), 320

    Parents Place, 319

    Pregnancy and Parenthood Project (Boston University), 96–110

    Pride in Parenthood Program, 261

parenting alliance, 68

parents, *see* adaptation to parenthood; adolescent pregnancy and parenthood; fathers; grandparents; infants, infancy; motivation for parenthood; parent–child interaction; parent–child separation; personality changes and parenthood; timing of parenthood

parent support groups, 319–21; *see also* childbirth preparation programs; family support programs; pregnancy decision programs

paternal instinct, 24–5

penis envy, 25

personal efficacy, parenthood and change in, 77–9

personality changes and parenthood, 25, 141, 348; *see also* adaptation to parenthood; psychopathological responses to first child

  affective states, 78–9

  impact of parenthood on, 67–9

  maturity, 79

  parenthood role and changes in, 63–7

  personal efficacy, 77–8

  process models of changes in adult and act-frequency approach, 14, 73–5, 80

  possible selves and, 14, 69–73, 80

  self-perceptions, 75–7

  social support networks and, 238

  values, 79–80

population research, 26–9; *see also* research

possible selves concept, 14, 69–73, 80

postpartum blues, 88–9, 252–4; *see also* depression

postpartum functioning, predictors of, 347–9, 352–9; *see also* adaptation to parenthood; depression; postpartum psychosis; psychopathological responses to first child

postpartum psychosis, 86–7, 166

poverty, family support programs and, 322–5, 335

power of parenthood, 13

pregnancy; *see also* childbirth preparation programs; Lamaze training

  adolescent, incidence of, 219

  adolescent mothers and, 216–18

  autonomy and affiliation and, 97, 106, 349

  high-risk, 178–80

  household chores and, 128

  marital conflict during, 131

  obstetrical perspectives on, 159–64

  planned and unplanned, 157–8, 219

  predictors of adaptation to, 350–1

  self-concept and, 72, 126

  social support during, 248–52

  technological considerations alphafetoprotein (AFP) blood test, 169–70

amniocentesis, 167–8
chorionic villus sampling (CVS), 168
electronic fetal monitoring (EFM), 170–1
fetal defects and, 166–70
future directions and, 171–3, 347–8
genetic testing, 166–70
obstetricians and, 163
ultrasound, 167
trimester-specific behaviors and feelings, 15, 159–62
pregnancy tests, 160
premature infants, see infants, infancy preterm and handicapped)
Preparenting (Fournier and Fournier, 1980), 57
prevention programs for marital dysfunction
concept of prevention and, 271–3
evaluation of, 273–4, 276–7, 298–9
goals of, 271
review procedures for, 270–1
pronatalism, 16, 23, 24
psychoanalytic theory, 25–6, 53–4, 85–6, 94, 210–15
development of adolescents, 210–15
motivations for having children and, 25–6, 53–4
object relations and, 87–8, 93–6, 210–15
psychopathological responses to first child
in men, 89–90
nonpsychotic postpartum depression, 87–8
postpartum blues, 88–9, 252–4
postpartum psychosis, 86–7, 166
predictors of, 89
psychosis (postpartum), 86–7, 166

quickening, 160

race
adaptation to parenthood and, 124
adolescent mothers and, 40–1, 43
adolescent pregnancies and, 219
birthrates and, 10, 314–15
family size and, 33
motivation for having children and, 32, 50
research design and, 357–8
values of having children and, 32, 33
reciprocal relations
family and friends and, 259–60
parents and children and, 100–1, 108–9
research
autonomy and affiliation study, alphafetoprotein, 96–110
childbirth programs and, 282–8, 291–3, 300–2

crisis perspective on parenthood and, 5, 63, 115–18, 209, 343
decision making, 277–9
disciplines involved in, 1
family roles, 148, 177
family support programs and, 335–6
follow-up
childbirth preparation programs and, 279, 297, 301
family support programs and, 334
future directions in, 354–9
instruments
Activity with the Child Questionnaire, 42
Dyadic Adjustment Scale, 100, 120, 146, 356
Hierarchy of Birth Planning Values, 27–8
How Are You Feeling Questionnaire, 42
Locke–Wallace Marital Adjustment Scale, 100, 120–1, 143, 146, 356
Parenthood Relations Questionnaire, 38
the Pie Role Analysis Instrument, 127, 145–6
Semantic Differential Measure, 39
Values of Children measure, 9, 29–31
marriage, 122–5
motivation for parenthood
adolescent parents and, 39–45
theoretical model (values of having children), 29–39
population, 26–9
prenatal, 202
prepregnancy programs and childbirth programs and, 280–8
separation of high-risk infant and parent and, 187
social support networks, 236–7, 264–5
retarded children, support programs for, 327–9
risk, see adolescent pregnancy and parenthood; infants, infancy; medical risks of pregnancy
rural populations
adolescent parents-to-be, 41
values of having children, 32, 43, 51

schizophrenia, 87
second-time parenthood, 342, 345–9
self-concept (adult) and parenthood and personality change, 69–73, 75–7, 126–8, 138, 344, 347
self-esteem, 141
adolescence and, 212
body image and, 76

self-esteem (*cont.*)
high-risk infants and parents, 183–4, 187
transition to parenthood and, 127
separation (infant–parent), 184–7, 191
sex roles, 27
gender identity and, 94
parenthood and changes in, 64–6, 137–8, 348
values of having children analysis, 37–9
sexual relations
adjustment to parenthood and, 100
affiliation in pregnancy and, 103
infant high-risk status and, 189–90
maternal instinct and, 24
pregnancy and, 126
siblings, 28, 36, 327, 328, 345, 346
social network, 16, 122; *see also* social support
composition of primary, 237
husbands' and wives' and, 238
informal, 16
parenthood and personality changes and, 66
preterm infant and, 177–8
social pressure, 160–1
social reform, 3
social services, 17; *see also* family support groups
social support; *see also* family support programs; social network
anticipated (during transitional period), 244–8
changes in, 235–6
childbirth and postnatal period, 254–60
couple's ties and, 239–41
density of, 238–9, 328
employment status and, 238
importance of, 9, 356
intervention programs and, 260–4
Lamaze program as, 252
marital and family adaptation model and, 135–6
measurement of, 236–7, 264–5
negative, 47–9, 160–1, 206, 247–8, 259
personality and, 248–52, 344
postpartum depression and, 252–4
preterm infant and, 177–8, 187–8
types of, 241–3
socioeconomic status, 318, 320–4, 355

technology, *see* contraceptive technology; medical technology
teenagers, *see* adolescent pregnancy and parenthood
teratogens, 169

Thank You, Dr. Lamaze: A Mother's Experience in Painless Childbirth (Karmel, 1959), 282
theory
ego psychology, 26, 210
Eriksonian, 26, 38, 54, 95–6
family systems, 85, 93, 96, 108–10, 346, 358
object relations, 85–6, 93–6
Piagetian, 215–16
psychoanalytic, 25–6, 53–4, 85–94, 210–15, 216–18
sociobiological, 24–5
timing of parenthood, 270
decision making and, 278
early childbearers and, 16
grandparents and friends and, 245–6
impact on men's and women's lives, 3
late childbearers and, 2–3, 91
life-span perspective on, 2–7, 68, 91
values in, 33–4
twins, 161, 167, 321–2

ultrasound, 167, 350
urbanization and values of having children, 32

values and beliefs
about timing of parenthood, 46, 68
parenthood and changes in, 79–80
"values of children" model, 13, 27, 28
adolescent parenthood and, 39–45
adolescent pregnancies and, 43–4
alternatives hypothesis and, 30
costs (negative values) and, 28, 30, 34–5, 37, 47–9, 55
fertility attitudes and, 26–9, 32–4, 53, 56
future research and, 53–8
historical overview of, 24–9
husband and wife differences and, 35–7, 51–2
international (seven-nation) study and, 30–2
methodological issues and, 50–2
values categories and, 29–30
venereal disease, 220
volunteer research subjects, 357–8; *see also* research
"vulnerable child syndrome," 182

weight
of infant and attachment to parent, 200
infant perinatal death and, 179
pregnancy and women's, 161
women; *see also* mothers
adaptation to parenthood and, 86–9, 92, 102–5, 216–18, 349–51, 352–7

autonomy and affiliation, 102–5
body image, 76, 126, 161
crisis and, 117
differences from men during transition to parenthood and, 137–8
marital conflict and, 140
parenthood and sense of self and, 3, 64, 69–71, 138
personality growth and changes, 13, 343
psychopathological responses to first child
  nonpsychotic postpartum depression, 87–8

postpartum blues, 88–9, 252–4
postpartum psychosis, 86–7, 166
predictors of, 89
role conflict and, 89
stress during pregnancy and, 126
stress and parenthood and, 64
temperament of child and, 77–9
values of parenthood and, 348
values of having children different from men's, 28, 31, 35–7, 51–2
weight during pregnancy and, 161
women's liberation movement and parenthood motivation, 38